The Psychology of Human Behavior

The Psychology of *Human Behavior*

Richard A. Kalish
California State College at Los Angeles

Wadsworth Publishing Company, Inc.
Belmont, California

Third printing: May 1968

L. C. Cat. Card No.: 66–25626
Printed in the United States of America

Instructors have often expressed the feeling that introductory psychology texts neglect students not intending to major in the field. *The Psychology of Human Behavior* has been written specifically for such students.

The first course will be the only academic encounter with the study of psychology for most, perhaps almost all, of these individuals. Therefore, although primarily interested in learning what the academic discipline of psychology is all about, they also wish to know about adjustment and the healthy personality—with some reference to problems involving them personally.

These students can best be served by a book with a minimum amount of jargon, by one that stresses concepts and that presents only the more important psychological terminology. They want a text that integrates research and nonresearch writings and ideas, rather than one that merely reviews the literature. They prefer a book with a point of view, rather than one with a totally eclectic approach, and—at the same time—a book that does not pretend to have all the answers.

They are also concerned with understanding the human personality as a possible aid in their future vocational and family roles. They come from a wide variety of backgrounds and are headed toward a wide variety of occupations, but their focus is the normal human personality. Methodological matters and scientific studies are relevant to the extent that they broaden and deepen knowledge of the human personality and aid in its evaluation.

The Psychology of Human Behavior is our response to these students. Since such a book must necessarily treat a number of topics relatively completely, and since some courses will last fewer weeks than others, the parts and chapters have been written so that they may be studied as units; therefore it is not necessary to cover the material in the exact order of its presentation. Cross references, included where helpful, further increase flexibility. Material has been included in the appendixes on the specific problems of college adjustment and effective study.

The personal teaching experiences of the author, covering several colleges and universities, as well as nurses' training programs and USAFI classes in the United States and Japan, have been supplemented through an advisory board of eight junior college psychology professors. Each of these individuals thoroughly evaluated the final two revisions of the manuscript, and their counsel contributed immeasurably to the final product.

A book may carry the name of only one author, but it is never the work of only one person. *The Psychology of Human Behavior* might have the following names on the title page: The members of the advisory board: Frank R. Blume, San Bernardino Valley College; Harry Cole, American River Junior College; Gerald L. Hershey, Fullerton Junior College; Victor J. Halling, Bakersfield College; Charles R. Kessler, Los Angeles Pierce College; William L. Sanborn, Vallejo Junior College; Frank W. Westfall, Ventura College; John E. Peters, San Diego Mesa College; the several hundred students of American River Junior College who suffered through an earlier draft of this book and who, along with their instructors, offered distressingly valid criticism; Richard Rosenstein, M.D., who evaluated some of the materials from the viewpoint of a pediatrician and who provided useful insights; Mrs. Val Davis for a fast, accurate job of typing; Albert Kallis, John G. Warford, and the files of Antioch College News Bureau, California State College at Los Angeles Public Information Office, and numerous other organizations for the photographs; Ed Fisher, whose cartoons the author has long enjoyed and who was so willing to participate; the Department of Psychology, CSCLA, and especially its chairman and secretaries; Mr. Stanley Kallis of CBS, who arranged for the use of the photographs credited to that network; my friends, my family, and my students, who provided—usually unknowingly—the ideas for most of the case histories; Harold Parnes of Wadsworth Publishing Company, who started the ball rolling; P. James Geiwitz, Stanford University, who reviewed the final manuscript; and my wife, Barbara, and children, Leah and Daniel, because they are so much a part of me.

Contents

I Introduction to the basic principles of psychology   1

1 Psychology and psychologists   3
2 Human needs   21
3 Perceiving the environment   47
4 Principles of learning and their application   63
5 An introduction to personality development   85

II Development of human behavior   105

6   The earliest years   107
7   The developing child and his relationships   131
8   Personality from twelve to twenty-one   155
9   The student at college   179
10 Courtship and marriage   205
11 The mature years   227

III The development and effects of stress   255

12 Emotions and stress   257
13 Reactions to stress   277
14 The troubled personality   297

IV Man and his society   325

15 Career planning and the world of work   327
16 The individual and his groups   351
17 The importance of values   377
18 Religious values and group memberships   399

V   *The healthy personality*   417

19   *The healthy personality*   419

Appendixes   437

Appendix I   College Orientation   439
Appendix II   Study Methods   463

Glossary   487

Bibliography   505

Index   521

I *Introduction to the basic principles of psychology*

Psychology and psychologists   **1**

Each person begins his first course in psychology with a different set of preconceived notions about what psychology *really* is. Some assume they will learn to "psyche out" all their friends; some are afraid of what they might learn about themselves; some are positive that psychology is merely common sense. None of these anticipations is likely to be found accurate. Perhaps the wisest course for a student to follow is to be actively curious and have as few preconceived notions as possible.

Few things excite people more than learning about themselves. In the science-fiction-like world of today, man has opened the vastness of space and the minuteness of the atom for exploration; yet the excitement of the universe is no greater than the excitement of our own thinking and feeling and behaving, nor is the solar system more complex than a single human being.

People readily accept the idea that it takes a great deal of study to learn about space. After all, space is unimaginably vast, and the problems are obviously highly technical. The idea that learning about **behavior*** also requires study is more difficult to accept. "I'm a person, and I've lived with myself for 18 (or 30 or 60) years. I should know myself by now—and I should know other people too."

Yet the realization eventually comes that understanding the behavior of others, or even of ourselves, is not as simple as it may seem. "Why do I sit watching television, when I know I have an exam the day after tomorrow?" "Why is it so often easier to ask out a girl I don't particularly like than one I do like?" "Why do I just smile when that girl makes nasty comments about my friend, instead of telling her what I really think?" These examples of everyday behavior are seldom easy to understand. How much more difficult it is to explain such phenomena as love and fear, marital success and vocational failure, mental illness and health adjustment.

Some claim to have found the key to understanding human behavior in statements such as, "Do unto others as you would have them do unto you," or "Man does not live by bread alone." Are these statements true? For the most part they express principles accepted by modern psychologists, but they hardly provide a comprehensive explanation of human behavior.

The purpose of this book is to introduce you to the world of human behavior, as explored by psychologists. You will read about things you already know and things you may not have considered. You will find some of your questions about human behavior answered, and—if you are a perceptive and inquisitive student—you will find many new questions to ask. You may gain a little better understanding of yourself and of those around you, and hopefully, you will find the study of human behavior to be both exciting and enjoyable.

Psychology: what is it?

Psychology is the scientific field that attempts to understand, describe, predict, and influence behavior—particularly human behavior. The psy-

*Words or phrases in bold type appear in the glossary.

chologist may study behavior scientifically or he may apply the theories and research findings of other psychologists to practical problems—or he may do both.

Psychology as a science

Psychology is defined as a scientific field, because psychologists make extensive use of the scientific method. As other scientists, the research psychologist begins by developing ideas from which he extracts a **hypothesis** or assumption he wishes to test; then he determines the proper method for testing the hypothesis; next he collects data; and finally he analyzes the data to determine whether they bear out his initial hypothesis. Good researchers conduct and report their work in such a way that others can follow the same procedures to verify the results. The psychologist uses strict research methods to assure the highest degree of objectivity and to prevent his own wishes or expectations from biasing his findings.

Psychologists direct a large part of their efforts at determining relationships between what are termed **variables** or things that vary or change. For example, psychologists are interested in learning whether the variable *spanking* has an effect upon the variable *obedience*. If the two variables are related, as they appear to be, psychologists will probe further into the problem. How will spanking affect obedience? Is it true that the more spanking a child receives, the more obedient he will become? Is there a point beyond which increased spanking no longer leads to increased obedience and may actually produce an increase in disobedience? Do some children respond favorably to spanking, while others indicate little behavior change? What predictions regarding obedience can be made from knowing about spanking? As answers to these questions become established, new variables are added. Under what conditions will spanking lead to obedience? Will it lead to behavior changes other than obedience? Will it produce anger toward the parents? Running away from home? Pinching baby sister when no one is looking? Piece by piece the puzzle is filled in; the ability to predict and describe is improved.

As new information and understanding are obtained through research, they are integrated into theories or systems of behavior. These theories or systems should generate new ideas and explanations, which can be tested through additional research. Slowly psychological scientists build, alter, and improve their theories.

In reporting their research, psychologists must use caution, since relationships are never perfect or even near perfect. If it is learned that children who are frequently spanked get lower-than-average grades in school, this does not necessarily mean that the spankings or fear of spankings produced the low grades. Perhaps parents who often spank their children are less intelligent than other parents; perhaps parents who spank are more concerned with obedience at home than with success in school. What other reasons can you think of? Nor does it mean that *all* children who get spanked get low grades. Psychologists speak in terms of either *tendencies* or **probabilities**—how probable is it or "what are the odds" that a particular event will occur.

Scientists do not expect to find final answers. New information, new understanding, new hypotheses are always forthcoming. Science progresses through many small steps and few large breakthroughs. A science may be compared to an immense brick house. Each piece of research is one brick that helps the house to grow. Some bricks are large, some are small, and some are not made of very good material and demand rapid replacement. The house is slowly built, but each time one part of it nears completion, the owners decide they need an additional wing. The work never ends.

Psychology applied

Although professional psychologists usually consider their primary concern to be research, some are more interested in applying the research findings and their own informed understanding of human behavior to practical problems. They are usually interested in the art of influencing behavior.

The psychologist who counsels a student regarding a suitable college is using the research of others to deal with an immediate problem. From previous research, he knows whether the grades and test scores of his counselee predict success in the college under discussion; he has also learned from research and experience those attitudes that seem to predict college success. Also his study of persuasion has probably convinced him that it would be poor judgment to argue with the student, if the latter appears to make a poor choice. By studying other cases and through much experience, the counselor has become sensitive to the feelings of students and has learned, along with the *science* of psychology, the *art* of helping counselees achieve their own goals, instead of trying to impose his goals upon them.

Other psychologists are hired by businesses or governmental agencies to deal with such practical problems as testing the effectiveness of a **propaganda** program to persuade the Brazilian people that Americans are their friends, or learning whether a new package for breakfast cereal is better than the old package, or determining the best methods to select the most promising volunteers for the Peace Corps. By building upon the research of others and adding research of their own, these psychologists will try to come up with the best answers to immediate and practical problems.

Psychology, then, is the scientific field that studies behavior in order to understand, describe, predict, and influence this behavior. Psychologists use research to lead both to theories of behavior and to effective, practical applications for solving immediate problems; they also use the *art* of psychology to aid in understanding and influencing behavior.

Psychology, not an isolated field

Human knowledge is not contained in a series of boxes, each set apart from the others and each representing one field of study. Human knowledge must incorporate many fields of inquiry and their relationships to one another. Psychologists are very much aware of the debt they owe others as well as the use these others may make of psychology.

The next time you look at a painting or statue, ask yourself how it affects you. Does it make you laugh or feel sad? Does it move you to anger, or does it leave you feeling pleased? Art not only expresses the mood of the artist, but it may also reflect ways in which people perceive the world. One philosopher has suggested that today's artists depict people as strange and distorted because man no longer has a true sense of who he is or how he relates to the world around him (Barrett, 1958).

The artist wants to understand human behavior, and he may wish to influence behavior. The psychologist and the artist may learn from each other about the influence of color upon mood, the effects of space upon the focus of attention, the degree to which feelings and attitudes are influenced by seeing artwork, or the significance of communicating through art. Consider, also, the relevance of these comments for the advertising layout artist, the theater technician, the beautician, the hotel manager, or the printer.

Literature also "holds the mirror up to man." A good novelist can communicate the feelings of his fictional characters and make them seem more lifelike than the real people whose behavior the psychologist attempts to describe. Plays and films can produce the same result. Writers can use the understanding provided by psychologists to enrich their stories, and psychologists can gain in their understanding of human behavior by drawing from the deep sensitivity of good authors.

The relationship of other social sciences to psychology is easily apparent. Sociology, anthropology, political science, history, and economics all deal with human behavior, although not in the same way that psychology does. Sociology contributes knowledge about the behavior of crowds, the structure of the family, and the functions of institutions such as the church and the school. Anthropology investigates the ways in which people live in other cultures to provide a better perspective of our own society. Political science is concerned with politics and government, but governments are made up of people, and political scientists and psychologists learn from each other.

While the political scientist and the political candidate are both interested in predicting the effects of political issues on the behavior of the voter, the historian desires a better understanding of the behavior of people in past generations. Both the historian and the psychologist could profit from discovering what factors enabled Lincoln to rise to such greatness; schoolteachers and parents would certainly appreciate understanding why Lincoln found reading books so exciting. Knowledge of the history of our country and of other countries helps explain the behavior of people today. To learn, for example, that the German army invaded France three times in one century may help explain the attitudes of the French toward Germans; to learn about the history of unions in the United States may help explain why your parents feel as they do about unions.

From biology and chemistry, psychologists gain knowledge of the physiology of the sensory and motor apparatus, the brain, and the nervous system in order to grasp better their effects upon behavior. At the same time, the medical doctor can use some of the findings of psychologists in treating his patients. Mathematics provides the statistical tools to conduct research; the study of grammar and linguistics suggests that language may actually affect the thinking process; processing data on large computers enables the psychologist to enlarge the scope of his research.

Parents, teachers, businessmen, office managers, skilled technicians, policemen, secretaries, government workers, military officers, and innumerable other groups draw upon the data of psychologists. They may wish to influence the behavior of children, potential buyers, employees, soldiers, or supervisors; they may want to predict the behavior of the competitor, the enemy, the criminal, or the boss; they may hope to understand the feelings of the spouse, the girl at the next desk, or the commanding officer. And they give to and receive from psychologists a deeper understanding of the world.

No field of study or work can exist in a vacuum. Each adds to its own store of understanding and knowledge from the efforts of others. What do you feel you can learn from psychology? What do you feel psychologists might learn from those in your chosen vocational field?

Psychologists: who are they?

Everyone, of course, uses principles of psychology in his work and personal life, just as everyone uses principles of mathematics and economics. However, the ability to use psychological principles does not make a person into a psychologist, any more than computing a batting average or maintaining a family budget makes a person into a mathematician or an economist. Most people properly considered to be psychologists have received a graduate degree, usually the Master of Arts, Master of Science, or Doctor of Philosophy, which normally take six to eight years of academic training plus the ability to pass difficult comprehensive examinations and to complete a satisfactory piece of research.

Most professional psychologists belong to the American Psychological Association, an organization of approximately 20,000 members. Thus, there is one psychologist for every 10,000 Americans—certainly a very small proportion of the population.

Specialties within psychology

Although all psychologists share the understanding of a common body of knowledge, this scientific field, as all others, has been divided into a number of specialties.

The specialty chosen by more psychologists than any other is **clinical psychology.** The clinical psychologist is primarily concerned with helping others deal with personal and emotional problems. He participates in the face-to-face relationship known as **psychotherapy,** a form of counseling that involves helping people with personal and emotional adjustment problems. In addition to performing psychotherapy, the clinical psychologist administers and interprets all types of psychological tests; he also does research, often involving various tests and various approaches to psychotherapy. He may have a private practice or work with a government agency, a hospital, or an educational institution.

The **social psychologist** focuses his attention upon the behavior of people and groups in a social environment. He studies the formation and change of attitudes and beliefs, the effects of society upon behavior, and the actions of people in small groups; he is also likely to be interested in how people communicate with each other, since communication is part of a social relationship.

Quite different from the social psychologist is the **physiological psychologist,** who studies the physiology, anatomy, and **biochemistry** of the body as they affect behavior. What changes occur to the human body when the person claims to feel anger or fear? Why do tranquilizer pills alter behavior? Why are some people color blind? How is memory stored in the brain?

The **developmental psychologist** is primarily concerned with behavior and behavior changes at various stages of development. He will try to discover why some infants learn to walk later than others, how adolescent interests change between ages twelve and eighteen, why some people seem old at 60, while others are still vigorous at 80.

Industrial psychologists study a variety of topics, including how to design efficient machines, how to evaluate worker morale and to improve it if necessary, how to devise training programs for workers, and how to improve marketing and advertising.

These five specialties were chosen to show what a wide range of human activity is covered by the term *psychology*. Other specialties are cited in Figure 1–1. Overlap, of course, exists between the areas. A clinical psychologist may become interested in emotional problems of industrial executives, while a social psychologist may find himself studying the effects of friendship upon the physical health of the aged. Your present psychology instructor may prefer any one of the specialties listed, or he may feel that he does not properly fit into any of them.

The job of the psychologist

The largest number of psychologists are associated with colleges and universities, where they teach, conduct research, counsel, and serve as administrators. Various agencies of federal, state, and local government also employ many psychologists; others work for industry, hospitals, social agencies, and public schools, while a few are self-employed (Ross and Lockman, 1963).

Psychologists use both the science and the art of psychology in their work, just as medical doctors use the science and the art of medicine in theirs. Some psychologists are involved almost completely with research, but most clinical and counseling psychologists must develop the art of being sensitive to the feelings of those they are trying to help. The industrial psychologist who is responsible for training foremen and managers must also develop a high degree of sensitivity to how others feel. And, of course, we may hope that the psychologists who teach in our colleges and universities develop the art of communicating the content and the methods of psychology to their students most effectively.

Some common sources of confusion about psychologists

Can psychologists control behavior? The only possible answer is "No!!" You learn that when a friend tells you his troubles he feels better afterward. The psychologist has learned a great deal more about this relationship. You find that you can influence your friend's behavior by listening to him; the psychologist has more sophistication and may have learned how to have more influence than you in the same situation, but neither of you come near controlling the behavior of the person with

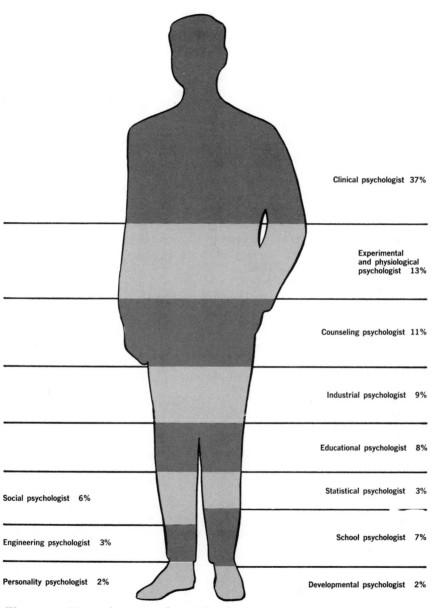

Clinical psychologist 37%

Experimental
and physiological
psychologist 13%

Counseling psychologist 11%

Industrial psychologist 9%

Educational psychologist 8%

Statistical psychologist 3%

Social psychologist 6%

School psychologist 7%

Engineering psychologist 3%

Personality psychologist 2%

Developmental psychologist 2%

Figure 1–1. The major areas of specialization in psychology and the percentage of American Psychological Association members identifying with each (Lockman, 1964).

troubles. Advertisers, ministers, politicians, and doctors all influence behavior, but do not control it. Psychologists have learned enough about people to increase the effectiveness of advertising slogans and political speeches, but this is far from control.

The greatest experiment in behavior control was undoubtedly the Chinese Communist **brainwashing** program, which was conducted both on the Chinese themselves and on non-Chinese in prison camps and elsewhere (Schein, 1958). These programs appear to have influenced behavior and attitudes, but they certainly did not allow total control. Although brainwashing is often believed to have caused American prisoners to be ineffectual in the Chinese prison camps, it rarely had long-range effect upon their behavior (Biderman, 1962).

If such thought control ever does occur, it is much more likely to come about through the work of biochemists or physicists, working with the chemistry of the body or the effects of certain electric impulses upon the brain.* Occasionally an uninformed person will claim that psychologists have some strange and secret method of persuading people to do things "against their will," but these claims are not supported by evidence.

Can a psychologist read people's thoughts? Not at all. A psychologist, because of his training and experience, may notice a movement that most people would ignore; he may see in a few words meanings that others do not see. However, a good automobile salesman can size up a customer very quickly; a competent policeman can quickly determine what happened at the scene of a crime. The psychologist has similarly developed a sensitivity to what people are thinking and feeling. Some psychologists, through their background, training, and experience, have developed the art of *understanding* people to a high degree.

How do clinical psychologists, psychiatrists, and psychoanalysts differ? Since clinical psychologists, **psychiatrists,** and **psychoanalysts** all perform psychotherapy, much confusion exists regarding the differences among them.

The clinical psychologist usually has received the Ph.D. degree with a major emphasis in psychology. In addition to his lengthy education, he has spent a year doing psychological testing and psychotherapy under supervision.

The psychiatrist must be, according to law, a medical doctor. His education includes a regular college degree, a medical degree (M.D.), a year of internship, and usually three to five years of medical residency,

Life Magazine (Coughlan, 1963) published an interesting series of articles on this topic.

often in a psychiatric hospital. Until his residency begins, his education is almost completely in medicine, rather than in psychology.

The psychoanalyst is almost always a medical doctor, and is frequently a psychiatrist before he takes the additional study, examinations, and supervised experience needed to be a psychoanalyst. Many psychoanalysts have practiced medicine or psychiatry for years before embarking upon the intensive training required to become an analyst; a very few have had no medical training.

Figure 1–2. Sigmund Freud. Courtesy Sovfoto.

Psychiatrists and psychoanalysts are more likely to base their therapy approach directly upon the theories of Dr. Sigmund Freud or one of his followers. Psychoanalysts in particular find their training heavily influenced by Freud's writings. Thus clinical psychologists, psychiatrists, and psychoanalysts all spend a substantial portion of their time helping people with personal and social problems; yet each group differs from the other in training and in emphasis. None, of course, can read minds or control behavior.

Methods used to learn about people

Although every scientist uses the scientific method, each field studies a different type of occurrence and, thus, needs to apply the scientific

13

method in somewhat different fashion. The psychologist, when he investigates the relationship between spanking and obedience, must use a much different approach from the physicist investigating the effects of temperature change upon spacecraft. The major approaches used by the psychologist to obtain information include observations, case histories, tests, and experiments.

The observational method

Everyone observes the behavior of others and makes certain assumptions from these observations. For example, have you ever observed what seem to be differences in behavior between commercial art majors and office management majors? Have you ever observed that left-handed

Figure 1–3. An example of the use of controlled observation. Courtesy University of Texas Visual Instruction Bureau.

baseball pitchers seem to exhibit different off-the-playing-field behavior from that of right-handed pitchers? If so, you have used observations, but probably not in a scientific, psychological way.

Such casual, uncontrolled observations may add to your understanding, but they are also very likely to be wrong. Whenever you notice an office management major or a left-handed pitcher behaving as you hypothesize, you feel your beliefs have been confirmed. When you see behavior that contradicts your hypothesis, you may tell yourself that it was only an exception, or you may find some other excuse for the behavior.

You can, however, apply the scientific method to your observations through careful controls. Commercial art majors, you hypothesize, are more likely to enter into class discussions than are office management majors. By making a careful count of how often each person comments in your class, you can obtain an average class-discussion score for commercial art students and for office management students. Of course, you should make certain that you collect your observations in several different classes, since commercial art students may talk more in certain classes and less in others. The final step is to analyze your data to see whether your hypothesis is borne out. (There are many possible pitfalls in the study outlined above. Perhaps you can figure out what they are and suggest ways for dealing with them.)

Of course, art or management majors in another college may differ from those you have studied, so you need to be cautious in extending the results of your research beyond the group you actually studied. Nonetheless, *carefully controlled observations* are a fruitful method of investigation.

The case history method

This refers to an intensive study of a single individual, utilizing a great variety of information sources, such as school records, vocational evaluations, psychological tests, and interviews with the individual himself and with those who know him. All this material is integrated to provide as complete a picture of the person as possible. Not only does the case history method give an understanding of one individual, but comparison of several case histories devoted to a specific topic may generate hypotheses to be tested on a larger scale.

Tests

A vast assortment of tests is available to the psychologist. These tests claim to measure everything from potential ability in art to moodiness, from reading ability to mechanical aptitude, from tendencies toward

Figure 1–4. An example of the use of testing. Courtesy University of Texas Visual Instruction Bureau.

mental illness to clerical skills. Tests have been constructed to measure achievement, aptitudes, interests, personality characteristics, memory, and other aspects of human behavior. Tests serve the psychologist-as-artist by giving him better understanding of the individuals he is trying to influence, and tests aid the psychologist-as-scientist by giving him an effective way to measure many human attributes.

Because of the importance of testing in psychology, a great deal of effort is expended in determining how good each test is. This determination is made by evaluating the **validity** and the **reliability** of the test. A test is valid to the degree that it really measures what it was designed to measure. It is reliable to the degree it measures consistently.

Consider your final exam in English last semester: what was it designed to measure? Knowledge of grammar? Ability to write? Understanding of literature? Did it measure what it was designed to measure? If so, it was valid.

Now, how consistently did it measure? If you had taken a very similar examination one week later, would you have gotten roughly the same score? After all, if you were to receive a high score on one test and then a low score a week later on a similar test, your scores would not have been dependable, that is, they would not have been reliable.

> An Air Force psychologist was approached by a young recruit who was unhappy about being assigned to the motor pool rather than receiving mechanical training to work on an engine crew. The psychologist pointed out that his test scores showed low mechanical ability, but the recruit objected. He had taken those tests, he explained, at seven in the morning after riding most of the night on a crowded train and arriving in time for about three hours of sleep and a hurried breakfast. Most of the others taking the tests had gotten to the base in plenty of time for a good sleep and leisurely breakfast. The psychologist agreed to retest the young man, and his scores were considerably higher the second time.

Sometimes a test can be valid in general, but not under a specific set of circumstances. How valid would a typing test be for a person with a fever and a terrible headache? Can you think of other examples of a normally valid test that is not valid under specific circumstances?

Since grades are based partly or completely upon tests, whatever factors affect the validity of tests also affect the validity of grades. Occasionally a student will believe his grade was not valid. If the grade is too low, he may complain to the professor, but he virtually never complains if the grade is too high. Most students seem to figure that the too-high and the too-low grades cancel each other out, and they do not make much fuss.

Some tests are based on national **norms**. In such instances, your score can be compared to scores of hundreds of other people. You may be told that you are in the thirtieth **percentile** (30%ile) nationally in clerical ability or the seventy-third percentile in scientific interest. This means that you have as much or more clerical ability than 30 percent of those who were used for comparison, or you have as much or more interest in science than 73 percent of the **norm** group. (Remember that this does *not* mean 30 percent of your answers were correct or 73 percent of your statements showed scientific interest.)

Surveys and questionnaires

Surveys and **questionnaires** provide a special form of test. Today's newspapers and magazines are filled with the results of public opinion surveys, attitude and personality questionnaires, and interviews. Statistics show how the Republican voters of California feel about who should be the next governor, how residents of Houston look upon a possible tax increase, how college students view their future.

However, the surveys you read in the newspapers form only a small portion of those actually conducted. Business and governmental organizations sponsor thousands of surveys annually. Our Department of State

"He's telling about how we believe in the Sacred Hippopotamus who created Man out of oyster shells—don't ask me how he keeps a straight face!"

Figure 1–5. Obtaining accurate information in surveys is not always possible. Courtesy Ed Fisher.

may wish to learn the attitudes of the Spanish people toward American soldiers stationed in Spain; a candidate for city council wants to know how the voters feel about the local issues; Campbell Soups may desire to test reactions to a new soup flavor; a nursing supervisor may want to learn how student nurses feel about their future work.

Questionnaires are used with more than immediate, practical problems in mind. A psychologist may, for example, hypothesize that attitudes toward education are related to college grades. He could construct a brief attitude questionnaire and administer it to his students, then check their over-all grade-point ratios at the end of the academic year. Or he might believe that a relationship exists between having emotional problems and being divorced. He could then administer a personality questionnaire, previously shown to be valid in measuring emotional problems, to a group of divorced people and to a *comparable* group of married people. His final analysis would show which group had more emotional problems. (Once again, the studies described have possible sources of error. Can you decide what they are and eliminate them?)

The experimental method

Psychologists like to use the **experimental method** in their research, since they feel that, in this way, they can best control all the factors involved. In a typical psychological experiment, one group of subjects (the experimental group) is given special treatment, while a comparable group (the **control group**) is left alone or given normal treatment. The psychologist then compares the two groups to see what effect, if any, was related to the condition he had arranged.

In one example, college students were given a long word and asked to write as many short words as possible, using the letters contained in the long word. One-third of the subjects (Group A) were told that the average number of words made by English professors was 31; one-third (Group B) were told that college freshmen averaged 31 words; the final third (Group C) were informed that prison inmates averaged 31 words. Interestingly enough, Group C made the most short words from the long word, and Group A averaged the lowest number. The same procedure was repeated many times, always with the same results.* Apparently the standards people set for themselves are affected by the nature of the group with which they are compared, and these standards influence the level of performance. Consider the implications for success in school or on the job.

In another experiment, subjects were told to write down words that

*Based on introductory psychology laboratories at the University of Hawaii, 1955–1959.

were to be flashed very briefly on a screen. One-third of the subjects received a paper telling them that the words would deal with travel; one-third were informed that the words would relate to birds and animals; the remaining third, the control group, were not given specific instructions. Among the "words" flashed on the screen were "s a e l" and "d a c k" (Siipola, 1935). What do you think each of the groups would write down when they saw the above "words?" The results indicated that a person's expectations will actually affect what he "sees." What relevance does this have to human behavior outside the experimental situation?

These are only two examples of thousands of experiments that have been conducted to learn more about behavior. Some psychologists prefer to use experiments to investigate behavior, while others use observations, case histories, tests, or combinations of all these.

SUMMARY OF IMPORTANT IDEAS

1. Psychology is the scientific field that attempts to understand, describe, predict, and influence behavior; psychologists make extensive use of the scientific method and the relationships among variables.

2. Some psychologists are more involved with applying the psychological understanding of human behavior to practical problems than they are with accomplishing research.

3. The thinking and the research findings of psychologists influence and are influenced by the thinking and research findings of scholars in other fields.

4. Everyone uses psychological understanding in his daily life, but to become a professional psychologist requires extensive study.

5. Psychology is divided into numerous, closely interrelated specialties.

6. Psychologists cannot "control" behavior nor "read minds."

7. The interests of the clinical psychologist, the psychiatrist, and the psychoanalyst overlap.

8. The research methods utilized by psychologists include controlled observations, case histories, tests, and experiments; surveys and questionnaires are types of tests.

9. Psychological experiments make careful use of control groups, whose behavior is later compared to the groups under investigation to determine whether the experimental condition produced a difference between experimental and control groups.

Human needs 2

Among the innumerable things that psychologists study are human wants or needs and how people try to satisfy these wants or needs. Many needs must be satisfied for a person to continue merely to exist, e.g., hunger and thirst; the human being, at birth, is unable to satisfy these needs without help. Other needs, such as the need for companionship, the need for self-esteem, or the need for safety, are not part of the behavior patterns of infants but develop over the years as the result of experience.

A Book of Verses underneath the Bough,
A Jug of Wine, a Loaf of Bread—and Thou
Beside me singing in the Wilderness—
Oh, Wilderness were Paradise enow!

Perhaps the famous poet Omar Khayyám felt that poetry, drink, food, music, and companionship (apparently female) added up to all the satisfactions he demanded, but most people are **motivated** by many other **needs.** What needs would you want satisfied to turn a wilderness into a paradise?

Motivated behavior is behavior set into motion by a need within the individual. A need indicates that some type of satisfaction is lacking and implies that the organism is activated to reduce the dissatisfaction. Thus, a need for food signifies that a person feels the lack of food, and it sets into motion hunger-motivated behavior. The need for money means a person feels he lacks money, and it sets into motion money-seeking behavior. Needs for affection, for prestige, for self-respect, and many more, operate in the same fashion.

> In the middle of studying for an accounting exam, Ned Rose began to feel uncomfortable. At first he was not certain why he was on edge, but he just could not concentrate. Suddenly he snapped his fingers, jumped up, and dashed to the telephone to call his steady girl friend. After he completed the call, he returned to his study and was now able to concentrate without difficulty.

Ned was motivated to telephone his girl, even though he was temporarily unaware of his need. Nonetheless, the motivation was strong enough to activate goal-seeking behavior, which began with agitated feelings and ended with behavior that satisfied his need.

Sometimes people cannot satisfy their needs. A woman on a diet, although perhaps helping to satisfy needs for popularity and self-esteem, may be perpetually hungry; a mediocre songwriter may never satisfy his need for achievement; an irritating and aggressive student may be unable to satisfy his need for companionship. A high proportion of needs, however, can be satisfied, and the behavior that leads to need satisfaction is rewarded and thus is more likely to occur on subsequent occasions when the same need arises.

Self-actualization: an important human need

The same qualities that distinguish the human personality from the personality of other animals also enable people to develop the need to grow, to improve, and to make use of their potential capacities. When a lower animal has had enough to eat, it rarely searches for food and when warm enough, it rarely seeks new ways of getting warm. The animal's needs seem satisfied when it has, for the moment, all the elements necessary to remain alive and to avoid discomfort and pain. Human beings, however, seem to have a need for more than this basic level of functioning.

The young child is eager to learn, to explore, to have experiences. Of course, his parents may have encouraged his learning, but many children enjoy learning and exploration even when they receive no parental encouragement—there appears to be something in learning and in having new experiences that, in itself, excites them.

> Nine-month-old Mike crawled slowly to the couch, reached up, grabbed the material, and painfully pulled himself to a standing position. In a moment, he had fallen and bruised his chin, but five seconds later he was again pulling himself up so that he could stand. His only reward seemed to be the satisfaction, perhaps excitement, of standing.

> A beautician in Santa Barbara, California, drove into Los Angeles every Monday for ten weeks to take a series of seminars in some recent techniques. Although her shop was so busy that she was turning away customers, she felt the 200-mile round trip was worth the effort, because what she learned enabled her to do a better job.

In both these instances, the people seemed rewarded by the feeling that they had done something that made the most of their abilities. They were **self-actualizing.**

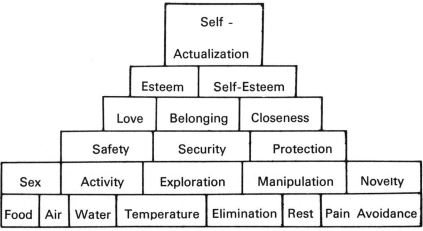

Figure 2–1. Hierarchy of motives.

What is self-actualization? According to one highly respected psychologist (Maslow, 1943), it is the tendency to "become more and more what one is, to become everything that one is capable of becoming." Also, to self-actualize is to make full use of potential abilities and talents and to be able to accept one's own real nature for what it is (adapted from Maslow, 1955). This concept implies that people have a desire, or a need, to make something of themselves, to do as much as their potential allows.

One person may self-actualize by doing a good job of framing pictures; another, by maintaining a happy home and bringing up healthy children; a third, by leading the debating squad; a fourth, by taking shorthand rapidly and accurately; a fifth, by writing poetry to express his own feelings.

Before you can do an effective job of self-actualization, however, other needs must be reasonably well satisfied. These, as described by Professor Abraham Maslow (1943), form a **hierarchy of needs** including **physiological needs, safety needs, love needs,** and **esteem needs** in addition to the self-actualization needs.

Physiological needs

The physiological needs can be divided into two categories: survival needs, which must be satisfied or the body processes stop and life ceases; and stimulation needs, whose function, although not well understood, appears more closely related to the appreciation of life than to the maintaining of life.

Survival needs

Survival needs include those produced by hunger, thirst, air hunger, elimination pressures, fatigue, temperature regulation demands, and pain avoidance. Relatively few Americans have suffered acutely from being unable to satisfy these needs (except, perhaps, for pain avoidance), but all of us have experienced these needs in milder form.

1. *Hunger.* For most people in the United States, being hungry means missing lunch and "starving" before dinner. Elsewhere in the world, and even in some American families, hunger is a major motivation, perhaps *the* major motivation, for the behavior of many people. Much of the world's population rarely receives the amount of food that an overweight American woman is allowed by a strict diet. The hungry have poor health, of course; their life span is low, and their rate of infant deaths is high. But consider the overwhelming importance of food as a motivating factor for these people; consider the motivation caused by hearing your children

cry constantly because they have not enough to eat. Communist and Western nations alike recognize the motivating force of food in their competition to maintain the friendship of hungry countries.

One group of Americans, during World War II, volunteered to undergo a starvation diet so that the effects of hunger might be studied. After several weeks of intense dieting, they displayed several types of behavior change: their dreams, thoughts, and conversations continually dealt with food; they became irritable; their activity level was reduced and they became apathetic (Keys et al., 1950). Thus, the stronger the need, the more its impact is felt on all aspects of living.

2. *Thirst.* Most Americans have experienced the dry throat and mouth that accompany thirst, but very few have gone through the serious discomfort of extensive thirst. Yet, those who have will acknowledge that the motivating qualities of acute thirst are overwhelming.

3. *Air hunger.* The need to breathe is so obvious, and breathing is so automatic that people often forget how essential oxygen is to the body. A very brief period without oxygen will produce permanent brain damage, and a few minutes will lead to death.

"And how was the food at your school?"

Figure 2–2. Satisfaction of basic needs, such as hunger, is necessary before higher-level motives can receive attention. Courtesy Ed Fisher.

4. *Elimination pressures.* The body must be able to get rid of its waste products in order to exist. Young children relieve the pressure in the bowels or the bladder without hesitating (just ask any parent who is forced to change diapers), but later learning reduces this freedom. Teaching children the proper conditions for satisfying the need for elimination consumes much parental energy in the early years of child rearing.

5. *Fatigue.* The human organism must have rest and sleep in order to renew its vitality. Occasionally this need becomes so strong that a person will fall asleep in class, on the job, or—more dangerously—at the wheel of his automobile. After having gone without sleep for nine days, one person displayed deteriorated thinking and emotionally disturbed behavior (Luby et al., 1960).

6. *Temperature regulation demands.* People have the ability to adjust to variations in heat and cold up to certain limits. The need to be in a comfortable temperature can be extremely motivating. As a result, man has gone to great pains to provide himself with clothing, with heating and cooling devices, and with protecting shelters. The popularity of Southern California, Hawaii, Florida, and Arizona both for residents and for tourists is partly based on climate.

7. *Pain avoidance.* Strangely enough, people often do not realize the role that pain plays in preserving life. If you felt no pain, you would not know when a part of the body was diseased or infected, and the disease or infection could spread and cause severe damage before you realized what was happening. Thus, pain avoidance is a survival need, not because pain is discomforting, but because pain is a signal that something has gone wrong with the organism. The few people who cannot feel pain must have frequent medical examinations. Why?

The survival needs are the most compelling needs people have. When experiencing hunger, pain, or extreme fatigue, we can concentrate on little else except satisfying the need. To obtain food, a starving soldier is likely to surrender to a hostile enemy even with the knowledge that he will possibly be executed. Under extreme pain, or the threat of extreme pain, people have been known to violate many closely held personal convictions.

Stimulation needs

The satisfaction of **stimulation needs,** including the need for sex, activity, exploration, manipulation, and novelty, does not appear necessary for survival. Nonetheless, complete lack of environmental stimulation is very distressing, as students who were completely shut off from their surroundings attested (Lilly, 1956). (See page 51.) And children deprived of activity and stimulating human relationships seem to suffer both physically and emotionally (Spitz, 1949). (See page 120.) Also, sex is obviously necessary for the life of the species, although not for the life of any given living individual. The evidence just cited, however, is not sufficient basis for assuming that stimulation needs must be satisfied for the organism to live.

Figure 2–3. How would this environment encourage the satisfaction of stimulation or self-actualization needs? Courtesy The Library of Congress.

At one time, these needs were believed not to have a physiological basis, yet recent observations have shown that animals and young infants respond to such needs as exploration and manipulation without any opportunity for learning them (Festinger, 1954; Harlow et al., 1950). Perhaps, in the future, scientists will find biochemical bases for all stimulation needs, as they have for the sex need.

1. *Sex.* Most Americans can satisfy survival and stimulation needs with relatively little difficulty—except for the sex need. Everything from the

professional writings in psychology to movie advertisements to college bull sessions indicate that the sex need is far from satisfied.

The desire for sex in humans results from biochemical changes within the body, but these changes are set off by information sent through the sense organs to the brain, or by thinking which began in the brain. Thinking of something with sexual meanings can lead to stirring up the sex need; seeing, touching, or hearing something with sexual meanings will also lead to sexual arousal.

Satisfying the hunger, thirst, activity, and other physiological motives is very easy to learn. Sometimes, as with the need for air or for sleep, no learning is necessary—we breathe and sleep without any help or learning at all. Sex is quite different. Human beings must learn how to satisfy their sexual needs.

2. *Activity, exploration, manipulation, novelty.* It seems clear that people do not desire a state of complete rest, but seek activity and stimulation. Total lack of activity produces boredom, fatigue, and apathy. Complete isolation from stimulation, brought about by being placed in an apparatus that completely cuts off all contact with the outside world, has led to symptoms of mental confusion such as fantasies and hallucinations (Heron, 1957).

> While studying deep-sea divers, one psychologist noted the reactions of some of the subjects when they were placed in their diving suit. These men were partially isolated from the outside world: they could feel nothing but the inside of their suits; they could hear only what was transmitted to them; they could see only directly ahead through the small window in the mask. "Some of these men will panic as soon as they are completely enclosed in their diving uniforms. I've seen men who had shown bravery in other situations break out into a cold sweat and shriek to be let out when I closed the glass face mask on them. Others are all right until they are lowered into the water and their heads go under—then they panic. Yet the same man may have no hesitation in swimming under the water without a face mask." (Paraphrase of personal communication from Ralph Kiessling, previously research psychologist with the United States Navy.)

Given the opportunity, children appear to wish to explore their environment; they wish to handle objects with their hands and—often to the amusement of older children and adults—manipulate the objects with their tongues. Frequently observers report that children will bypass a familiar object in order to explore and manipulate a new object, implying that novelty may be a factor in their behavior. Even monkeys will spend much time and effort manipulating mechanical equipment with no apparent reward (Harlow et al., 1950), indicating that the act of manipulation is rewarding itself. However, both infants and monkeys will eventually tire of any given object and will prefer to go on to something else.

You may have observed similar behavior in adults and older children, but these individuals have had the opportunity to be rewarded for having performed such actions. Infants, however, have not had the same opportunities for learning, and their responses to stimulation needs have probably resulted from inborn characteristics. Like so much of the world's store of knowledge, the degree to which stimulation needs might be inherited is still under debate.

Adults would rarely wish to restrict the chances of children to satisfy their survival needs, yet many adults appear unaware that the satisfaction of stimulation needs is similarly very important. Limiting the opportunity for a child to explore his environment or to be physically active may actually harm the child's normal process of development. The hunger need, of course, cannot be ignored without risking the death of the child, but punishing the child for expressing his needs for activity and exploration may also turn out to be harmful. How do adults encourage or discourage the satisfaction of stimulation needs?

Stimulation motives appear related to each other and to the general desire to receive more from the environment. For this reason, they support the contention that people have the need to make the most of their talents and capacities. In this instance, you might say that people desire to make the most of their environment by manipulating and exploring it, by being active and having new experiences.

Social aspects of physiological needs

The satisfaction of survival and stimulation motives involves more than biological satisfaction. Unless the needs are acutely disturbing because they are not being adequately met, people respond in keeping with certain customs, traditions, personal tastes, and habits. You can also attempt to increase your pleasure in the process of satisfying your physiological needs: eating fish eyes would help reduce your hunger need, but you might refuse, although residents of other countries consider fish eyes a delicacy; sleeping in the flower bed by the entrance to the college library would satisfy your need for sleep, but you would be unlikely to behave this way. You would undoubtedly prefer eating a medium rare steak to eating fish eyes, and sleeping in a comfortable bed with clean sheets to sleeping in the flower bed. Can you see the relationship between the way in which you satisfy your physiological needs and the possibility of self-actualization?

"Man does not live by bread alone"

The history of the world is filled with examples of people who gave up the satisfaction of a physiological motive in order to satisfy a motive higher on Maslow's hierarchy of needs.

In wartime Europe, starving parents gave their only food to their children; their love, duty, and responsibility were stronger than their hunger.

A music student lived in near poverty, without adequate food or warmth, to save money to pay for lessons.

A student, his nose completely cut from his face, helped pull his friends from a wrecked automobile before running for his personal relief (*Los Angeles Times*, July 1, 1964).

Early in World War II three military chaplains drowned because they had given their life jackets to others.

Hundreds of college students risked abuse, beatings, and even death to help Negroes win voting rights in certain communities in the United States.

Rituals, restrictions, traditions, and laws affect the methods permitted to satisfy all survival and stimulation needs. Certain foods are eaten and others are refused because of early learning experiences, not because of food value. Eating in a clean environment, preferably with pleasant companions, seems to improve the enjoyment of food. A person who enters a smelly restaurant and notices lipstick smudges on his water glass and dried bits of food caked on his fork is very likely to lose his appetite.

And food also has great symbolic meaning. Some societies place restrictions upon doing violence to a person with whom you have recently eaten; to "break bread" with someone is an indication of friendship.

Eating habits are important to the major religions of the world. The Orthodox Jews accept the *kosher* laws, which forbid them to eat any meat from pigs, goats, or shellfish; Catholics must not eat meat on Fridays; Moslems will not eat pig meat; Hindus will not eat any part of the cow; and many Protestant groups have replaced the traditional ceremonial wine with grape juice.

Food preferences also vary greatly. In Japan, raw fish (sashimi) is very popular, but oysters are eaten cooked; in the United States, oysters are eaten raw, but never fish. Many enjoy rabbit meat, while others become sick to their stomach at the thought of eating such a cute, furry creature—although they do not hesitate to eat young chickens.

Eating customs extend to how the food should be eaten. American parents teach their children to cut meat with the fork in the left hand, then transfer the fork to the right hand and pick up the meat; English children are taught the simpler method of keeping the fork in the left hand. Japanese drink soup from a bowl, while Americans and Chinese spoon it slowly from a dish.

The list of social influences upon the way people satisfy their physiological needs could be continued indefinitely. What examples can you think of?

Figure 2–4. Private ownership of guns (confiscated by police in this picture) can be used to satisfy safety needs. Do you feel guns are an appropriate solution? Courtesy Columbia Broadcasting System.

Safety and security needs

If you are deeply involved with satisfying your hunger need or your need to avoid pain, you will have little time or energy for anything else. However, once you are able to satisfy these needs, at least at a minimally adequate level, and can feel reasonably confident that the need will not return to disrupt you for a period of time, you can turn your attention to satisfying safety and security needs.

Everyone needs to feel safe from such harm as meeting with physical violence, fearing that things they value will be taken away, or fearing that the care of parents or other protectors will be removed. People who fear that the Secret Police might suddenly burst in and arrest them certainly will find it difficult to concentrate on satisfying any except the basic physiological needs. The child whose parents are constantly arguing and threatening divorce will also have unfulfilled safety needs, and his behavior may be strongly influenced by attempts to assure himself that his parents or some substitute will continue to protect him. What is the effect of the threat of atomic war upon your own safety needs?

Sometimes, however, people with normal physiological or safety needs will satisfy needs higher on the hierarchy of needs in preference to those lower. Example 2–1 contains several examples. This involves the study of values, which are discussed in Chapter 17. Does anything motivate you so much that you would risk survival or safety to achieve it?

Love and belonging needs

Although the claim that "love makes the world go around" is at least slightly exaggerated, no doubt exists about the motivating properties of the need for love and a sense of belonging. Some evidence exists that, at least for infants, love may be necessary for maintenance of good health. Infants who lack the love of a mother or mother-substitute have been observed to become depressed (Spitz, 1949), apathetic, and physically and emotionally retarded (Ribble, 1943). Since such infants are also usually deprived of normal satisfaction for stimulation needs, we cannot be certain whether the ill-effects resulted from the lack of love or the lack of opportunity for stimulation.

In any event, the need for love and for belonging is important. People with an unsatisfied need for love or for the feeling of belonging to a group may go to great lengths to satisfy this need, even though loss of self-esteem might be the cost.

> Mrs. Leonard had been widowed when her son was ready to finish high school. She and her husband had had an excellent marriage, and she had been very dependent upon her husband's love. At her husband's death she felt lost and, subsequently, became very demanding of her son for signs of love; she could not tolerate even the thought of his going away from home to college. Although the family was in very modest financial circumstances, Mrs. Leonard bribed her son with an automobile to make him agree to go to the college a few miles from home. At the beginning of his second year, the boy's "steady" enrolled at a college some distance away, and he wanted to transfer there, but once again Mrs. Leonard bribed him to stay home, this time with the promise of a summer at the University of Hawaii. He was an obliging son, reluctant to leave his mother alone anyway, and he again agreed to the arrangement.

He liked Honolulu so much, however, that, when they were to return home at the end of the six-week session, he accepted a job with a large Waikiki hotel. His mother tried to persuade him to return. When that failed, she literally begged him to go back with her, crying and shrieking and moaning like a thwarted child.

A parallel to Mrs. Leonard's unhappy situation occurs in a one-sided romance when one member of the couple needs love so much that he will expend all his energies and sacrifice his self-respect to gain even unimportant tokens of love from the other.

The reference to love needs is not restricted to romantic love and parent-child love. We are concerned with the entire area of the feeling of closeness between two good friends, the feeling of neighborliness that exists in some communities, or the feeling of good fellowship that occurs in social clubs or other social groups. Those who feel friendless and unloved exert a large portion of their efforts to satisfy love needs.

Esteem and self-esteem needs

Once physiological, safety, and love needs have been satisfied, attention can turn toward gaining the respect of others and having respect for yourself. Mrs. Leonard sacrificed this opportunity when her unsatisfied love needs became so demanding that she had to beg her son to remain with her.

We are all human beings and, as such, feel we have the right to be treated as people of worth. The strongest word one three-year-old can call another is "baby," because this implies a lesser level of competence and worth (at least in three-year-old eyes). The person who feels inadequate may channel his energy into proving his adequacy *to himself*. Of course he may also wish to establish his adequacy in the eyes of others, but he is mainly motivated to convince himself.

When he lacks self-esteem, he is likely to be too busy trying to establish his self-esteem to be able to make the most effective use of his abilities and potential talents.

Self-actualization needs

Only when more basic needs have been at least minimally met can the individual turn his attention to satisfying his needs for self-actualization. Self-actualization, as explained earlier, refers to the process of making maximum use of your abilities, of developing your talents, and of being the sort of person you really are, rather than the sort of person you believe others wish you to be.

Just as the young infant seems to need to explore his environment, just as the monkey seems to need to manipulate puzzles for the challenge, mature human beings also wish to develop their capacities. No one is constantly self-actualizing, just as no one is constantly in the process of satisfying any one other need, but each individual has the potential within him to feel the need to self-actualize and to satisfy this need. Perhaps a few examples will help clarify this complex concept.

John Ferguson had gone to dental school only because his mother had insisted that he follow in his late father's footsteps. One month before he would have finished the three-year graduate program, his mother died, and John dropped out of school immediately and entered another college where he earned a degree in political science and eventually obtained a position with the State Department. When his friends told him he was foolish to sacrifice so many years of training, he merely answered, "Dentistry is not me." He felt he could be himself and make use of his real abilities as a political scientist. As you might imagine, he was very successful, although his income never reached that earned by most dentists.

An English professor told the following story:

"At the small town college where I teach, older people rarely take daytime courses, so I was surprised to notice a shiny, bald head among the more youthful ones, and I was doubly surprised when I realized this head belonged to the owner of the nearest thing to a department store our town had. He later explained that, by the time he was 45, he had made all the money he needed and had proved to himself he could run a business. But all his life he felt he could be an excellent furniture designer, and now he was returning to college to learn both the techniques and the artistic background, so that he could develop this capacity. The truth is that he didn't have much talent, but he certainly had fun."

Mary Welch was brought up in a family which believed women were not capable of being educated, and—at 17—she married a man who believed the same. Suddenly, after five years of marriage, an automobile accident left her a widow with two small children and no source of income. She took a job as waitress at a Howard Johnson restaurant and enrolled in a course to learn IBM keypunching at night, while her mother cared for the children. Slowly she realized she had ability and that she actually enjoyed the excitement of a busy restaurant, as well as the challenge of trying to improve her keypunching ability. She felt that her hectic schedule enabled her to use her talents and become more the sort of person she really was, whereas the years of living in homes that treated women as inferior and unintelligent had only held her back. However, she felt uncomfortable because she was unable to spend the time with her children she felt necessary.

At the age of ten, Mark's parents were told by his teachers that their son spent all his time sketching and doodling; when he was 15, his father begged him to forget his drawing and study accounting so that he could eventually support himself; at 19, Mark finished business college and went to work for an accounting firm but was soon fired because he drew some uncom-

Figure 2–5. Which of Maslow's needs is this man satisfying? Courtesy California State College at Los Angeles.

plimentary pictures of his boss. Mark got another job but went to art school at night. The job pays poorly, but "I don't really care much about pay, as long as I can concentrate on art. I just have to paint. It's just as important for me to paint as it is for you to eat."

All of these people were motivated by the need to develop their capacities and to be "themselves." At the time of this writing, only one of the four had shown himself professionally successful, but all received satisfaction from their endeavors. Each one of the four was fulfilling his need for self-actualization, regardless of what the rest of the world thought.

How can you tell whether or not you are self-actualizing? First, it is necessary to realize that self-actualization is not as sharply defined as many psychological concepts, and you may have a difficult time deciding whether you are applying the concept properly. However, four situations occur when a person self-actualizes.

(1) People raise their standards and demand more of themselves. By so doing, they also demand more of life and expect greater value from the things they do.

(2) Self-improvement becomes continuous. This improvement may occur through a course in Chinese cooking, through reading books and magazines, or through a summer camping trip to the National Parks. If the end result is that the individual gains in understanding the world or himself, or if he has become better able to do something, then he has been self-actualizing.

(3) The individual improves his self-understanding and becomes more the kind of person he wants to be. It may seem strange to say that many people do not really like themselves, but it is true. People are ashamed of certain things they have done or wish to do or have not done or are afraid to do. The self-actualizing person behaves so that he can respect himself.

(4) The self-actualizing person makes the fullest use of the abilities he has and also tries to develop new abilities. Most people will attempt only a small proportion of the many things they have the potential to do. People self-actualize when they develop present competencies and investigate new and untried areas (adapted from Coleman, 1960).

The need for self-actualization motivates people to grow and to develop their talents, but some needs produce behavior that can only compensate for deficiencies, rather than lead to growth.

Deficiency-motivation and growth-motivation

Behavior motivated by hunger or by fear of physical punishment is **deficiency-motivated**; that is, it is motivated by things the organism lacks. You sense an uncomfortable inner tension, you wish to reduce this tension, and so you seek food or escape.

A starving man does not worry about how his food is seasoned; a child, frightened because his parents have left him alone at night without warning, would probably welcome a spanking, if that was the price of his parents' return. These are deficiency-motivated people. When they satisfy their hunger or safety needs, they have not attained any degree of personal growth; they have merely reduced a deficit.

On the other hand, when you are motivated by the possibility of truly enjoying the meal or by the pleasure of warmth and security in being with those you love, the behavior is **growth-motivated**. It is not so much tension-reduction, but the opportunity for personal growth and pleasure that provides the motivation. You may even create a mild tension on purpose, such as by eating a very light lunch when anticipating an excellent dinner, so that the enjoyment is heightened.

Thus behavior occurring in response to any need may, on the one hand, lead to the reduction of a deficit or, on the other hand, lead to some form of personal growth. Satisfying the hunger need can merely reduce hunger, or it can be an enjoyable process with good, exciting company and pleasant surroundings; satisfying the esteem need may merely compensate for lack of self-esteem, or it can be a wonderful experience that leaves you with a warm glow of pleasure, e.g., being commended by your employer

Figure 2–6. The satisfaction of a deficiency motive, such as hunger, can still be fun. Courtesy A. Devaney, Inc.

for having done an excellent job with a task on which you worked particularly hard.

Here, then, is the hierarchy of needs: physiological needs, safety and security needs, love and belonging needs, esteem and self-esteem needs, and self-actualization needs. In order to focus upon the higher needs, the more basic ones must be reasonably well satisfied. In satisfying each need, you may be motivated by deficiency and tension-reduction, or by growth and enhancement. The hierarchy, of course, is not a rigid one, but must be considered in light of the specific background and values of each individual.

We will return to the concept of self-actualization at many points in this book. In the meantime, consider a few of the implications of this idea:

1. Everyone, yourself included, has potential capacities and talents.

2. These capacities and talents are often never developed.

3. Before developing them effectively, you usually must deal with such other matters as physiological, safety, love, and esteem needs.

4. You are wasting a certain segment of yourself if you leave your potential capacities and talents undeveloped.

5. Developing these capacities and talents is enjoyable and natural, not dull or strained.

6. By trying to influence others to be what *you* want, you may be limiting their possibilities of developing themselves as *they* want.

Each individual has a unique personality. When he is able to satisfy his physiological, safety, love, and esteem needs adequately, he is able to attempt to develop his unique personality to the utmost that his capacities allow.

Some specific social needs and their description*

1. Achievement—the need to accomplish things well and quickly, to be successful in what is done, to overcome obstacles.

2. Deference—the need to follow someone else, to have a leader.

3. Order—the need to be neat and orderly.

4. Exhibition—the need to attract attention, to be noticed.

5. Autonomy—the need to be independent, to gain freedom, to defy authority.

6. Affiliation—the need to form friendships, to love others, to join groups, to please people.

7. Introception—the need to be imaginative, subjective, to participate in romantic action.

8. Succorance—the need to get help or sympathy, to be dependent.

9. Dominance—the need to influence or control others, to lead, to organize.

10. Abasement—the need to apologize, to accept punishment.

11. Nurturance—the need to help others, to express sympathy.

12. Change—the need to avoid routine, to be involved with change.

13. Endurance—the need to work hard, to avoid distractions.

14. Heterosexual—the need for relationships with the opposite sex.

15. Aggression—the need to express aggressive feelings, to harm, to punish.

Example 2–2.

---

* These categories are those used in constructing the Edwards Personal Preference Schedule (Edwards, 1954). They are based on the list of needs developed by Professor Murray (Murray, 1938).

Other human needs and motives

Other systems of classifying motives have been developed. One of the most respected is outlined in Example 2–2. This system deals only with nonphysiological motives, fifteen of which have been described here. Notice that most of these needs may be deficiency-motivating or growth-motivating, depending upon the circumstances.

Individual differences in need strength

Individuals vary considerably in the degree to which they are motivated by each need. John may have a great need to attract attention and to express aggressive feelings, while Jim needs to follow others and form friendships. Jane, who is studying nursing, wants to be good enough to become a supervisor while Jean will be happy remaining a staff nurse.

Figure 2–7. What would you assume the need for achievement to be for the five men coming through the door? Courtesy Columbia Broadcasting System.

Mac has a high need to help others, but Mort has little need to be of service.

Level of aspiration

As the result of the strength of his needs, in interaction with other personal characteristics, each individual develops a **level of aspiration** for many areas of his life. Your level of aspiration refers to the goal you

anticipate achieving. The person who intends to be a straight B student has a higher level of aspiration for grades than someone else who anticipates a straight C average. In the earlier example, Jane had a higher level of vocational aspiration than Jean.

A person's happiness and satisfaction are closely related to the gap between his actual accomplishments and his aspiration level. Thus, the farther a person falls below his level of aspiration, the less happy he is, *even if his achievement level is objectively high* (Block and Thomas, 1955; Rosenberg, 1962).

When a person's achievement level begins to approach his aspiration level, he will usually raise his sights. If he finds that he is unable to succeed in fulfilling his level of aspiration, his goals may become less ambitious.

> Ralph Gardner had a good intelligence and knew it. He decided to become a medical doctor, and began college with that in mind. However, because of his need to have a lot of money to spend, he devoted his energies to an outside job, and his grades remained low. After his first year of college, he lowered his level of aspiration from physician to social worker, which required graduate work but not nearly so long a training period as medicine. By the end of the first quarter of his sophomore year, he had been dropped from college because of low grades. He returned the spring quarter, now aspiring to a degree in social science, but he continued to hold his outside job, and his final grades were so low he decided not to return to college.

> Ralph then got a job selling encyclopedias and was quite successful. His success reminded him that he had a good brain, and his work schedule left him free between noon and four in the afternoon; so he enrolled in a junior college to earn an Associate of Arts in Sales Management. Although his educational level of aspiration had dropped, his financial level of aspiration began to rise. He was soon selling an average of four sets of books a week, which earned him more than an average social worker makes, and he aspired to more. After ten months, the area supervisor asked Ralph to open a new territory and recruit and train other salesmen. He persuaded some of his college friends to sell during the summer, and he made a commission on every set of books they sold, plus the normal commission on what he sold. Within two years, Ralph had received his junior college degree, had opened up two additional territories, and was next in line for assistant regional supervisor. He was now aspiring to the average income of a medical doctor, which he achieved at about the same age he would have completed his long medical training and begun to practice.

When Ralph first entered college, he had high levels of aspiration in both income and education. Eighteen months later, he was deeply depressed and felt he would achieve neither aspiration. He was only partially successful in achieving the educational aspiration, but he was completely successful in his financial goals.

Ralph's aspirations changed because he was able to judge himself fairly accurately. Others are less fortunate. Some set a level of aspiration beyond their abilities to achieve, then refuse to change it. Others set their level so low that it is easily achieved, but they never fully develop their talents, since they need to use only a small portion of their abilities to gain their goals.

Your levels of aspiration are learned as all social motives are learned. Among the factors influencing the level of aspiration are the actual maximum potential ability level; the degree to which parents and others in the environment encourage success; personality factors such as security or anxiety, which might work for or against success; early childhood experiences; and, like Ralph, the person's unique history relevant to the particular aspiration.

An individual's level of aspiration is influenced by his **reference group,** i.e., those people with whom he compares himself. If you attended a high school where 80 percent of the graduates went to college, your reference group would most likely have been a college-preparatory group, and you would probably aspire to more educational achievement than your friend who went to a high school that sent very few graduates to college. One of the reasons for Ralph's not feeling highly successful was that he retained his old college friends as a reference group, and he knew that they would have admired academic success more than financial success.

Group differences in need strength

Differences in the motivating force of needs are found not only between individuals, but between groups as well. Men, for example, show a greater need for achievement than do women (McClelland et al., 1953); students majoring in engineering have a greater need for order and neatness than those majoring in other fields (Izard, 1960); in Hawaii, high school students from different national backgrounds were found to differ greatly in the relative strength of those motives described in Example 2–2 even though all were born and reared in the United States, spoke only English as a native language, and attended the same schools (Fenz and Arkoff, 1962).

As you might expect, differences in the strength of needs are often found between comparable groups in different countries. University stu-

an (Berrien, 1964) have been shown to demonstrate less need
...ance than do students in the United States, while junior executives in the United States had a much greater need for achievement than
those in Turkey (Bradburn, 1963), and American adolescents had a
greater need for achievement than Brazilian adolescents (Rosen, 1962).

People are motivated by needs that must be satisfied in order to sustain
life; they are also motivated by needs learned through the years. Some
people are motivated to attain high levels of aspiration and to self-actualize, while others are primarily involved in satisfying deficiency motives,
and are unable to pay attention to growth-motives and self-actualization.

Unconscious motivation

People often behave without knowing why, i.e., without knowing what
their motives are. When behavior results from motives you are unaware
of, the behavior is **unconsciously motivated.** You may become aware of
the motives in the future, but—for the moment at least—you are behaving
without really being conscious of the underlying causes.

Many people like to believe that they always understand their own
motives, that they never do anything without knowing why. Psychologists do not agree; they feel that much human behavior occurs without
the behaver actually understanding all of his motives.

Consider some situations involving unconscious motivation.

> Clayton Black sits in English class biting his nails. Whenever he
> realizes what he is doing, he quits. As soon as he becomes
> absorbed in the lecture again, he returns to his biting.

> Jan Sturm spilled salt during lunch. He immediately threw some
> over his shoulder, then laughed about "silly old superstitions."
> Yet every time Jan spills salt, he repeats this action, although he
> swears he is not superstitious about spilled salt bringing bad
> luck.

> The first moment you walk into class, you know you will not
> like the instructor, even though your friend has recommended
> him to you. Everything the professor does irritates you, from
> the tie he wears to the examination questions he asks. However,
> you are uncertain why your friends do not share your dislike.

> Harry's regular girl was Cynthia, but she was away at another
> college, and Harry had been dating Jeannie during her absence.
> Although Harry spoke of Cynthia as being a "fine wife," Jean-
> nie was more submissive and flattered Harry more. During
> Christmas vacation, when Harry took Cynthia home the first

evening they had been together in several months, he kissed her goodnight, looked into her eyes—and said, " 'Til tomorrow night, Jeannie."

Craig Kelly has a great fear of being immersed in water, especially of getting his face wet. He even hates to have a heavy shower spray on his face; yet he admits his fear is foolish, and he cannot explain it.

The motivation for all these behavioral acts was unconscious, as far as the participants were concerned. How would you, as an outside observer, interpret the motivations underlying the various actions?

Repression

When behavior results from unconscious motivation, it is often said that the basis for the behavior is **repressed**. Repression, like forgetting, is the inability to recall something. Unlike forgetting, however, repression occurs not because of passing time or disuse, but rather because you are motivated to be unable to recall. You may quite easily *forget* your dentist's telephone number, but you are not likely to *forget* an appointment made two days earlier. You may have repressed the memory of the appointment, but you have not forgotten it.

Repression does not occur because you consciously want it to occur. A person does not purposely decide to repress something; it happens without his awareness. Why do people repress certain feelings and events? Because they have a need to do so—because the incident or feeling is so upsetting or so threatening or so disturbing to their self-esteem that they are strongly motivated to be unable to recall what happened. People repress experiences, feelings, wishes, even thoughts. In our culture, sexual and aggressive feelings are especially likely to be repressed, because we are so reluctant to accept ourselves as the "sort of person with *that* kind of feeling."

Repressed motives may influence behavior in ways that are not always understood, although people try to make their behavior appear rational.

> When I was still in the primary grades, my parents had a strict rule that I could never hit my younger brother unless he hit me first; so I would goad him into hitting me, so that I could hit him back. Being bigger and stronger, of course, my blows were more painful than his, and, to make things even better, I always felt justified in my actions. It wasn't until I was in college that I realized what I had actually been doing.

The unconscious motivation was, of course, the desire to be able to hit his brother. Even a third-grader realizes that hitting a child five years younger is unacceptable, and his self-esteem would suffer if he felt he had picked the fight himself. So, without being aware of why he was doing it, the older boy irritated his brother into attacking. He could thus act out his need to hit the younger boy without losing self-esteem and without bringing his parents' wrath down upon him. The basis for the motivation was, however, repressed until a psychology class discussion provoked his memory. At that time, he had much less need to repress his motivation, since the hostility he felt toward his brother had long since disappeared.

How about the person who tells his friend, "I'm only saying this for your own good," and then proceeds to criticize him with considerable vehemence? Is he really motivated by the desire to help the other person? What motives might be repressed? What would be his need to have them repressed?

SUMMARY OF IMPORTANT IDEAS

1. Motivated behavior is behavior set into motion by a need within the individual; a need indicates that some satisfaction is lacking and implies that the organism is activated to obtain the satisfaction.

2. A hierarchy of needs has been suggested, with the more basic needs having to be adequately satisfied before the individual can turn his attention to needs higher on the scale.

3. The most basic needs are the physiological needs, including the survival needs (produced by hunger, thirst, and fatigue) and the stimulation needs (exploration and manipulation); when the former are not adequately satisfied, the organism dies; psychologists are not certain of all the effects of lack of satisfying the stimulation needs, although lowered effectiveness will result.

4. People usually satisfy the physiological needs in keeping with certain customs, traditions, personal tastes, and habits.

5. The second most basic needs are the safety and security needs.

6. Next are the love and belonging needs.

7. And then the esteem and self-esteem needs.

8. When the above are reasonably well satisfied, the individual can concern himself with satisfying his needs for self-actualization; this means making maximum use of his ability, developing his talents, and becoming the sort of person he really is.

9. Some behavior is motivated by deficiencies or the things the organism lacks; some is motivated by growth or the desire to be better or do things better.

10. Another system describes motivation by a number of needs not occurring in a hierarchy.

11. Each person develops, in many spheres of his life, a level of aspiration or goals he anticipates achieving.

12. Groups differ in the strength of their various needs.

13. Much behavior occurs because of unconscious motivation or motivation of which the individual himself is not aware.

14. When behavior results from unconscious motivation, the basis for it may be repressed; repression occurs when a person does not recall something because he needs to be unable to recall, rather than (as in forgetting) because the matter was not important enough to recall.

Perceiving the environment 3

Psychologists have always been deeply concerned with how man determines what is going on in his environment. The interest carried over from philosophy and can be traced far back into history. Much of the early research in psychology, dating back some 90 years now, involved the relationship between what is actually, objectively, in the environment, and how man interprets and analyzes it. Psychologists, in conjunction with physiologists and physicists, studied these problems in many ways and are still interested in them, although at a much higher level of sophistication than they were in the nineteenth century. The awareness that man could develop research methods to evaluate his own behavior came partly through the studies of sensation and perception.

The human organism is highly sensitive to its environment. It becomes aware of colors, shapes, sounds, tastes, pressures, odors, temperature change, and other environmental **stimuli*** through the senses, which might be compared to windows in a house. Without these windows, the residents of the house would not know what was going on outside.

Everything that enters through these windows is transmitted to the brain, where it is interpreted, largely in light of previous experiences. As the individual matures and has more experiences, he is better able to understand the information communicated through the senses.

Each sense is represented by **receptor** organs which receive the "message" from whatever in the environment is presenting a stimulus. **Visual** receptors are in the eye; **auditory** receptors are inside the ear; taste receptors are on the tongue.

After being received by the receptor, the "message" is transmitted through the nerves to the brain, where it is interpreted and its significance communicated to the appropriate part of the body, so that the organism may take some form of action. The visual receptor receives the stimuli that show the traffic light to be green instead of red; this pattern of shapes and colors is transmitted to the brain, which interprets it and then communicates the pattern's significance to the various parts of the body that get the automobile into motion. Of course, all this happens so rapidly that it appears instantaneous.

Sensation is the term applied to what occurs each time a receptor organ is stimulated. **Perception** is the process through which the various sensations are interpreted and organized into meaningful patterns.

Sensation

Tradition states that man has five senses: sight, hearing, taste, touch, and smell. (Some people add a sixth, **extra-sensory perception** or ESP, to explain certain mysterious occurrences, such as a person's dreaming of an event before it happens, "mental telepathy," or mind reading. However, few psychologists presently believe that ESP actually occurs (Warner, 1955).)

Psychologists have changed the list of senses somewhat, adding the **kinesthetic sense** (sense of body movement, posture, and weight), the **vestibular sense** (sense of balance), and the **internal** (or interoceptor) **senses** (sense of hunger, thirst, and so forth). Also touch has been broken down into four different senses, pressure, pain, warmth, and cold, which

*Stimuli is the plural of the word stimulus, which refers to any object or event that stirs up or stimulates behavior.

Figure 3–1. Receiving, interpreting, and responding to stimuli.

are usually referred to as the skin senses. Each of these four senses has its own receptor organs consisting of nerve endings located all over the body. However, nerve endings are more closely grouped in places like the lips and the tongue, which are very sensitive as a result.

Often, one experience involves several receptor organs. For example, when you drink hot coffee, you are stimulating several senses: taste, smell, vision, pressure, temperature, and—if the coffee is very hot—pain. Close your eyes and rub them: not only do you feel the pressure, but you see various colors and shapes, even though your eyes are closed, because the visual receptors are being activated by the pressure.

Although the human being has extremely sensitive receptors, his senses respond to only a small portion of all possible stimuli. Some sounds, sights, and smells, for example, can be sensed by certain lower animals, but not by man. These stimuli are said to be outside man's **sensory threshold**. Bloodhounds can sniff their way along a trail; hawks are very sensitive to movement (Sanford, 1965); dogs can hear specially constructed whistles barely audible to the human ear. And many stimuli, e.g., X rays, atoms, extremely high-pitched sounds, are not recognized by any form of mammal.

Human beings can develop their sensitivity for their own enjoyment and satisfaction, if they wish, but other animals cannot. A forest ranger develops his ability to see movement; a wine connoisseur develops his ability to distinguish wine bottled in 1957 from the same kind of wine bottled in 1958; an opera lover can recognize when the tenor is the slightest bit flat. What sensitivities are developed by a safe cracker? A perfume tester? An art historian?

Thus humans can develop their senses to aid in self-actualization. At the same time, because we are completely dependent upon the senses for contact with the world, any reduction in sensory accuracy will reduce knowledge of what is happening in the environment; when one sense is not able to function at all, the individual is deprived of one phase of knowledge about the world. Consider the added barriers to need satisfaction that occur when someone is unable to see or hear. Ironically, even the sensation of pain is necessary; without pain, you would not know that your tooth was infected or that your toe was sprained, and the ailment could become much more serious, perhaps causing grave illness or death.

Fortunately, people have learned ways to overcome the disadvantages produced by sensory handicaps. Eyeglasses and special braille books have been developed for those with visual handicaps; hearing aids and sign language enable those with auditory defects to communicate. Nonetheless, personal determination, rather than mechanical devices, often seems

the major factor in compensating for sensory handicaps. Many handicapped individuals can fulfill their needs for self-actualization as well as or
better than nonhandicapped people.

However, even blind or deaf people retain several "windows on the
world." What happens when an individual is completely isolated from his
environment? In prison, solitary confinement is one of the most dreaded
punishments. Investigations have been conducted to observe people
placed in an apparatus that deprives them of any contact with their
environment and any stimulation of their senses. This means, of course,
that they could not participate in *any* sort of activity. After a period of
time, these subjects became upset and temporarily displayed symptoms
commonly associated with the mentally ill (Heron, 1957).

Thus, the importance of sensory stimulation becomes increasingly obvious. When such stimulation is absent, serious emotional problems may
occur; when it is restricted, the individual needs to adjust to his condition
and find ways to compensate; and sensory stimulation can be used to
provide pleasure and satisfaction and to help in self-actualization.

Figure 3–2. What clues inform you that the pillar on the right is closer to the
camera than the last one down the line? Photograph by John G. Warford.

Perception

Perception is the process of organizing and interpreting sensory stimuli into meaningful patterns. It includes "becoming aware of objects, qualities, or relations by way of the sense organs" (Hilgard, 1962). To explain further: the visual stimuli received by your visual receptors (eyes) of the cover of this book do not tell you that you are looking at a book; they merely communicate a pattern of colors and shapes, and the brain, as the result of previous learning, interprets this pattern as a book. The auditory sense communicates only sounds, and the brain interprets these sounds as words with meanings. People who suddenly gain their sight after having been blind all their lives report that the patterns of color and shape are meaningless until they can learn to distinguish what the patterns represent.

To some extent, certain types of perception seem to occur inevitably, as the result of **maturation**. Some infants as young as six or seven months will crawl to the edge of a bed, but will not venture beyond or even put their hand out to see if they can continue, although they may have had no opportunity to learn through experience that the end of the bed indicates a sudden drop (Gibson and Walk, 1960). By and large, however, perception entails some learning.

In early infancy, it is hypothesized, the infant perceives his environment as a mass of shapes, colors, and sounds, along with miscellaneous pressures, temperature sensations, pains, smells, and tastes. Order slowly develops out of this chaos. One set of colors and shapes becomes identified with the coming of food or warmth; another set, which appears less frequently, may add an uncomfortable scratchy sensation to the sensation of warmth and wetness (that is, when "daddy" kisses him). The infant explores his world by touching, biting, and moving through it, and he is continuously

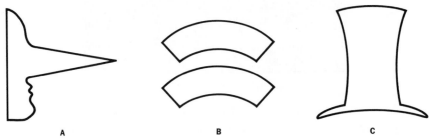

Figure 3–3. Distances are not necessarily what they seem. In A, the "nose" is as long as the figure is high; in B, the two arcs are identical; and in C the brim of the hat is as long as the hat is high.

testing to learn what it all means. Gradually he learns to identify people and objects, to locate sounds, to anticipate tastes and pressures, and to recognize relationships among the various stimuli.

Perceptions are influenced both by the objective characteristics of the stimuli themselves and by the perceiver's own characteristics, such as needs, experiences, **set**, and some personality **traits**. Because of these characteristics, all people do not notice the same stimuli, nor do they perceive and interpret the same objective stimuli in identical ways.

Attention, perception, and stimulus characteristics

Stimulus characteristics, such as size, color, shape, movement, contrast, uniqueness, and repetitiveness, obviously have a dominant effect upon perception. These, after all, describe the essence of the sensory materials that stimulate the receptors. These qualities not only help determine the sensory stimuli, but they also influence **attention**, a familiar term presently used in a more technical fashion to refer to the process of responding to only a portion of the stimuli in the immediate environment.

Since people do not attend (that is, give their attention) equally to

Think small.

Figure 3–4. Attention-getting advertisement. © 1962 Volkswagen of America, Inc. Used by permission.

every environmental stimulus, certain things are selected for increased attention. Look at the advertisement shown in Figure 3–4. Notice that the words "Think Small" and the small automobile are the only things appearing in the very large space of the advertisement. In this instance, the uniqueness and the contrast affect your perception and attention. Uniqueness results from the unusual nature of the sign; contrast results from the large blank area and the small picture. Even a person who had never seen a billboard before (and who, therefore, would not realize that this billboard is different from other billboards) would find his attention caught by the contrast.

Consider some of the following principles of perception and attention: (1) Size influences attention, with larger pictures and louder noises receiving more attention than smaller pictures and softer noises (although the VW billboard does not utilize this principle). (2) Certain colors and color combinations attract more notice than others; food packaging and automobile license plates are both designed with clarity and attention-getting color combinations in mind. (3) A moving object is more likely to be noticed than a still object: flashing neon signs will capture your attention more effectively than still signs of similar color and size. Can you think of other principles?

Characteristics within the perceiver

Perception and attention are also related to conditions within the individual, such as physiological and other needs, personal experiences, set, and personal rigidity.

1. *Needs.* A hungry person may notice, for the first time, a restaurant he has walked past on a hundred unhungry occasions. Research has shown that hungry students were more likely to "see" food in a highly blurred picture than are less hungry students (Levine, Chein, and Murphy, 1942). The physiological need "hunger" has an influence both on which stimuli are attended to and on how these sensory stimuli are perceived and integrated into meaningful patterns.

Love needs may function in a similar fashion. You vaguely notice a group of six people talking together, and suddenly you realize that one of them is a person for whom you have strong affection. A few moments later you are able to give a complete description of the clothes, posture, and mood of the loved person, but you are not even certain who the other five are, because you did not attend to them.

Psychological needs affect not only attention, but also perception itself. One investigation showed that the need for self-respect and the respect of others affected the perceptions of some subjects.

A group of students were placed in a half-circle facing a pair of posters. One of the posters contained three lines of different heights, while the other contained one line identical to one of the three lines on the original poster. Each student called out in turn, the line on Poster A that was the same as the one on Poster B. Then another pair of posters was presented. On the third pair of posters, all the students but one called out the *wrong* line (since all but one had been trained by the experimenter to do so); the student who was not "in" on the study sometimes called off the correct line and sometimes called off the same line as all the others, even though it was obviously incorrect to the objective observer.

When later asked why they responded incorrectly, the subjects gave several reasons: (1) "I figured the group was wrong, but I thought I'd better go along"; (2) "I saw them differently than the others, but I felt something was wrong with me"; (3) "I saw them the same way the group called them" (Asch, 1951).

Thus, in the first instance, group pressure won out; in the second, the personal insecurity and uncertainty of the student caused him to answer against his better thinking; in the third, the student stated that he actually perceived the lines as being a *length they were not*!! If the perception of the length of line can be so affected by the need to go along with the group, many other perceptions must be similarly affected. If one boxer is strongly favored by the crowd, will the referee and judges be affected in

Figure 3–5. Interpretation of environment is based on familiarity. How do you think these Africans, shopping at their market, would respond on a tour of an American supermarket? Courtesy Columbia Broadcasting System.

their decisions? "I know it happened because I saw it with my own two eyes." Is that always sufficient proof?

2. Experiences. Needs are not the only qualities within people that affect attention and perception. Previous experience also enters in.

> A four-year-old American child, living in Paris while his father was assigned there by his company, was playing in a sandbox at a large park. A French child his own age approached and, holding his shovel above his head, called out in French, "Do you want to play with me?" The American was unable to understand the words, but he responded in light of previous experience with children who held shovels over their heads—he slugged the French boy in the stomach.

People necessarily interpret the environment in terms of their own background. If your experiences are such that a raised shovel means "fight," you respond accordingly.

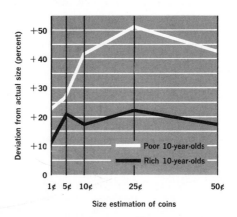

Figure 3–6. Motivational factors and perception. Reproduced by permission of the American Psychological Association. The top curve in Figure 3–6 represents the size estimation made by poor 10-year-old boys, when asked to adjust a circle of light so that it was the same size as a designated coin. The bottom curve shows the results from well-to-do boys. While all the boys tended to overestimate the size of coins, the poor boys overestimated more than the well-to-do boys. (Bruner and Goodman, 1947).

When you observe two Japanese men bowing and smiling to each other, you perceive them as being friendly, whereas their culture demands that people show such behavior, even when they do not like each other. An American observer may have no idea which Japanese man is the manager and which is his assistant, while a Japanese observer could easily tell by the depth and frequency of the bowing because *his* experiences have taught him what cues to attend to for such information.

3. *Set.* Because of previous experiences and learning, we often anticipate that certain things will occur before they actually happen. That is, we have a *set* or expectation that they will occur. The basketball referee knows that the visiting team's center has fouled out in three successive games, and he develops a set that this man is likely to foul. The referee is, then, more apt to interpret the center's actions as a foul than he would be to interpret the same actions on the part of another player as a foul.

Even simple instructions can produce a set in a group of students that will lead to inaccurate perceptions:

> Professor Blanchard, a friend of the author, told of this demonstration. First he set a bottle of yellowish liquid on the table in front of him and turned to the large class. "I want to test your power of smell today. This bottle contains a very bad-smelling chemical. When I take the stopper out, the odor will slowly drift back, and it should be strong enough to reach even the back rows. Please raise your hand when you first smell the chemical." Professor Blanchard then removed the stopper. First a few hands in the front of the room went up; within a few minutes most of the students had raised their hands.

The chemical solution in the bottle was colored water, without any odor at all. Yet, well over half the students believed they smelled something, or, at least, raised their hands to indicate they did.

4. *Personal Rigidity.* Some people display the personality characteristic of being rigid or inflexible, and this quality appears to affect perception as well. In one well-known study, subjects were shown a series of simple drawings of a dog; in each new drawing, however, the dog looked a little more like a cat, until the dog was obviously no longer a dog but a cat. People who had indicated a high degree of racial prejudice were more likely than average to continue to insist the animal was still a dog, while the more flexible subjects recognized the change more rapidly (Frenkel-Brunswik, 1949). This is an excellent example of the close relationship that exists between perceptual processes and personality.

Although everyone is susceptible to the sorts of perceptual distortions described above, frequent or extreme distortions are probably not often made by individuals successful in self-actualizing. These people can see the world more nearly as it really is, rather than as they want it to be. Also, misinterpretation of sensory stimuli would produce errors in judgment to go along with the errors in perception and would reduce the chances a person has to make maximum use of his abilities.

Perception without external stimuli

Under certain circumstances, perception occurs without the activation of the sensory receptors. This may happen when a person is dreaming, when he is recalling an incident in "the mind's eye," and when he is hallucinating.

Dreams

Everyone dreams every night. As a matter of fact, strong evidence has accumulated to indicate that people dream four or five times each night, for an average of twenty minutes per dream (Dement, 1960). You may not remember your dreams—you may even insist you do not dream—but the weight of scientific research has reasonably well established that dreaming is a normal and usual, probably necessary, process. Recent studies show that not being allowed to dream is very upsetting. If dreams are interrupted one night, the number of dreams will increase the following night; if dreams are interrupted several nights in a row, anxiety and irritation result (Dement, 1960).

During the day, everyone has feelings, desires, and fears which he cannot admit, even to himself. One explanation of dreams is that these feelings cannot make themselves known during the day, when you can control your thoughts, but at night when—in a sense—your guard is down, they do appear in disguised form. What you actually "see" in your dreams, according to this theory, is called **manifest content**; the real significance of the dream, which is often disguised because the dreamer finds it impossible to admit to himself that he has such thoughts and feelings, is termed **latent content**. The manifest content is often bizarre, making no apparent sense, but the latent content, if interpreted correctly, makes very good sense. Psychologists and psychiatrists often interpret dreams in an effort to help people understand certain feelings they may not be able to admit, even to themselves.

The following incident is a good example of how dreams and their interpretation can affect normal human relationships. Notice that it was the student, not the psychologist, who finally recognized the full significance of her dream.

> Penny Joseph, a lively and very attractive graduating senior, entered my office close to tears. She had been having the same dream, off and on, for about four weeks, and she always awoke from it in a state of panic. Her fiance, an army lieutenant with a psychology major, had encouraged her to discuss it with me. The dream setting was at the family dinner table, where

Penny, her parents, her two brothers, and her fiance were eating Sunday brunch. But, Penny insisted, someone else was at the table, although no one could see him and only Penny seemed aware of his presence. This "presence" came closer and closer to Penny, until she woke up drenched with perspiration, her heart pounding.

I suggested that the "presence" might represent certain hesitancies Penny had concerning her coming wedding, and that she had some common fears about getting married. She agreed that this was part of the solution, but not all of it. After about 30 minutes of discussion, I asked whether anyone in her family disapproved of the wedding. She shook her head, then her hands began to clench. "Now I know," she said.

It turned out that Penny had been married when she was 18, but the marriage was annulled the following year. Since this had occurred in a distant state and few people knew about it, she and her family had agreed never to tell anyone (her ex-husband had subsequently been imprisoned for several counts of robbery, and the entire incident was a very painful one). When she fell in love with Robert, her fiance, she had intended to tell him, but "the moment was never right." Robert's family was known to be "stuffy" in their concern about reputation, and Penny feared that they would not approve the marriage if they learned of her past. When the wedding was eventually planned, Penny totally lacked the courage to talk to Robert about her past.

The "presence," of course, was her ex-husband. When I asked if anyone in the family disapproved of the marriage, she suddenly realized that he was, in a way, a member of the family and that he would certainly have disapproved. He had often hit Penny during their marriage, and he had beaten up an old high school boy friend who he felt was "just too friendly." He also threatened to kill anyone who "lays a hand on my woman." Penny was afraid to tell Robert, yet felt guilty about not telling him and fearful that her first husband would find her. His "presence" certainly overshadowed the entire family and the happiness of the future marriage.

If you had been the psychologist, what would you have done to help Penny? What do you think the eventual outcome was? (Remember, this is real life, not a Hollywood film.)

Consider Lorrie's dream, which occurred during her freshman year at college.

"I dreamed I was running after a little pig. I chased the pig through the town, in and out of houses, across streets, to the edge of town, and back to our house. I finally caught the ugly little thing, picked her up and started to carry her to the butcher, when she suddenly turned into my baby sister."

When Lorrie was 16 and deeply involved in dating, cheerleading, and high school dramatics, her mother gave birth to a baby girl. Lorrie's brothers were both in college at the time. You can interpret this dream yourself.

Very few dreams, however, lend themselves to interpretation as easily as these. Each dream must be considered in light of the unique personality and life circumstances of the dreamer. Penny's dream, for example, could never have been understood without a full knowledge of her background. For this and other reasons, psychologists consider dream-interpretation books as having little or no merit.

Fantasies

Human beings have the ability to recall a situation in "their mind's eye," or to create a situation that has never occurred. These are called daydreams or **fantasies.** Before calling a girl for a date, one college freshman rehearses the event through fantasy; a student in police science "pictures" what he will say when he catches one of his professors speeding—especially if that professor had flunked him; an unpopular girl fantasizes dating the most popular boys at the college.

Fantasies and daydreams may actually be helpful in achieving self-actualization. You rehearse the future to see "how it fits"; you anticipate, through fantasy, things that may happen, and you are better able to cope with them when they do occur; you blow off steam harmlessly by yelling at your professor, arguing with the policeman who gave you a speeding ticket, and making your girl friend's ex-steady look foolish—all through fantasy. Fantasy can also help in other ways: have you ever created, through fantasy, a short story plot, a new office procedure, or an improvement on the dress pattern you recently purchased?

However, fantasy can be carried too far. When you begin to find daydreams easier than making an effort, when your fantasies become so interesting that real life seems dull, then fantasies can become harmful. People with severe mental illness confuse fantasy with reality, so that their fantasies seem true to them.

Hallucinations

From time to time, someone reports hearing voices or seeing visions. These are **hallucinations,** or perceptions that occur without external stimuli. Although hallucinations are most commonly associated with severely mentally ill or alcoholic individuals, they can occur to normal individuals under extreme circumstances.

Perceptions that occur without external stimuli can be either an indication of a serious emotional problem or a sign of true creativity; they may help a person adjust to the real world, or they may remove him from the real world. They may even be necessary, in the case of dreams and some degree of fantasizing, to normal functioning.

SUMMARY OF IMPORTANT IDEAS

1. The human organism is aware of the world around it through the senses; these senses include vision, hearing, smell, taste, the skin senses, and others.

2. Perception is the process of interpreting the sensory stimuli received by the sensory apparatus.

3. People deprived of sensory stimulation may become emotionally upset.

4. The infant explores his world through sensory stimulation.

5. The term *attention*, when used technically, means the process of responding to only a portion of the stimuli in the immediate environment.

6. Attention and perception may be affected by needs, past experiences, set or expectation, or personal rigidity.

7. Some perceptions, including dreams, fantasies, and hallucinations, occur without external stimuli.

8. Dreams take place frequently, are experienced by everyone, and appear necessary to normal behavior; fantasies can be useful but may be carried too far; hallucinations are associated with an unusually stressful situation or mental illness.

Principles of learning and their application   4

Once the investigator becomes interested in how human beings are stimulated by objects in the environment, he wishes to know how learning and thinking take place. Obviously, learning affects the interpretation of the stimuli, and so perceptual processes and learning processes are closely related. Interest in learning principles also descended from philosophers of centuries ago, and—again like the material of the previous chapter—led to the development of techniques for the study of behavior. Sensation, perception, learning, thinking, motivation, and emotion (emotion will be discussed in a later chapter) are usually considered to constitute the basic processes of human behavior.

Throughout history men have been curious about the process of human **learning**. How do people learn language, values, motor skills, social behavior? Very little behavior is totally uninfluenced by learning, and much behavior would be impossible without a great deal of learning. As a result, the study of learning principles has become basic to the study of the psychology of human behavior.

For practical reasons, much learning research has been conducted with lower animals, and the findings have been extended to people. (This is true of many areas in psychology, as well as in medicine, biochemistry, and other research fields.) Although this book focuses upon the human being, and most of its examples are drawn from human behavior, the debt owed to studies of rats, dogs, cats, monkeys, and even amoeba must be acknowledged.

Organisms, of course, are not merely a collection of assorted processes, such as sensing, perceiving, learning, and thinking. A person must be looked upon as a unified whole rather than as a series of parts. Thus, although perception and learning are discussed in different chapters for the sake of convenience, try to keep in mind the continual interplay between these and all other behavior processes. Your perceptions are based upon what you have learned through previous experiences; your learning is most strongly influenced by what you perceive.

Only through learning can people even begin to satisfy their physiological, safety, love, esteem, and self-actualization needs. Initially, of course, parents take responsibility for satisfying their children's needs, but this is a temporary situation; people must eventually learn how to satisfy their own needs and how to help others help them satisfy these needs. Even the young infant soon learns that crying will bring parents to satisfy his hunger, thirst, and pain-avoidance needs.

Learning takes place whenever a relatively permanent change in behavior results from experience. Almost all behavior involves some learning. You learn to talk, eat, be interested in politics, feel insulted, want money, thread a needle, love your parents, plan a budget, drive an automobile, and respect or dislike yourself. Without the ability to learn, people would be little more than vegetables and would need constant care to continue to exist.

Kinds of learning

In developing principles of learning, psychologists must account for both simple learning, such as an infant learning that he can stop crying for his bottle when he sees his mother enter the room, and complex learning, such as learning how to design the plans for a skyscraper. The present discussion will include two forms of simple learning, classical conditioning and operant learning, and two forms of complex learning, problem-solving behavior and concept formation.

Classical conditioning

Physiologist Ivan Pavlov conducted the first systematic studies of **classical conditioning** over 60 years ago. After observing dogs salivate when their food was brought to them, Pavlov demonstrated that they would learn to salivate to the noise of a buzzer sounded a moment before the arrival of the food (Pavlov, 1927). Originally the **stimulus** *food* produced the **response** *salivation*; after many trials during which the buzzer was sounded prior to the presentation of food, the buzzer became the stimulus for salivation. This, in essence, is classical conditioning.

Similar conditioning can be observed in human beings. Let's begin with a reasonably well-accepted statement: year-old infants enjoy being cuddled by their parents. That is, the stimulus

Figure 4–1. Ivan Pavlov, the great Russian physiologist. Courtesy Sovfoto Agency.

of the warmth and physical contact with the parent will produce a response indicating pleasure, such as gurgling and smiling. Assume that this year-old infant has had many such experiences with both his mother and his father. He has, by now, come to associate the presence of his parents with the warm, pleasant physical contact that produces the gurgling and smiling. What happens? He now responds to the sight, perhaps even the sound of the step, of his parents with gurgling and smiling. His response, in this simplified example, occurs virtually inevitably to the presence of his mother or father. Gurgling and smiling did not originally occur in response to his parent, but through the constant association of warmth-and-affection with parent-close-to-me, the infant has become conditioned to respond in this fashion.

The original stimulus *warm-human-contact* produced the response *gurgling-and-smiling;* after many experiences with the parent, the stimulus *sight-of-parent* produces the response. Thus, it can be said that the infant is conditioned to gurgle and smile at the sight of the mother, that is, he has learned to give this response.

After a while, the infant responds with gurgling and smiling to all adults. This is called **stimulus generalization** since his response to his parents has been generalized to other adults. Then his older brother, who is unfortunately jealous of the baby, enters the picture. Whenever the brother comes by, the baby is likely to get a pinch or a squeeze. The baby then learns to **discriminate** between adults and older brothers; if his brother's friends are pleasant to him, the baby will hopefully learn further discrimination, this time between his older brother and other boys the same age.

Each time the situation occurs, we say the learning is **reinforced.** That is, each time the sight of the parent is followed by cuddling, one reinforcement occurs. The more reinforcements, the more thoroughly the infant learns to respond to his parents with pleasure, and the longer it would take for his responses to cease if his parents ceased their cuddling.

The findings of Pavlov and those who followed him have led some people to believe that all human behavior can be controlled as easily as the salivation of dogs or the smiles of babies, but this is not the case. Psychologists do explain some human behavior through principles of classical conditioning (which are much more complicated than indicated above), but few would argue that *all* human behavior can be understood by applying these principles: human behavior is not as easily explained as salivation in Pavlov's dogs.

Operant learning

In classical conditioning, the original stimulus-response sequence is already part of the person's potential behavior. That is, the infant gurgled and smiled in response to being cuddled *without* having to learn to smile. Much learning, however, is of a different nature, and involves having the proper response rewarded and improper responses either unrewarded or actually punished in some way. Eventually the individual learns to follow the stimulus with the proper response.

Operant learning can be understood through a four-step sequence: first, the person has the desire (is motivated) to do something; second, he recognizes certain cues in the situation which indicate possible responses; third, he responds (or behaves); fourth, he receives a reward if the response is correct, or, if the response is incorrect, he tries alternative responses until the correct response occurs (after Miller and Dollard, 1941).

Each time the correct response occurs and is followed by a **reward,** learning has taken place. On each successive occasion, the correct response should occur sooner and the number of incorrect responses will diminish, until, finally, the correct response will regularly follow the stimulus.

In classical conditioning, the person can change his behavior, but he does not affect the surrounding environment; the response of the dog was to salivate and of the baby, to smile. In operant learning, the individual does something to the environment; that is, he *operates* on the environment. Some examples may be helpful:

> A young girl wants to thread a needle (motivation); she observes the thread and the hole in the needle (cues); she tries to put the thread through the hole (response); she fails, so she continues to try until she at last is rewarded by success (reward). The next time she tries to thread a needle, she succeeds more quickly.

> A clumsy student decides to learn to make lay-ups on the basketball court (motivation); he observes other students shooting baskets (cue); he tries one type of shot (response); it fails but he tries others until he succeeds (reward). Slowly he learns, through success and failure, how to sink a high proportion of his shots.

> A college student wants to be a professional writer (motivation); he learns he must write and submit his pieces to magazines (cue); he writes a short story and submits it to one

magazine (response); it is rejected, and he tries other magazines until he succeeds (reward). He has learned the type of magazine that is likely to buy his stories, and he has also learned something about the magazines that rejected his story.

Each time the individual responds is termed a **trial**; each time he is rewarded is termed a **reinforcement**. The more rapidly and the more frequently a person's trials are reinforced, the faster he will learn.

The increasingly popular teaching machines also illustrate operant learning. A question appears in the machine, and the learner writes down the answer or says it to himself (this covers motivation, cue, and response). Then, through some action on the part of the learner, such as

Figure 4–2. Teaching machines are finding increasing acceptance among teachers and students. Courtesy Western Design.

turning a handle or pressing a button, the actual answer to the question appears. If the learner's response is correct, he is rewarded, and a reinforcement occurs on that trial—a sort of a psychological pat on the back. By repeating the sequence of questions with the machine several times, it is possible to answer all the questions correctly.

Students both in high school and in college have stated their approval of teaching machines for a variety of types of learning; over 75 percent of one group of college students believed that machines enabled them to get more out of their introductory psychology course than they otherwise would have (Holland, 1960). Teaching machines offer many advantages to the student, such as enabling him to work at his own speed and to check immediately whether his response was correct or incorrect. Teaching machines are undoubtedly very useful as a supplement to the instructor and the text; they are an effective way to study for examinations, and under some limited circumstances, they may actually replace an instructor or a textbook, but—at least at present—they cannot substitute for a competent teacher or a well-written book.

Learning symbols

As you have undoubtedly observed, people not only learn to do things for immediate satisfaction, but they also learn when rewarded by symbolic reinforcers, such as money, which has value not in and of itself, but in terms of what it can purchase. Chimpanzees can learn to work to receive poker chips that could be exchanged for food a day later (Wolfe, 1936), which indicates that they had learned a relatively sophisticated symbolic relationship. People, of course, also work for money to buy things, but—for some people, at least—money eventually seems to become important in its own right, perhaps because of its association with safety needs, such as security, or esteem needs, such as prestige; people will often work hard to obtain far more money than is needed to purchase the goods they desire.

Problem solving and insight learning

Much human learning involves seeing relationships and working out new solutions. Sometimes this occurs in an obvious, step-by-step sequence, but more often it seems to happen all at once. Such experiences may actually result from some step-by-step process that has gone on wthout our knowing it, but we end up with the feeling that the solution came suddenly.

> A young child wanted to turn on the lamp in her room, but the switch was above her head. Previously her parents had lifted her

up, so she knew how to manipulate the switch. She had also had the experience of standing on a stool to reach the bathroom faucet. She looked at the lamp for a few moments, then looked around the room and began to whimper. Suddenly her face brightened, and she went directly to the bathroom, returned dragging the stool behind her, and climbed on it to turn on the lamp.

Her behavior indicated that she had understood, or learned, a new relationship. Her previous learning was combined into a successful solution to a new problem. Her behavior seemed to indicate her solution occurred through what would be called **insight. Problem solving** need not occur this way, however, as the following example shows:

Our newly purchased French automobile seemed to intrigue and baffle all American mechanics who were entrusted to repair it. As long as we remained in Los Angeles, we had little difficulty, but one summer we decided to take a cross-country camping trip, and the car's water pump fell off twenty miles from Kansas City. The local dealer (there was only one in the entire city) was reassuring, but his mechanics were less so. They put on three successive water pumps, none of which lasted more than a few miles. A total of five man-hours went unsuccessfully into what should have been a one-hour task. Finally, just before closing time, the head mechanic came back over for the ump-teenth time, leaned over to face the water pump, touched and twisted and yanked and pushed every conceivable contrivance. Then I noticed he began turning a bolt that had been partly hidden and completely unnoticed. As he turned it, he began to grin, then he got up, said "Try 'er," and walked away. The water pump lasted the remaining two years we owned the car.

This was also problem-solving behavior, but using a succession of trials and errors, rather than a sudden burst of insight. Insight has been differentiated from other problem solving as occurring to a person (1) suddenly, (2) smoothly and without hesitation, (3) before he actually tackles the task, (4) and with a novel solution (Osgood, 1953). The young girl figuring out how to turn on her light, according to these criteria, used insight, while the auto mechanic did not. More dramatic examples of insight are available:

The author was a college sophomore when confronted for the first time with the puzzle shown in Figure 4–3. He made a few false starts, which quickly turned out to be incorrect, then stared at it for ten minutes as though in a trance. Suddenly he knew what the correct words were, although to this day he cannot figure out the process through which he solved the problem. See what you can do with this task, then try to analyze your problem-solving processes. One suggestion: try to overcome your previous set in doing crossword puzzles.

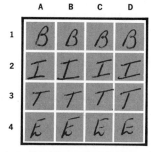

1. Buzzing insects
2. Organs of vision
3. What older brothers do to younger sisters
4. Without difficulty; with _____
A. Lions do it
B. Mosquitoes do it
C. Dogs do it
D. Snakes do it

Figure 4–3. Rigidity of thinking. Complete this crossword puzzle. Hint: the correct words are easy, but the correct *form* demands that your thinking not be rigid. The answer is at the end of the chapter.

Concept formation

We have still not coped with the problem of how human beings develop their understanding of concepts. How do you learn what is meant by the terms democracy, manly, three, total, blue (the color), opposite, or Swedish? This problem is undergoing extensive investigation today among psychologists.

One way in which concepts develop is through abstracting as the result of experience with the concept in a number of different settings. The young child hears the word *blue* applied to a blue coat, the blue sky, his

Figure 4–4. Concept formation consists of learning that one response describes a number of related things. Courtesy Fillmore H. Sanford.

sister's blue eyes, and his blue blanket; slowly he recognizes that blue refers to the color. Of course, if he has previously formed an under-standing of the concept, *color*, he could merely be told that blue was the color of the sky, coat, etc. Once the child has learned what common quality of the coat, the sky, his sister's eyes, and his blanket is encom-passed by *blue*, he can generalize blueness to other objects. Through the responses of others, he will gain an understanding of the outer limits of blueness: when does blue become black or white or purple or green? And, if he hears his father ask his mother why she is so blue, he may become confused all over again.

Very young children tend to develop concepts through concrete fea-tures shared by various items, e.g., automobiles and trains are similar because they are both hard, fast, and have horns. A later step in **concept formation** is to respond to the function of the items, e.g., automobiles and trains are similar because "you ride in them." The most mature phase of concept formation is to recognize the similarity between trains and auto-mobiles because both belong to the abstract concept *vehicle* (Reichard and Rapaport, 1943).

Figure 4–5. Man can deal with abstract concepts, making science possible. Courtesy Electro-Optical Systems, Inc.

Thinking

Where does the topic of learning stop and the topic of **thinking** begin? The answer, of course, is an arbitrary one of definition. Concept formation and problem solving form a borderland between learning and thinking.

Human beings are able to combine the many symbols, concepts, and other results of learning into thinking. Imagining the future or trying to make sense of the past is thinking. Creating a comic strip, designing the body of a new sportscar, or solving a problem in algebra all involve thinking. Criticizing a movie or deciding to break a date are forms of thinking. Whether the thinking will lead to good or poor results is not the point; the point is that thinking takes place. Animals show a form of behavior that can be called thinking, but the difference between men and animals is tremendous in this respect.

Thinking has been described as "any process or activity not predominantly perceptual. . . . Judging, abstracting, conceiving, reasoning, and . . . imagining, remembering, and anticipating are forms of thinking" (English and English, 1958).

Thinking may work under our control—or it may be partly or completely outside our awareness. In working out an accounting problem or in trying to figure out the identity of the criminal in a murder mystery, we use controlled thinking—we try to guide our thought processes to gain a particular goal. Thinking for school or work is frequently controlled thinking.

Thinking without conscious control

More often than you may realize, however, thinking occurs without conscious control. While you are driving alone in an automobile, thoughts come and go quickly, move from one idea or image to another with relatively little control. Creative people often make use of this type of thinking, since controlled thinking tends to run along the same paths as before. All forms of dreams, daydreams, and fantasy are at least partly uncontrolled, affected more by occurrences within the individual than by stimuli from the outside. (Although these forms of behavior were discussed in Chapter 3, they could equally well have been covered here.)

> Sitting in psychology class, you hear the instructor remark, "The birth of a new infant into the family often produces a problem for the older children." Your thinking begins to wander back to when your sister was born, the way your parents sent you to stay with your aunt and uncle for a month, how

nice your aunt is and how bald your uncle is, whether you will be bald when you are as old as he, how old he looks today, why he looks older than your father, how your father reacted to your little sister when she was born, how you did not really begin to like her until she was about 14 years old. Then you find yourself listening to the lecture again. Your daydreams might have taken a minute or two, but the thoughts, although set off by the professor's statement, were really carried on by your own associations.

Sometimes uncontrolled thinking can be used to solve problems.

> "My short story's hero was about to be killed, and I couldn't figure out a decent way to get him out of the spot. Nothing seemed right. I sat and looked at my typewriter for 30 minutes, but nothing came to me; so I decided to hit the sack. Suddenly, just as I was squeezing the toothpaste tube, the idea hit me: let him get killed and rework the ending. I used the idea and it worked beautifully."

The writer had a *set* that his character had to remain alive, and he had "written himself into a corner," but kept persevering along one line: how to get the character out. Later, while thinking of some trivial matter, his thinking was no longer controlled or channeled—in a sense he had been freed from the rigidity that had controlled his thinking—and he was able to arrive at a new type of solution not previously considered.

Language and thought

Thinking is communicated through symbols; these symbols are most often words, but they can also be gestures, facial expressions, body movements, or mathematical formulas. To communicate the theory of classical conditioning, you might use a combination of words, diagrams, and—perhaps—an actual example you can observe.

Feelings are also expressed through symbols. When you are angry with another person, you may call him a name, swear at him under your breath, push him, or stamp away. All of these responses will communicate the feeling of anger. In expressing anger your voice tone, facial expression, and body movements will all be quite different than when you are explaining classical conditioning. All are part of the process of communication.

Words, of course, are concepts and are learned as other concepts are learned, through abstracting and generalizing. Can you explain how the concept of operant learning can be applied to the process through which a young child learns the meaning of new words?

The meaning of words is often difficult to interpret to people from other cultures. Frequently the subtle points of a language will never be properly learned unless they are absorbed in childhood. Verbal symbols often have meanings that are not easily translated.

> Assume a language uses the same word for "my house" and "my home." How would you explain, in simple English, the difference in the meanings of those words to a person speaking that language?

> Assume you were asked to escort a foreign student around campus. He speaks good English, but does not know American slang. He asks you the meaning of the expressions *Big Man on Campus, rat fink, it isn't kosher, Mickey Mouse course*, and *snap exam*. Try to explain in simple English the real meanings of these terms; for example, you would need to explain the subtle difference between *snap exam* and *easy exam*. (Keep in mind how foolish a literal, word-by-word translation would be—Big Man on Campus might mean someone seven feet tall.)

Nonverbal communication

Words are not the only methods of communicating, although they may be the most common. Communication occurs through a raised eyebrow, a cough, blushing, spitting, taking a girl's hand, crying, sending a gift, or kicking someone in the shins. All these approaches, and many more, communicate feelings, ideas, beliefs, and intentions.

Folklore has it that a hearty handshake and a firm glance mean a man is honest. The truth is that the salesman who is trying to persuade you to buy an encyclopedia or a new back porch you do not need is also aware of this folklore. **Nonverbal communication** can easily be as complex as verbal communication.

> A college freshman on a blind date to the movies tries to hold hands. What does this mean? Is he showing honest affection? Is this the lead-up to "making out"? Does he just enjoy holding hands? Then his date slips her hand away from his. What is she communicating? Is she trying to get rid of him? Does she want him to think she is a "nice girl"? Do her hands perspire and embarrass her?

Nonverbal communication can also produce misunderstandings between people of different cultures who have established differing patterns of the kind of behavior they expect.

> An over-friendly American doing business in Manila came to like one of the Filipino businessmen with whom he was dealing. They met for dinner that evening and the American, who was

feeling the effects of two martinis, slapped the Asian across the back. The Asian looked at him in amazement, then realized he had meant it to be a friendly gesture. However, the business deal fell through and the two companies did no further business.

Whether we communicate through words or through actions or through physiological change, communication is vitally important. In order to make the most of your abilities, you need to be able to communicate effectively to others and to receive the real meanings of what they are communicating to you.

Creative thinking

A great deal of thinking combines the use of both controlled and noncontrolled thought. Creative thinking is one example. One well-known sequence suggested for creative thinking has four steps (Wallas, 1921).

1. *Preparation.* Obtain the background necessary to deal with the problem, the accumulation of a lifetime.

2. *Incubation.* Let the idea "simmer," thinking about it, talking about it, mulling it over, and considering its significance.

3. *Illumination.* The solution to the problem occurs. It may occur suddenly or gradually, through controlled thinking or through uncontrolled thinking.

4. *Verification.* Check the idea, try it out. The creative scientist must conduct research; the creative artist must observe how his work appears when it is finished.

Creativity has undergone extensive study recently. Creative people have been found to be more independent and less likely to accept the values and standards of the general society (Getzels and Jackson, 1962). Governments and organizations that attempt to eliminate deviant or "odd" types of thinking may also be eliminating creativity. However, psychologists still know very little about the actual creative process, whether it is in the sciences, in social relationships, in business, or in the arts.

Rigid thinking

Many people are rigid in their thinking. They seem to say "Don't bother me with facts or new ideas—I know what's right." They are referred to as closed-minded people, because they are not willing to consider new information. People who are racially **prejudiced** tend to be more rigid in their thinking than people less prejudiced. They have more difficulty in discarding old ways of thinking and trying new ways (Frenkel-Brunswik, 1949).

A person's prejudices against (or for) other people may make his thinking less effective. A man who is prejudiced against a particular newspaper may not believe something they write, even though it is obviously true; a person prejudiced against Italians may not recognize the important contributions made by Italians. To be prejudiced means to prejudge or judge in advance; if a judgment is made in advance, its accuracy may be reduced.

Prejudices may be based on **stereotypes.** A stereotype is a "rigid and oversimplified or biased perception" (English and English, 1958) that leads to rigid and oversimplified thinking. Even the origins of the word emphasize this: the term comes from printing, referring to something that is difficult to change once it is set in type.

Think of the stereotype "All sailors like to drink heavily." This particular stereotype, often held in communities located near navy installations, may make it more difficult for sailors to get dates or make friends off base. Therefore, they tend to drink more, and the stereotype is made to appear true. When a person holding such a view meets a sailor who claims he does not drink, the individual may not believe the sailor; he has a set for the sailor to be a heavy drinker, and this set reduces the logic and perceptiveness of his thinking.

The above situation is also an example of the **self-fulfilling prophecy.** The stereotype that sailors will drink actually increases the chances that sailors will drink, thus making the original prophecy appear valid. If adults prophesy that teen-agers are troublemakers, they will treat teen-agers accordingly, and the teen-agers are more likely to respond by becoming troublemakers. Stereotypes can easily lead to self-fulfilling prophecies. What other examples occur to you?

Rigid, stereotyped, and prejudiced thinking may distort the accuracy of perceptions, hinder the effectiveness of learning, and provide an untrue picture of the world. Since, under these circumstances, we "know" certain things to be true when they are actually not, the effectiveness of efforts for achievement and self-actualization may be negated. When people insist on doing things the same old way and when they allow their biases to interfere with the accuracy of their thinking, they reduce their competence to run a business, enjoy leisure, or help their children to mature.

Learning is, therefore, basic to the entire study of human behavior, and psychologists are hopeful that they may discover principles that will be applicable both to simple and to complex types of learning—principles that will explain the learning of a simple motor task or a complex system of values. Although psychologists are far from agreeing upon one theory of learning, there is relative agreement regarding how specific learning principles can be applied to practical problems, such as effective study.

Learning principles applied to effective study

Many principles of learning, developed through research, can be applied to the problems of effective study. These principles are not magic formulas for success or clever gimmicks that can be used for an easy A. They cannot be substituted for self-discipline or ability, but—with proper motivation and sufficient effort—they will help students make maximum use of their abilities.

Now—what are the principles?

Warm-up is time-consuming

It takes a few minutes, or more, for an athlete to get **warmed up.** The same principle holds for students. Each time you begin to study, you need a little time to warm up. A typist does not work at top speed in the first ten seconds of typing; a mechanic called to the telephone in the middle of a complicated task may take several minutes to figure out where he was before he left; an accounting student who allows two or three days to elapse between work sessions may take ten minutes or more to get back into the problem he left.

Since warm-ups do consume time, study should be planned to minimize the number of warm-ups. One way is to avoid shifting frequently from one task to another, since each shift demands another warm-up period. What other ways can you think of?

Planned number of repetitions and spacing of repetitions

Football players do not merely learn their plays until they go through them correctly one time: they drill and drill until a mistake is almost impossible. The same is true for actors in a play. This is repetition to the point of **overlearning.** Such overlearning will both improve learning and reduce the rapidity with which forgetting takes place.

However, boredom and fatigue may decrease learning and the effective use of intelligence. Therefore, going over the same material in the same way again and again and again, until boredom occurs, is not efficient. Fortunately, repetition and overlearning need not be so boring. As an example, consider the following program of repetition for studying class notes:

(1) Take notes as the instructor talks.

(2) Study them for a few minutes after class is over.

(3) Summarize the notes into a brief paragraph.

(4) Read them over before the beginning of the next class meeting.

(5) Read over all notes for the week each Sunday evening.

(6) Study the notes thoroughly before the examination.

These six repetitions are spaced to reduce boredom. In addition, the spacing fulfills another principle of learning: **distributed practice**, *on the whole, is more effective than* **massed** **practice** (McGeoch and Irion, 1952). In nontechnical language, this means that study repetitions that occur very close together in time are less efficient than the same number of repetitions spread out in time.

Massed practice, which includes cramming, means that all learning repetitions occur one right after the other; monotony and boredom are frequent. Distributed practice, or proper spacing of learning, not only reduces boredom and fatigue but also appears to slow down forgetting. However, under some circumstances, massed practice is better; for example, when warm-up takes too long or when motivation is so great that boredom does not occur.

The examination is often thought of as the final repetition, but this is not really true. To think of the examination as the end is to assume you are studying for the benefit of your instructor, rather than for your own benefit, but the purpose of study is to understand more and to recall more at later times. Thus, review of returned exams is another useful repetition; it should involve not only figuring out what you missed, but trying to understand better what you did not miss.

Meaningful material is remembered longer

Psychologists have shown that people learn facts, ideas, and relationships faster and remember them longer when they have meaning (McGeoch and Irion, 1952). For this reason, you can improve your ability to recall by trying to understand the relationships between what you are studying and other aspects of your academic or personal life. You may find it difficult to memorize the battles of the Civil War, but by plotting them on the map and trying to understand their consequences to the politics of the Civil War, the battles are no longer isolated incidents to you, but part of a meaningful pattern. To make the study of the Civil War meaningful to you, you might contemplate how its outcome changed our country and how different the United States might be today if the South had won.

Think about the courses you find the least interesting: how can you relate the material to your own life? How can you find a meaningful pattern that ties the material together? How does it fit in with other courses you are taking?

Interference in learning process reduces efficiency

Anything that breaks the train of thought, that makes concentration difficult, or that increases fatigue, will interfere with learning effectiveness. Not only does such interference lead to unnecessary warm-ups, but it reduces concentration, since we cannot concentrate efficiently on two activities at the same time. One author has suggested four major categories of distractions: people, noises, personal problems, and study-area problems (Kalish, 1959).

People as distractions. No matter where a person attempts to do his learning, other people are likely to interfere. College libraries often provide so many distractions that some students spend less time studying than they spend doing other things. Observations made over 30 years ago (cited in Robinson, 1961) showed that one-half of the library interruptions were caused by other people—the remainder involved daydreaming, looking around aimlessly, flipping through pages, and working on clothing or makeup.

One very sensitive problem is how to deal with parents who, in spite of good intentions, interfere with studies. Four out of five college freshmen in one survey complained that parents hindered their studies in one way or another, the most common interferences being family conversations, walking in and out of the study room, inconsistent parental attitudes, and television or other noisy household equipment (Feinberg, 1963).

Whether you live at home, in a dormitory, or with friends, you are likely to find that people will interfere with your plan for study and with your ability to concentrate. How can you best cope with these problems? Can you ask people to leave you alone? Can you compensate by concentrating harder?

Noises as distractions. Our world is full of a fantastic variety of noises. When motivation and interest are high, the sound of the family television or the construction of a new science building are not even noticed. Studies in industry have shown that industrial noises reduce efficiency and increase fatigue (Laird, 1929); extra determination or concentration compensate for noise, but the added effort leads to more rapid fatigue. When the noise is interesting, such as a television show or a conversation, interference with learning is probably even greater.

Another type of distracting noise seems to be devices that claim to teach you while you sleep. The manufacturers claim that, by playing a record while going to sleep and setting it to play while getting up, a person can learn without effort and during sleep. Research, however, indicates that, although learning does occur, sleep appears to be sacrificed (Simon, 1955). Much professional thinking is that sleep-learning is really inefficient and a relative waste of sleep.

Personal problems as distractions. Daydreams of the future and memories of the past seem to meet head-on during the time set aside for learning. Students with more serious personal worries, such as a recent family death or a broken engagement, may find that preoccupation with their problems interferes with concentration. However, less important, day-to-day problems can also interfere. Have you ever had any of these concerns disturb your concentration?

> You think the parking meter has run out.
>
> You said something that you believe your closest friend interpreted as an insult.
>
> You have a bad toothache, and you hate the thought of dentists.
>
> You have to break your date for Saturday night, and even though your reason is good, you know your date-to-have-been will not believe you.
>
> If you do not finish what you are doing in time, your ride home will leave without you, and if you keep worrying about your ride home leaving without you, you will not possibly finish in time.

If, in spite of all efforts to concentrate, a personal problem continues to spoil your concentration, you may need to deal with it first, and then return to your study. Sometimes a few moments of quiet concentration or jotting down some brief notes will be sufficient to get rid of such preoccupations.

Study-area problems as distractions. The place where you study often contains many distractions; no one of these by itself is especially distracting, but each may provide a little bit of interference. Examples of study area distractions include:

> poor lighting—both too little light and too much direct glare are harmful;
>
> overcrowded desk—uncluttered surface space should be adequate;
>
> improper room temperature—between 65° F and 72° F is probably best;
>
> unavailable study tools—pen, pencils, dictionary, ink, and so forth, should all be within arm's reach.

Active set improves learning and recall

How often have you been introduced to someone, only to find a moment later that you do not have the slightest idea what his name is? This common experience arises because, in those instances, you lack the active set to learn. You are not paying any attention to the auditory stimuli communicating the name.

How often have you had to reread the same paragraph four or five times, because none of the ideas seem to "stick"? The principle is the same as above: you were not actually attending to what you were reading; you did not have an active set to learn. One method has been evolved that helps establish an active set for learning when reading. This approach is called *SQ3R* and consists of five steps: survey, question, read, recite, and review (Robinson, 1961).

> Survey. In order to gain an active learning set, it is useful to have an idea of what is ahead. Before taking a long automobile trip, you usually look at a map of the entire route; similarly, you can survey the book you are going to read by skimming the material and reading the summary carefully.

> Question. To encourage an active set, it is useful to be searching for something. If you look for the answer to a particular question in a book, you are more likely to have an active set than if you are only trying "to cover the pages assigned." Make up your own questions by turning each major heading into a question and writing this question down. If you were applying SQ3R to this text, you would jot down, "How does an active set improve learning and recall?"

> Read. You obviously need to read the material. With the question in the back of your mind, read actively to answer the question.

> Recite. To complete the process, you need to answer the question. It is suggested that you do this at first aloud, then by jotting the answer down under your question in your notes. Once again, you are forced into activity so that you can better check your own reading adequacy.

> Review. The previous three steps are repeated for each major heading, probably between four and eight per chapter. The final step, which is more repetition than active set, is to reread the summary and review your notes. This gives a useful repetition and helps you to see the entire chapter as a meaningful pattern, rather than as isolated segments.

Proper use of SQ3R will not only produce an active set for learning, but will also supply you with a brief chapter outline, enable you to recall the material longer, and reduce daydreaming. (See Appendix for examples and some additional suggestions in using SQ3R.)

Studying with a group can also improve your active set to learn. By having other people ask you questions from the text or your professor's lectures, you must answer these questions aloud. This forces you to learn the material well enough to explain it to the satisfaction of the others in the group.

One important purpose of teaching machines is providing an active set for learning. Both the *Question* and *Recite* steps are usually incorporated in programmed instruction procedures.

Knowledge of results improves learning

When you learn the results of previous behavior, you are in a better position to improve your performance. Teaching machines make use of this learning principle by telling the student immediately whether his response was correct or not. Imagine how little improvement a typist would show if she never learned whether she had struck the proper keys. How can you apply this learning principle to your own study?

Applying these learning principles to day-to-day study efforts can improve study effectiveness. Since each student is a unique individual, certain changes in the procedures suggested above may increase their usefulness for any given person.

SUMMARY OF IMPORTANT IDEAS

1. The study of learning is basic to the study of psychology.

2. Only through learning can people satisfy their needs.

3. Learning occurs whenever a relatively permanent change in behavior results from experience.

4. In classical conditioning, a stimulus is presented a moment before a second stimulus; if the second stimulus elicits a response, the first stimulus will eventually elicit the same response, assuming the procedure is repeated often enough.

5. Additional learning takes place through generalization and through discrimination; reinforcement strengthens the bond between the new stimulus and the response.

6. In operant learning, the organism is motivated to behave, and the behavior that satisfies the original need is more likely to occur on subsequent occasions.

7. People learn not only when their needs are satisfied imme-

diately, but also when they are rewarded by symbolic reinforcers.

8. Problem solving can take place through numerous trials and errors, or through what seems to be an all-at-once insight.

9. The understanding of concepts occurs when the individual is able to abstract and to generalize.

10. Thinking is closely related to learning; it may occur with or without conscious control.

11. Creative thinking may follow this sequence: preparation, incubation, illumination, verification.

12. Thinking is communicated through symbols; these symbols are most often words, but they can also be gestures, facial expressions, body movements, or mathematical formulas.

13. Rigid thinking and stereotyped thinking reduce an individual's ability to behave effectively.

14. Stereotypes can lead to self-fulfilling prophecies.

15. Learning principles can be applied to effective study.

16. Warm up is time consuming.

17. The number of repetitions and the spacing of repetitions of study are related to study effectiveness.

18. Meaningful material is remembered longer than nonmeaningful material.

19. Interference with the learning process reduces learning efficiency.

20. Having an active set improves learning and recall.

21. Immediate knowledge of results improves learning.

	A	B	C	D
1	B	B	B	B
2	I	I	I	I
3	T	T	T	T
4	E	E	E	E

Here is the answer to the crossword puzzle shown in Figure 4–3. Did you figure it out?

An introduction to human personality and development   5

From the preceding three chapters, you might assume that the human being was a combination of separate elements rather than a single, unified structure. The divisions were only matters of convenience, and the present chapter will discuss the individual as a whole, rather than as a series of parts. The discussion will involve various ways of looking at the human personality and will close with an introduction to the next section, which deals with human development. You may find it helpful to relate the ideas of the previous chapters, particularly the hierarchy of needs as expressed by Professor Maslow, to the materials in the first half of this chapter, especially to the section *Introduction to personality*.

When psychologists look at people, what do they see? Do they see living things whose behavior is beyond their own control, who are helpless in the face of the pressures of their environment? Or organisms that will harm others unless kept in careful check? Or animals that differ from other animals only because they can walk upright and talk?

Different psychologists, of course, look at people differently. This book presents the view that people will try to make use of their capacities, if given the opportunity, and that people can become successful in using these capacities in spite of great environmental pressures. Further, the author assumes that most, perhaps almost all, behavior called "good" and "evil" is learned. And finally, the book takes the position that factors distinguishing humans from lower forms of animal life are numerous and vital.

Human behavior: some apparent contradictions

Nothing illustrates the complexity of human beings better than some apparent contradictions in their behavior. Men are adaptable and creative, yet strangely rigid. Their behavior varies according to their culture, yet shows consistency from culture to culture. They can communicate across space and time, yet are often unable to understand those they love the most. Their behavior results from the most subtle and intricate factors; yet this complex behavior is still, to some extent, predictable. To consider these apparent contradictions is to become aware of man's fantastic range of abilities, feelings, and achievements.

Adaptable, yet rigid. More than any other creature, the human being can change his environment to please himself. Over the centuries he has learned to build structures and manufacture clothing to protect himself against extreme cold and to create air-conditioning devices to protect himself against extreme heat. He has devised medicines to prolong life and bombs to destroy life.

He can produce enough food to feed the entire world (although he has not yet learned how to distribute this food adequately), and he can establish schools and write books (although he has trouble persuading his children to profit from these schools and books).

He can live on the earth, under the earth, in the air, in outer space, on the water, and under the water. He has obtained power from lower forms of animal life, from water, from heat, and from splitting the atom. He can create clothing out of chemicals, build computers that play chess, and send words and pictures thousands of miles in a matter of seconds. He can establish laws and customs to control his own behavior, so that millions of people can live within a short distance of each other without constant conflict.

Yet, in spite of this amazing ability to alter his environment to suit himself, man displays disturbing signs of rigidity. Once he takes a stand on an issue, he is extremely reluctant to admit he is wrong. He gives up his superstitions very slowly, if at all, and hesitates a long time before altering any of his more important values, even when the world around him is changing rapidly. He likes new gadgets and appliances, but has a difficult time accommodating himself to new architectural styles and teaching methods. He is much more adept at finding ways to win wars than at finding ways to stop wars.

Thus, although men have made immense strides in creating and adapting their physical world, they have been less successful with their personal and social world.

Changeable, yet consistent. "There are only two indisputable truths in psychology," one professor remarked in his first psychology lecture. "The first is that people are similar, and the second is that people are different."

For example, every society has a family system of some sort, but the systems differ. In the United States, the family usually consists of mother, father, and children, but the Tibetan woman may marry two brothers simultaneously (Peissel, 1965), and a married couple in Japan is likely to reside with the husband's parents and take care of them as long as they live.

Such emotions as love, anger, joy, and jealousy are known throughout the world; yet each society permits different ways of showing emotions. And the members of any given society may express emotions differently from each other. In France and Italy, anger is often shown directly; in Japan, however, anger toward a child or a servant may be expressed directly, but not anger toward an equal. Yet *some* Japanese express anger toward equals, and *some* French and Italians are inhibited in showing anger.

Effective in communicating, yet ineffective in communicating. Man is the only creature that can communicate effectively across time and space. A telephone call can connect a travel agent in Kansas City with a hotel manager in Calcutta; a radio enables an astronaut to communicate with people hundreds of miles beneath him; a television set allows a track fan in Dallas, Texas, to watch an Olympic track meet in Tokyo.

Not only do men send and receive communications across space, but they can also send and receive communications across time. A technique has been developed that will determine the age of a rock; ancient scrolls have been found recently that report what life was like 2000 years ago; records of our present civilization have been buried, and civilizations in the future will, hopefully, uncover them and understand the present era

Figure 5–1. People are the same, and people are different. People receive satisfaction from dance, but they choose different forms. Courtesy Columbia Broadcasting System.

better. Only man has such wonderful ability to send messages into the years ahead or to understand the messages left by people years and even centuries ago.

Yet people often cannot communicate with those closest to them. Parents show their children great love and care, yet these children often find themselves unable to explain their deepest feelings to their parents. A wife wants desperately to tell her husband that she needs more of his

Figure 5–2. With this radiotelescope, man can receive radio signals from outside our galaxy. Courtesy Columbia Broadcasting System.

attention; a high school student wants to ask his parents to respect his privacy. But fear and inhibition prevent the expression of these feelings, and the person to whom we are trying to communicate is often unable to sense what is being felt. Men have learned more about the scientific techniques of communicating across time and space than about communicating deep feelings to those they love.

Behavior: complex, yet predictable. No two individuals look or behave exactly alike—even identical twins are slightly different. Each person combines physical appearance, personality, abilities, and attitudes in a unique fashion.

Nonetheless, psychologists have found that, within limits, human behavior may be predicted. In spite of its complexity, behavior is not a complete mystery. A psychologist can administer a brief test to 100 entering freshmen and judge which ones are likely to graduate; his judgment will be far from perfect, but it will be much better than guesswork or making the decision from an interview. If you are more stubborn than average, you are also likely to be neater than average (Sears, 1936)—not every time, by any means, but the relationship has been shown to exist.

If you marry at 18 or younger, you are more likely than average to be divorced. If you are forced to express your views in public, those views will be less likely to change later (Hovland et al., 1957). If you are under stress, you may run faster than you normally could, but if the stress is too great, you may "freeze." Thousands of such predictions can be made with varying degrees of accuracy, although the uniqueness of people has prevented psychologists from making their predictions with complete accuracy.

The behavior of humans and of lower animals

The human being is considered the highest form of animal life. Yet, although he is, *by definition*, an animal and has many characteristics of other animal species, the human being differs from lower animals in distinct ways. Both humans and other animals seek food and shelter, care for their young, exhibit aggression and fear, and enter into relationships with other individuals and with groups. Yet humans have vastly higher intelligence, the ability to walk upright, and the ability to use tools. You can easily add many other examples.

But, more important to the purpose of this book, people differ from lower animals in six ways having major implications for the study of human behavior.

1. *People develop more slowly.* Therefore, the effects of the environment have more time to operate. Since infancy and childhood are longer for the human than for other forms of animal life, his experiences during these periods may have more lasting effects.

2. *People study themselves.* No other creatures study themselves. As a matter of fact, no other creatures seem aware that they exist and, thus, can be studied.

3. *People develop interests having nothing to do with keeping alive.* Many animals enjoy play, new experiences, and companionship, but only at a relatively primitive level. People can become interested in such

activities as reading, travel, television, sports, talking, collecting match-books, studying ancient civilizations, and playing poker.

4. *People use symbols in thinking and communicating.* The symbolic language of animals is very limited, but people have developed a tremendous variety of symbols, including words, gestures, and numbers, which open entire new worlds for them.

5. *People can govern their behavior by occurrences far away in time or in space.* A man may wish to have future generations think well of him; a student can learn what happened in 1492 or in 1933, or he can anticipate

Figure 5–3. Cosmopolitan man. Photograph by Shinichi "Tony" Yamashita.

what might happen in 1984 or 1999. In the same way, people can alter their behavior by learning what is happening in Bogor, Indonesia, or Indianapolis, Indiana (the above were adapted from Diamond, 1957).

Although any individual is influenced primarily by occurrences in his own country, he cannot help but be affected by what is going on in the rest of the world. In Figure 5–3 a young Japanese man in a western-style business suit sits barefoot in Japanese position next to an American type-writer on a Japanese desk. The room is heated by a British gas heater supplied with fuel from Kuwait.

6. *People change the environment of each generation.* You are living in a world much different from the one your grandparents knew when they were your age. Most of the change is the result of human accomplishments. The dog or the horse, on the other hand, would live in the same sort of world as his grandparents', except for those changes produced by human beings. Humans can acquire, accumulate, alter, and

transmit values, ideas, and material goods (adapted from Sanford, 1965).

These differences between human and animal behavior allow the human being wonderful opportunities for personal growth, for controlling his environment, for using his abilities, and for enjoying his life. They also offer him great destructive potential. How well do you feel the human being has used the abilities and opportunities he has? You can see immediately the importance of knowing history in order to consider this problem.

An introduction to personality

The theme of this book is human behavior and, therefore in final analysis, the human **personality:** its development, the way it adjusts to the world, its feelings, its values, its problems, and the ways in which it deals with these problems. Although you all have an idea what the term *personality* implies, the psychologist's definition may differ from yours in several ways.

Personality can be defined as "the **dynamic** organization of characteristic attributes leading to behavior, and distinguishing one individual from other individuals. It refers to the total individual and includes (but is not limited to) needs, motives, methods of adjusting, temperament qualities, self-concepts, role behaviors, attitudes, values, and abilities." The term covers behavior the individual himself is aware of, behavior of which he is not aware, behavior evident to others, and behavior evident only to the person himself.

This definition is extremely broad and demands some additional explanation of the terms used.

Dynamic. A dynamic person is forceful, always moving, filled with energy. In psychology, to refer to personality as dynamic is to say that the human being is constantly changing and that each change affects the entire personality. No element of personality is isolated from any other element—nothing operates independently, in a vacuum. Consider the impact of a seemingly insignificant behavior change in a hypothetical case:

> Jack Sweeny stops smoking. His girl friend admires his willpower; his roommate, who hates the odor of tobacco, decides Jack is not such a bad fellow; his mother tells his three aunts (which Jack resents); Jack has two dollars a week more to spend; he starts chewing pencils. And each of these actions will affect the chances that Jack will or will not smoke again in the future.

Personality is dynamic, interacting, changing.

Organization. Personality is not a single entity nor a combination of entities, but an *organization* or a "whole." An automobile is not a shell, nor is it merely a large number of separate parts. In order to work, an automobile must become an organization of the individual parts into a whole automobile. Personality also is organized into a whole.

Characteristic. An example of behavior fairly typical of an individual is said to be *characteristic* of him. If a man is consistently kind and gentle, but will strike anyone who threatens to strike him first, we would still call him kind and gentle, because such behavior is more typical of him.

Behavior. Any observable action is behavior. Eating a ham sandwich is behavior; so is each separate step in eating a ham sandwich, such as making the sandwich, raising it to the lips, biting it, chewing it, swallowing it. Two people may both eat ham sandwiches frequently enough to consider this act to be characteristic or typical, but each will make it, bite it, and chew it in different ways.

Thinking is also behaving, since thinking involves brain cell activity, which is indirectly observable through such devices as the electroencephalograph. Any expression of an attitude or a need, even if only a thought, is thus an act of behavior. Other examples of behavior include figuring out whether you received the correct change at a store, wondering whom to vote for in the next campus election, becoming angry when you hear someone tell a lie about your friend, and trying to listen to the professor who speaks so quietly you can barely hear him.

To repeat the initial definition in other terms: Personality is defined as *"the changing and interacting organization or whole of typical qualities that lead to a man's behaving as he does and that make him different from other people."*

The self-concept and other approaches to personality

A very useful way of gaining an understanding of the human personality is through consideration of the **self-concept**. The definition of self-concept is deceivingly simple: Self-concept is your picture or image of yourself. Like personality, self-concept is a dynamic organization of characteristic qualities, but—unlike personality—self-concept is those qualities *as seen by the individual himself.* Your self-concept includes *your* picture of your abilities, of your effect upon others, of your temperament and other elements of personality, and of your physical qualities, such as health and appearance.

When we talk about **self**, we are talking about what you really are.

When we talk about self-concept, we are concerned with what you think of yourself, your picture or image of yourself, or what you really *feel* you are.

> Ron Vance had two older brothers, both brilliant and outstanding college students. Ron was constantly expected to live up to the standards set by his brothers, which he could not do although he was well above average in intelligence. Over the years he developed a self-concept of being "not too bright," and he increasingly avoided situations that called for intelligence or schoolwork.

Your self-concept reflects how you feel about yourself. Like any feeling, it may be partially unconscious or based on unconscious needs. You are likely to have some elements in your self-concept you are not fully able to recognize.

> Patricia Tratner, a highly intelligent girl, was more than 30 pounds overweight, even though her friends had been telling her for years that she would be very attractive if she would reduce. Consciously, her self-concept became "I would be attractive if I could only reduce." However, until she sought help from a psychologist, she was unable to realize why she had never lost weight. Pat's unconscious self-concept was that of a hopelessly unattractive person. She was unconsciously motivated to remain overweight because, if she did lose weight and was still unattractive, as she perceived herself, she could no longer make excuses. Once she gained insight into her unconscious self-concept, she was able to lose weight and, more important, to worry much less about whether she was physically attractive or not.

Many forms of behavior that appear inconsistent or irrational on the surface begin to make sense if you can learn about the self-concept of the people involved. For example, a 14-year-old girl became furious during Christmas dinner because she was seated, as she had been for years, with the children; her self-concept, however, was that she had attained sufficient age and status to eat with the adults, and being seated with the younger children disturbed her self-concept.

The self-concept has been extensively investigated. The results of one study (summarized in Figure 6–2, p. 115) suggest that the self-concept in combination with attitudes toward others, can tell a lot about the behavior of an individual. Research has shown that people whose self-concepts are unpleasant are more likely than average to be poorly adjusted (Calvin and Holtzman, 1953).

The ideal self

The self-concept reflects the image an individual actually has of himself; the **ideal self** reflects his image of himself as he would like to be. The ideal self of a young child is usually a parent; older children tend to idealize glamorous or historical figures; adolescents and adults select a combination of several people or an imaginary or hypothetical person for their ideal self (Havighurst, Robinson, and Dorr, 1946). Thus, as we mature, the ideal self becomes more complex.

People try to live up to their ideal self, but they usually fall short. When a person's self-concept falls too far short of his ideal self, he is likely to show greater maladjustment (Rosenberg, 1962) and more confusion (Block and Thomas, 1955). He is dissatisfied with himself and feels that he has failed to become the sort of person he wishes to become.

At the same time, people who claim that their self-concept and ideal self are almost identical may also be unstable. Research has shown that these individuals have an unusually great need to be liked and accepted by others and that they dislike expressing their emotions (Block and Thomas, 1955). All in all, the self-concept of the healthy personality is close, but not too close, to the ideal self.

Traits and roles

In addition to the self-concept, two other ways of describing personality stand out as being particularly useful: **traits** and **roles**. Each of these has its place in the study of human behavior.

Traits. A personality trait is a behavior characteristic that differentiates people from each other. Psychologists talk about such traits as thriftiness, boastfulness, friendliness, foolishness, or honesty. To describe an individual in terms of a trait implies that the trait is fairly typical of his behavior.

People talk in terms of traits all the time. "John seems to be a happy guy." "Jeanne just isn't as thoughtful as she used to be." "Greg is too shy to be a good salesman." However, it is important to remain aware that describing a person by using traits is oversimplifying, since his actual personality is both unique and dynamic. John is not always happy; Jeanne is still thoughtful in many ways; Greg might make an excellent salesman for a company that allowed him to contact people he liked.

Role. Any given society has many *positions*, such as male and female, leader and follower, minister and doctor, teacher and student, and so forth. In each society, certain patterns of behavior are expected of individuals who occupy those positions. These anticipated behavior patterns form the *role* associated with that position. Thus, the role of the minister is to be concerned with spiritual matters, and many people become upset when a minister seems to be trying hard to make a lot of money for himself, since that appears inconsistent with his role. The role of the adolescent male in the United States is much different from his role in many other countries. In what ways do you suppose these roles differ?

Whether you prefer to approach personality through an understanding of the self-concept, of traits, of roles, or of some combination of these, or —indeed—any other way you might wish, you need to become concerned with the origins of human personality. Personality does not begin suddenly at a particular point in time; it develops and changes very slowly but constantly throughout the life span.

Personality influences before birth

By the time the human infant has emerged into the world, he already displays certain characteristics and has achieved a particular level of development. These characteristics and this development have taken place as the result of **inherited factors** and nine months of existence.

Inherited factors

The very first moment of life occurs in the mother's womb, when the sperm from the father combines with the ovum from the mother. At this instant, the future individual inherits certain characteristics from each of his parents, through tiny, microscopic bits of life called genes and chromosomes. Among the **hereditary** or **genetic** characteristics, determined at the moment of conception, are eye color, hair color, and head shape.

Other characteristics are believed to be heavily influenced by genetic factors but also affected by the environment. Your height and weight, for example, depend both upon your gene structure at conception and upon health and nutrition and eating habits in later life; your *potential* intellectual capability appears to be inherited, but your ability to make use of this intelligence arises from the environment.

People often make such statements as "He has his father's temper," or "He cries easily, like his mother." The implication is that temper and tendency to crying are genetically inherited. Geneticists and psychologists are not at all certain how important heredity is in determining this kind of behavior. We assume that environment is probably dominant in causing a hot temper or frequent crying, but heredity will also play a part. Nor is it necessary that heredity and environment contribute the same proportion to the temper or crying behavior of every individual.

Not all human characteristics are necessarily influenced by heredity. Your political attitudes, your religious preferences, your enjoyment of television quiz shows, or your interest in watching or playing baseball are virtually completely the result of what you have learned.

In essence, heredity influences certain behavior and characteristics substantially or almost totally, but is limited, perhaps almost nonexistent, in its influence on others. Thus, assuming proper motivation, an individual is capable of changing certain of his characteristics but will remain unable to change other personal qualities.

Some relevant research. Careful observations of patients suffering from certain medical problems have led scientists to talk about **inherited predispositions**. Thus, if two people who lead the same sort of life and are equally healthy both become ill with a strep throat, Person *A* will contract rheumatic fever, while Person *B* will not be affected. Person *A*, therefore, may have genetically inherited a predisposition or weakness toward rheumatic fever. He did not inherit rheumatic fever, but he inherited a susceptibility to contract the disease, while Person *B* inherited a strong resistance to the illness. Considerable evidence is available that one person may have a greater inherited predisposition to become mentally ill than another, although they both lead equivalent lives and face equally stressful situations (Kallmann, 1953).

Many studies, including the one mentioned above, investigated differences between **identical twins** and **fraternal twins**. Since identical twins come from the division of a single fertilized egg, they share an almost identical heredity; they are nearly identical to each other in appearance and are inevitably of the identical sex. Fraternal twins occur when two separate eggs are fertilized; their heredity is no more the same than any two children of the same parents, and they need not look alike or be of the same sex.

Fraternal twins share with each other a highly similar environment, just as identical twins do, but they share a much less similar heredity than do identical twins. As a result, in behavior presumed to have some genetic basis identical twins should resemble each other more than fraternal twins resemble each other. Research results bear this out. Identical twins have been found more similar than fraternal twins on measures of various types of maladjustment, on the length of time it takes to react to stimuli, on numerous personality traits, and—as mentioned above—on the likelihood of becoming mentally ill (Harsh and Schrickel, 1959; Kallmann, 1953).

Other studies have shown that the intelligence of foster children is more similar to that of their biological parents than to that of their foster parents (Honzik, 1957), even though a good foster home appears to increase the IQs of the foster children beyond that otherwise expected (Skodak and Skeels, 1949).

Research on twins and on adopted children has been used as evidence of the importance of inherited qualities in influencing some types of behavior, although there has been no attempt to assume that environmental factors are not also involved.

Environment and its interaction with heredity. Much of what was once considered to be genetically inherited is now recognized as learned, often during the early years of life. A young girl whose mother is always arguing with her father may learn to feel that men are crude and must be argued with. When she grows older and marries, she argues with her husband, much as her mother had argued with her father. The casual observer may assume such behavior to be genetically inherited, whereas most behavioral scientists believe it is learned.

Of greatest importance to the proper understanding of human behavior is the recognition that heredity and environment interact with each other. Neither stands in isolation. Being tall or short, being Caucasian or Polynesian, being male or female, being what our society considers beautiful or what our society considers homely, these are all genetically determined characteristics. Each of these qualities affects the way others respond to us. Since the response of others to us helps determine the self-concept, the degree to which needs may be satisfied, and the opportunities for self-actualization, genetically transmitted characteristics thereby have an important indirect influence upon human behavior. Genetic qualities affect the individual's environment, which inevitably affects his behavior. Can you see how the resulting environment might act to affect the genetic inheritance of the next generation?

Think of some people you know and try to understand how their heredity interacted with their environment to make them the sort of people they are. How about Napoleon? Marilyn Monroe? Albert Einstein? Martin Luther King, Jr.? Mickey Mantle?

In summary, inherited characteristics probably affect personality in four basic ways: (1) people inherit certain physical characteristics, such as facial features and certain medical conditions; (2) people inherit predispositions to certain psychiatric and other illnesses; (3) people inherit predispositions to certain types of behavior; and (4) all these qualities interact with the environment to influence personality indirectly as well as directly.

Prenatal influences upon later development

A newborn infant has already had a history of roughly nine months of existence. Although his brain and senses were not well developed during that period, his condition was still influenced by the health of his mother and by what is termed the **intrauterine environment**. Thus, his later appearance, intelligence, and behavior *may* be affected by what occurs between conception and birth.

Women who maintain an adequate diet during pregnancy are not only more likely than poorly nourished women to give birth to healthy babies, but the birth itself and the mother's recovery will be much easier (Ebbs et al., 1942).

Although being undernourished is certainly harmful for the mother and the fetus, "eating enough for two" is not the proper alternative. Moderate amounts of food, with particular attention to a well-balanced diet, undoubtedly are most effective. In countries where women cannot receive adequate food and medical care, many infants die during the **prenatal** period.

When the mother contracts certain illnesses during her pregnancy, the future health, intelligence, and physical condition of the infant may be adversely affected. These illnesses include German measles (during the first three or four months of pregnancy), syphilis, tuberculosis, and some strains of influenza (Montagu, 1958).

Women who are unhappy about being pregnant appear to have more pregnancy problems and less well-adjusted children than do women who are pleased with their role (Wallin and Riley, 1950). Although it is not known why such unhappiness is related to future problems, observations of pregnant rats may shed some light on the topic. An experimental population of pregnant rats was treated in such a way as to make them fearful, while the control population was left alone. The offspring of the experimental group definitely showed more anxiety, when they eventually matured, than the offspring of the control group (Thompson, 1957). Since emotions cause physiological changes in the human body, it seems possible that anxiety felt by unhappy mothers might cause a physiological change that affects the offspring.

Other conditions of the mother that may disrupt the normal development of the fetus include heavy drinking (which usually reduces the likelihood of a healthy diet), certain narcotics, smoking (which seems related to low birth weight and prematurity [Lowe, 1959]), X rays, lack of oxygen, a major illness or accident, a condition occurring when the parents have a specific inconsistency in blood type, and atomic fallout.

The neonate

The first two or three weeks of life are called the **neonatal** period. A century ago, this was considered a time of danger to the future health and life of the individual, and the proportion of infants who died before they were two weeks old was quite high. Improvements in maternal health, hospital conditions, and general medical care have been major factors in producing an amazing drop in the death rate at birth and during the neonatal period. This very improvement in health, however, has been an important contributor to the present-day **population explosion.** Can you explain the significance of this term and its relationship to reduced infant mortality?

Behavior differences at birth

"To be honest, I didn't really enjoy my son until he was about a year old—that's when he began to have a real personality." In spite of a common belief that all babies are alike, definite individual differences are evident at birth.

Neonates differ in the amount of crying and sucking they exhibit. Observations during the first few months show differences in motor behavior (movements), reactions to frustration, and readiness to smile (Diamond, 1957). Some infants are generally more responsive to their environment, more easily stimulated by what goes on around them. These personality differences occur so early and with so little opportunity for learning that they seem to be at least partly the result of inherited factors.

Birth and right after

Many physicians and psychologists feel that modern American women become so tense and fearful about giving birth that the birth process becomes more difficult and painful. This, in turn, may create a negative attitude toward the infant, who caused the discomfort. Medical men try to encourage mothers-to-be to look upon childbirth as a natural event, neither very dangerous nor necessarily especially painful.

A few expectant mothers follow a program termed **natural childbirth,** which combines various physical exercises with encouragement to develop mentally healthy attitudes regarding childbirth (Dick-Read, 1960). In some instances, the husband will remain with his wife during her labor and, sometimes, even during the delivery itself, if his presence is felt to contribute to the security feelings of the mother.

Although only a small proportion of women use the natural childbirth methods, medical and social attitudes toward proper behavior of mothers-to-be have changed considerably over the past 50 years. At one time, expectant mothers were encouraged to rest as much as possible, to stay off their feet, and to remain at home unless it was necessary to leave. Today they are encouraged to get mild exercise, to remain moderately active, and to follow their normal schedules to the degree they can do so without discomfort or danger to the fetus.

After the infant is born, some mothers prefer to use **lying-in** in the hospital. With lying-in, the newborn is placed in a small room adjacent to the mother's bed or in the same room as the mother, so that the baby is immediately available to her, instead of being in a special ward some distance away.

Some expectant mothers have the sort of attitudes that make natural childbirth and lying-in very rich, worthwhile experiences. Other women are undoubtedly better off adhering to the more traditional methods.

Physical development

At birth, infants have only a minimal awareness of their environment. Although their senses are fairly well developed at birth and mature quickly in the following weeks, neonates have little basis for interpreting those stimuli they do receive. Even very young infants, however, will exhibit certain responses to some noises, odors, tastes, colors, and tactual stimuli, e.g., avoiding an unpleasant odor or looking for longer time periods at one color or pattern than at another (see Kidd and Rivoire, 1966).

Because of the infant's immaturity, his early movement is largely mass activity. That is, his entire body will move in response to stimulation of one part of the body. Neonates can suck and swallow, which allows them to take food, but these are **reflexes,** which occur automatically, without learning. Motor behavior, such as grasping, crawling, and walking, progresses more slowly than sensory abilities and varies considerably from child to child. Figure 5–4 shows the average age at which certain behavior is first observed, but it is perfectly normal for children to develop much later or much earlier than these averages.

The neonate sleeps about two-thirds of the time, but—as parents learn to their dismay—will wake up every few hours, crying to be fed. Slowly, as his body grows larger, he can take more food at a time and will need to eat less frequently.

During the first few months of life, physical growth and development are rapid. Birth weight is usually tripled by the end of the first year and height has increased by 50 percent. At the same time, the body proportions change, with the head growing less rapidly than the rest of the body.

The significance of maturation

Some behavior results from **maturation,** which means that it develops almost inevitably, assuming a normal environment, without being taught.

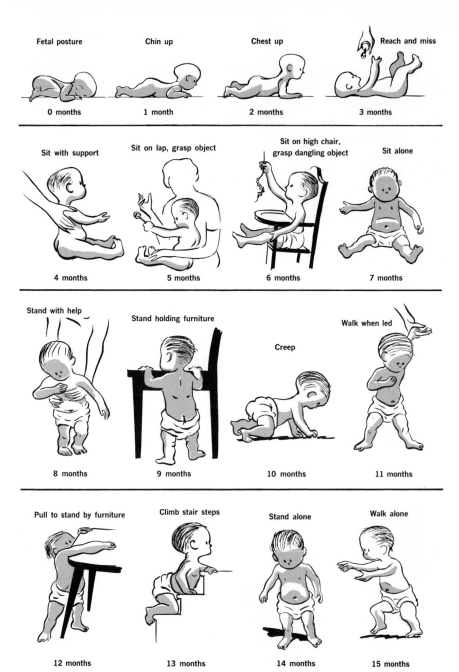

Figure 5–4. Motor development in children. The averages pictured do not, by any means, imply that infants developing quickly are bound to be highly intelligent or those late in development are doomed to slow learning throughout their lives. Normal infants show a wide range in development. Adapted from Shirley, 1933; by permission of the University of Minnesota Press.

For example, walking is largely the result of maturation. The human being must reach a certain level of maturation and readiness before he can learn to walk; at that point, he will probably learn to walk with or without aid. Effective help and encouragement might hasten the process by a few weeks, but no more.

Maturation is almost impossible to speed up, and the rate of maturation is primarily the result of heredity, although inadequate physical health, nutrition, or learning opportunity can retard maturation. Parents who pressure their children to learn certain tasks, such as climbing stairs or buttoning, before they are ready, will find this has little long-range effect upon the ability of the child to do the particular task. If, however, the parents push too hard, the results may be unpleasant, because the child is being forced to do something he cannot do successfully. He may become anxious and fearful over his inevitable failure and develop feelings of inadequacy and a lowered self-concept.

SUMMARY OF IMPORTANT IDEAS

1. People will try to make use of their capacities, if given the opportunity; most behavior called *good* or *evil* is learned; differences between the behavior of humans and lower animals are numerous and vital.

2. Human behavior is adaptable, yet rigid; it varies from culture to culture, yet displays conspicuous consistencies; it is subtle and intricate, yet predictable; people communicate across time and space, yet have trouble communicating with those they love most.

3. Personality is the dynamic organization of characteristic attributes leading to behavior and distinguishing one individual from other individuals.

4. The self-concept is the picture an individual has of himself; the conscious self-concept and the unconscious self-concept are usually similar, but are not necessarily identical.

5. The ideal self is the image an individual has of himself as he would like to be.

6. Personality may also be described in terms of traits and roles.

7. Heredity influences certain characteristics and behavior sub-·stantially or almost totally, but it is limited—perhaps almost nonexistent—in its influence upon others. A person need not accept all his characteristics as fixed.

8. Evidence exists that people vary in their inherited predispositions to many characteristics.

9. Heredity and environment constantly interact with each other.

10. The physical condition of the expectant mother influences the well-being of her future child; her emotional state *may perhaps* also have such an influence.

11. Behavior differences exist among infants at birth.

12. At birth, infants have a minimal awareness of their environment, although their sensory apparatus appears adequately developed; development is rapid in the first few months.

13. Some behavior results from maturation, i.e. it develops relatively inevitably and at a fairly well-anticipated pace.

II Development of human behavior

The earliest years 6

The previous chapter formed a bridge between the basic principles of human behavior and the development of human behavior. Psychologists and others emphasize the study of the early years of life, because they usually feel strongly that experiences at this stage leave an unerasable mark upon responses to situations in later years, even though an accurate memory of the early experiences may be lacking. The previous chapters have discussed behavior principles; the following chapters will emphasize behavior development.

Experiences during the earliest years of life probably have a greater effect upon later behavior patterns than do experiences at any other time in the life span. Even though the infant and young child face a limited range of situations, and even though this age group lacks a conscious memory of what occurs, the first two or three years are tremendously important. The mature personality is largely the product of early parent-child relationships, early experiences of all sorts, and—of course—the interaction between these factors and the genetic qualities the infant inherits.

Child-rearing methods and personality

Psychologists believe that experiences during the first few years of life are vitally important in shaping the entire personality. As a result, they have spent a great deal of time and effort exploring the methods parents use to rear their children and the various parent-child relationships that occur. Some of the specific aspects that have been studied include early feeding experiences, early toilet-training experiences, and early sex-behavior training.

These experiences are very important for several reasons: (1) Early experiences set the stage for later expectations. (2) Very young children cannot use speech, and their memories are very inexact; so they are not able to communicate early experiences or to recall them with accuracy. (3) Since early experiences have not been contradicted by other experiences, they may have greater and more lasting impact. (4) The child's attitudes toward himself begin to develop at a very early age. (5) Early experiences may affect later unconscious motivation.

Attitudes of parents toward children may be described in many ways, but two dimensions occur frequently in research and theories: (1) warmth (or acceptance) versus hostility (or rejection); and (2) control (or restrictiveness) versus permissiveness (or independence) (Maccoby, 1964). It is generally assumed that these two factors, rather than the specific techniques of child rearing, are of primary importance. Thus, in considering the topics to follow, we must consider the behavior of individual parents according to the degree of warmth they show and the degree of independence they allow their children.

Early feeding experiences

For the infant, hunger needs and their satisfaction are among the most compelling forces in life. If the hunger need remains unsatisfied too long, he may develop fear or anxiety regarding his ability to obtain food; children who suffered severe hunger during their very early years were later observed to stuff food into their pockets, even when the supply was plentiful. If early eating experiences are tense, uncomfortable occasions, the child may develop negative attitudes not only toward eating but toward those individuals associated with early eating experiences.

The most meaningful experiences infants have with eating are the initial breast or bottle feeding, weaning from the breast or bottle, and contact with solid food.

Breast feeding. For many years, most physicians and psychologists have strongly advised those women who were physically capable to breast feed their babies. Among the reasons frequently mentioned were: (1) Breast feeding leads to close physical contact between the mother and the child, providing a sense of security for the infant and pleasure for the mother. (2) As the child begins to learn, he will associate the warmth of his mother's body and the satisfaction of his hunger with his mother as a person, helping to build a strong affection between the two. (3) Breast feeding often helps a woman to "feel like a mother" (Spock, 1957). (4) Mother's milk is more likely to be right for the baby and free from germs, while bottled milk often necessitates preparation and adjusted formulas. (5) Breast-fed babies have fewer illnesses and better chances for survival (Jeans et al., 1954).

Although a considerable body of research findings exists on the later personality of nursed versus bottle-fed infants, no final conclusions can be drawn. While many of the studies find breast-fed children healthier, happier, better adjusted, and more successful in school (e.g., Hoefer and Hardy, 1929; Rogerson and Rogerson, 1939), other studies discovered no differences between the two groups (e.g., Sewell and Mussen, 1952; Sears et al., 1957). (No research, however, has shown bottle-fed babies to be better off than breast-fed infants.)

One psychologist (Watson, 1965) suggested that the breast feeding itself is less important than the possibility that mothers who breast feed have more positive attitudes in general toward their children (Newton and Newton, 1950). Therefore, breast feeding is just part of a pattern of warm, positive responses toward infants, and it is this pattern, rather than any one aspect of it, that leads to better physical and mental health. Since most authorities recommend that the baby be held (rather than propped) during feeding, the main value of breast feeding could be the cuddling and affection the infant receives during this social period.

One unfortunate outcome of the emphasis upon breast feeding is that many women who are physically unable or personally unwilling to breast feed may feel guilty and inadequate. If, as hypothesized above, the main value of breast feeding is the cuddling the infant receives, mothers who use bottle feeding can compensate by other forms of care and affection.

This is particularly important, since American mothers are less likely to nurse their infants than are mothers from most societies in the world (Whiting and Child, 1953).

Weaning. Eventually the young child must be removed from the breast or the bottle and taught to drink without sucking. According to the famous Dr. Spock, most infants are ready to begin this step between seven and ten months, although they may begin taking sips from a cup as early as five months (1957). Anthropological investigations of small, less-developed societies show **weaning** of the child from the breast to begin typically between two and three years. Of 52 groups investigated, only the Marquesans weaned their children earlier than Americans (Whiting and Child, 1953).

Weaning should occur gradually, preferably by the elimination of one feeding at a time (Spock, 1957). An infant who is shifted suddenly from the breast or bottle to the cup may find the experience upsetting. Mothers in some of the societies described by anthropologists wean their children very gradually, allowing them to continue feeding from the breast from time to time, to as old as five years of age (Whiting and Child, 1953), and in one society actually until around the age of twelve (Gorer, 1938).

Feeding. Feeding problems in childhood, especially in infancy, often plague mothers. Unfortunately for parents, the appetites of their children are rarely predictable. Sometimes children eat a great deal; at other times, very little. Without warning, a child may go on a hunger strike and eat nothing at all or refuse to eat solid food. Since the mother often becomes frantic, she communicates her anxiety to the child, who is likely to respond by becoming more anxious and unhappy himself. Unless something is medically wrong, a child will eat when he becomes hungry; and a jumpy, frightened mother is not going to increase his appetite.

Feeding problems among one group of children studied could not be traced to bottle feeding, weaning, or strictness of the feeding schedule. In this research, children with feeding problems were found to have had more severe toilet training, more physical punishment, and less warmth from their mothers than children without feeding problems (Sears et al., 1957). Here, then, is additional evidence that the degree of warmth and of parental restrictiveness, rather than the specific training techniques, is important in determining later personality adjustment.

Toilet training

Primitive societies usually do not begin **toilet training** until the child is around two—and the Bena of Africa, as late as five (Whiting and Child, 1953). American families, however, usually start toward the end of the first year, sometimes placing the child on the "potty" as early as five months and finishing toilet training at about 18 months on the average (Sears et al., 1957).

Some parents feel a glow of pride in toilet training their child before he is nine or ten months old, even though pediatricians and psychologists discourage any attempts at toilet training too early. Being toilet trained demands a certain degree of maturation: the child must learn to associate the physical pressure within his body with the acts of elimination; then he must be able to withhold the waste until he can get (or be taken) to the toilet. Many children will toilet train themselves if left alone; when they are around two years of age, they wish to imitate their parents and their older friends or brothers and sisters. The later training begins, the less time it takes (Sears et al., 1957).

It may seem strange that psychologists and pediatricians place so much stress upon toilet training, but there is a good explanation. Toilet training is likely to be the first attempt of the parent to train his child; it often involves the first taste of real discipline and the first fear of disappointing the parents. Perhaps most serious, the child is often frustrated because he cannot please his parents by doing what they expect of him. He may thus develop a self-concept of inadequacy, which could generalize to other phases of living. Since toilet training, unlike other types of child training, continues for many weeks, or even months, the possible failure to satisfy the parents becomes even more disturbing. The child may even come to feel that being toilet trained is the most important thing in his life. His parents praise him when he is successful, scold him when he is unsuccessful, and discuss it constantly. Sometimes the child thinks that the valuable thing is the feces itself, not the act of getting to the toilet.

> Karen Reiter's parents placed great emphasis upon toilet train-ing, and they were very unhappy at Karen's slow learning. At 26 months, Karen made many mistakes, and the family did everything they could to get her trained. Karen was a sensitive child who wanted to please her parents but seemed unable to learn this particular trick. One evening, while her parents were entertaining three other couples for dinner, Karen called to her parents to ask whether she might bring out "something to show you." Her father, thinking she wanted to show the guests her brand new furry slippers, called back "Yes." And Karen trooped out, her pajama pants around her knees, pulling the bowl from the "potty"—full.

Parents may also demand too much of their child during toilet training. Some children are physiologically ready to be trained much earlier than others, and even children who have been trained will have accidents from

111

time to time, especially on occasions of stress, such as at the birth of a new brother or sister or when the parents are arguing. The severity of toilet training, rather than the age at which it begins, is more closely related to emotional upset (Sears et al., 1957).

Children may consciously or unconsciously ignore their toilet training as a form of aggression against their parents: a child who is apparently trained, then suddenly wets or soils, not only has insulted the control of his parents but has produced a job of cleaning up that parents usually abhor. Chronic bed wetting, sometimes interpreted as aggression against the parents, is more frequent among children who received very severe toilet training (Sears et al., 1957).

> While the author was working with young children, he developed a particularly close relationship with three-year-old Barbara, who was living in a type of orphanage. After several months of frequent contact, he told the child that he had to leave for another job. Although he did all he could to break the news gently, and another psychologist had agreed to take up where he left off, the child was very upset. During each of their last three meetings, she soiled her pants at least once, although her most recent previous mistake had been nearly a year earlier. Was Barbara expressing aggression or responding to stress or both?

Toilet training is closely related to cleanliness training. Parents who desire rapid toilet training often emphasize other forms of cleanliness and neatness (Sears et al., 1957). The child who fails in his toilet efforts is reminded how "dirty" he is. A few years later, the same body parts will again become the center of attention as a place where modesty must be maintained. The demands for cleanliness and the demands for modesty interact to make that part of the body a forbidden, exciting, "dirty" area.

Perhaps you feel the importance of early feeding and toilet-training experiences have been exaggerated in this chapter. If so, discuss these topics with friends who have young children. Regardless of their specific experiences, you will quickly see what an important part this early training played in the lives of the parents, and you can imagine how important it was to their children, who had much less in the way of outside activities to distract them.

Sex training

Young children invariably locate their genital areas during the normal process of becoming familiar with the sight and feel of their own bodies. Exploring or handling the sex areas is likely to elicit punishment from parents, although most mental-health authorities would probably say, "Ignore it."

In some societies, sex play among children is accepted as natural (Whiting and Child, 1953). Even in the United States, children frequently explore each other's bodies, perhaps while claiming to play *Doctor*, although they usually hide their game from adults. Parents often oppose

Figure 6–1. Modesty is not "natural"; it must be learned. Photograph by John G. Warford.

any sort of sex activity among their children, over one-half of a group of mothers expressing definite opposition to sex play (Sears et al., 1957).

When punishment for sex play is severe, it may produce sexual-adjustment difficulties that work against future mental health. The early training of many American adults has created fear, anxiety, avoidance, and even impotence and frigidity in sex behavior and affection.

To convince their children to avoid any sex behavior, some parents make up stories or relate "facts" that are not accurate. For example, "If you touch yourself there, you will get sick or go crazy." Statements of this nature may create an immediate sense of panic, as well as long-range fear and avoidance of all forms of sex. The usual types of sex exploration and manipulation, in which children often indulge, are unlikely to be harmful, unless the children feel anxious or guilty because of being persuaded that their activity is sinful and unclean.

Nonetheless, adults are often frightened and offended by children's sex play, occasionally with justification. If the sex behavior involves two or more children, or if an older child is participating, one expert suggests that adults consider trying to get the child to stop (Spock, 1957). Distracting children, getting them involved in other activities, or expressing mild and general censure (i.e., "That game isn't really so good—why don't you ride your bikes for a while?") are among the effective approaches. They reduce the behavior without drawing attention to it.

Methods of child training are considered important by most societies, and contemporary America is certainly not an exception. If infants are fed, toilet trained, and trained regarding sex as part of a pattern of basically loving and affectionate parent-child interactions, the specific training techniques probably are of secondary consequence. What is of primary consequence is how these factors affect the development of the individual's self-concept and his relationships with the important people in his life.

Significant figures and the development of the self-concept

The self-concept develops through interaction with other people, beginning in infancy. A young child's judgment of himself can be only a reflection of how he feels others are judging him, and those "others" who have a particularly great impact are referred to as **significant figures**. For most infants and young children, significant figures are the parents, and it is through his parents' eyes that the child evaluates and pictures himself. Significant figures form a sort of psychological mirror (Cooley, 1902; Sullivan, 1953). The child looks to his parents to learn who and what he is; what he sees reflected back forms his picture of himself.

Thus, if the child feels his parents love him, he will feel he deserves this love; if he feels his parents think him stupid, he will believe it of himself. He is not able to judge himself or them but tends to accept their viewpoint of himself (and of much else in the world) as right and proper. If his parents have treated him well or cruelly, paid attention to him or ignored him, shown him love or shown him nothing but the back of their hand, he can only feel, "If these people do this to me, I must deserve it." He has no other basis for comparison at his age.

Figure 6–2. Relationship of acceptance of self and acceptance of others to certain personality variables.*

Acceptance of self	Acceptance of others	Personality traits exhibited
Good	Good	Healthy self-confidence, accepts responsibility, has faith in mankind, optimistic.
Good	Poor	Critical of others, over-estimates own acceptability.
Poor	Good	Timid, modest, popular, feels open to attack.
Poor	Poor	Dissatisfied, dependent, frightened, great need for security, impulsive.

* Adapted from Fey, 1957.

Elaine Lander's parents were well into their forties when she was born, and her sister and brother were both in high school. She was, by any definition, an unwanted child. Her mother, a private secretary to a business executive, quickly hired a housekeeper to care for her and returned to work; her father was irritated with having to worry about diapers and baby-sitters again, especially when he was working unusually hard to save money for the older children's college. Whenever either parent had to feed or change or otherwise handle Elaine, they did it as quickly as possible, not really caring whether she was bounced around a little in the process. They rarely bothered to give her that extra attention and affection that babies need.

Both parents constantly referred to her as a "damned nuisance." They had no sympathy for her crying and little interest in how she developed, other than making certain she received good physical care. As Elaine grew older, she began to recognize how her parents felt about her. When she played imaginative children's games, she would yell at herself, "You're a bad girl, Elaine, and a nuisance and a damned and a not-hurry-up. You're an icky."

She matured into a quiet, reserved, fearful girl who was constantly apologizing for bothering others. She hated to approach people for friendship, since she viewed herself as being unworthy of friendship; also, her parents had rejected her attempts at gaining their friendship, and she feared similar rejection from others. She later became a successful and popular nursery school teacher.

As a very young child, Elaine accepted her parents' view of her as valid. She was unable to say to herself "I'm really a very good person, but my parents are too busy to notice me." All she could feel was "If my parents (who are my world) do not notice me, then I am not worth noticing." By the time she was mature enough to evaluate herself with greater objectivity, her self-concept and her behavior patterns were well formed, and change was extremely difficult. Why do you think she was able to succeed as a nursery school teacher? Do you think she ever married? Why?

To make matters worse, children who feel unacceptable often behave in ways that irritate others. They may be so hungry for people to accept them that they are unable to disagree or turn down the request for a favor, and they gain a reputation for being weak. Or they may react in just the opposite way: having been unable to trust the significant figures in their lives, they are unable to trust or wholeheartedly like anyone else. Since most people respond to being disliked by disliking in return, the self-concept of inadequacy is made to appear true. This is another example of the self-fulfilling prophecy discussed on page 77.

As the child matures, he is constantly coming into contact with other people who may influence his self-concept. They respond to his appearance, intelligence, verbal ability, temperament, friendliness, and so forth. Being treated by others as an attractive, intelligent, capable individual will help encourage a corresponding self-concept. If this agrees with the very early self-concept developed through the parents, the child is likely to mature into a healthily adjusted adult.

On the other hand, being considered by others as an unclean, unintelligent, lazy person can create a corresponding self-concept. Even if the parent-child relationship is healthy, the negative reactions of later contacts with other people can partially undo the good the parents have accomplished. If, and this is more serious, the parent-child relationship was not good, later negative experiences will reinforce, perhaps make worse, the already negative self-concept.

In any case, it would appear that changing the self-concept in a direction that contradicts the early learning from significant figures becomes increasingly difficult as the person becomes older. This is why psychologists place such great emphasis upon the importance of early parent-child relationships: they set the stage for the entire life.

Self-perpetuating aspects of the self-concept

Although the individual's self-concept develops in response to the response of others, the response of others is a direct reaction to the individual's self-concept. For example, the more frequently people on welfare are condemned as "no good and lazy," the less likely they are to seek work. They seem to be saying, in essence, "Since I'm lazy, I couldn't find work or do a good job anyway. Since I'm no good, why bother trying." When they do get jobs, they may be unnecessarily sensitive to criticism. Then the rest of the community reacts by condemning them more strongly for being lazy or for being irritable when criticized. A few people rebel against the evaluation of others and do better than they otherwise would, but most accept the evaluation as largely true.

Community responses to welfare cases are self-perpetuated through the children of those on welfare, who recognize that many people stereotype their parents as lazy, unintelligent, and unclean and that these stereotypes are extended to them as well.

> These youngsters do not know who they are, what they can be, or even what they want to be. They are afraid, but they do not know of what. They are angry, but they do not know at whom. They are rejected, and they do not know why. So they make up answers. . . . And perhaps worst of all, they accept without question the world's judgment of them as not simply unlovable, uncultured failures, but as one such failure in a vast sea of failures (Washington, 1964).

If the children are also members of certain minority groups, such as the Negro American, the American Indian, or Americans of Puerto Rican or Mexican ancestry, these feelings may be intensified.

Other influences of significant figures

Significant figures influence the lives of their children in other ways than in the development of the self-concept. First, they serve as models for behavior. Regardless of what parents tell children, the examples set by the parents themselves are vitally important. When parents who swear insist that their children not swear, they are not really saying that swearing is wrong; they are saying swearing is wrong if someone is around to punish you for it, or swearing is wrong if you are a child.

Second, parents provide most of the rewards and punishments in the early lives of their children. It is their smile or frown, their gift or slap, their love or rejection that means the most to the child. Later in life, other people also become important, but the parents are the most influential, or significant, figures in the first few years, and they usually remain so.

Development of love

Significant figures are associated with warmth, love, and affection. They are also associated with the satisfaction of the infant's hunger, thirst, and temperature-regulation needs. When the parents are not there, discomfort remains; when they are there, discomfort ceases. When the parents are not there, love and affection are missing; when they are there, love and affection are with them. Thus, the absence of parents is associated with the absence of those things that are important.

As the result of being associated with such important satisfactions, the

Figure 6–3. Love can be expressed in many ways: Matthew not only accepts love; he also is able to give it. Photographs by Albert Kallis.

parents become valued for themselves. Just as some people like money for the sake of money rather than for what it will buy, infants come to love their parents for themselves rather than just as bringers of good things. This is the beginning of true love and affection.

Psychologists and psychiatrists have emphasized the importance of love and affection for infants in many ways, but a series of studies conducted over the past several years has captured the imagination of both laymen and professionals. Although this research has been carried on with monkeys rather than people, the implications for human beings are obvious.

Two false "monkey mothers" were constructed, identical to each other except that one had a wire body and the other's body was made of sponge rubber and covered with terrycloth. Baby monkeys showed a strong preference for the terrycloth mother, even when they were fed by a bottle inserted through the wire mother. When frightened, the animals would run for the soft, cuddly mother (Harlow, 1958). The soft mother offered a type of reassurance, which might be compared to the human mother who offers her child physical affection. Later, these monkeys who were raised without normal mothers were themselves unable to perform adequately as mothers (Harlow and Harlow, 1962a). This indicates that inadequate mothering will affect not only the children but even later generations.

Offering a child love—not only physical affection but emotional warmth—is a great help in establishing a later healthy personality. The child develops the self-concept "I am lovable," which leads to feelings of adequacy and self-worth. You may recall that the needs for love and for self-esteem must be reasonably satisfied before an individual can become concerned with self-actualization.

When a significant figure leaves. A parent often must leave his child. The absence may be permanent, such as through death or some divorces; it may be temporary, when a parent is very ill, takes a long business trip, or is in the military or in prison. If the absence occurs before the child is three or four months old, his awareness of the world is probably not well enough developed to cause him to be upset. After this very early age, however, the infant has established enough rich associations with his parents that their extended absence might be very disturbing.

When a significant figure leaves, the child may suffer **separation anxiety.** He fears that the source of love and satisfactions has left him, and he becomes fearful. Parents may notice that even when they leave for an evening, their child resents their absence. A child who wakes up in the middle of the night and finds a strange baby-sitter, rather than his parents, will become very frightened or upset. Of course, if the child knows the baby-sitter and has expected her to be there, his fear will be negligible.

Even a schoolchild who comes home after school to find his mother unexpectedly away is likely to be frightened.

When a child whose mother died before he was five reaches maturity, he is more likely than average to be emotionally disturbed, to show signs of mental illness, or to be delinquent, unless an adequate replacement can be found or the remaining parent can do a good job of compensating. Types of separation other than death also lead to increased chances of later emotional problems (Barry and Lindemann, 1960).

Being separated from a parent produces emotional upset in two major ways: (1) The child has lost an important person upon whom he depended for many satisfactions; and the loss, which is also reflected in great excitement and confusion in the home, is very disturbing. (2) A home with only one parent is often less stable because of pressures of money, the time of the remaining parent, and other factors. If the separation is caused by death, the child may become confused about the meaning of death and its effect on him; children often think of death as a punishment, and they may become afraid that they, too, will die soon.

The topic of death, in our society, is rarely discussed. People get fidgety and irritable when the matter is brought up, often claiming that it is too depressing to talk about. Nonetheless, death is part of life, and even children eventually learn its significance. The relationship between separation anxiety and death is not fully understood, but at least one authority (Muensterberger, 1963) has suggested that fear of death in adulthood may be a direct result of early fears of being separated from a parent.

Separation anxiety has also been observed in children who entered a hospital or other institution when they were between 15 and 30 months of age, especially when circumstances allowed little or no contact with their parents. Their reactions occurred in three stages: (1) *protest*, when they showed active distress, crying, and eager searching; (2) *despair*, when they became withdrawn and inactive; and (3) *detachment*, when they seem to have recovered from despair, but have actually attempted to avoid emotional involvements with people (Bowlby, 1960).

Since infants and young children in hospitals and institutions often receive little personal attention and no affection from the busy nursing and institutional staffs, they lose their spirit and enjoyment of life. Even when given good physical care and diet, children in institutions develop more slowly and have a higher mortality rate than children raised in private homes. The institutional children are also more likely to have later behavior problems and show apathy (Spitz, 1949).

> Barbara (the child discussed on page 112) lost both her parents
> when she was 18 months old and was placed in an institution for

children. A year later she was a tense, tearful child who fought constantly with others and could not adjust well to the nursery school the institution supported. At that point, she was referred to the institution's psychological clinic. For several months she met with one of the psychologists there twice a week and did nothing but play; the psychologist gave his full attention to Barbara, sometimes playing with her, sometimes just watching as she played. At the end of ten weeks, both Barbara's housemother and her nursery school teacher commented spontaneously that her behavior had improved greatly.

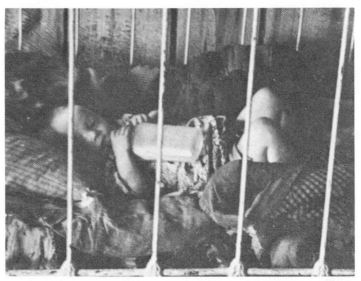

Figure 6–4. Apathy and withdrawal are commonly observed results when adult attention is lacking. Courtesy The Library of Congress.

The changes in Barbara's behavior illustrate the importance of feeling loved and cared for. Although replacement figures can compensate for the absence of significant figures to some extent, the best life situation for children undoubtedly occurs when significant figures do not change.

The developing personality

Life is not a series of time categories but a continuing flow, which we describe in time periods for convenience. The total human personality and all aspects of this personality develop and change continuously throughout the life span. The development of **conscience**, of **sex roles**, and of aggressive and dependent behavior patterns have been selected for more thorough discussion as examples of personality attributes that begin their formation in the earliest years and have important implications for behavior for the remainder of life.

Development of conscience and internalized attitudes

Before a child is three, he has begun to develop a sense of what is considered "right" and what is considered "wrong." At first this occurs without his questioning, without his actually knowing what he is doing. As his parents punish him for this, reward him for that, and show pleasure or displeasure for the other, the child learns what is expected of him. He also learns from observing how his parents themselves behave.

Since his significant figures are *the world* for him, he accepts their ideas and their behavior as correct. This leads to the process of **internalization,** through which the child accepts his parents' ideas and values as his own. When he is older, the ideas of others in his society will also be internalized; the child will learn these ideas through his friends, through the schools, through what he reads and hears and sees about him, but—at the beginning —the parents provide almost the only source of **values.**

The values that the child internalizes have a strong influence upon his behavior, because his own sense of right and wrong, rather than fear of outside authority, controls his actions. This value system, through which a person approves or disapproves of his own actions, thoughts, and feelings, is the **conscience.**

To some extent, the development of the conscience and of other internalized values is conscious. The child sees his father walk with a long stride, and so he walks with a long stride; he observes his parents enjoying reading, and so he picks up a book—even though he may hold it upside down. And he internalizes the values that walking with long strides or reading are "good" and "proper."

The greater part of the process, however, is **unconscious.** As the mother and daughter walk down the street, the mother spies a mangy stray dog and yanks her child away. Shortly after, the girl wants to pet another dog, but her mother tells her not to, that it is probably dirty. Slowly the child builds into her own belief system the value that dogs are to be avoided. She has internalized, or taken for herself, her mother's attitude toward dogs. Thereafter, when she wants to pet a dog, her conscience may tell her that it is wrong. These values will interact, in a dynamic fashion, with her personal experiences with dogs.

Sometimes, personal experiences contradict internalized values, but more frequently they are interpreted to support previously held beliefs:

the child who had internalized the belief that dogs are bad may see a friendly dog run toward her but will interpret its behavior as potentially vicious. Since the sight of the dog has undoubtedly created a feeling of fear and tension, avoiding the dog will reduce the tension; thus, the act of avoiding the dog is reinforced because of the reduction of fear, and this behavior, therefore, probably will be repeated on later occasions. In this way the value that dogs are bad and that avoiding them is good will be reinforced, just as the infant's pleasurable response to his mother was reinforced (see page 66).

The process of internalizing values can be seen very clearly in young children:

> Seth Regan, a bright three-year-old, had been carefully taught not to color on the floor. One afternoon, his mother heard loud shouts and slaps from Seth's room. She raced in and saw Seth slapping his hand as hard as he could, shouting, "No! Naughty! Don' do dat!" Then she saw he had accidentally crayoned off the drawing paper and onto the floor.

Shame and guilt. There are three basic reasons why an individual avoids doing something he would like to do and has the capability to do: (1) he recognizes that the punishment will be too great; (2) he feels that his family or country or some valued group would be **shamed** by his actions; and (3) his conscience or internalized values will not let him—that is, he feels it is "wrong," or feels **guilt.** In many situations, all three occur. For example, many young men would like to avoid military service, but very few pretend they have poor hearing or vision, which would allow them to stay out. Why? Because (1) they are afraid of the punishment if their faking is uncovered; (2) they know that their friends and family would be ashamed of them; and (3) they feel such behavior is unethical and unfair to others. The last two reasons may be understood in terms of the unhappiness produced by too great a difference between self-concept and ideal self.

For most Americans and Europeans, internalized values and conscience are the major restraints against committing unethical and illegal acts. Americans will feel a sense of guilt when they do something to violate their consciences. Not only overt behavior but even thoughts and feelings may elicit guilt so disturbing that the individual will avoid the action, the thought, or the feeling, in order to avoid the disrupting sense of guilt.

You often are confronted with the knowledge that you could do something unethical or illegal with little chance of being punished; yet you behave honestly. The feeling of shame may enter into your decision, but the chances are that you wish to avoid the extreme discomfort caused by a guilty conscience.

In Japan, and elsewhere in Asia, the emphasis is not upon guilt but upon shame, especially upon bringing shame to the family (Benedict, 1946). Thus, Japanese tend to be very polite to their friends and in their own homes, because they wish to avoid shame. However, they may be very rude in crowded department stores and rush-hour subways, where no one can identify them and cause shame to occur. The American, who typically is more polite in public, is more likely than the Japanese to show rude behavior to family and friends.

In both **shame societies** and **guilt societies,** the family and the home are probably the greatest influences upon behavior. The American conscience and the Japanese sense of shame will not develop adequately if they are not given encouragement by significant figures. If children do not have respect or affection for their parents, they will not internalize parental attitudes (if American) or worry about bringing shame to the family name (if Japanese). Samoan children, who, like the Japanese, tend to be controlled by shame, were compared with American children in a situation that allowed them to cheat at a game without (so they thought) their being observed. As predicted, the Samoan children, being less influenced by internalized values, were less likely to resist the temptation to falsify their scores (Grinder and McMichael, 1963).

American children who were reported to have strong consciences had been brought up in families that used praise and reasoning rather than physical punishment. These children were shown warmth and acceptance by their parents and thus were more inclined to internalize the values of their parents while maintaining a positive self-concept. When warm and loving mothers frequently threatened their children with withdrawal of love, their children were likely to develop healthy consciences; when cold and aloof mothers threatened their children similarly, the children were much less likely to develop a healthy conscience (Sears et al., 1957). Although parents usually wish their children to be influenced by their consciences, some individuals develop an unnecessarily strong conscience.

> Mary Fogarty was a physically affectionate mother, but she also demanded a great deal from her children. Whenever one of her children showed the slightest sign of misbehaving, Mary threatened to withdraw her love from him, and she would give extra attention to her other children. By being so affectionate, Mary gained the devotion of her children. Once having gained their devotion, she was able to force them to meet her demands, because failure was punished by rejection and obvious favoring of the other children. As the Fogarty children grew older, even

thoughts of disobeying their mother caused anxiety and feelings of guilt.

Jack Fogarty, Mary's oldest child, was especially afraid of his mother's disapproval. He developed an exaggerated sense of guilt. On one occasion, his teacher stated that one of the students had broken a classroom window during the lunch hour. Although Jack was in the cafeteria with several of his friends the entire lunch period, he felt compelled to explain to his teacher that he had not been responsible, even though no one suggested he had been. Another time, a teacher announced that she had caught a student cheating on an examination. Again, Jack, who had never been accused of the incident, needed to tell her he was innocent.

In Western nations, if no sense of guilt exists, there is little control upon behavior, since, in many instances, neither fear of punishment nor avoidance of shame provides adequate motivation. However, although lack of conscience is undoubtedly a matter of serious concern, the opposite is equally a problem. Some people have an exaggerated conscience and feel guilty about actions, thoughts, and feelings that are not expected to elicit guilt.

Some typical behavior patterns that emerge from chronic and intense guilt feelings include: the person who is always apologizing for anything that might even remotely be interpreted as wrong; the person who is afraid to make a decision for fear that his decision will hurt someone's feelings; or the person who is so worried that his actions will be seen as "bad" that he is unable to concentrate upon the important, day-to-day tasks of living.

Psychologists attempt to reduce these irrational or exaggerated guilt feelings through psychotherapy. Have you ever experienced guilt that was so strong you could not concentrate on your studies?

The development of sex role

The impact of internalized values is especially strong when sex role becomes involved. The proper behavior for males and females is a part of the social structure of every society, and the person who behaves inconsistently with what is expected of his sex is a partial outcast in his community.

From the very earliest years, boys and girls are treated differently. Children learn what sex they are almost as soon as they learn their name. They are dressed differently, given different toys to play with, and rewarded for different sorts of behavior. Young girls are given dolls and encouraged to hold them like "Mother holds baby sister." Young boys are given trucks and airplanes. Boys are often allowed to get dirty or to be noisy, while girls may be punished, if only by a hard look, for exactly the same behavior.

The older the child becomes, the more important he finds it to behave in ways considered proper for his sex. He learns this sex-role behavior from three basic sources: first, from observing the parent of the same sex as a model, by behaving as he does; second, by internalizing his values as they relate to sex role; and, third, from being rewarded by significant figures (and, to a lesser extent, by others) for appropriate behavior, while being punished—or at least unrewarded—for inappropriate behavior.

Contact with people of both sexes is necessary to help young children learn the proper sex-role behavior. The girl, for example, needs a woman whom she can imitate and whose values she can internalize; she also needs a man, so that she can observe how men treat women and how women respond to this type of treatment. If one parent is missing, the children may turn to other relatives, family friends, teachers, or other community members to learn their sex role. What would you predict to be the sex-role development of a boy brought up in a home where the parents are divorced, the father has disappeared, and the mother frequently criticizes men-in-general in the harshest terms?

When the wife completely dominates the husband, the children may not know whose behavior patterns to internalize: the strong mother or the weak father. The same problem occurs when one parent is very cold or hostile to the children, while the other is warm and affectionate. The child of the same sex as the unpleasant parent does not want to be like that parent; yet, if he becomes like the admired or affectionate parent, he will internalize the attitudes and behaviors of the opposite sex.

Freud's explanation for the development of the sex role suggests that the male child, around three years of age, develops an extremely strong attachment to his mother, even to the point of wishing to replace his father in his mother's affections. At the same time, he begins to fear his father, who, being bigger and stronger, might hurt him if he really competed for the mother. During the next few years, the boy learns that although his mother loves him, she restricts her more intimate feelings to his father. Finally the boy realizes that he cannot win in the competition with his father, and so he attempts to become as much as possible like the man his mother loves. In this way, boys begin to imitate their fathers and to internalize the fathers' values and behavior and, thus, the male sex role.

There seems little doubt that the best situation for proper sex-role development occurs when both parents are warm, have a good relationship with each other, provide a good parent-child relationship for their children, and do not deviate too far from acceptable sex-role behavior.

Development of aggressive and dependent behavior patterns

Aggressiveness and dependency, like the conscience and the sex role, develop through interaction between the child and his significant figures. All people have aggressive feelings, especially after a frustrating experience; similarly, all people have the need to be dependent upon others on occasion. Both aggressive behavior and dependent behavior are frequently punished when children exhibit them openly. The child who hits a playmate over the head with a metal truck is more likely to be punished than the child who never leaves his mother's side, but neither behavior is considered appropriate for a growing child.

Aggression. Most healthy, normal children express some aggressive behavior. Parents who punish aggression, especially when the punishment is physical, seem to encourage further aggression by their children; if the children are afraid of expressing their aggression directly, they may do so indirectly, perhaps through their play or their fantasies (Sears et al., 1957).

However, mothers who completely overlook aggressive behavior do not reduce aggression either. The least aggressive children have parents who showed they dislike aggressive behavior but did not use physical punishment or extreme threats of punishment. The most aggressive children had parents who provoked aggressive behavior by using physical punishment themselves frequently, but did not show particular disapproval when their children were aggressive (Sears et al., 1957).

Dependence. When a child is punished for aggressive behavior, he feels frustrated, and his own aggressive acts increase. Similarly, when a child is punished for being dependent, he becomes more dependent, probably because of fears that his parents are rejecting him as an individual when they reject his attempts at being dependent. Recent research has verified that these relationships exist (Sears et al., 1957; McCord et al., 1962).

Healthy dependency will cause the child to wish to please his parents, so that he will internalize their values and, eventually, the proper sex role. In Sears' study, the unhealthily dependent children had parents who were either rejecting and punitive or else **overprotective** (Sears et al., 1957).

Figure 6–5. The role of the American boy differs from the role of the boy in Saudi Arabia. Courtesy Standard Oil Company (N.J.).

Children who are prevented from exploring the world while they are young, either because their parents are too fearful of their actions or too restrictive, may be afraid to explore later.

Such children develop a self-concept of being people who need their parents, rather than a self-concept of being independent and self-sufficient. Children given the security resulting from being loved have a self-concept of being adequate people and are not afraid to venture into the world at the proper time.

SUMMARY OF IMPORTANT IDEAS

1. The degree of warmth and of independence provided by the parents, rather than any specific child-rearing technique, seems to have primary influence on later behavior and adjustment.

2. Breast feeding is considered, *on the whole,* superior to bottle feeding, but parental love and affection are more important than the method of feeding.

3. Child-rearing practices in the United States are more severe than they are in most preliterate societies.

4. Toilet-training methods are important to the development of children, largely because parents place so much emphasis upon control.

5. A young child's evaluation of himself reflects the reactions of others toward him; the most important of these others, usually the parents, are termed "significant figures."

6. Young children accept the views significant figures have of them, usually without criticism or evaluation.

7. The self-concept is somewhat self-perpetuating; it develops in response to the response of others, and the response of others is a direct reaction to the individual's self-concept.

8. The love of a child for his parents develops from the satisfaction by the parents of the child's biological needs, in combination with the child's receiving warmth, affection, and independence from the parent.

9. When a significant figure leaves, the child may display separation anxiety and emotional upset.

10. Life is not a series of time categories, but a continuing flow which we describe in time periods for convenience.

11. The child begins to develop a conscience before he is three years old.

12. He tends to accept the values and behavior of significant

figures as his own; that is, he *internalizes* these values and behavior patterns.

13. Much of the process of internalization occurs unconsciously.

14. Inappropriate behavior is prevented by shame, by guilt or conscience, and by fear of punishment; some cultures emphasize shame, others emphasize guilt as methods of control.

15. Appropriate consciences are more likely to be developed by children brought up in warm, loving homes.

16. Feelings of guilt can become unnecessarily strong.

17. Proper sex-role behavior is part of the social structure of every society.

18. Contact with people of both sexes aids in the development of acceptable sex role.

19. All people experience aggressive feelings and dependent feelings.

20. When parents punish aggressive behavior, they provoke more aggressive behavior; when they punish dependent behavior, they provoke more dependent behavior.

The developing child and his relationships   7

The previous chapter focused largely upon the infant or child himself; the present chapter emphasizes the world that surrounds him and his responses to it. Thus, intelligence is discussed not only in terms of the child's development, but also in terms of how environment may affect the ways in which the individual uses his intelligence. Similarly, personality development is presented as evolving from interactions of the child with his surrounding world of peers and parents.

Growth and development during the years of childhood are truly phenomenal. By his twelfth birthday, the average child has attained about half his future body weight and well over half his adult height (cited in Thompson, 1946); his motor skills have improved tremendously, and he is able to do many adult tasks. Most impressive, perhaps, is what he has learned: a language consisting of thousands of words, the ability to adjust to numerous minor frustrations and some major ones, the values and attitudes of the surrounding society, and the behavior considered proper by each of dozens of different individuals and groups.

The ability of the child to learn about the world around him depends in part on his personality and self-concept, the particular needs he develops, and his early relationships with significant figures. In addition, the relationships a child has with others, both children his own age and persons older or younger, influence his competence in dealing with the world. And, inevitably, the ability to learn is related to intelligence.

Intelligence: its development and measurement

Look again, for a moment, at the characteristics listed on pages 90–92 that distinguish human beings from other forms of animal life. Notice the extent to which these factors are the result of the greater **intelligence** of men. Although all animals, even the lowest forms, have some intelligence, no animal—not even the relatively intelligent monkey or porpoise—approaches the intelligence of a normal human being.

Without his superior intelligence, the human being would lack the self-awareness to study himself, to attempt to self-actualize, or to transmit his values, ideas, and material goods across time and space. He would be unable to build upon the knowledge and products of past generations and to plan for future generations. He would not be able to extend life through science and medicine or to destroy life through wars and other forms of destruction. Man's intelligence even enables him to search for ways to improve his intelligence.

What Is Intelligence?

Intelligence refers to the ability to grasp abstract concepts and symbols (such as language), the ability to learn, and the ability to cope with new situations (English and English, 1958). It also includes the ability to profit from experience and the ability to solve problems of all sorts. This explanation is necessarily broad, since a tremendous variety of specific acts may be termed intelligent.

It is intelligent behavior to ride a bicycle, recognize a person you met last week, and know the difference between a bush and a tree; it is intelligent behavior to count, to read a blueprint, and to spell; it is intelligent behavior to learn the meaning of concepts such as afternoon, love, round, and democracy; it is intelligent behavior to know what to do when your best friend is in trouble, when you see an automobile accident, and when you have a fight with your brother. In the following imaginary argument, Pete and Mike are in a hopeless deadlock because each is referring to a different type of intelligent behavior.

Pete: My kid brother is really bright. He can take his bike apart and put it back together all by himself, and he gets along great with the other kids—he's a real leader.

Mike: Yeah? Pretty good, but my sister is a real whiz. She cracks top grades in her class, and she won an award in Sunday School.

Pete: She may be bright, but she isn't *that* bright. She doesn't have more than one or two friends. Besides, she still thinks Santa Claus is a real person.

Mike: Well, your brother isn't so smart either. He forgot his lines in the school Christmas play, and he was a semester behind in his reading for a long time.

Thus, numerous difficulties can occur when we talk about an "intelligent person." An individual might exhibit a high degree of intelligence in his verbal behavior, yet display very limited intelligence in any acts that demand an understanding of mechanics. Because of such occurrences, psychologists have become interested in "factors of intelligence." Some of the factors more commonly described have included the following:

—the ability to use words effectively (verbal ability)

—the ability to reason effectively

—the ability to memorize easily

—the ability to know how to behave effectively in social situations

—the ability to work well with numbers (numerical ability)

—the ability to act quickly when necessary

—the ability to perceive spatial relationships

—the ability to work effectively with the hands (motor ability)

—the ability to understand principles of mechanics

A person above average in one factor of intelligence is likely to be above average on others. A child with a good memory is also likely to be above average in handling numerical concepts, in reasoning, and in adjusting to new social relationships. Exceptions, of course, do exist, and psychologists are constantly conducting research to determine more accurately the nature of factors of intelligence and the relationships among the various factors.

The meaning and measurement of the IQ

Intelligence cannot be measured directly. To measure a friend's weight, for example, you could use a scale, but there are no scales or yardsticks or electric gadgets to measure intelligence directly. The only available approach is to observe behavior and decide whether it is intelligent behavior. This, of course, is a very difficult task.

The usual measurement of intelligence is the **IQ** (Intelligence Quotient) test. Technically the IQ is the ratio of **mental age** to chronological age, multiplied by 100. Or:

$$IQ = \frac{MA}{CA} \times 100$$

A person's chronological age is the number of years and months since his birth; his mental age is determined by comparing his test performance with that of normal children at various age levels. A child, therefore, who is exactly ten years old, but does as well as the average eleven-year-old, would have an MA of 11, a CA of 10, and an IQ of 110; a child of five whose mental age is four has an IQ of 80. Can you compute the IQ of a seven-year-old with a mental age of eight? (Computing the IQ for persons over the age of 15 is somewhat different. Can you see why?)

The IQ test has three major limitations. First, it is only an estimate of intelligence. Even though shown to be a good estimate in most instances, a variety of situations may interfere with its accuracy. The child may react negatively to the person giving the test and, therefore, become unwilling to respond; he may have been brought up in a home where a foreign language was always spoken; he may have a bad cold that interferes with his test performance; or he may have been upset by an argument between his parents that morning, which keeps him from concentrating effectively. In addition, of course, he may just not care whether he does well or not.

Second, the IQ test can measure only the kinds of intelligent behavior related to items on the test. Most tests given in schools measure such intelligent behavior as memory, vocabulary, following directions, verbal reasoning, and arithmetic, which are related to school success. They say much less about the sorts of intelligence that enable a person to be popular, to repair a transmission, or to make a wise choice in a presidential election.

Third, although psychologists have tried to construct IQ tests that are not influenced by previous learning experiences, this is clearly impossible. Therefore, to some extent the IQ scores reflect the opportunity the person has had to learn, although—in theory—a measure of intelligence should not be affected by learning opportunity.

In spite of its shortcomings, the IQ test can predict success in academic work at all levels from elementary school through college, in vocational achievement, and even in leadership (Anastasi, 1958; Mann, 1959). However, the IQ test is a measure of intelligence and, as with any measure, is subject to error and to misinterpretation.

Factors influencing intelligent behavior

Most psychologists and educators believe that intelligence is influenced both by heredity and by environment, both by what we are born with and by what happens to us after birth. We are not certain, however, *how* important heredity is and *how* important environment is. We know, for example, that the IQ of a child is substantially related to the IQ of both his mother and his father (Conrad and Jones, 1940). Does this mean that he inherited the IQ through genetic means? Or does it mean that intelligent parents help their child learn more than do less intelligent parents? Both elements probably enter into the situation. (See previous discussion, pages 96-98.) What, then, are some of the major environmental factors?

Home and family. Some families do a great deal to encourage their children to develop intellectual abilities, while others do nothing. Families who take time to talk intelligently to their children, even when the children are very young, aid in the children's use and development of intelligence. The attitudes of the parents toward learning, books, and school are also important: children whose parents ignore or make fun of education and books are less likely to be successful in intellectual tasks related to school progress.

Parents not only influence their children's intellectual competence by their attitudes, but also by their use of language. A person whose language ability is poor will not do well on IQ tests or in school. When a child is reared in an environment where parents seldom talk to children, the children do not learn much language in the home. They are, then, not adequately prepared for schoolwork and quickly fall behind. As a result, they come to dislike school and pay even less attention to language, which further reduces their IQ scores. A vicious circle is set up. This is particularly likely to occur to children from socially and economically poor homes.

The lower-class child . . . tends to have a poor attention span and to have great difficulty following the teacher's orders . . . he generally comes from a nonverbal household: adults speak in short sentences, if indeed they speak at all. . . . The child has never been obliged to listen to several lengthy sentences spoken consecutively.

Figure 7–1. The average annual income of migratory workers is $900 per family! How might the early experiences of these children affect their school performance and IQ scores? Courtesy Columbia Broadcasting System.

In school, the middle-class teacher who rambles on for several sentences might just as well be talking another language . . . lower-class children have a limited perception of the world about them: they do not know that objects have names . . . , or that the same object may have several names. . . . They also have very little concept of size or time.

The lower-class youngsters are poorly motivated, because they have had little experience in receiving approval for success in a task or disapproval for failure; but school is organized on the assumption that children expect approval for success. And since the parents . . . do not ask the youngsters about school, the children have no way of knowing that the parents *do* very much want and expect success (Silberman, 1964).

Some children are faced with another problem: the language spoken in their home is different from that spoken in the community. Living in a home in which English is either not spoken or poorly spoken, the child uses English less frequently, and may have more difficulty thinking in English. He will probably not speak English as well (Soffietti, 1955), which may lead to lower performance on IQ tests and in classroom work.

So far we have largely emphasized the ways in which parents can affect that aspect of intelligence known as verbal ability, but the parent-child relationship has an effect upon intelligence that extends beyond language and verbal symbols. The willingness of the parents to encourage, rather than stifle, the child's needs to explore and manipulate his environment might affect many of the factors of intelligence. Can you suggest ways in which the parents may influence the child's mechanical ability or social ability?

The home also influences IQ indirectly by affecting the physical health of the individual. For example, where diet is poor, intelligence seems to suffer (Harrell, 1947), and certain types of physical handicaps, such as limited hearing or arthritic fingers, make learning more difficult, which would lower performance on IQ tests.

Many factors influence the degree to which an individual can make maximum use of his potential abilities, including his potential intellectual competence. The IQ test, a normally valid measure when we become aware of its limitations, can nonetheless also be influenced by environmental and personality factors.

Intelligence is one aspect of the total personality, and it inevitably interacts in dynamic fashion with other personality attributes. Self-esteem, for example, affects performance on IQ tests, and performance on IQ tests affects self-esteem. The case of Eddie illustrates many of the principles discussed in this chapter.

Eddie: a case history

At the time of testing, Eddie was finishing second grade at a highly respected school near St. Louis. He was reported to the principal because he was totally unable to read, he could not draw even the simplest house or person, he constantly daydreamed, he paid little attention to the teacher, and he did not get along well with the other children. His teacher believed he was well below normal in intelligence and might need special treatment.

The psychologist who tested Eddie had been his counselor at summer camp, and he and the boy liked each other. In addition, being tested gave Eddie an excuse for leaving class and an opportunity for individual attention. While with the psychologist he was talkative and happy, unlike his apathetic, classroom self.

The first test Eddie took was drawing a person (Goodenough, 1926). The maturity level of his drawing, compared to others of his age, showed Eddie to be in the upper 5 percent, an amazing performance for a child whose teacher stated he could not draw a man that even remotely resembled a man. He then took the Stanford-Binet Intelligence Test, and scored in the upper 10 percent. Eddie scored in the top 10 percent on every test, except one that demanded reading, which he could not do.

Eddie was obviously a child of high ability. Why was he doing so poorly? The answer was mainly in his family relationships. His father, frustrated in his work, constantly criticized the teachers and the school system and sometimes even made fun of the entire process of education, claiming it was a waste of time; at the same time, he demanded that Eddie study hard and get good grades. His mother, a weak person who worried more about her imaginary illnesses than she did about her children, both feared and resented her husband and gave Eddie neither affection nor discipline. Eddie admired his father, but did not know how to please him, so he withdrew by becoming apathetic.

Several years later Eddie had become an aggressive, disliked child. He still did poorly in school and was now impossible to handle at home. He was alternately very friendly, then very nasty and aggressive, and the other children avoided him. His school performance remained poor and he was sent to a special private school to receive help.

Eddie's case is a good example of the value of intelligence testing as an aid in understanding the problems of the individual. It also points up the importance of thinking in terms of different kinds of intelligence, since Eddie had good verbal and reasoning abilities, but was not able to learn how to behave socially. The effects of his home environment upon his personality and his school performance are very dramatic.

Will Eddie be able to self-actualize at a later time? What do you think? At last report, his parents had satisfied only one set of needs: his physiological needs. Eddie did not feel secure, loved, or esteemed, and the effects had become so intense that he withdrew from the school learning situation. But he expressed his need to display aggression by fighting with his playmates. His prospects for leading a fully satisfying life in his mature years seem dim today, but things can change. What do you think might be done to help Eddie? How would you talk to him and his parents, if you were a close friend of the family?

Healthy parent-child relationships

The satisfaction that a child feels with himself, his life, and the world around him often reflects the satisfaction felt by his parents. Parents happy in their marriage, in their work, in their social relationships, and in their general approach to life seem to be better parents. Parents (like Eddie's) who are bitter, frustrated, and unfriendly often allow their unhappiness to interfere with their relationships with children.

> The mother, unable to have the concert career she had desired, pushes her daughter into seeking a concert career for which she is not capable.

> The father, disliking his wife and distrusting women in general, convinces his son that women are to be avoided.

> The father, a failure at work, is a tyrant in his own home, the only place where anyone listens to him.

> The mother, unhappy in her marriage to a cold, aloof husband, turns all her attention to her son, whom she coddles and over-protects.

Unhappy and poorly adjusted children do not inevitably result from unhappy parents, nor do happy parents inevitably have happy children, but the chances are much more favorable for these relationships than for the opposite. Among the many factors related to healthy parent-child relationships are the parents' ability to allow freedom and responsibility, the opportunity of the children to express their feelings, the degree to which the children have been aided in self-actualization, and parental methods of controlling or disciplining behavior.

The following maternal characteristics were associated with general family adjustment according to one study (Sears et al., 1957):

1. Mother has high self-esteem.
2. Mother has high esteem for father.
3. Mother is very satisfied with her present life.
4. Mother feels confident about her ability to bring up children.

5. Mother was delighted at becoming pregnant.

6. Mother believes father was also delighted when she became pregnant.

7. Mother and father have no disagreements about bringing up children.

8. Mother enjoys affection with baby.

9. Mother believes father feels affectionate toward child.

10. Mother can follow through on her disciplinary actions.

Allowing freedom and giving responsibility

Freedom and responsibility go together; children need to receive freedom and responsibility when they are young and to an increasing degree as they mature, so that they will be accustomed to independence when they begin college, move away from home, or take their first job. Parents who overprotect their child, for whatever reason, are not preparing him adequately for adult life. Children need to be allowed to grow up and, eventually, to leave home, without feeling that they are hurting their parents. (In some societies grown children would not wish to leave their parents, but we are presently concerned with the mainstream of Western culture.)

Parents face a major dilemma. On the one hand, children have definite limitations, and they will inevitably fail at certain tasks and make incorrect decisions. On the other hand, in order to mature into self-sufficient adults, children need to try difficult tasks and make difficult decisions. Adults may "know better" than children, but children have to find out for themselves much of the time; adults may "do it better," but children want to "do it myself."

> Danny, at 12 months, refused to take any food that he could not get to his mouth through his own efforts, and this included ice cream, which he loved. His parents had to watch him go through strenuous effort and many spills in order to eat. It was hard on the floor, on his clothes, and on his parents, but Danny showed great pleasure in his achievements.

> Lee's parents were in a hurry, and her father lifted her into the family car for a quick get-away. Lee protested loudly, scrambled out of the car, glared at her father, then pulled herself into the vehicle without help.

Riding a bicycle, getting dressed, drawing grandmother a birthday card, crossing the street without help, all are ways in which children establish that they are independent, competent individuals. Parents who are overprotective prevent their children from developing freedom and responsibility and may encourage them to become highly dependent or else may provoke aggressive rebellion.

Children mature at different rates, of course, and not all children of the same age will be sufficiently mature to take the same responsibilities or be given the same freedoms. One ten-year-old can be trusted to go shopping for his mother, but another cannot; twelve-year-old Ted can be believed when he says his homework is completed, but twelve-year-old Tom must be checked.

It seems logical that children who are prevented from taking appropriate responsibility and freedom will develop a self-concept of being inadequate: "My parents don't think I'm competent, so I guess I'm not competent." On the other hand, children who are pushed into responsibilities long before they are ready may feel their parents are rejecting them; also, they are likely to fail at their tasks and similarly develop a self-concept of inadequacy. The most successful children seem to be those who are encouraged to take responsibility at appropriate age levels and whose parents can tolerate mistakes and misjudgments as part of the child's process of growing up.

Statements children can get along without.

1. You know I love you—look how much money I spend on you.
2. Your brother likes to kiss me—he must love me more than you do.
3. You're my child—you're supposed to love me and respect me.
4. When I was your age, things weren't so easy.
5. If I only had had the chances you kids get today.
6. Do you always have to do what the other kids are doing? If they all jumped off the Golden Gate (or Brooklyn or any other) Bridge, I suppose you would jump off also.
7. I used to love helping my mother around the house.
8. When you get older, you'll think back to all the time you wasted.
9. I don't know what's going to become of you when you get older.
10. It took me a long time to realize that my parents knew what they were talking about, and I always regretted not paying attention to them sooner.

11. Do you always have to spend your money on such trash?
12. Is that any way to talk to your parents?
13. I don't know why you can't do it—your sister always did it that way.

Expressing feelings

Parents have feelings, and so do children. Both have the right to express their feelings. There are occasions when a mother is entitled to become angry with her child; there are times when children are entitled to express unhappiness with their parents' actions. If the basic relationship is good, and if the parents do not threaten to withdraw their love or administer violent physical punishment, an expression of anger may actually improve the situation. Children and parents can learn to respect the emotional expressions of each other, if they are secure in their relationships.

Helping children self-actualize

Most parents wish to see their children make as much of their own talents as they possibly can, whether the talents involve artistic ability, sales ability, administrative ability, technical ability, or social ability. Parents are often less aware of their role in enabling their children to become more and more themselves, which is also part of the child's process of self-actualization. Adults are often intent on bringing up their children to be as much like the parents as possible, regardless of how the child feels.

Consideration of Maslow's need hierarchy may be useful in discussing how parents can help their children self-actualize. Parents, of course, would never purposely deprive their children of adequate food or sleep, and lack of fulfillment of survival needs is rarely a problem in the United States.

Nonetheless, parents may, often without realizing it, not allow sufficient satisfaction of the stimulation needs. By doing too much for a child, an unthinking adult may inadvertently stifle his need to explore and manipulate his environment.

> Maureen, a very pretty three-year-old whose parents both worked, was left with a full-time maid. The maid, a gentle, elderly woman, became very much attached to Maureen and soon developed the need for Maureen to be dependent upon her. She slept with Maureen when the child napped, refused to let her play at other children's homes, and even fed her although Maureen could easily feed herself. Maureen did become dependent upon the maid and soon internalized the self-concept

that she was helpless, a self-concept the maid unknowingly encouraged.

Not only was Maureen overprotected, but she was overindulged. She was always able to get what she wanted by crying or throwing a tantrum. The maid was so afraid of losing the child's affection and so devoted to her that she frequently spent her own salary on gifts for the girl. Maureen made occasional attempts to break away by playing with other children, but the maid hovered around, and the other children soon preferred to avoid this well-meaning, but irritating, supervision. When offered the alternative of a dish of ice cream with "the kids" or a walk to the store with the maid, Maureen decided to take the walk. (P.S. The maid bought her ice cream anyway.)

Overprotection is not the only way of restricting the satisfaction of children's stimulation needs. Some parents are overly punitive and frighten children from exploring their environment; others are worried that new activities might be too time consuming, too demanding, or too dangerous for the child, so the parents always do it for him.

Safety needs and love needs can be discussed together, because, in the parent-child relationship, they interact dynamically with each other. Parents who show their children a great deal of love and affection are also providing security for the child. And a parental show of affection can rarely be an error, unless the love has strings attached or is so overwhelming that it smothers the child. "I'll love you if . . ." is not really giving love, but trading for love. What husband would appreciate his wife's saying, "If you buy me a new dress, I'll love you."?

In the example on page 124, Mary Fogarty had caused her children to develop extremely great needs for safety and love, so that they felt anxious at the threat of loss of the mother's approval. The children's tremendous concern over that possibility generalized to other of their relationships and prevented them from accomplishing many things for which they had the ability.

Some parents, because of their own upbringing, find it difficult to show physical affection or even other forms of love. Nonetheless, children seem to sense when they are loved and, also important, respected. To say that parents should respect their children does not imply that the children be allowed to dominate their parents, but that they be treated as unique and worthwhile individuals, in spite of their immaturity.

Even adults who provide security and love for their children do not always show their children this sort of respect. Like Mary Fogarty, these parents repeatedly communicate to their children how immature they are and how dependent they are upon the parents. By emphasizing their children's inadequacies, the parents may be encouraging a lack of self-esteem in the very individuals they are so anxious to help.

But what about self-actualization itself? How can parents take positive steps, over and above more general considerations such as love and respect, to help their children use their talents? There are innumerable answers to this question, but we will be able to discuss only a few:

(1) Reading to children, even before they can understand all that is said, will expose them to the immense world of words and books. Children whose early contacts with books are happy ones are not so likely to find books and words a problem in school. Perhaps equally important, a period set aside each day for reading will assure the child that he can share a pleasant, relaxed few minutes with his parent—even when he knows every word of his favorite book by heart.

(2) Children ask many questions, often foolish ones and sometimes impossible-to-answer ones. This is their way of learning about the world, and the adult who tries to answer their questions truthfully is reassuring and satisfying.

(3) Children need time with their parents, doing things together. Having a picnic, going for a drive, or taking a walk are simple things families can easily do together. Fathers in particular, since they are away from the home so much, can greatly enrich the father-child relationship by having some type of activity they can share with their children. In France, it is not unusual for a father to take his children somewhere on Thursday afternoon (school is not in session then), while mother stays home.

(4) There comes a period for each child when he wants to learn to count or read or tell time; this is the opportunity for the parents to encourage him, without pushing him. A warm, noncritical parental attitude of encouragement will probably do more good in the long run than any specific learning that might occur. Success in school is not improved by knowing the alphabet sooner than other children, if the child has been bribed or pressured, but if his knowledge grew out of his own motivation, such learning may be advantageous.

(5) Children benefit from an appreciation not just of books, but of art and music, of nature and science, of the behavior of machines and the behavior of people, of white-collar work and blue-collar work. The ability to appreciate a diversity of activities, interests, and people will help a child discover his own talents and respect the talents of others.

Self-actualization does not come about automatically because parents follow a rigid set of rules. Rather, it develops slowly when parents satisfy the more basic needs and provide an exciting and stimulating environment, while respecting the child's individuality and his need to succeed in his own unique way.

The problem of placing limits on behavior

When children are born, they do not know how society expects them to behave. Their parents take on the responsibility of placing limits upon what is acceptable. In different families, of course, different sorts of limits will be established. One family will allow the child to play in mud; another will not. One family will keep the child out of the living room, while another will give their children freedom in any room.

Once the limits are set, children appear to be better adjusted if the limits are enforced consistently. To discipline a child for throwing the jelly spoon at his sister on one occasion, but to laugh about it on another,

Figure 7–2. Children enjoy expressing themselves through art and through music. A, courtesy Antioch College News Bureau; B, courtesy California State College at Los Angeles.

is an example of inconsistent limits on behavior. The child is uncertain of the limits to his behavior.

Of course, the methods used to keep behavior within limits are also important. All parents hope that their children will quickly accept the values of the family and the general society, so that the children will do the desired thing without external controls. For most children, this desire is not realistic, and some way to discourage inappropriate behavior and to encourage acceptable behavior is necessary.

Whereas punishment is probably the most common approach to maintaining limits, other methods are also available. Too much use of punishment merely draws attention to the forbidden act, but does not reinforce the correct response. Like the teaching machines that give no response for a wrong answer, but reward the right one, parents can often find a way to ignore the improper behavior and reward correct behavior.

Punishment has other dangers: it may cause the child to become angry with the parent for the punishment, instead of with himself for the improper act; it can induce frustration, which may lead to future aggressive behavior; it can become unnecessarily severe and cause undue pain or overly severe restrictions; it indicates the incorrect path, but may ignore the correct path.

This is not to contend that discipline, controls, or even punishment are never effective. The child may endanger himself by shoving a nail into an open socket; he may endanger others by ramming his tricycle into a playmate; he may endanger property by twirling a large stick dangerously close to a breakable lamp. In each of these instances, the adult may be able to reduce the danger from the child's behavior without actual punishment, but sometimes the unique demands of the situation require punishment. How would you approach each of the above situations, to change the behavior without the use of punishment?

Interestingly, children may interpret parental lack of limits as an indication that the parents do not "really care."

> "It was raining cats and dogs that day—I must have been about nine—and I asked my father if I should wear my rubbers. He told me to do what I thought was best. Well, I knew what was best, but I wanted him to tell me, because it seemed like he didn't really care. He wouldn't, so I went without my rubbers and caught a terrible cold. I hated my father for giving me that cold, and I hated him more because he reminded me that I made the decision."

The maturation level of children is an important factor in the type of limits set upon their behavior and the sort of enforcement used. Very young children do not understand language well enough to respond to

"Don't!" So a mild slap on the hand may be necessary. Of course, parents who take necessary precautions in child-proofing their house will avoid many problems.

At certain ages, children do not recognize the significance of what they are doing. They may spread jam on the tablecloth, shoot big brother's dart gun at the neighbor's baby, or curl up and sleep underneath Aunt Molly's car parked in the driveway. Sometimes they will hit another child as a release for their own frustrations. Constant punishment for acts they do not understand may be highly frustrating, especially for very active children. Still worse is disciplining a child for failing at something beyond his physical or intellectual powers to achieve. A child who is not ready to be toilet trained or who is not ready to memorize the alphabet will find punishment extremely frustrating, and of little value in producing the desired behavior.

Some parents still hold to the ancient fiction that the more a child is beaten, the better his behavior will be. Evidence certainly does not support this view. Although children can be frightened into good behavior by extreme punishments, they often become sullen, resentful, withdrawn, or anxious.

Considerable question exists about whether a spanking is more cruel or less cruel than having to miss a planned-for movie or being kept in from playing. We do know, however, that a spanking in combination with reasoning works much better than a spanking by itself, and that warm, loving mothers get better results from spanking than do cold, aloof mothers (Sears et al., 1957). We also know that men with criminal records received more physical punishment and threats of harsh physical punishment during childhood than a fairly comparable group without criminal records (McCord et al., 1963). Studies of underdeveloped societies indicate that more theft occurs in groups that are very punitive than in groups that show great love to their children, implying that stealing may be a way to make up for not feeling loved (Bacon et al., 1963). In these instances at least, harsh physical punishment certainly did not lead to more responsible behavior.

Each parent has to work out a system of enforcing limits that is appropriate for his own personality, his child's personality, and the specific set of circumstances involved. After an argument with her father-in-law, a mother may be harsher in punishing her son; after a fatiguing day at work, a father may not have the energy to control his daughter; after an especially exciting birthday party, a child may be so overtired that he needs to unwind before going to bed. Children and parents can adjust to each other's habits and to individual circumstances, as long as the children never feel that parental love may be withdrawn.

Real love does not depend upon eating cereal, not hitting baby sisters, or getting good grades in school. Parents who threaten to withdraw their love for any reason imply that their love is neither very strong nor very dependable. Their love is not given freely, but must be earned. Such threats—like brutal physical punishment, which is more to satisfy the parents than to discipline the child—may produce the immediate behavior desired but will also bring about long-range feelings of anxiety, resentment, and fear. Such parental behavior will probably have more harmful effects in the long run.

Giving children "anti-parent" weapons

Children, except in **overindulgent** homes, cannot command their parents directly; they must find indirect methods. Infants may learn that going for long periods without eating is a good way to gain attention; spitting up food and vomiting are also effective in upsetting and controlling parents. At about two, bed-wetting or soiling, especially if the parents have been bragging about how clean the children are, is a wonderful way to annoy adults. Even if children are punished, they have learned how effective their behavior is—the punishment may actually convince them that they "have a good thing." Constant whining may be the best way for three-year-olds to get a rise out of Mom and Dad.

Older children may use more obvious forms of aggression. When four-year-old Tod says, "Daddy, you're pooey," his father merely responds, "Oh?" But the father of four-year-old David gets angry and gives a stern lecture. David now has a weapon he can use against his father, whenever he is willing to risk punishment.

In essence, although punishing children may be pertinent, it draws attention to the incorrect behavior and does nothing to emphasize the proper behavior. Parents who insist upon the correct behavior and then reward the child for doing the correct thing are usually doing a more effective job of inducing the child to behave in an acceptable fashion than are those who punish the wrong behavior, but do nothing more. Nonetheless, mild punishments, even spankings, may be useful in certain situations, and no evidence is available that mild punishment is, in itself, harmful.

Relationships with other children

Although the parents are the most meaningful significant figures, other people become increasingly important to children as they grow older. Both playmates and **siblings,** a term used to include both brothers and sisters, are among the most influential of these other people.

Brothers, sisters, and competition

The first child in the family has no competition at all—until a sibling is born. The first child has the full attention of his parents—he is king. Then a competitor appears upon the scene. Not only is he a competitor, but he seems a very successful competitor. All the aunts and uncles and grand-parents and friends who used to tell four-year-old Joey how cute he was, now tell Joey how cute Lisa is. And, to top it all off, Joey's mother was taken away to the hospital; Joey was shipped off to live with grand-mother, and, as soon as he returned, he was warned to "Shut up, keep out of the way, and don't bother the baby."

After this introduction, Joey is expected to show love, loyalty, devo-tion, and respect to the little monkey that cries at all hours, cannot even talk, and is absolutely no fun to play with. The result is often **sibling rivalry**, an intense competition between two children in the same family, frequently leading to hostile feelings.

To some extent, older children can be prepared for a new sibling.

> Leah, aged two-and-a-half, was well prepared for the birth of a new sibling. She felt the movement in her mother's "tummy" and even claimed to "have a baby in my tummy, too." She took great pride in becoming a big sister, a feeling her parents encouraged, and she was made to feel that the baby would be hers as much as her parents'. When the baby did arrive, her parents made an extra fuss over Leah and acted as though they depended upon her help in various ways, such as getting diapers out of the drawer and patting the baby's back when he needed to be burped.

> Jerry was three-and-a-half when his sister was born. His parents talked about the coming baby and told Jerry he would love her and protect her, but when the baby came, Jerry was shushed, ignored, told to play outside, and rarely allowed to see the baby. When he did see his sister, he was instructed to kiss her and fuss over her. Within a few months, Jerry had learned that the best attack was to pretend to be showing affection; while apparently kissing his sister, he would bite or pinch her. His parents punished him severely, and Jerry withdrew completely from his sister. In later years, his sister turned out to be a very pretty girl and was much fussed over; Jerry had very little to do with her.

When the older child is not properly prepared for his new sibling and not allowed to play a part in the new infant's life, several forms of reaction can occur: (1) active or subtle aggression directed against the baby; (2) increased attempts to gain attention from the parents, including —if necessary—naughty behavior, even though it may be punished; (3) attempts to get even with the parents; (4) withdrawal from parents, to avoid the possibility of further emotional hurt; (5) **regression,** or returning to earlier forms of behavior such as bed wetting, crying, or wanting a bottle. Fortunately, children can respond as Leah did, exhibiting a true big-sister attitude.

Sibling rivalry can become intense and bitter, since the children are fighting for the attention of the most important people they know. Some parents make matters worse by comparing them with each other: "Robert made good grades in school—why can't you?" "Mary Jean didn't wet her panties when she was three."

In a few instances, sibling rivalry is so intense that grown children are afraid to leave home, for fear that the remaining sibling will oust them from the good graces of the family. Most incidents of severe sibling rivalry disappear after the children go to college or establish their own homes, although, unfortunately, the effects do not always disappear. By then, the individuals have achieved a sense of personal adequacy without being so dependent upon their parents.

Playmates and friends

Friendship among young children is usually limited to the immediate neighborhood and to children brought to visit by family friends. These **peer**-group friendships become more stable over the years, until—by third or fourth grade—a child may feel very uncomfortable when moving into a strange community (Hurlock, 1959). Such early relationships may be very important for later adjustment. Generalizing from laboratory studies with monkeys, good friendships are not only enriching but may partially compensate for inadequate parent-child relationships (Harlow and Harlow, 1962b). Motherless monkeys who were allowed to play with each other showed normal social development, while comparable monkeys with no play opportunity were severely retarded socially.

Children are not very subtle in their behavior. If they do not like a particular child, they will let him know it. The unpopular preschool child is described as one who "attacks vigorously, strikes frequently, or pushes and pulls." Other traits which lead to unpopularity include overdependence upon adults, unwillingness to accept the routine of other children, and not respecting the property of others (Hurlock, 1959).

In later childhood, playmates are usually of the same sex; social class, race, and religion have begun to influence friendships. Personality is undoubtedly as important as any other quality that leads to the avoidance of certain people. A group of fifth- and sixth-graders indicated who the least-liked children were. These outsiders fell into three major groupings: (1) dull, lacking in energy, not especially intelligent; (2) not interested in the same activities as the other children; (3) noisy, rebellious nuisances (Northway, 1944). The value of being accepted by a friendship group is very important to people of all ages. Children are no exception.

The importance of play

Children's play is very important to proper development, although adults may think of it merely as a pleasant way for children to pass time. One reason for the importance of play is that it provides initial experience in entering into social relationships with others of the same age. At first, children merely play by themselves, but they soon enjoy having another child around during their play. Initially, a young child will play with his own things, although liking to have another child nearby. The only contact between the two may be arguments when both want the same toy at the same time. This is known as **parallel play**, since they are not interacting. When they are about two-and-a-half or three, children begin to play with each other, although if one child is older, play may begin much earlier. Through such play, they learn the need for sharing and for give-and-take.

Play also allows children to use their imaginations. They can act out the behavior of their parents, through playing house; they can travel to the zoo, take an airplane trip, or visit the planet Mars, all through the wonderful device of play. At the same time, they can try out new roles by being Mommy or Daddy, and thus experiment with their future behavior.

Third, children have many aggressive feelings that are not permitted direct expression but can be expressed through play. A young child who is angry with his parents may gain some satisfaction by punishing a doll; a boy who has been spanked for breaking a dish can build a skyscraper of blocks and smash it to the floor.

Not only feelings of aggression, but also many other feelings can be expressed through play. The little girl who is so attentive to her doll may be behaving as her mother has behaved with her, or she may be trying to compensate for a lack of maternal affection.* She, in a sense, becomes the doll, and thus can receive from mother (herself) the love she does not receive from her real mother. This possibility of two different interpretations from the same behavior shows the danger of making snap judgments.

A fourth reason for play is that it leads to new learning. This learning

---

*There are, of course, other possibilities. Can you suggest some?

may take the form of new motor skills, such as hopping or skipping; increased verbal ability, which results from trying to communicate with others; and increased ability to understand and get along with others. Play also gives children exercise, stimulates their imagination, provides excitement, and is entertaining.

Figure 7–3. Healthy play allows children (and adults) to let off steam. Photograph by Albert Kallis.

The attitude of adults can contribute to the value and pleasure of play or can detract from it. Adults limit the value of play when they demand quiet, interfere or make frequent suggestions, constantly ask questions, tease, or try to show the child "how to do it right." To encourage appropriate play, adults can treat each individual child with respect, give him the freedom to make noise and get dirty (unless there are good reasons not to), enjoy the child's enjoyment, and provide him with toys that allow him to be creative.

Childhood friendships and the play of children are part of the normal development of each child, and they provide an important channel for the satisfaction of many important needs. Nonetheless, healthy parent-child relationships are undoubtedly the major factor, for most children, in producing healthy adjustment and the possibility of self-actualization in later years.

SUMMARY OF IMPORTANT IDEAS

1. Growth and development during the years of childhood are truly phenomenal.

2. The ability of an individual to learn about the world around him and to deal with this world depends upon many factors, including intelligence.

3. There are many kinds of intelligence, including the ability to grasp abstract concepts and symbols, the ability to learn, the ability to cope with new situations, plus numerous others. An individual can show a high level of competence in one kind of intellectual task, but a limited level of competence in another.

4. Intelligence cannot be measured directly, but the IQ test determines whether a person can perform certain tasks that have been defined as intelligent.

5. The IQ test has limitations, however, and is influenced by home and family, by familiarity with the language in which the test is given, by motivation, and by other factors.

6. Personality and intelligence are interrelated.

7. Parents who are satisfied with their own lives seem to be better parents.

8. Effective social development of children requires a proper balance of freedom and responsibility.

9. Children need the opportunity to explore their environment.

10. Parents can encourage self-actualization in their children.

11. Certain limits need to be placed upon the behavior of children; these limits should be enforced with consistency, but with the minimum amount of punishment.

12. Rivalry often develops between two children in the same family.

13. Even children as young as three or four seem to profit greatly by healthy relationships with other children.

14. Play allows children to learn to get along with others, to use their imaginations, to express many feelings (including aggression) indirectly, and to learn new motor and verbal skills.

Personality from twelve to twenty-one 8

As your reading has progressed from Chapter 6 to the present chapter, you may have noticed that the orientation shifts. No more is the individual discussed solely in terms of how the world affects him; he now becomes responsible in varying degrees for his own behavior. The six-month-old has little to say about how people respond to him, but the sixteen-year-old has a great deal of control over his life situation. Also, Chapter 6 had nothing to say about the relationship of the infant to those his own age, because—by and large—no relationships exist; Chapter 7 had a section on peer-group relationships; Chapter 8 is largely a discussion of the interaction between individuals of the same age level.

The decade from twelve to twenty-one is often considered a time of preparation for eventual maturity. By the end of this period, the individual is ready to take his place as a self-sustaining member of the community. Physically he attains full strength, mature growth, and reproductive ability. His formal education is usually completed by the end of this period, and he steps into a job side by side with older people. Socially, he has gone through a period of trying out a variety of relationships with the opposite sex and is beginning to consider marriage seriously—if he is, indeed, not already married.

Figure 8–1. Teen-agers spend a large proportion of their time in class. Courtesy Columbia Broadcasting System.

But the years of adolescence and the beginnings of young adulthood are more than merely preparation and transition. The process of maturing occurs with dynamic interaction among physical changes, personal changes, social changes, and changes in the surrounding environment. This is a decade in the individual's life that finds him awakening to the world around him and to his own sense of identity.

Postponing the entrance of the adolescent into adult society until his twenties is a recent development. In a sense, the idea of adolescence as a distinct period in the life process is relatively new, is probably the result of the extensive education demanded in the modern world, and has possibly come about because this age group is no longer needed in the labor force. In past centuries, the individual assumed adult responsibilities while still in his teens, probably married before 20, and seldom lived beyond 50.

Even recently, many **preliterate** (or primitive) societies inducted the male child into official manhood at around age 13, when he becomes physically and sexually mature. Known as **puberty rites,** these ceremonies often included painful rituals and demanded that the boy show his ability to fend for himself. At this time, the boy was taught some of the tribal secrets and was thereafter considered in many ways to be an adult. (Why do you suppose the girls were usually ignored in this procedure?) In these communities, the male moved directly from childhood to manhood, without an intervening adolescence. Our society, however, recognizes adolescence as a separate phase. We are especially aware of changes in the physical body, in the sense of individual identity, and in the form and meaning of social relationships.

The changing human body and its consequences

The growth rate of children, which was very rapid during the early years, begins to taper off until the girls are about ten and the boys are about twelve (Tanner, 1961). At these ages, the growth rate suddenly spurts ahead for about two or three years. Since this **growth spurt** begins sooner for girls, there is a period of a year or two when girls are taller than boys, the only time during the entire life span when this occurs.

Puberty

Before the end of the growth spurt, the child begins to enter **puberty,** the time of his life when he becomes sexually mature. Most girls begin puberty, which is defined in this instance as having the first menstrual period, between the twelfth and fourteenth birthdays, although the range is from ten to seventeen (Cole and Hall, 1964). The determination of when puberty begins is less precise for boys, but it occurs about one year later than for girls.

Have you heard your parents make the comment "Kids certainly seem to be growing up faster these days than when I was young"? Their observation is not merely the result of their having forgotten what it is like to be young. Puberty does begin at an earlier age today than it did 30 or 40 years ago. Data from Norway show that girls in 1950 reached puberty nearly four years earlier than their great-great-grandmothers (cited in Cole and Hall, 1964). The change is very likely the result of improved health and nutrition, which has also led to an increase in weight and height of teen-agers; boys in the United States, for example, are an average of 10 pounds heavier and nearly 2 inches taller than boys forty years ago (Metropolitan Life Insurance Company Statistics, 1961).

Physiological changes accompanying puberty are well known. They include the growth of body hair and—primarily for boys—the growth of facial hair; the change in the outlines of the body and the beginning of breast development for girls; the cracked voice, which embarrasses boys so frequently and which eventually matures into the adult male voice; and the beginning of menstrual bleeding for girls—at first irregularly, and later, every month.

The body-image

The physical changes occurring during puberty (and, of course, at other times as well) are accompanied by changes in our self-concept and in our **body-image,** which is the picture we have of our physical appearance, or—to express it in other words—the body-self-concept.

During the early years of adolescence, the body-image must change quite rapidly to remain accurate in light of the actual physical changes that occur. Like all facets of the self-concept, your body-image is largely a reflection of how you feel others perceive you. If you feel you are considered physically attractive, you are likely to have a corresponding body-image. This will inevitably affect the rest of your self-concept, your behavior and responses to others, and—therefore—the responses other people have toward you. As a result, a dynamic interaction takes place, involving your body-image, your self-concept, and the responses of other people.

If the way others respond to you satisfies your needs, you may try to do something with your appearance to encourage more such responses; if the reactions of others are displeasing, you may try to alter your appearance. A girl who is complimented upon her hair may take better care of her hair as a result; a boy who is teased because he is so skinny may try hard to gain weight.

The desired body-image is not the same in every country, nor does it remain the same in every generation. The American woman today prefers a body-image different from her mother's during the 1920s, when the Flapper Age decreed the most attractive female figure to be slim and straight.

A person with a good self-concept will not be overly disturbed by not being considered physically attractive, since he accepts himself as a worthy individual. The individual, however, whose self-concept causes him to feel insecure may place too much emphasis upon the need to be thought physically attractive. You can make some interesting guesses about a person's self-concept and body-image based on what he does to his physical appearance: notice clothing, hair style, cleanliness, use of make-up and jewelry, style of eyeglasses, posture, walk, smile, and so forth.

The body-image extends beyond the outward physical appearance, and includes physical health and handicaps that cannot be seen. Being colorblind, having a rheumatic heart, or needing a filling for a cavity are all part of the body-image.

Body-image and the physically different. Just like the racially different

Negro and the religiously different Jew, the physically different person suffers job discrimination, social discrimination, and ridicule.

> Mary Frost had been severely burned as a child, and her face was badly scarred. After becoming a skilled stenographer, she found jobs difficult to obtain. One executive commented to his assistant, after Mary left his office, "The rest of the staff would have nightmares after looking at that face all day."

> Sam Ishikawa, the highest-ranking officer in his university ROTC, won a national award for his competence. However, the Army refused to commission him because he was only a shade over 5 feet tall.

Physical problems, even relatively minor ones, can have a negative effect upon a person's body-image. The ability to adjust to problems involving physical appearance and the body is only partly the result of the appearance itself; it is also related to the general self-concept and feelings of adequacy of the individual.

Figure 8–2. How would you evaluate the body-image and self-concept of this boy? Courtesy Crippled Children's Society of Los Angeles.

Dave Korngold lost his leg when he was four years old, and was fitted with a wooden leg almost immediately. His parents, wisely, did not overprotect him, but treated him like a normal child, needing the love and care and the freedom to explore his environment that all children need. During World War II, when Dave was still in junior high school, the director of social work at a nearby veterans hospital asked Dave to show the returning amputees how well he could get around.

A popular person with both boys and girls, Dave never lost his sense of humor. His favorite story concerned a junior high school touch football game when he became angry with several members of the opposing team; after a particularly long run by the opposition, Dave casually leaned up against a tree and suddenly pulled off his wooden leg and waved it like a club at his opponents. They were so startled that their playing completely disintegrated, and Dave's team won. Dave had a normal, healthy childhood and adolescence, and is now successful in the entertainment field. He says he rarely even thinks of himself as a person with one leg.

Although Dave's body-image certainly included the recognition that he was lacking one leg, he did not find this body-image unpleasant—it was merely one of the facts of life. If his parents had been less understanding or too protective, Dave might have considered himself a cripple. As it was, he considered himself a normal person who happened to have one leg.

Another physical difference affecting body-image is being overweight or underweight (although the former is presently a more serious matter). Being too heavy, which is primarily the result of too much eating and too little activity, often produces an unpleasant body-image. Overweight people, unlike the stereotype, are not jolly. They are often unhappy. Not only do they dislike their body-image, but certain types of social relationships, such as dating, are often difficult to find. Obese people are also the source of humor on television and in movies, which further worsens the body-image and resulting self-concept.

Body-image and acne. Acne is the medical problem which "causes more . . . maladjustments between parents and children, more general insecurity and feelings of inferiority, and greater [emotional] suffering . . ." than any other (Sulzberger and Zaidens, 1948). No really effective cure has been found for acne, or pimples, even though it is extremely common, particularly during the late teens and early twenties (Cohen, 1945).

The major problem caused by acne is its effect upon the body-image.

Many sufferers, particularly girls, become frantic at the sight of even a few red or white or black marks. They buy creams, salves, soaps, and special cosmetics; they go on special diets, use sun lamps, and take X-ray treatments. Whether these methods work or whether the acne merely disappears in time, most cases are eventually cured.

The specific causes of acne are not known, although dermatologists believe that the following factors are contributory: poor diet, particularly eating too much oily food, such as chocolate and peanut butter; constant touching and picking; inadequate cleanliness (which might include over-use of cosmetics and hair spray); poor general health and fatigue; and emotional stress (Sutton, 1941). Since cleanliness is only one of many possible factors, it may be overemphasized both by adolescents and by adults.

The degree to which emotional stress affects acne is not known, but research indicates that a combination of genetically inherited skin qualities and stress may interact to aggravate acne. Severe acne sufferers give off a large amount of facial oil when under stress, while those with little acne produce much less of this oil, which is believed to contribute to acne (Lorenz et al., 1953).

Displeasure with body-image may arise from unpleasant childhood or adolescent experiences, such as being teased by other children or over-hearing parents apologize for their appearance. Of course, people whose basic self-concept is poor may generalize their feelings toward their body-image. The importance of physical appearance is often overestimated during adolescence, but increasing maturity leads to a greater ability to accept the body-image and to concentrate upon more significant aspects of the self.

The developing self

In 1962, the *Saturday Evening Post* published a lengthy article called "Youth," based on the results of interviews with over 3,000 Americans from 14 through 22 years of age. The description below is the typical interviewee. How accurate do you feel this description is? Do you feel it has changed since 1962?

> . . . he is a pampered hothouse plant and likes it that way. The beatnik is a rarity; the delinquent is a minority.

> Our typical youth will settle for low success rather than risk high failure. He has little spirit of adventure. He wants to marry early—at 23 or 24—after a college education. He wants two or three children and a spouse who is "affectionate, sympathetic,

considerate, and moral"; rarely does he want a mate with intelligence, curiosity, or ambition. He wants a little ranch house, an inexpensive new car, a job with a large company, and a chance to watch TV each evening after the smiling children are asleep in bed.

He is a reluctant patriot who expects nuclear war in his time and would rather compromise than risk an all-out war. He is highly religious, yet winks at dishonesty.

He wants very little because he has so much and is unwilling to risk what he has. Essentially, he is quite conservative and cautious. He is old before his time; almost middle-aged in his teens. While he has high respect for education, he is critical of it—as he is about religion—and he is abysmally ignorant of the economic system that has made him what he is and of the system that threatens it.

In general, the typical American youth shows few symptoms of frustration, and is most unlikely to rebel or involve himself in crusades of any kind. He likes himself the way he is, and he likes things as they are.

The United States has bred a generation of nice little boys and girls who are just what we have asked them to be and what we so frequently say they are not. They will one day shape the nation. . . . (Gallup and Hill, 1961).

By the time an individual has reached early adolescence, he will have developed the basis for his later self-concept, a knowledge of the society around him and his place in it, a recognition of what behavior is approved and what is disapproved, and—to a large extent—insight about what he must do to get what he wants (Hollingshead, 1949).

Nonetheless, even though personality and self-concept changes are neither so extensive nor so frequent during later years, changes do occur. In our country, the decade following puberty is a period of certain significant types of growth and maturity. We will discuss three of these here: (1) the adolescent **search for identity**, (2) the adolescent approach to dealing with adult discrimination, and (3) eventual emancipation and adult status.

Gaining a sense of identity

Who are you? Not your name or your physical appearance or your family history, but the *real* you. What is the real you? The you no one else really knows, that perhaps you do not really know yourself. In other words, what is your *self?* Not your self-concept, but your actual self.

A confusing question? Certainly, but a question that begins to have meaning during adolescence. According to one well-known psychoanalyst, this is the major "psychosocial crisis" that faces people between twelve and twenty-one. In order for them to continue toward self-actualization, they must—and usually do—overcome this crisis (Erikson, 1956).

How do you know when you are being yourself? As you behave, you become aware of your behavior and decide, partly consciously and partly unconsciously, whether the behavior represents "the real me" or not. When the behavior is not consistent with "the real me," you may feel "I am not myself." This feeling is upsetting and causes emotional discomfort. You may also be concerned about the effect you have upon others when you are not yourself (adapted from Jourard, 1963).

People become unhappy when others treat them as though they had no identity—no "real me." We talk disparagingly of large, impersonal universities as factories, even while recognizing that their educational programs may be of high quality. You are probably pleased when someone remembers your name, because that signifies his awareness of your **identity**; you are an individual, apart from the thousands of other people he has met. People talk longingly of small towns, where "everyone knows everyone else," because the individual has identity in these communities that he may lack in the large and rapidly changing city and suburban areas. Repetitious tract home designs, impersonal treatment in large medical clinics, the way colleges use numbers instead of names to identify students, the vast growth of computers, all are cited as examples of the loss of identity of the individual, regardless of their contributions to efficiency and "the better life."

In a world where many people complain about a lack of identity, it is not surprising that the adolescent is still seeking his, still wanting to know "the real me." To do this, he tries out new behavior patterns and new styles of living, to see which ones are comfortable. For example, adolescents experiment with styles of handwriting, with variations in spelling their names, with an assortment of nicknames, with hairstyles and clothing styles, with speech mannerisms. The adolescent tries each of them on like a new pair of shoes, walks around with each a bit, then decides whether it fits comfortably or not.

> "About two months before I finished college, I went out and bought my first pair of loafers (I'd had only laced shoes before); then I got my first crewcut. I'd thought of these things before, but they never seemed exactly right for me. But this time they seemed fine. I was so pleased that I replaced my old yellow-pink eyeglass frames with new heavy black frames. That was 14 years ago, and I still feel comfortable with loafers, a crewcut, and dark eyeglass frames—they are me."

During the teen-age decade, we also try out more important styles of behaving.

> "It's some years ago, but I can still remember. One day I thought I'd be romantic and dashing, but that didn't work too well, so the next day I was the sweet-and-understanding type. That was better, but I still tried out a few others: I was the silent-and-in-emotional-pain type, the happy-go-lucky type, and the big-spender type. But each time I came back to the sweet-and-understanding type. Even though I was aware of what I was doing, I kept feeling that I was really being myself. Today I don't try to be any type any more, but I guess that I still think of myself as more like the sweet-and-understanding type than anything else. Of course, I do know I'm not always either sweet or understanding."

Adolescents are strongly motivated to find out "who am I?" and then to behave consistently with what they feel this self to be.

A portion of the adolescent and college-age population seems uncertain what part they are to play in today's world. Perhaps because their own lives have included so many luxuries and so few hardships, they feel little challenge in just earning money or following the socially acceptable standards, and they firmly reject the earlier description as referring to them—now or ever. Many of these students turn to various political and social movements to give them a feeling of self-fulfillment or self-actualization; others, like the beatniks who were so talked about some years ago, retreat into fads; some will find satisfaction through the arts. These students are frequently criticized because their behavior does not follow social standards, but they may eventually turn out to be among the most productive and creative individuals of their age group. They are trying to be unique individuals in a world that seems to them to have forgotten the individual.

Others of the same age respond to the lack of identity in a different fashion. They seem unable to find worthwhile goals, so they turn to frantic activity, perhaps including heavy drinking or even narcotics. They need to be moving all the time, and at one time they symbolized their restlessness by attaching the expression "a-go-go" to their favorite hangouts.

All of the above groups satisfy the need for a feeling of identity, but each does it in a much different way.

A discriminated-against minority

Strange as it may seem, those of adolescent age form a minority group that is the object of **discrimination**, **prejudice**, and **segregation**, just as many other groups are. And they respond, much as other minority groups, by forming their own society with its own rules and customs, a society that resembles the general society in most ways, although with some behavior distorted or exaggerated.

Adolescents in the United States are given no real place in their country. They are no longer satisfied with being children; yet the adult world has no room for them. Adult opportunities, such as regular employment, sex and marriage, and independence and responsibility for their own behavior, are not available. They are reminded of their second-class citizenship by everything from restrictions on buying a bottle of beer to editorials in newspapers. Adults often consider them unstable, immature, and potentially violent. They are treated as being dependent and ineffective (Ausubel, 1954).

Perhaps the adults are correct; perhaps adolescents are actually all these things. If so, the adult population has participated in making them so, partly by inducing a self-concept in many adolescents that corresponds to the adult view. Since this is a painful self-concept, many adolescents try to prove that it is not valid, and the attempts may merely persuade the adults that the original beliefs were all too true. Fortunately, many adolescents are successful in changing their self-concepts to their own satisfaction and through appropriate behavior.

Since adolescents are essentially told they have no place in adult society, they inevitably turn to each other for support. In this way, they become extremely dependent upon what other adolescents think of them. The teen culture becomes much more important than the adult culture. After all, the adult culture says KEEP OUT! and the teen culture says WELCOME FRIEND AND FELLOW SUFFERER!!

In years past, and in many parts of the world today, adolescents received a great deal of responsibility, ranging from household chores to working side by side with adults in the field and the factory. This was not just busy work, but work essential to keep the family going. In our country today, we do not need adolescents to take these responsibilities, but—simultaneously—we have deprived them of the feeling that they are making a real contribution. The Latter-Day Saints (Mormons) encourage their young people to participate in community responsibility—perhaps their low rate of delinquency and school dropout is partly a result of their willingness to allow youths a mature role.

Of a large sample of teen-age boys, 43 percent considered that responsibilities and opportunities that allowed them to take on the adult role contributed greatly to making them feel important and useful. Nothing else was nearly so highly rated (Boys' Clubs of America, 1960).

In spite of the importance of their own culture, teen-agers exhibit very much the same values as the general adult culture that surrounds them. True, there has been much teen-age violence, which seems to be a way for them to handle frustrations they are too immature to cope with otherwise. We might, however, draw a parallel to the murder of literally millions of civilians in Nazi concentration camps, the ruthlessness of Russia under Josef Stalin, or the violence ordered by the Ku Klux Klan in our own country. If teen-agers exaggerate the importance of the automobile in building their self-esteem, think of the symbols of status that their parents exaggerate.

Perhaps adults overemphasize differences between the teen culture and their own. It has been shown, for example, that the social, political, religious, and other values of teen-agers closely resemble the values of their parents (Hyman, 1959). Also, adolescents have (a) a higher opinion of adults than their parents have of themselves, and (b) a higher opinion of adults than their parents believe they have (Hess and Goldblatt, 1957). Like many minority groups, adolescents admire the majority group and internalize their values.

Emancipation and primary status

As long as teen-agers live with their parents, are almost completely dependent upon them for financial support and guidance, and are either unable or unwilling to be responsible for their own behavior, they are identified as their parents' children. One author has described this as **derived status**, because these individuals *derive* their *status* and identity directly from the status and identity of their parents, and the parents are considered largely responsible for what their children do (Ausubel, 1954).

In their own teen-age culture, of course, they have **primary status**. Here they are not known as Mrs. Johnson's boy, but as Jack Johnson. They are responsible for their own status.

Although parents encourage their late-adolescent children to take responsibility and behave in a mature fashion, they often find it difficult to allow these children an equivalent amount of decision-making power and acceptance as mature and responsible individuals (Ausubel, 1954). The adult seems to be saying: "I'll give you freedom and decision-making power when you prove to me that you are mature." The teen-ager responds: "How can I prove I'm mature when you don't treat me as a responsible person." Even 33 percent of college freshmen agreed that "Parents demand more, but won't let you grow up" is a greater problem for them than for their parents' generation (Harris, 1965).

Sometimes, in an effort to emancipate himself and establish primary status, a teen-ager will leave home against his parents' wishes. Boys may enlist in the military, while girls often seek marriage; and both, of course, can get work. Our society seems to perceive a married person or a working person as deserving primary status, and the main purpose for teen-age working is rated as becoming financially independent of parents (Boys' Clubs of America, 1960). Many college students need to learn to cope with the frustrations of remaining financially dependent upon their

Figure 8–3. One way to achieve an adult role is to join the military service, in which this young man is receiving useful training. Courtesy United States Air Force.

parents, while friends are emancipating themselves through marriage and full-time jobs.

Not all adolescents really seek emancipation. Freedom can be frightening, particularly for people whose physiological, security, and love needs are not adequately satisfied. To leave home and become established demands giving up many of the comforts and satisfactions that you have been accustomed to. More than that, it demands that you make your own decisions and take responsibility for your own actions. Many people prefer to allow others to make decisions for them. If they leave home, they quickly find a person or an organization to tell them what to do and how to behave. The German Nazi party prospered partly because people were so confused by the turmoil in Germany that they preferred to sign away their freedom. In the United States, the head of a small but very aggressive political group has told his followers that free speech and questioning are unnecessary in his organization and only lead to arguments; he insists upon making all the decisions. Adolescents and adults who are very uncertain of themselves and have little self-respect may find freedom too difficult and may prefer others to do their thinking for them. (Erich Fromm, an internationally known psychoanalyst, has written a book called *Escape from Freedom.* Does the title make sense?)

Slowly, however, often painfully slowly to the adolescent himself, he gains freedom from his parents and emerges into the community as a person in his own right. Once the general community of adults gives him primary status by accepting him for himself, he no longer needs the teen culture for support. He can now take his place in the adult community and will very quickly become responsive to their demands, rather than those of the teen-agers whose ranks he has left.

In discussing the development of self during the decade following puberty, we have emphasized the search for identity and its dynamic interaction with the position of the adolescent in an adult world, his relationship with his parents, and his eventual emancipation. Since most readers of this book are at the end of the age period under discussion, or slightly older, you are in a particularly good position to evaluate what has been said and determine how it might apply to you.

Social relationships

Since his peer group gives the adolescent primary status and individual identity, acceptance or rejection by this group looms as vital to most teen-agers. Unlike the adult who knows the limits of what he can do and still be socially acceptable, the adolescent is less sure of his identity and is not willing to risk a blunder that might cost him status in the group that does accept him.

Because he is uncertain how far he can safely venture from the demands of the group, the adolescent is willing to accept pressures from his peers that he would violently reject from his parents. When he was young and his parents were the major significant figures, he accepted their demands with little questioning. Now his friends are more than ever involved in the satisfaction of his security, love, and esteem needs, and the adolescent wants to do his best to see those needs continually satisfied.

When adults criticize the adolescent friendship group, they are attacking the basis of the adolescent's status and esteem, and he becomes very defensive. He may become even more defensive if he recognizes the adult comments as largely true, since this possibility is very damaging to his self-concept. In the long run, however, and with some obvious exceptions, the qualities that make an adolescent popular with his peer group and acceptable as a date are qualities that adults approve.

Popularity

Popularity is greatly desired by Americans of all ages. The advantages are considerable: the popular person is assured of friends, dates, better job opportunities, more leadership opportunity, and a potentially busy and exciting life. His self-concept is bolstered since he learns that others look upon him as a worthwhile person.

Sometimes a situation arises requiring popularity to be sacrificed for other values. Military officers, newspaper reporters, policemen, and teachers are only a few of the groups that must risk becoming unpopular in order to carry out their duties. Examples of men hated by many during their lives would include Lincoln, Darwin, Socrates, Voltaire, Robert E. Lee, both Franklin D. and Theodore Roosevelt, Gandhi, and—of course—Christ.

Popularity also has its dangers. The popular individual may overestimate his competence, and his level of aspiration may extend beyond his actual ability. Also, his popularity can become so satisfying that, rather than lose the rewards of popularity, he will sacrifice other values in order to please everyone and retain his status. By so doing, his behavior may become inconsistent, and his self-concept may become confused and uncertain—he no longer knows whether the popular person with the peculiar standards is the "real me" or a false front. Eventually he may lose many of the qualities that produced his popularity initially.

Qualities that lead to popularity

The bases for student popularity have been studied frequently by psychologists. Different groups, of course, value different personality and ability traits. A scholarship to Harvard is admired by one group, while a record of three arrests and no convictions is admired by another; getting married at 18 is considered wonderful by some girls and foolish by others. However, certain characteristics seem to be generally admired by a variety of groups.

One extensive study was conducted in ten different high schools in the Chicago area. When asked what got a person into the leading crowd, both boys and girls specified personality as most important. The girls placed secondary emphasis upon good looks and clothing, while the boys stressed good reputation and athletic ability. Neither boys nor girls believed grades contributed much to getting into the leading high school crowd, but students with good grades plus athletic ability were especially popular (Coleman, 1961).

(If the observations of this author and of others are accurate, athletic ability is less likely to lead to popularity in college than in high school, and is less important in college today than in the past. Some college athletes even complain that they are stereotyped as stupid and conceited, merely because they are athletes.)

Investigators in a second study, conducted in California, selected students on the basis of how often their names were mentioned in the student newspaper. (The assumption was made that the more active and more popular students would be mentioned more frequently.) The popular students were rated as having better grooming and appearance and as having more pep and eagerness; they were also cheerful, relaxed, and poised (Jones, 1958).

Other psychologists have found the following characteristics contributed to popularity: cooperativeness, helpfulness, unselfishness, courtesy, considerateness, intelligence, self-control, initiative, dependability, conversational ability, humor, and politeness (Ausubel, 1954).

Dating

Between puberty and engagement, the American student is immersed in the problems of dating. Success or failure in dating means much more than a way of spending time and having fun. Dating influences attitudes and behavior in many ways.

(1) *Dating affects the self-concept.* A girl knows she is well-liked when she receives many calls for dates and is frequently asked to go steady. Her self-concept develops accordingly. The self-concept of the boy will follow the same course, if he finds girls are interested in dating him.

(2) *Dating is an indication of prestige and reputation.* Students are judged not only by their own accomplishments, but also by the popularity and accomplishments of those they date. Dating a less-popular girl or boy will certainly do nothing to raise prestige. Prestige is gained by dating a popular person or member of the leading crowd, a student leader, or—particularly for high school girls—an athlete.

(3) *Dating affects other aspects of social life.* The girl tends to find herself in the social group selected by her date. If the dating relationship is a continuing one, or if other fellows in the crowd ask her out, she is likely to develop friendships with other girls similarly dating in the

crowd. Much of her nondating social activity may also become centered in this group. Of course, when the boy and girl sever the relationship, they are often embarrassed or upset by having to face the friends who had known them as a couple.

(4) *Dating is an opportunity for learning.* Often overlooked in discussions of dating is the learning that can take place. The demands of married life in the United States are great because so much is expected of marriage. Both the husband and wife *expect* the other to understand

Figure 8–4. Just before the prom. What are her thoughts? Courtesy *Ladies Home Journal*. Photograph by Werner Stoy.

them, to be sensitive to their needs, and to supply love, affection, and companionship. To deal with the great complexities of selecting the correct spouse and living enjoyably with that person, a great deal of experience and understanding are needed. Some of this, of course, occurs through observation of the relationship between the parents, but much can be learned through the give and take of dating.

Dating thus allows young people to get to know many potential spouses in a very personal, face-to-face situation, which is a preliminary to the marital relationship in some ways. The teen-ager can test out certain behavior, attitudes, and roles in a relatively harmless arrangement. He can gain an understanding of the type of behavior that appeals to him in the opposite sex, and what of his behavior appeals to the opposite sex. He learns to know people of the opposite sex as individuals, rather than merely as members of a group. In many societies, marriages are arranged and dating opportunities are limited or nonexistent, but the expectations each married person has of his spouse are usually different from those of Americans. Talk to people from other countries, and see if you can learn how different marital roles require different sorts of experience before marriage.

Jack Soph wants to date Mary Frosh. Jack is ready to make the date. Hopefully, he is two weeks ahead of time, but a briefer time, even a last-minute date, is permissible. Jack shouldn't be surprised, however, if a last-minute call is refused. By and large, Jack should state what they will do. If he does not know, he can say "I'm not too sure what we'll do, but we can always catch the movie on campus if nothing else turns up." He will, of course, clear final plans with Mary. Jack knows that the etiquette books insist he have the evening already planned, but the life of a college student is not always that certain.

Nonetheless, Jack is willing and able to make the decision. He knows how weary girls get of the fellows who constantly say, "Gee, I dunno what to do—what do *you* wanna do?" His role is to make the decision, then—out of courtesy—make certain Mary has no objections.

If Mary turns him down, Jack might try to figure out whether he is getting the brush-off. It all depends upon how disappointed Mary sounded and whether she implied she would like to see him at another time. However, Jack does not want to push Mary into a date she does not want, so he will never ask her out for more than two dates on any one telephone call. If she continues to turn him down, he should start looking for another Mary.

Jack should arrive on time for the date, perhaps a few minutes late. Conversation with Mary's parents or dormitory mother is useful and a good way to kill time until Mary emerges. (Jack might even get some inside information on his competition if he listens carefully and does not ask questions.)

The evening may be a party, movie, dance, picnic, swim, play, skate, dinner, concert, stockcar race, baseball game, television party, or . . . A long drive or a long walk with a soda in the middle can be a great deal of fun if Jack and Mary are the right sort of people. Jack may try an expensive evening if he thinks that will impress Mary, or he may try an inexpensive evening to see if Mary is worth spending more time and money on. During the evening Jack should keep the conversational ball rolling. The etiquette books say this is up to the woman, but that is only for men who are very shy or very dull. If Jack is worth his salt, he will be able to carry on a conversation.

Also, Jack recognizes that Mary is not an idiot merely because she is a woman. Mary is a person with feelings and hopes, and she enjoys being treated like a woman *and* like a person who has something to say worth listening to. If Jack needs a Mary to spend the entire evening asking him questions about himself or telling him how wonderful he is, Jack is a sad excuse for a man. (Almost one-third of a group of college women had purposely pretended to be inferior to men on at least several occasions—Wallin, 1950.)

If the evening is dull, Jack still must make the best of it. Perhaps a little extra attention will bring Mary out of her shell. If it was a blind date, Jack has just as much obligation to be nice about a dull evening—after all, he knew he was taking a chance.

If Jack wants another date, he can ask when he takes Mary home. If he does not want another, he is certainly not obligated. There are a lot of fish in the sea. Of course, there are a lot of other fellows fishing.

Mary Frosh is asked out by Jack Soph. If Mary wants a date with a particular Jack, she must either be aggressive and hint that he ask her out, or she must put herself in a position where Jack will think that asking her out is his own idea. Some popular devices are: suggest to a friend to suggest to Jack that he ask her out; find out Jack's favorite table in the library and be there before he arrives; find some honest reason to ask his advice or help.

When Jack does ask her out, she should not play hard-to-get. If she has a date for the night he asks her, she should encourage him to try another night. On the other hand, if Mary does not really want to go out with Jack, she should find some way to let him know so that he does not keep calling back. Or, if she is not certain, she might try to arrange a coffee date during the day to get to know him better. Some etiquette books claim this is dishonest, but it would be more dishonest to accept a date under false pretenses.

When Jack announces the plans for the evening (and if he does not, Mary can ask), Mary has the right to suggest something else, as long as (a) she does it gently, (b) it does not cost more money, and (c) it does not affect other people Jack may have involved.

Mary can be ready when Jack comes, or a few minutes late. To keep someone waiting is not only rude, but may be a subtle way of trying to be boss.

For a first date or a blind date, Mary may suggest spending the evening with other people, both to ease the conversational stiffness and for protection. She must help keep the conversational ball rolling, but she should not have to spend the entire evening building Jack's self-esteem. If Jack needs that form of support, let him find some girl that cannot get dates any other way. Mary is a person with a mind of her own. While she will not try to out-talk Jack, she need not try to be the idiot some Jacks want their dates to be.

Dating: other places and other times. Dating as practiced by most college students is a recent phenomenon, occurring mostly in the United States, Canada, and some European countries. The idea of a boy asking a girl to spend an unchaperoned evening was unknown a century ago. The couple might have gone for a Sunday afternoon walk or they may have sneaked away from the community picnic to be together, but these are a far cry from the present dating behavior. Not only have styles of dating changed, but the age at which teen-agers begin to date has been getting steadily younger.

In African, Asian, South American, and some European countries, dating "American-style" is either virtually unknown or else is limited to a very small proportion of the population, usually the more wealthy and sophisticated. Even in European countries where dating is common, group activities occur more frequently than the single date or double date, and going steady is usually avoided until the students are in their late teens.

Chaperones are still very common in such places as the Philippines and Latin America. A young couple going to the movies is accompanied by an older relative or a trusted family friend. One young American, teaching in the Philippines for a year, told of dating a local girl and being chaperoned by her married brother and sister-in-law, both younger than the teacher. Sunday afternoon strolls are popular in many parts of the world, although parents may demand that even these walks be chaperoned, at least from a distance.

For a boy in Iraq to meet a girl he has seen, he must first ask his parents or a close friend to learn about the girl. Then he will try to arrange for his parents to call upon the girl's parents and take him along, or for the mutual friend to introduce them. Eventually he will be admitted to the girl's house without his parents, but they would never be left alone until they were engaged. In the meantime, the couple may be passing exciting love notes back and forth to each other through a mutual friend or a servant. This may be poetic and romantic, but how far it seems from American dating problems.

A Japanese girl expressed what many students around the world probably feel: "I would like to be more free than I am, but I would not like to be free like American girls. They do too much with boys that is wrong. American parents are not strict enough with their daughters. And I know from talking to American students that their freedom does not make them any happier than we. No nice Japanese boy would marry a girl who behaved like an American girl."

Attitudes toward dating. Nearly half of a large group of teen-agers stated that they began to date at 13 or 14, while most of the rest began at 15 or 16 (cited in Cole and Hall, 1964). Girls begin to date earlier and often date older boys. By their senior year in high school, about 80 percent of all students claimed to be dating regularly (Gallup and Hill, 1961).

Many investigators have asked high school and college students to list the most important characteristics for a date or a future husband or wife. The lists are all a little different, but a University of Michigan study of qualities wanted for a date is fairly typical. These students selected as most important (1) being pleasant and cheerful, (2) having a sense of humor, (3) being a good sport, (4) being natural, (5) being considerate, and (6) having a neat appearance (Blood, 1956).

The same University of Michigan study had other significant results. For example, men seemed to feel they needed a car in order to date, while girls did not consider cars so important. Similarly, men felt their dates preferred them to be in a good fraternity, have money, dress sharply, go popular places, be a good dancer, and be able to drink. The girls, however, put much less stress on these factors than the men thought they did (Blood, 1956).

Attitudes of parents. Most adults these days recognize dating to be an inevitable part of growing up. Although parents frequently set limits upon the dating of their high school children, college students are given a high degree of freedom. When parents do interfere, it is likely to be because the college student's schoolwork is falling down, because he seems to be dating too frequently, or because they disapprove of his companions. Disapproval of dates may be based upon personality or intelligence, or upon religious, racial, nationality, or social-class differences. Most dating is between people of the same social class (Hollingshead, 1949), reflecting parental preference also.

Often parents recall the attitudes *their* parents had toward dating. Because their own attitudes are usually more flexible, they somehow feel that their dating children should appreciate them more; they do not recognize that this generation is probably just as different from its parents' generation as they were from *their* parents.

Going steady

College students frequently go steady or have previously gone steady by the time they finish their education. About one-fourth of a large group of high school students indicated they were going steady at the time they

---

Changing prospectives on going steady

In 1925. "None of the popular girls will go with the same fellow more than a couple of times a month—unless they really intend to marry him. Why, I dated eight different men last month alone. I guess that's why I'm considered just about the most popular girl around."

In 1945. "I've been going steady with Chuck for six months, but I think we're going to break up soon. That's a shame, because I went steady with Eddie for over a year before that. The really popular girls are the ones that go steady with someone they really like for at least several months, because anything less than that just isn't worth it."

In 1955. "I've been going steady with Jerry for three weeks already, but it's all over now. Besides, I want to go steady with Frank—he attracted me even last month when I was going steady with Rich."

In 1965. "This going steady business is for kids or for almost-engageds. Marty and I are going *steadily*, but not steady. None of that exchanging rings or anything. We like each other and we're what you might call a couple, but we're each free to do what we want. I get kind of a kick out of playing the field once in a while, and we don't want to be too involved."

In 1975. ? ? ? ?

---

were asked (cited in Cole and Hall, 1964). Going steady offers the advantages of getting to know one person very well, of feeling accepted by at least one person, of giving and receiving emotional warmth, and of not having to worry where the next date is coming from.

The disadvantages include the possibility of getting bored with each other but being unable to break the habit, of moving into an overly intense sex relationship, of having limited social contacts, and of the emotional strain involved in threatened break-ups and suspected unfaithfulness. The biggest problem of going steady, however, is that it can lead to marriage before the individuals are ready.

Going steady does not necessarily imply future marriage, but may be simply a matter of obtaining a secure relationship. On the one hand, it can be a retreat for the insecure who do not wish to face the competition and games of dating around. On the other hand, it can be a wonderful, although often painful, emotional experience for those who are emotionally and intellectually mature enough to keep it in perspective.

> Joe Porter was not very popular in high school. When he got to college, he began dating Karen Himmel, a rather plain, dull girl, and they quickly decided to go steady, both of them feeling very much alone in the large college they attended. One day, Joe was told that Karen had been rushed to the hospital after a suicide attempt. This incident occurred right after Joe had told Karen he felt they should break up. Joe felt so guilty for causing such drastic behavior, that he proposed to Karen in the hospital, and she accepted. They were married at the end of the school year, and are still married, now with two children. Joe has never loved Karen, but he feels he is paying his debt for the anguish he caused her. He never learned that Karen had called the dormitory mother just after taking the sleeping tablets and had dramatically announced, "I'm going to kill myself."

Joe and Karen were certainly not mature enough to become involved in the relationship they had. Yet they were perfectly persuaded they knew what they were doing. Not many steady couples are married because of a faked suicide attempt, but less-dramatic incidents are common. Fortunately, many young couples deal with a steady relationship in a mature way.

SUMMARY OF IMPORTANT IDEAS

1. The decade from twelve through twenty-one is not only a transition from childhood to mature responsibility and opportunity, but it is also a time of increased concern regarding the world and regarding a personal sense of identity.

2. Adolescence is not considered a distinct developmental period in all societies.

3. The growth spurt begins shortly before puberty.

4. The body-image is the picture, or self-concept, an individual has of his physical appearance and physical self.

5. The body-image can extend to physical health and handicaps that may not be obvious to the observer.

6. Many adolescents are involved with the search for identity, i.e., the desire to understand *who* they are.

7. Adolescents are a discriminated-against group; they reject the role of children, but are not accepted by society as adults.

8. The peer group is very important to the adolescent because it is the only group that allows him primary status.

9. Popularity is both helpful and potentially dangerous.

10. Qualities leading to popularity differ in different groups, but certain characteristics are generally admired by a variety of groups.

11. American students are deeply concerned with dating; dating relationships are valuable in developing mature roles in our society but also involve certain hazards.

12. Going steady is common during adolescence in the United States.

The student at college   9

Awareness of increasing personal responsibility with maturity is now more important than ever. College provides, at least for many students, freedom and responsibilities that are new, often exciting, and sometimes frightening. The college student, unlike the high school student, can drop out of school whenever he—or his college—sees fit. At the same time, the close, warm relationships with significant figures, emphasized in Chapters 6 and 7, have changed considerably; even the dating relationships, mentioned in Chapter 8, change in meaning as marriage becomes a real possibility.

"Make the most of your capabilities!" This is easy to say, but its actual accomplishment takes more than good intentions—it demands that certain skills and knowledge be acquired. College offers one excellent source for some of these necessary skills and knowledge and simultaneously opens up new opportunities and helps develop interests and capabilities you may never have realized you had.

The importance of education, particularly college education, is receiving increasing recognition. The great majority of 14- to 18-year-olds are now in school, around 90 percent today as opposed to less than 9 percent in 1889. Approximately 43 percent of those between 18 and 22 are attending college or a comparable institution, a much higher percentage than in other countries (Cole and Hall, 1964) or in past generations in the United States. College enrollment more than doubled between 1955 and 1965.

The percentage increase in college students is particularly dramatic in two-year colleges that award an Associate in Arts or comparable degree. Of the nearly six million students in the United States, about one-seventh are presently studying in junior colleges or community colleges, and one estimate suggests that half of all college freshmen will be in junior colleges within the next few years (Gleazer, 1963).

Junior colleges and four-year colleges are, of course, only two of the many types of institutions offering education and training beyond high school. We also find business colleges; technical institutes; art and drama schools; secretarial schools; specialized schools to educate nurses, morticians, key-punch operators, and photographers; and a host of other institutions ready to offer the understanding, information, and skills that enable us to realize and use our capabilities.

What is a college?

Is a college just a group of buildings? Is it the students? Or the faculty? The administration? The spirit? Is it all these things together?

Try thinking of college as a community of scholars, coming together to share their learning and to try to learn more. Students learn not only from the faculty, but also from other students; faculty members not only teach students, but also learn from students and from each other. The learning occurs through the formal channels of textbooks, lectures, library assignments, audio-visual aids, teaching machines, and demonstrations. Learning also occurs informally, such as in conversations in a faculty office or over a cup of coffee, in hearing a faculty member or student talk of his original project or research, in disagreeing so violently with a professor that you search for some additional information yourself.

Figure 9–1. The nature of the physical plant differs considerably from college to college. Figure 9–1 A courtesy Antioch College; B courtesy California State College at Los Angeles.

In this community of scholars you can be like the gas tank of a car: you can sit back and let information be pumped into you, then run on it for a while, and eventually return for more. Or you can be active in seeking information and understanding: you can go beyond the formal part of college education and enter into the spirit of the community by reading on your own, by seeking new ideas, by evaluating what is told to you and relating it to your own experiences, by questioning faculty members, by learning from other students, and by being alert to the meaning of your own experiences.

Attending a classroom lecture will not produce the heart thumping of getting a date with the best-looking girl on campus or of holding the winning ticket in a contest for a new Cadillac, but learning in college can be exciting. A new insight into the workings of the federal government, learning how to program a new computer, finding a line in a poem that describes exactly how you feel, the sudden jump in typing speed, discovering that your constant anger with your younger sister not only is common but even has a technical name—these are just a few examples of learning that can be exciting.

Some of the great variety of learning tasks that are part of college include developing the ability to

(1) Express your own ideas and understand the ideas of others through effective and meaningful reading, writing, talking, and listening.

(2) Understand human behavior, including your own, through a knowledge of historical and cultural traditions and human motivation.

(3) Prepare yourself as a future citizen, a member of the work force, and a spouse and parent.

(4) Be familiar with the physical world, technology, and the scientific method.

(5) Understand good mental and physical health practices, and apply them to yourself and in dealing with others.

(6) Enjoy social relationships in the neighborhood, on the job, and with the family, and be able to give to and receive from these relationships.

(7) Appreciate artistic and creative contributions of others and receive satisfaction from your own creative and artistic talents.

(8) Recognize the problems of the local community and of the world and determine the type of contribution you can make.

(9) Evaluate ethical principles and develop your own.

(10) Think, solve problems, and plan for the future.

(11) Evaluate your own behavior and be self-critical.

(12) Gain knowledge and understanding in a wide variety of areas, so that you can evaluate critically what others say and reach your own independent conclusions (suggested by a similar list by Bennett and Lewin, 1957).

The deficiency-motivated person is restricted from participating effectively in the college community of scholars because his activities are controlled by a need to satisfy his security or self-esteem motives, and he may not see the excitement and adventure of acquiring knowledge and skills; the growth-motivated student can see beyond need restrictions and obtain great satisfaction from his learning.

In describing what the college student should be, one psychologist has suggested a combination of "College Chap," "Vocational Man," "Scholarly Student," and "Intellectual Rebel" (Wrenn, 1962). What sorts of attitudes and behavior do these types represent? If you had one hundred points to describe yourself, how many points would you allocate to each type?

The student looks at college

So far college has been discussed from the viewpoint of what many educators feel *should* take place. What do the students themselves say? A number of colleges, scattered all over the country, participated in a study to answer this question. Although all the responding students were male, their answers are relevant to everyone. Here are the reasons they gave for going to college, with the number in parentheses indicating the percent believing each statement to be "highly important" (Goldsen et al., 1960):

(1) To obtain a good general education and to be able to appreciate ideas (74).

(2) To be better able to get along with others (72).

(3) To acquire necessary vocational skills (60).

(4) To become a better citizen (50).

(5) To acquire information helpful in determining "right" from "wrong" (45).

(6) To contribute to a happy marriage and a pleasant family life (22).

A more recent survey inquired into the beliefs of college freshmen throughout the country and compared these beliefs to beliefs held by the parents of high school students of equivalent background. The most conspicuous difference between the students and the parents was that the students were interested in college more for noneconomic advantages (79 percent emphasized these), while the parents were primarily concerned with the vocational aspects (74 percent). Getting a broad education, finding their "own identity" (recall the earlier discussion of this), and getting ahead socially were much more important to students than to their parents (Harris, 1965).

Talking more informally, students mention other reasons for college attendance, although parents and professors might not consider them appropriate. These include avoiding arguments with parents, staying out

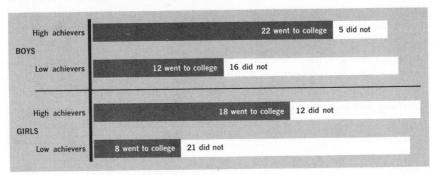

Figure 9–2. Comparison of able boys and girls who went to college with those who did not (Adapted from Havighurst et al., 1962).

of the army, postponing the need to get a job, having fun, finding a husband, and "because all my friends are going." In most instances, of course, the decision to attend college is based not on one factor only but on a combination of several.

Not all the intelligent students enter college. Motivation and other factors are also important. Figure 9–2 refers *only* to students in the upper quarter of their high school class on measures of intelligence, so that all clearly had the potential to enter college. Notice that those whose high school achievement was better tended to go on to college. The factors that led to their success in high school most probably were the same factors that encouraged them to enter college.

A logical question follows: Does college accomplish the things these students expected? The answer is that it does to some degree. Those who finished college were much more likely to become business executives and professional men than those who did not, and they definitely had higher incomes and better job opportunities. Only 2 percent of a large group of college graduates stated that college did not help them at all vocationally, while 70 percent said it helped "a lot" (Havemann and West, 1952).

Also, college men are more likely to marry and less likely to divorce than noncollege men; so we can *tentatively* assume they achieve happier marriages, although we do not know whether college attendance actually leads to the lower divorce rate or whether college attracts individuals who would be less likely to get divorced anyway. On the other hand, college women are less likely to marry than noncollege women, although the gap between the two groups has been shrinking consistently over the years (Havemann and West, 1952).

College has also been shown to help increase critical thinking ability and to decrease rigid and inflexible thinking; interestingly enough, most of the change occurred in the freshman year (Lehmann, 1963). On the other hand, it does not seem that college attendance necessarily leads to better citizenship. American college students were less interested in participating in public affairs than students from the six other countries studied. American students did not feel that such activity would give them much satisfaction (Jacob, 1957). This study, however, was conducted before the active political participation of college students in the 1964 presidential election and the civil rights movements which began a year or so earlier.

Are college graduates satisfied with what they got from college? Although they naturally have criticisms, a resounding 98 percent would go to college if they had it to do over again, and 84 percent would return to the same college they attended (Havemann and West, 1952).

Thus, learning in college is expected to perform many functions, from providing job skills to helping critical thinking to giving a broad education. In spite of their criticisms, college graduates appear to believe that they benefited considerably from their education.

New freedom, new identity, new relationships, new responsibilities

As little as three months or even less may separate the high school senior from the college freshman, but the change in freedom and responsibility can be immense. College life requires increased self-discipline and responsibility. College professors and administrators do not feel it is their role to tell a student how to schedule his time, how much he needs to study, or how much he should read each day. At the same time, parental supervision usually decreases. For those who live away from home, the new demands are even greater.

Freedom from supervision

In high school, parents and teachers kept a close eye on students, but this supervision—of academic activities and of personal life—diminishes considerably in college. Students who miss a class must learn for themselves what they missed; although most professors are happy to talk to students after class to explain some point in the lecture more thoroughly, the student must take the initiative for these conferences himself. Attendance is not always taken, and there is little, other than his own planning and motivation, to keep a student from falling impossibly far behind in his studies. Even parents do not supervise their college-age children as closely

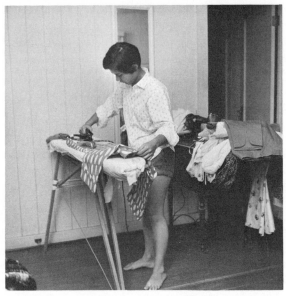

Figure 9–3. College often requires new responsibilities. Courtesy *Ladies Home Journal.* Photograph by Werner Stoy.

as previously, partly because they feel their children must now use their own initiative and partly because parents usually do not understand college assignments and demands as well as they had understood those from high school. College students are expected to be responsible for their own behavior without constant parental and professorial reminders.

> In her first semester at junior college, Helene Gould signed up for an average load of courses and a heavy load of social activities. Although many of her professors did take attendance, her instructors in English and in psychology did not bother. Her psychology professor stated at the first class meeting, "Attendance is strictly up to you; you are in college because you choose to be, and your success depends upon your performance. If you decide something else is more important than class, that is

up to you, but it is your obligation to make up what you missed." Since English and psychology classes were held on Monday, Wednesday, and Friday afternoons, Helene found that cutting these classes gave her a great deal of free time. At first she cut only Friday classes, to give herself more time to set her hair for Friday-evening dates; then she began to cut Monday and Wednesday occasionally. Neither professor said anything to her, so she felt safe—especially since she had low C grades going into the finals. The axe fell when she received her final grades: a D in psychology and an F in English. She visited her psychology professor, tears in her eyes, and asked whether she could do work to bring her grade up. He listened patiently but said "No." Then Helene told him it was his fault that she had gotten the low grade, because "you should have insisted that everybody come to class every time." The professor merely sighed deeply and reminded her of his warning at the first meeting: "It's up to you to stay in or flunk out, not me."

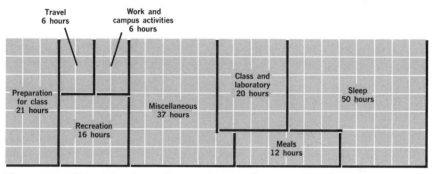

Figure 9–4. This chart shows how a sample of University of Hawaii students used their time during a seven-day period (Dole, 1959). How does it compare to your college?

Helene had not learned in time that college students are expected to be responsible for their own success. Since students are not forced by law to attend college, and since colleges are not forced by law to keep students who do poorly, the situation in college differs considerably from that in high school. The student is expected to solve problems and to gain knowledge and understanding on his own; when he needs help, he is expected to seek the help, not to wait for the help to find him. The watchful eye and commanding voice that Helene had been accustomed to in high school were lacking at college.

Even the scheduling of classes places more demand upon students to organize themselves. After a high school schedule of five days a week from 8:30 A.M. to 3:00 P.M., the college schedule of 15 to 20 hours a week in class seems "a breeze." Knowing that the week has many free hours reduces any sense of urgency, and assignments may be all too easily postponed.

The independence demanded by college is too much for some students, even though they live at home. Those who live in dormitories may have still more difficulty. They need to contend with all-night bull sessions (often valuable, always interesting, but rarely substitutes for study), noisy roommates, and no one to remind them that work must be done. Some students thrive on such freedom; they work better and mature more than when closely supervised. Others simply cannot manage this much freedom.

Continuing the search for identity

In Chapter 8 we stated that the adolescent wishes to answer the question "Who am I?" He wants to find his identity. This desire continues into the college years. Although most entering freshmen have read a great deal about college, have talked to college students, and have probably visited the campus, they cannot fully comprehend the meaning of being a college student until they actually become one.

In high school, the senior is high man on the totem pole. He knows his way around, has many friends, and is probably proud of his status as a future high school graduate. Three months later, as a college freshman, he is low man on the totem pole. He is new and does not know his way around, and he will probably not be especially proud of his freshman status.

Perhaps more important, he does not know exactly how to act. He wants to behave like a college student, to have an identity as a college student, but he is a little unsure of what this means. The author had the following experience as a freshman:

> During high school, I had learned to smoke a pipe, and I rather fancied myself with it. I had a few sieges with upset stomachs, but those were all in the past, and the girls I dated in high school seemed to admire my pipe. Knowing that college men smoked pipes, I was puffing around campus during my first week, rather pleased that I was able to present such a mature and scholarly picture: Young Man With Pipe. Then, at the Coffee Shop one evening, I overheard one of the older and well-respected students, a veteran just out of the navy, comment to his friend, "You know, you can always spot a freshman—they're the ones who smoke pipes." And they both laughed. I packed my pipes and tobacco away that evening and did not dig them up again for two years, when I was secure enough in my status not to fear being considered a freshman.

The author was extremely deflated to learn that what he thought was mature, typical-college-student behavior merely marked him off as a naive, young freshman. His identity as a college student had not yet been established. Each freshman, whether he enters college at 17 or 47, must learn for himself what it is to be a college student.

At the same time, college studies may open new and exciting, sometimes frightening, avenues for consideration. What is your relationship to God? To the universe? To nature? To other human beings? Who are *you* in relation to these phenomena? Here again the problem of identity becomes important. These are problems that cannot be answered in a lecture or through a textbook, but only through living and thinking and feeling and experiencing. These words may seem strange and confusing. What do you think they mean? How do they apply to you?

Dealing with new social relationships

High schools draw students from the surrounding community; thus students at any particular high school are likely to share common interests and backgrounds, especially in urban and suburban communities, where large areas of similarly priced homes are found. Friendships and dates are drawn primarily from members of the same race, social class, religion, and financial grouping.

Attending college often changes these circumstances. College students usually represent a wide variety of races, religions, social classes, and even foreign countries, so that any one student has an excellent opportunity to meet others from diverse backgrounds.

Some students have difficulty in being with others whose backgrounds are different and whose behavior may, therefore, not be so predictable. They may feel socially inadequate or fearful of making blunders; so they avoid stress by returning to more comfortable ground—in a sense, they are unable to establish their identity as college students.

> Mel Peterson lived within twenty minutes drive of a good state college, and he decided to enter there, along with many of his old friends. However, Mel felt lost among the 14,000 students attending; to get a date he returned to his old high school, where he felt more comfortable. Being a college student gave him new prestige, and he was soon dating the most popular cheer leader on the squad. The next year she also entered State, where she quickly started dating the men on the football team, so Mel returned to his high school again. This continued for four years, until all Mel's prestige and glamor wore off, and he gained a reputation as a person who could not make the grade with college girls.

Mel's behavior was obviously not in response to growth motives. He lacked self-esteem and feelings of security. Little growth can occur in a person who does nothing but repeat over and over again his earlier experience.

The college student needs to gain a sense of identity as a student both in on-campus relationships and off-campus relationships. Many parents and friends, less familiar with the actual situation at colleges, may have inaccurate perceptions of college students, and students find themselves treated in terms of stereotypes that may be upsetting and discouraging. For example:

> *Spoiled.* "Kids in my day didn't have it so good. College kids today got it easy. Easy life, good job, lots of money. They don't know what real work is."
>
> *Wild.* "Boy, the things I've heard about you college people— Wow!! I was just reading where every college man has at least two girls just aching for loving."
>
> *Snobbish.* "You guys aren't as good as you think you are. You're no better than anyone else; so don't put on airs with me."
>
> *Brilliant.* "I know how hard you have to study to stay in college. You must be real brilliant."
>
> *Bohemian.* "All you college guys with beards and those girls with long hair and no make-up. Nothing but oddballs."
>
> *Rich.* "I guess you have to have real money to go to college."
>
> *Radical.* "You guys are mostly Commies, aren't you? Always yelling about peace and equal rights and stuff."

Only when a student is secure in his identity as a college student can he interact effectively with those who maintain these pictures-in-the-mind regarding college students. Although the new social relationships on campus can be somewhat difficult at first, they eventually become more satisfying and allow for more personal growth and maturity.

Responsibility to contribute to the dialogue

Communication in education should be a two-way street. Not only does the instructor send information to the student, but the student has a responsibility for active participation and response. You might say that education should be a dialogue, not a monologue.

One example is active participation in the classroom. In some classes this may consist only of active listening; other courses will demand participation in group discussions, laboratory work, field trips, and oral presentations. From time to time, a student will want to use class time to mention a personal experience, ask a question, request clarification, or refer to some recent reading he has done. He may want to pursue some issue after class. These are all part of the dialogue.

Some students ask whether disagreeing with the instructor can be part of the dialogue. The answer must be "Yes and no." A dialogue assumes that each has something meaningful to contribute, and when a student disagrees with his professor in a calm, intelligent manner, he may precipi-

Figure 9–5. Informal conversation among students and faculty members can be an important part of the educational dialogue. Courtesy Antioch College News Bureau. Photograph by Axel Bahnson.

tate a significant discussion or even a healthy argument. In education, no source or authority is the absolute final word—we can have only relative degrees of certainty about most matters. Presumably the professor and the textbook should provide more accurate information than the students, but new information or different interpretations of old information are sometimes better known by a student from other available sources. However, the dialogue is not enhanced by argument for the sake of argument, prolonged insistence upon a point, or disagreement without adding anything new.

No comment or question that a student offers, with thought and sincerity, in class can be termed "stupid." Students may fear that asking a question will expose them as ignorant, but the professor usually welcomes the question, because it signifies to him that he has not done an adequate job of explaining the material. How do you think the instructor of this class feels about questions from students?

The academic dialogue does not cease when the class period ends, nor even when college graduation occurs. It should be a constant and continu-

"So you see, my opinions on the stock market were not
derived entirely from books."

Figure 9–6. Students need to recognize that even experts do not always agree.
Courtesy Ed Fisher.

ing process. Learning occurs on campus and off campus, during the
college years and later. Personal growth and vocational success both
depend upon a constant questioning of the old ways and investigation of
new ways.

Cheating

You cannot hold a real telephone conversation with a recording on the
other end of the line, and you cannot maintain a true academic dialogue
when there is cheating on one end of the line. Surveys, nonetheless,
indicate that nearly half of all students *admit* having cheated during their
college careers, although cheaters still end up with lower grades than
noncheaters (Goldsen et al., 1960).

Students at one large state university in the Southwest went so far as to
hire a professional safecracker to get an examination from the trunk of a
professor's car, then rented out copies for five dollars an hour. Their
ingenuity netted them a good income but few friends, since the professor
noted that his car had been tampered with, figured out that a copy of the
exam was missing, and made a last-minute switch.

Students generally do not respect cheaters, and they will become furious if a congressman receives special privileges or if a businessman bribes a police officer to avoid a drunk driving charge. However, the same students seem afraid to expose cheating on campus or even to bring pressure against the cheater by criticizing him. Yet the person who says nothing and does nothing about others who cheat may seem to be offering his silent approval. How do you feel about students who cheat? Why do they do it? Would you ever inform on another student? Would you ever tell a cheater that you disapprove of his behavior?

College success: What is it? What produces it?

What is success in college? Is it getting high grades? Getting a degree? Learning about the world? Receiving effective job skills? Getting married? The answer obviously varies from person to person, but it is important to keep in mind that the individual student's definition of success shapes his motivation and behavior.

When the term "college success" is used in this book, it will refer to learning as measured by grades and the receipt of a degree, although the author realizes the shortcomings of such an approach. What is your measure of college success?

College success has increased in importance as more and more people receive degrees; as a result, the individual with no college at all is now at a definite disadvantage in getting a good job and may even be considered less desirable as a husband or wife. Research has shown that a college education is seen as "acquiring greater self-esteem and a feeling of personal power. Not acquiring an education is perceived as being quite a deflating experience" (Sinnett and Stone, 1964).

Grades and graduation: an international comparison

Grades as measures of college achievement do not have the same meaning in all countries. In some European universities, grades are not given. Instead, students must pass lengthy, two- or three-day oral and written examinations to receive their diplomas. If the student fails these exams, which cover his entire course of study, he must wait six months or a year to try again.

In Japan, on the other hand, high school students are under tremendous pressure to get into good universities—much greater pressure than students in the United States. However, once they have been accepted, they worry less about grades, since almost no one leaves college because of low grades. College graduation occurs when the student has passed all his required courses and the necessary number of electives. If he fails a few courses along the way, no one cares much.

"I think the American university system is cruel. It forces so much competition that students come to dislike each other. Our Japanese system is much better—students do not need to be afraid they will have to leave the university. When they have learned enough, they receive their degree. In America, if I take a very difficult course and get a D, the grade hurts my record, and no one cares if I learned anything from the course—it would have been better if I had not taken it. But in Japan, no one cares that I get a D, and I may learn a great deal."

In spite of her complaints, however, this Japanese student admitted that American university students study harder than Japanese students (although she felt Japanese high school students studied harder than Americans in order to get into college).

Each of these three systems, the American, the European, and the Japanese, has a method of determining the amount a student has learned in order to decide whether he deserves a diploma. Which system do you feel uses the most valid measurement system? How much tension is produced by each system?

Factors in college success

What enables one student to succeed in college, while another *with equal potential* does not succeed? Part of the answer we have already discussed—the ability of the student to handle the new freedoms, responsibilities, and relationships he finds in college.

The best *single* method of predicting success in college is to examine high school performance (McCormick and Asher, 1964; Reiter, 1964), since the tasks to be accomplished in college are similar to those in high school. The second best single method of prediction is achievement on tests of academic ability (Reiter, 1964). The relationship between academic aptitude and college success is not, however, a simple one. Other factors, such as personality, attitudes, study methods, and goals, interact in a dynamic fashion to affect college success.

Personality. Much effort has been spent trying to learn whether successful students and unsuccessful students each show different personality characteristics. Results of research indicate that the successful student is more self-confident, more mature, more dependable, better able to overcome his personal problems, more efficient, and more realistic in his future goals (Taylor, 1964). He is also more ambitious and shows greater curiosity but places less importance on social relationships (Gebhart and Hoyt, 1958). In addition, his need for achievement is higher (Reiter, 1964).

Personal adjustment problems reduce a student's study effectiveness, and the success or failure of poorly adjusted students often depends more upon the method they use to deal with their personal problems than upon their actual academic aptitude (Malnig, 1964). In general, a positive self-concept leads to increased probability of academic success.

Attitudes. The student who shares the likes and dislikes of college students in general and who enjoys behaving as college students are expected to behave also tends to do well in college (Armour, 1954). Attitudes toward study and toward college are also related to college performance, better students having more positive attitudes (Brown and Holtzman, 1955).

Study methods. The use of good study methods, although apparently less important than attitudes toward college, is definitely related to college success (Brown and Holtzman, 1955). The application of the SQ3R method (see pp.473-479), for example, was shown to benefit a large proportion of students who used it seriously, and it helped the better students more than it did the poor students (Robinson, 1961). Numerous studies have verified that students enrolled in study methods courses do better than comparable students who did not enroll (Kalish, 1959; Robinson, 1961).

College goals and motivation. Why are you in college? Do you really know? Students who have a goal in college seem to do better than those who do not (Wrenn and Crandall, 1941). Furthermore, the student preparing to enter the occupation of his own choice does better than the student who expects to work in a field about which he is less enthusiastic (Weigand, 1953).

As the survey cited on page 183 indicated, goals are not limited to vocational preparation. They may involve searching for identity or being a better citizen or trying to satisfy needs for self-actualization. However, the person with no goals at all has no real motivation to succeed. As one wise Indian philosopher said, "If you don't know where you are going, any road will take you there." Do you know where you are going?

Even having a goal does not ensure college success. Sometimes students accept the goals their parents or others have set for them, without considering whether the goals fit them as individuals. Often these students have taken their goals for granted for so long that the very thought of an alternative is ignored. If the imposed goal fits the student's interests and abilities, the path to success is made easier; if, as often happens, the imposed goals reflect the parents' values without any consideration for the student's unique characteristics, motivation is likely to be poor, and future success and happiness are dubious.

A second reason that goals may impede, rather than aid, college success is that certain students feel their goals are not best attained through college. Whether they are right or wrong in this feeling, the important fact is that they feel it.

> Susan Clay had wanted to be an actress since she was a young child, although her parents had planned college for her. When she entered a junior college near her Los Angeles home, she enjoyed her courses but could not concentrate upon them. However, she did work part-time to pay for private acting lessons and had no trouble concentrating on these. She eventually dropped out of college and devoted all her attention to acting, singing, and dancing studies—which demanded more time and effort than most students put in at college.

Sue was more fortunate than most, since she eventually got a few bit parts in television and—after three years of hard work and study—an occasional major role. College did not give her the feeling that she was making the most of her talents, but her private lessons did. Success in television gave her a great sense of fulfillment.

Susan Clay had **long-range goals,** and she was willing to work hard to achieve them. Her present success, she feels, is just a stepping stone to the long-range goal of being a highly respected actress. College also requires the ability to work for long-range goals. Otherwise the temptation to get a full-time job and leave college altogether becomes too great.

When the goals of students from the United States were compared with those from nine other countries, the Americans were found to be very frank and cooperative, more self-centered, more anxious to get money and material goods, less concerned with the welfare of their country and the rest of the world, and less likely to have pioneer spirit (Gillespie and Allport, 1955). This study was conducted several years ago. Do you think American college students have changed since then? What effect would such student goals have upon the country itself?

Personality, attitudes, study methods, and goals are not isolated factors, but part of a total picture. Good study methods seldom occur in conjunction with poor attitudes; students very highly motivated by safety and security needs may have difficulty concentrating on their studies. Success in college is the result of a combination of intellectual and personal elements.

Sex behavior in college

Dr. Alfred Kinsey published his famous reports on the sex behavior of Americans almost two decades ago, but a continuing and highly emotional debate has been raging around these books ever since (Kinsey et al., 1948, 1953). Although his statistics are open to criticism, they appear to be reasonably accurate and have been found similar to those resulting from other studies. After reading the following paragraphs, you can decide whether student behavior has changed since Kinsey's books were written.

Although some people believe college students are highly immoral, Kinsey found their sex experiences more limited than those of the non-college population. People from the middle class, which includes most college students, were less likely to have been sexually intimate outside of marriage than those from the lower class.

Almost all college students had kissed and necked at one time or another, many doing so on numerous occasions. Petting (involving the breasts or genitals) is less common, but over nine out of ten college men and women had done some petting by their twentieth birthday, about one-third reaching complete sexual release through orgasm in this fashion.

In many instances, necking and petting do not lead to intercourse but consume enough time and allow enough excitement so that intercourse does not take place. Rather than hazard the risks of sexual intercourse, college men frequently indulge in mild love-making, then receive release through masturbation at a later time. Although some people still believe masturbation leads to mental illness, no evidence exists for this assumption, except that guilt arising from fears over masturbation can be emotionally disturbing. Middle-class parents often accept masturbation as a way of keeping their sons from intercourse, but lower-class people consider it both foolish and dirty. Almost all boys and many girls use masturbation as a form of sexual release, so that it hardly can be considered strange or unnatural, and its use is especially frequent among college students.

A form of sexual release common among adolescents is the sexual dream. In these cases, the sleeper will dream about sexual activity. The manifest content (what you "see") may or may not be sexual, but the latent content (what the dream represents) will be. (See page 58 .) During the dream, he (and it is usually the male) will have an orgasm, which may or may not wake him up. Such an experience may be very distressing to adolescents not aware of what is happening, but college students are accustomed to these dreams and cease to be bothered by them, since they realize the dreams are normal.

Homosexual and other deviant relationships occur more often than is usually realized, although most of those reporting homosexual experiences were involved only in isolated incidents. About 10 percent of the adult men had maintained homosexual behavior over an extended period of time (Kinsey et al., 1948).

Some people claim that Kinsey's data were highly exaggerated, while others contend that the sexual involvement of today's college students exceeds Kinsey's figures. In either case, college produces a new set of responsibilities and freedoms in regard to sex behavior.

New freedoms and new responsibilities

Less parental supervision and more flexible time demands give the college student increased freedom for social life and dating—and, inevitably, for sexual relationships. His (and her) concept of the role of a college student may also encourage a freer attitude toward sex behavior. College freshmen are no longer as sexually innocent as they were (or as others liked to think they were) 50 years ago. Although they participate less in sexual intercourse than nonstudents the same age (Kinsey et al., 1948, 1953), they are aware of what occurs in the world around them. If television shows and high school reading lists are sometimes censored, the daily newspaper, popular monthly magazines, and bull sessions are not. With the increased freedom and increased awareness comes an increased need to understand the consequences of what he is doing and to be willing to accept responsibility for what is done.

There are many types of sex behavior. A mature and complete sexual relationship between two people who love each other is one type; a group of eighth-graders giggling at a bunch of obscene postcards is another. A world of difference stands between these two kinds of behavior. Sex behavior may satisfy growth motives, or it may satisfy only deficiency motives.

> John Small entered my office rather timidly and asked if he might talk with me a few minutes. After much embarrassment and hesitation, he finally got to the point. John had begun dating only a year earlier; he was fairly popular with the girls, although very shy in his dating behavior. Many of the other fellows had talked freely of their sex experiences, and John had begun thinking something was wrong with him for never having had any.
>
> Now, the middle of his first semester, he had reached a point with a girl he had been dating that he felt he could "go further" than kissing, but he did not know whether he should. He did not ask his sister or his parents, although he was close to them,

because he knew they would merely say "No" and not wish to talk about it. John did not want an answer—he wanted an opportunity to discuss. For over an hour that afternoon, he calmly discussed his feelings about sex in general and his behavior with the girl in particular. At the end of the discussion, he had not made up his mind, although he had explored most of the pros and cons.

A month later he returned. He told me he did not really know what he was going to do until the moment came. He suddenly realized that he did not wish to "go further." He had thought so much about it, not because of his own desires, but because he wanted something to tell the other fellows. His opportunity to discuss his problem with me freed him from behavior that would have caused him embarrassment and guilt for the sake of status in his group.

Not all students have the insight and maturity that John showed, but he had reached the point in his life where any such decision he made had to be his own—others could no longer make decisions for him.

Sex can be used to deepen and enrich a happy marriage, or to degrade a human relationship as one person uses sex to exploit the other. Sex can bring pleasure, satisfaction, even fun, or it can bring guilt, fear, and anxiety.

Each individual has internalized values regarding sex. Beginning with toilet training and modesty training, children are taught to keep the genital area private and clean, touched as little as possible. When they are mature enough to understand, they learn that sex without love and affection is not appropriate. Although many were fortunate in internalizing the value that sex in marriage was to be enjoyed, others had early learning experiences and faced parental and community attitudes that made difficult any sort of later sexual enjoyment without ensuing guilt and anxiety.

Other cultures differ from ours in their sexual attitudes. Some restrict sex so effectively that even sex in marriage is not enjoyed. Others teach that sex is a basic part of affection. Still others restrict nonmarital sex officially but allow it to occur unofficially: "Don't do it, but if you do it, don't get caught." And a number of cultures allow premarital sex to occur with little objection but demand complete faithfulness in marriage (Ford and Beach, 1952; Murdock, 1957).

Nonetheless, behavior in other cultures does not determine appropriate behavior for our culture. There are people who contend that complete sexual freedom would improve mental health. However, many circumstances having no relationship to sex contribute to our emotional problems, e.g., intense competition, need for status, social role uncertainty, desire for material possessions. There is no sufficient evidence that Americans would suddenly become mentally healthier if they became sexually free (Ausubel, 1954).

The major problem is undoubtedly the conflict that arises between (a) the values we have internalized and the religious and legal pressures, all of which demand that we avoid sex outside of marriage, and (b) the constant barrage of stimuli from movies, publications, conversation, and just plain knowing what is going on, all of which suggest "Have fun—do it now." This conflict, however, is part of the world we live in, and each person must work out the most effective way that he, as an individual, can adjust to the dilemma.

Those who cannot cope with their sex conflicts may have difficulties which originally arose from other sources such as (1) inadequate parent-child relationships, (2) poor marriage relationships between parents, (3) poor family attitudes toward sex, (4) personality adjustment problems, (5) insufficient social learning opportunities, (6) misleading sex education, and (7) extremely disturbing childhood or early-adolescent sex experiences. Such occurrences can lead to inadequacy in later sex relationships. Strangely enough, feelings of sexual inadequacy can lead both to withdrawal from sex relationships *and* to unusually strong desires for sex relationships. The person who is not secure in his own sexual adequacy often feels the need for sexual exploits to prove to himself and others that he is adequate.

The "new" college sex morality. Is there a "new" college student code of morals? Some experts and many students claim there is. They believe that sex relationships on college campuses are increasing. Others claim that the actual behavior has not changed, but the attitudes and values have changed. A third group claims that neither behavior nor attitudes have changed, but people are just talking more about them.

What are some of the specific claims?

> (1) College men used to have their sex relationships with women they did not respect, such as prostitutes, off-campus girls, and an occasional coed with a bad reputation. Now their relationships are with women students whom they do respect.

> (2) College men are no longer as likely to wish their future wives to be without sexual experience. (Remember, these are only claims.)

> (3) College students feel they live in an impersonal world, attend an impersonal campus, and must find needed security

through both sex and affection with a student of the opposite sex.

(4) The consciences of college women are not so strong. They do not feel so guilty about participating in sex behavior.

(5) College women are more willing to discuss their sexual activities. Years ago, college girls would only reluctantly discuss having kissed a boy. Today they discuss with other girls, and occasionally with boys, much more intimate relationships.

(6) College women today worry less about gaining a bad reputation if they are known to have had sexual intimacies, especially intimacies with boys they believed at the time they loved.

(7) Promiscuity is frowned upon, but not sex relationships that can be justified by affection.

Is this picture accurate? If so, it means, among other things, that factors inhibiting sex behavior are disappearing, which may well lead to an increase in sexual intimacies on college campuses. We may then ask whether college students are setting the pace for the rest of the country, following what others have set, or behaving relatively independently of what others are doing.

Opposing the idea of sex behavior change among students, a recent study concludes that most college girls have never been sexually intimate and that they intend to restrict any premarital relationships to their future husband. According to this study, the sex behavior of college women has changed little over the past 20 years, but willingness to discuss sex values has become greater (Freedman, 1965).

The truth is that we do not know whether the sex behavior of college students has actually changed, since the evidence conflicts. Based on your own observations and comments you hear, what conclusions would you offer?

Sex behavior: reasons and justifications. Students justify their sexual activities in many ways. These include the belief that sex experience before marriage is an advantage for the marriage; the feeling that love is enough reason for sex, even without marriage; the desire to gain security by receiving physical as well as emotional closeness; the enjoyment of pure physical pleasure; the attempt to hold on to a relationship through sex when it cannot be held together in other ways; the belief that prestige or daring is gained through sex; and "everybody does it—why not me?" An additional reason, although rarely expressed or even consciously felt, is the desire to punish parents. The student is, in a sense, saying to his parents, "I know how much it would hurt you to know what I am doing. I have so much power over you now to hurt you."

The reasons opposing sex relationships outside of marriage are also many. They include the possibility of pregnancy (which occurs even when preventive measures are used); the possibility of gaining a bad reputation; the fact that many men, in spite of their willingness to "make out," still wish to marry a girl they consider "pure"; the fear that sex can lead to a one-sided relationship, the girl perhaps loving the boy and finding only sex can hold him; the danger of drifting into a marriage neither wants; and the obvious fact that religious beliefs and the law both oppose such relationships.

From a psychological point of view, one additional problem in nonmarital sex is important. A great deal of **guilt** and **anxiety** can develop, not only for the girl but also for the boy. Whatever our present beliefs, almost all of us have been raised in an environment that condemned nonmarital sex, and we have internalized these values. Participating in a sex relationship, even though we may find many ways to justify it, still opposes the values we internalized as a child and is very likely to arouse strong guilt feelings. Not only does each person feel guilt for what he has done, but he may feel doubly guilty for the fear and anxiety he has caused his partner.

> Rick Kelley and Brenda Taylor met during their freshman year, and were soon deeply involved. A complete sexual relationship seemed quite natural, and—within a few weeks—they were making love regularly at Brenda's home, while both her parents worked. After eight months, they realized they had no intention of marrying each other—their love now seemed like infatuation, and they calmly and rationally decided to cut abruptly. On the surface, it seemed to be a good example of trying something out, then quitting before it was too late.

> But it was too late. Rick and Brenda had planned their course schedule to take classes together, and they saw each other several times a week. Also, because of mutual friends, they continued meeting at parties. Each began to feel guilty about taking part in a relationship that, as they looked back, was not based on love but on physical appeal. They made nasty comments about each other, behind each other's back; then the whole thing erupted in a vicious argument when Rick criticized Brenda's present steady to her face.

> They made life miserable for each other. Each felt the other had been the cause of the sex, and each resented the other. At the same time, each recognized his own role and felt guilty. This continued for an entire semester. Then Brenda, her grades now very low, decided she had to drop out of school.

During the relationship, guilt had seemed impossible. Even their breaking up was done without anger. Everything seemed calm and sensible. But Rick and Brenda lived in a culture where their behavior was disapproved not only by others but, unconsciously, by themselves. A few months later Brenda married a much older man with two divorces behind him. This inappropriate marriage was partly due to Brenda's confusion after breaking up with Rick.

It would be an obvious exaggeration to insist that every sexual relationship ends in tragedy. It would not be an exaggeration to state that things happen that the couple cannot anticipate and that affairs with tragic endings often have had apparently sensible beginnings. Too many people are confident that pregnancy, venereal disease, or reputation loss will not occur; they overlook the more dangerous problems of guilt, anxiety, and remorse. In the final analysis, sex behavior, like all behavior, is the responsibility of the individual.

SUMMARY OF IMPORTANT IDEAS

1. One definition of "college" is "a community of scholars, coming together to share their learning and to try to learn more."

2. For any given individual, learning can be active and exciting, or it can be passive and boring.

3. College students believe their education to be very important, both for personal and for vocational reasons; their parents emphasize the vocational aspects of college education.

4. College requires the student to take more responsibility for his own behavior; he has relatively little supervision in college.

5. College offers new social relationships.

6. The educational dialogue must occur between instructor and student and not be merely a monologue from instructor to student.

7. The definition of success in college varies with the individual.

8. High school performance is a reasonably good predictor of college performance; personality, attitudes, study methods, and goals are all factors in college achievement.

9. College student sex activity, although extensive, is probably less extensive than that of nonstudents of comparable age.

10. The new freedom allowed in college demands new willingness to accept responsibility for sex behavior.

11. Sex can be used to deepen and enrich or to degrade and exploit.

12. Allowable sex behavior differs from culture to culture, but people living in Western society must deal with Western values and restrictions.

13. There are claims that college students today have created a new morality.

Courtship and marriage 10

The period between 18 and 21 is often a transitional time for American youth. In past centuries this transition may have come earlier, but demands for both vocational and personal competence have extended the time of dependence upon parental and school authority. During this brief period the adolescent becomes an adult in the eyes of the law, either by turning 21 or by getting married. In either case, since the responses toward him of those in his environment tend to mirror the legal definition, he is labeled "of legal age" and "mature." He is forced to make decisions for himself that had always been left to others, and none of these decisions is more important than those relating to marriage.

Throughout the history of the world, thoughtful parents have taken great pains to see to it that their children enter into appropriate marriages. So concerned were most of the parents that they would never dare leave the decisions to their children; the parents themselves made these vital arrangements. The parents, of course, desired to find someone their child could like or even come to love, but family finances, family reputation, social class, religion, and various forms of bride payment or dowry were the deciding factors.

Even today, in many parts of the world, marriages are arranged by parents, often without either member of the couple having much to say. Committing a child to marriage shortly after his birth or sending a female child to her husband just after puberty were also widely practiced until recently. Child marriages, for example, were not outlawed in Nepal until 1963 (Rowse, 1964).

Although Americans are frequently upset when they hear of arranged marriages, our own high divorce rate has been used by other nations as evidence that marrying primarily for love is not successful in the long run.

Marriage and divorce are matters of immediate concern to every high school graduate. Today, more than half the girls in this country are married before their twenty-first birthday (*Information Please Almanac*, 1966); more girls are married for the first time between their eighteenth and nineteenth birthday than during any other year (Havighurst et al., 1962). One-half of American men are married by the age of 23 (*Information Please Almanac*, 1966). Thus, almost every college student has seen some of his personal friends marry—and perhaps divorce.

Courtship and engagement

The term "courtship" is commonly associated with that period between the beginning of serious dating and either breaking up, engagement, or the wedding. For our purposes, we will consider courtship as meaning the same as serious dating.

Purposes of courtship

The major purpose of courtship is for two people to get to know each other well enough to decide whether they wish to marry. If they decide they like each other and the general situation well enough, they become engaged. If not, they can break off, which, as painful and embarrassing as it can be, is still far better than breaking an engagement and infinitely better than breaking a marriage. The following is such an example:

Evan Mann matured later than most of his friends and rarely dated until his senior year in high school. In the middle of his freshman year in college, he started going steady with Toni Bailes, a very attractive girl who was a senior at a local high school.

They dated with increasing frequency for four months, and although Evan tried feebly to break up on two occasions, he always called Toni again. Suddenly Toni's parents began to talk about marriage, and the first thing Evan knew, he had proposed and had been accepted. Toni's father was going to take him into the retail clothing chain he owned, and Evan's parents were pleased with his opportunities. The wedding was set for the Christmas holidays during Evan's second year of college, by which point Toni would have finished enough secretarial school to get a job and support Evan through the remainder of college.

Evan had persuaded himself that he loved Toni completely; Toni knew she did not love Evan, but realized he would be an honest, faithful, hard-working husband, and she was not at all sure she could ever really "love" anyone. When Evan's mother became ill, he decided to transfer back to the community college in his home town. At first he missed Toni tremendously, and would hitchhike to see her three or four times a month. Slowly, however, it dawned on him that, when he thought of Toni, he thought of sex, not affection. He began to notice other girls on campus and saw a couple for informal afternoon coffee dates.

Just five days before the wedding, Evan wired Toni to cancel everything; he then wrote a long letter explaining that he could not marry her, and he willingly took the blame himself. Toni was at first heartbroken and embarrassed, then understandably bitter. Most of their mutual friends sided with Toni, and Evan faced great hostility when he returned for a final visit. However, all the unhappiness was slight compared to what would have occurred had Evan allowed himself to be drawn into a marriage he knew he did not want.

The courtship period may begin with the couple still playing games: both trying to impress each other, playing hard-to-get, trying to read deep meaning into harmless statements, hoping for flattery, and being on best behavior. Each is interested in the other but wants signs of returned interest and affection for assurance that the interest is mutual. (For an amusing and enlightening discussion, see *Games People Play*, by Eric Berne, 1964.)

As courtship continues, the couple usually become more relaxed with each other. Instead of the formal dating relationship, they spend a lot of time together informally. They do not ignore each other's feelings, but they behave with each other more as they behave in their parents' home and more as they will behave in their own future home.

Problems in courtship

One author has listed seven major causes of problems during engagement: (1) difficulty with families, (2) difficulty with friends, (3) conventions, such as manners and dress, (4) conflicting values, (5) the use of money, (6) religious differences, and (7) affection and sex (Merrill, 1959).

Difficulty with families. "I'm marrying you—not your family." This statement is very true, but . . . Families come as part of the package, and the importance of the family to a marriage is great, even if all the relatives live a thousand miles away—or even if no relatives are still alive.

Couples can use the period of courtship to get to know one another's family, to spend time with them, and to learn to adjust to their habits and manners. It is definitely not the proper role of the younger person to try to change his future in-laws' political beliefs, religious philosophy, or automobile preferences. To build family hostility serves no purpose.

Parents will disapprove of a marriage for a variety of motives. Many parents become so attached to their children that they hate the idea of giving them up. Some parents need to have a child around who depends upon them so they feel they have a place in the world. Others have difficulty in accepting the fact that their child is mature enough to leave home. Still others have such high standards for their children—after all, the person your child marries reflects credit or discredit upon you as well —that no one can possibly be good enough. Sometimes parents object to religious, social-class, or nationality differences. Although parents try to think of the happiness of their children, the end result of their behavior does not necessarily promote that happiness.

However, parents can be correct. They can see the prospective mate more objectively. They know their child, and they may see trouble ahead. Particularly with teen-age courtship and engagement, parents are anxious to avoid letting anything become permanent too quickly. Our attitudes and aspirations at 18 often change by 22. Adults, having had more experience in judging people, may be better able to predict the future behavior of a 20-year-old than can other 20-year-olds. The boy who seems so romantic at 18 may be unable to hold a job at 30; the girl who is so lovely at 17 may be more worried about getting to the beauty parlor than to the grocery store after she is married. (And these are things "your best friend won't tell you.")

There is another excellent reason to learn about the family—after all, they are the significant figures in the life of the person you are going to marry. A perceptive boy will learn a great deal about his girl by seeing the way her parents treat each other, by observing for himself the social and religious values in her home, and by looking for important little things. Do the parents bicker? Is her younger brother totally undisciplined? Are the parents gossips? Is the home always noisy? These behavior patterns provide indications of what might be expected later from the daughter. The emotional climate of your childhood home cannot help but affect the later emotional climate of your adult home after marriage.

Difficulty with friends. In dating, the couple usually spends its time with the social group of the male, but courtship is a more permanent situation, and the woman may be more inclined to spend time with her friends as well. Since it is rare to meet anyone and like *all* his friends, it is rare that one member of an engaged couple does not dislike at least a few friends of his partner. Sometimes, rather than disliking any individual friend, the girl may resent her fiancé's spending so much time with "the boys," while he feels her girl friends are "just a bunch of gossips." These problems need to be dealt with early in the relationship.

Previous romances also intrude upon the couple. The newly engaged girl may be very jealous of all the dates her fiancé ever had, and his talking about them does not help matters, especially when the engagement is new and both are a little insecure in their new roles. Nor does it help for either one to describe all previous dating relationships "because I want to be honest with you."

Adjusting to conventions. Everyone has certain kinds of behavior that others might find difficult to accept on a long-term basis. Many of these actions are merely habits or manners and are so unimportant that they cannot interfere with an otherwise healthy relationship, but they can become a great annoyance far out of proportion to their real importance. For example:

> Claudia smokes two packs of filter cigarettes a day, and her fiancé cannot tolerate the smell of tobacco. He feels that, once married, she will give up smoking out of love for him.

> Mac likes to walk around the house in his undershirt. Frequently he will sit on the front porch or walk to the corner drugstore in his undershirt. His fiancée finds this very irritating.

> Jonathan's mother is an immaculate housekeeper, and Jon demands that everything be neatly in its place. He acts like a hurt little boy when things are not just so.

> Marlene puts her hair up in curlers right after supper, then reads until after midnight. Her fiancé cannot stand women with their hair in curlers. He argues that it is unfair for a husband to spend most of his life seeing his wife's bare scalp, so that she can look attractive for strangers on Friday and Saturday nights.

Courtship and engagement enable two people to learn each other's manners and habits and to determine whether the feelings of attraction are sufficient to overcome these irritations. Unfortunately, the effects of some such habits can often be understood only after marriage, at which point the couple must make the best possible adjustments.

Conflicting values. No two people have the exact same values, and two people may be happily married with very different values. When important values are in direct conflict, however, both the engagement and the eventual marriage have problems. If the man demands peace and quiet and the girl prefers noise and loud parties, their values conflict; if the girl insists upon owning a home and having a stable life while the man enjoys freedom from responsibility and wandering from town to town, their values conflict; if he favors leisure and she admires hard work and high achievement. . . .

The use of money. How important is money? How should money be spent? In courtship and engagement, there is more feeling that the money is jointly possessed. When it is spent, even though earned by the man, the girl feels *her* money is being spent. How much should be spent, how much should be saved, how much should be used as down payment on credit buying, and how much for inexpensive, used furniture? In our society, disagreements over money can become a major problem between an engaged couple or a husband and wife.

Religious differences. Church affiliation and religious values can create two major types of courtship problems. First, you feel yourself a member of a particular religious group and have a sense of loyalty to that group. Therefore, you are likely to prefer the person you marry to be part of the same group and to bring up your children similarly.

Second, as a member of a particular religious group, you tend to internalize the group's values, some of which may conflict with values of other groups, e.g., birth control, church attendance, eating habits, or religious education. Two people who differ widely on these and other matters might find religious values somewhat of a barrier to a satisfactory marriage.

Motives for interfaith dating and marriage vary widely. In some instances, the major motive is to defy parents or show independence; occasionally it seems easier to "make out" with a girl of another religion, perhaps because her parents are less likely to know your parents; some people find interfaith dating daring or exciting. However, the usual motives for interfaith dating are the same as the motives for any other dating.

As old community ties become weaker and more students attend college, especially college away from home, they are bound to meet those of different religions. Also the general behavior and values and mannerisms of Protestants, Catholics, and Jews are becoming more similar, and there is less to restrain their dating and subsequent marriage outside their religious group.

People often claim that those entering into interfaith marriages are neurotic or trying to throw over the values of their parents. More recent evidence, however, shows there is no difference in emotional health between those who had intermarried and those who had not (Sklare, 1964).

Many parents would accept interfaith dating if they did not fear interfaith marriage. Ironically, even parents who do not personally attend church or follow religious rituals may object vociferously if their children date outside the religious group. Some such feelings result from nothing more than prejudice. Many objections, however, come about because parents have developed a strong sense of identification or association with their own religious group, even if they do not follow its beliefs and rituals carefully. They wish their children to affiliate with the same group when they marry and especially when they bring up their own children.

At the same time parents want their children to be as happy and successful as possible in their marriage. Interfaith marriages have consistently higher divorce rates (e.g., Gordon, 1964), and you often hear the statement "Marriage is so difficult at best, why make it more difficult by marrying outside your own religion?" When religious values and habits are different, the relationship can lack an important basis for sharing. Students themselves indicate that marrying outside their religious group would be more difficult than marrying outside their educational, nationality, or economic group (Gordon, 1964).

Also, the general community may disapprove and bring pressure to bear. A member of one church may be embarrassed to tell her friends that her daughter has married a boy of another religion. Since parents recognize they are largely responsible for their children's values, it seems as though they had failed by not being able to keep the children in the fold.

In spite of these potential problems, of a sample of 5,400 college students drawn from 40 colleges across the country, only 8 percent would "break off at once" if they fell in love with someone of another faith, while nearly half would continue to date and another 20 percent would feel uncertain. Perhaps these reactions occurred because 40 percent of the students had already observed an intermarriage in the family, and only one in ten had never himself dated a person of another religion; one-third of the students implied that they dated people of other religions as often or more often than they did people of their own religion (Gordon, 1964).

Many factors relate to the success of interfaith couples: the intensity of their identification with their church group; the attitudes of their community and their friends; the acceptance by the families; and—probably the most important—the similarity in their values and beliefs.

Marriage can be compared to a rope consisting of many strands of different thicknesses. Each strand represents some quality joining a couple, for example, educational background, food preferences, enjoyment of travel, liking each other's family. Religion is one strand. If religion is important to either of the couple, that strand is very thick; if it is unimportant, the strand is thin. If the strand is cut (that is, if religion is not shared), the rope is that much weaker. Cutting a thick strand would obviously be more dangerous than cutting a thin strand. For some couples, the rope itself is very thick, and a severed strand is not important; for other couples, so little is shared that the marriage rope is thin. When pressure is applied to a thick rope, little happens; when pressure is applied to a weak rope, it pulls apart (adapted from personal communication with Dr. Abraham Stone).

In other words, if the marriage is basically good and religion is unimportant to the couple, interfaith marriage is no problem. If the marriage is not secure or if religion is very important, the marriage will pull apart more easily in an interfaith marriage. If the marriage does occur, certain hazards may be avoided by the husband and wife who show special respect for each other's beliefs.

After some couples marry, they drop away from organized religion altogether. Others work out a method by which each continues to attend his own church. Often one of the partners will convert to the religion of the other, perhaps through conviction but often for convenience. Over a period of years, however, the couple tend to drift toward one or the other religion, if an actual conversion does not occur, so that religious splits within marriages are usually not permanent (Lenski, 1961).

Sex and affection. A great deal is said in popular literature about sexual compatibility, perhaps so much that many people overestimate its value. While sexual compatibility is a great addition to a marriage, it has value only if the other elements are appropriate. (See Chapter 9 for additional discussion.)

When an unmarried couple decide to test their sexual compatibility before marriage, they may be fooling themselves. For many people the sexual act changes its significance so much after marriage that the premarital experience may have little relationship to later satisfaction. For example, a person who had internalized the value that premarital sexual intimacies are totally inappropriate may seem sexually cool before marriage, but very warm after the wedding when the fear and anxiety are reduced. On the other hand, some people find great excitement in an illicit sex relationship but do not respond physically to the long-range affection required in marriage.

Sexual enjoyment reaches its greatest moments within a marriage between two people who love each other. Yet, a good marriage can exist where sexual enjoyment is only moderate or even low. This author believes that people oversell the thrill of sex in marriage in an effort to persuade young people to avoid sex outside marriage. As a result, many young people are disappointed when they do begin their sex life, since it has been overemphasized.

Sex is only one way of expressing affection. A look of understanding, a touch on the arm, a smile, all express affection between man and woman. In a healthy engagement or marriage, these forms of affection are more common and, perhaps, more important than the strictly sexual side.

Love in courtship and marriage

Have you ever really loved someone in a man-woman relationship? How did you feel? What is love? Love is usually defined as a very great affection or a very great liking for a person or, sometimes, a thing. Love is an emotion or feeling that may be expressed through actual behavior or may, for many reasons, be kept unexpressed or even repressed. Healthy mutual love is likely to increase over the months and years and to help both parties grow as individuals *and* as a couple. It begins with mutual respect, a strong feeling of affection, the desire to be together, and the willingness to make more of yourself for the other person *and* to help the other person make more of himself as well. In order to lead to marriage, love should also include physical attraction, but physical attraction often grows from love.

Can everyone love? Some people claim not. They feel that those who were not themselves loved cannot feel love for others. It has also been said that you cannot love others unless you can accept yourself and trust others (Blood, 1955). These statements emphasize the importance of early experiences and relationships with other people, particularly significant figures. It is claimed that, if these experiences and relationships are unhappy, you may find it very difficult to enter into healthy mutual love later in life. Do you feel the above statements to be true? Why or why not?

In much popular fiction, in movies, on the television screen, you find a type of love called *romantic* love. The Rock Hudson-type or the Pat Boone-type meets the Doris Day-type or the Ann-Margret-type; they find themselves romantically, excitingly in love, and overcome great odds in order to marry. You put down the book or leave the theater or turn off the television with a warm, happy glow, feeling that if you are lucky, something like this might happen to you. Not only does this sort of romance rarely exist, but even when it does occur, it is seldom the sort of relationship that would last through 40 years of marriage.

The overly romantic is not the only sort of misguided love. Some people persuade themselves they are in love, when they merely seek to marry for money, for status, for security, or to get away from an unhappy home situation. People who wish to marry for these reasons will often rationalize their feelings as being love, since their self-concept would find it unacceptable to marry without love.

Courtship and engagement allow two people to get to know each other very well before entering into the permanent relationship of marriage. During this period, both people have the opportunity to anticipate many of the problems their marriage might entail, such as uncooperative relatives or highly irritating mannerisms, and evaluate these problems in light of their feelings for each other. In the United States, we expect people to love each other before becoming engaged and most certainly before marrying. Romance and sex appeal are occasionally one part of love, but they are not the same as love.

Marriage

Marriage, for most people, leads directly to the most important new human relationship of adult years. Only vocation can even begin to compete with the family in its impact upon a person's life. The success and stability of marriage influence the emotional health of all concerned, especially the children, and—as a result—influence the vitality of the entire country.

In the United States we believe that the goal of marriage is to make the two involved people happy—it should be a worthwhile, self-actualizing, enjoyable experience for the couple. Carrying on the family name or taking care of the parents in their old age or bringing a dowry are no longer important to most Americans. These values are quite different in other areas of the world. As a matter of fact, our belief that marriage should include only one husband and only one wife is far from universal. Among preliterate (or primitive) groups, the one-wife-one-husband (monogamous) arrangement is far less common than one allowing the husband several wives (Murdock, 1949).

Who marries whom?

What brings two people together so that they wish to marry? The immediate answer is *proximity*, i.e., they live or work or go to church or do something near each other, so that the chances are high that they will meet frequently and have the opportunity to get to know each other.

In addition to proximity, we find that husband and wife are similar to each other in numerous characteristics. These include race, religion, education, intelligence, social class, age, previous marital status (that is, divorced people tend to marry other divorced people), attitudes toward drinking, and the number of children desired (Berelson and Steiner, 1964). Husband and wife also have similar personality characteristics, although these relationships are not as consistent as those cited above. Similarities occur in excitability, social behavior, attitudes and values, tendency to become depressed, and tendency to withdraw (Smith, 1961). When people select the characteristics of an ideal mate, they select characteristics similar to their own (Prince and Baggaley, 1963). Thus, the old idea that opposites attract is certainly not upheld.

Among college students, women prefer to marry older men, and men prefer to marry younger women;* all the college women wanted to marry men with more or at least as much education as they had, while the men preferred the women to have about the same amount of education as they had themselves. College women wanted to marry when they were about 22 or 23, while men selected 24 and 25 as the best ages for marrying (Goldsen et al., 1960).

Early marriages are more frequently entered into by certain types of individuals. For example, school dropouts, less-intelligent girls, non-church-attenders, and teen-agers from broken homes were found more likely to marry early. In addition, the husbands of early marriages are less likely to have training and job skills and are more likely to have an

---

*What effect does this, in combination with the longer life expectancy of women, have upon the family structure in later years?

unstable work career (Havighurst et al., 1962). How will these factors affect the success of early marriages?

What makes marriages successful?

Successful marriage depends upon many factors, some of which are far from being understood. Nonetheless, research into this matter has been extensive, and we can predict with some success those marriages that will be happy and those that will be unhappy.

Background factors in happy marriages. Thirty years ago an outstanding psychologist found that many childhood experiences were related to later marital happiness. Although his findings will probably not surprise many readers, they are worth remembering since they are still accepted as valid today.

First, and in some ways most important, he learned that happily married people had happily married parents and a happy childhood. Thus we find that a good marriage produces emotionally stable children who, in turn, produce their own fulfilling marriage. Second, good relationships with parents produce later happy marriages. The person who was attached to his mother and father and did not have much conflict with them will make a better mate. Third, children who were disciplined firmly but not too harshly or too frequently were later able to have good marriages. Fourth, if parents were frank regarding sex and communicated healthy attitudes toward sex, their children seemed to be happier in marriage (Terman, 1938).

You have undoubtedly also heard that early marriages are less successful than later marriages. In one midwestern city, 40 percent of those who married before 21 wished they had waited, compared to less than 10 percent of those married after 21 (Inselberg, 1961). The early life of the individual and his age at marriage are definite factors in his marital success, yet they are certainly not insurmountable barriers.

Personality and self-concept. Marital happiness is greater when both husband and wife come from emotionally stable families and are themselves emotionally stable (Burgess and Cottrell, 1939; Lippmann, 1954). In addition to emotional stability, other personality characteristics have been found related to happy marriages: (1) consideration for others, (2) willingness to yield rather than demanding to dominate, (3) being a good companion, (4) having self-confidence, and (5) being able to accept emotional dependence (Burgess and Wallin, 1953), but not necessarily becoming so dependent that nothing matters except the relationship— after all, a good relationship should build people up, not reduce their effectiveness.

Personal maturity also improves the chances for marital success and happiness. The immature person is unable to make the necessary adjustments and is more likely to fail in marriage. The high rate of divorce in teen-age marriages is evidence for this.

People who accept themselves and admire their spouses are more happily married than those who have low esteem for themselves and their spouses. Lower marital satisfaction is found when one or both parties have a self-concept involving impatience, lacking self-respect, being distrustful, being unwilling to accept help, being uncooperative, lacking warmth, and being gloomy (Luckey, 1964a, 1964b). Whether or not these descriptions are accurate was not learned—the important matter was what the various individuals *felt* was accurate.

Similarity of attitudes, values, interests, and activities. Husband and wife need not share everything—indeed, there is merit in being apart from each other occasionally—but enjoying many of the same things can enrich a marriage. Liking the same movies, the same sports, or the same books adds a common bond; having similar religious, social, political, and child-rearing values produces the same effect.

It is interesting to note that not only do husbands and wives share political attitudes, but each assumes the other agrees with him more than the other actually does (Byrne and Blaylock, 1963). That is, husbands and wives overestimate the degree to which their spouses think as they do.

Needs and their satisfaction. Married couples may have similar psychological needs. However, it is more important that their needs be complementary, i.e., that the needs of each be satisfied by the other. Thus, if the husband has a need to be admired and the wife has a need to admire others, their needs are complementary. If the wife has a high need for achievement and the husband has a need to have an achieving wife, their needs are complementary. Good evidence exists that husbands and wives tend to have needs that are complementary (Winch, Ktsanes, and Ktsanes, 1954).

> Betty Williams was 30 years old before she married. She was attractive, intelligent, and popular, and few people could understand why she did not marry sooner, especially since she had had many proposals. Her husband, Marv, although pleasant-looking and of equal intelligence, did not share either her vivacious personality or her popularity. In addition, he had a lower income than her parents and most of her friends. Many of Betty's friends could not understand why she married Marv, since she had the opportunity to marry men with more money and status.

The answer can only be understood in terms of Betty's needs. Betty had no need for a talkative companion or for someone to keep up with a hectic social life. She enjoyed talking, and her husband enjoyed having a sociable wife. Also, Betty wanted a strong, dominating man like her father. Marv was strong to the point of being stubborn—so was Betty's father. Betty had a need for someone to understand her as a woman, not a social companion. Marv recognized her femininity and paid no attention to her surface bossiness which had dominated previous admirers. All in all, Marv and Betty satisfied each other's needs, so that the prediction of future success was good.

Women and men often do not want the same things from each other. Women show more need for love, affection, sympathy, and understanding; men have a greater need for a mate who will be neat and tidy, adjust to routine, and be even-tempered and dependable (Langhorne and Secord, 1955). Thus, the woman who needs affection and can be neat will probably be happiest with a man who needs neatness and can be affectionate, because they satisfy each other's needs.

Role behavior. Each person enters marriage with a self-concept, an ideal self, and an idea of how he expects his mate to behave. Happiness in marriage occurs when you behave as you expect to and your mate also behaves as you expected (Ort, 1950).

The role of the husband has traditionally been the dominant role. Throughout history, in most societies, men have been the warriors, while women have cared for the family. Even the God of the Judeo-Christian tradition is referred to as *He*, rather than She or It.

One author states that marital happiness is related to role behavior in three major ways. The marriage is happier when: (1) the husband's self-concept and ideal self are similar; (2) the husband's self-concept resembles his concept of his father; and (3) the wife looks upon the husband as being like *her* father (Tharp, 1963). Also, when the concept each partner has of himself corresponds to the concept the spouse has of him, the marriage is happier. Thus, in a happy marriage, the husband is the sort of person he wants to be; he has internalized the masculine role from his father; his wife has learned to judge the masculine role from *her* father and finds her husband lives up to her father; and both husband and wife have a self-concept consistent with the concept the other has of him. This, of course, is not to say that the previous conditions are *necessary* to marital success, but that they are helpful.

In the United States, our marital roles are relatively *egalitarian*. That means that the husband and wife share the power to make decisions and are considered fairly equal in the marriage. In most of the world, marriages are husband-dominated. College men are, perhaps understandably, less favorable than college women regarding egalitarian marriages (Kalish, Maloney, and Arkoff, 1966).

In spite of this *relative* egalitarianism, the American husband tends to make certain decisions, such as car buying and jobs; the wife tends to make certain decisions, such as food buying; and they share in some decisions, such as where to go on vacations and the sort of insurance to get (Blood, 1960). Each home has a division of labor. Wives usually are responsible for doing the dishes and the cooking; husbands take care of the lawn and home repairs. However, when the wife works, the husband must share some of the wife's tasks, and the wife finds that she has less time to help him with his (Blood, 1960).

Marital happiness not only depends upon how you feel your mate should behave, but also upon how your parents feel about marital role behavior. After World War II, many American men of Japanese ancestry returned to Hawaii with war brides from Japan. The mothers of these soldiers were very happy to see the Japanese girls, because they believed these girls would behave in the traditional Japanese young-wife role, which is to take care of her parents-in-law. The girls, however, thought more like American girls than did their in-laws, and they wanted the egalitarian marriage they knew existed in America. As a result of this and other factors, these marriages often produced frustration both for the Japanese brides and for their Japanese–American in-laws, since the *role expectancies* of both groups did not concur (Kimura, 1957).

To some extent, each person recreates in his marriage the marriage he lived with in his parents' home. He will behave much as the parent of his own sex behaved and will expect his mate to behave much as his other parent behaved.

> Marcia Sohn was the daughter of an aggressive woman who pushed her to "go with the right people" and "do the proper thing." Marcia's mother pushed her father also, until he was wealthy and terribly unhappy. Marcia swore to herself as a child that when she married she would never push her own husband to become wealthy. Marcia eventually married a very pleasant man who enjoyed building up his business. Marcia did not push him to become wealthy, but she did push him to become better educated. He tried, but he decided he did not like college. Unlike Marcia's father, her husband refused to be bullied beyond a certain point, and he suggested a divorce. The couple decided to see a marriage counselor, and through his help, Marcia realized that she had been repeating the same pushing pattern that her mother had shown, although she se-

lected education rather than money. The marriage has continued, and Marcia is slowly succeeding in breaking the pattern she had internalized from her own mother.

Obviously, the role behavior of children is not always the same as the parents. In some instances, it will be quite different or even apparently directly opposite. Nonetheless, children tend to behave much like their parents. Since we assume role behavior is learned, largely through **identification** and **internalization**, the behavior of parents becomes a vitally important influence upon the role behavior of their children.

Behavior in marriage

When two people enter into marriage, they usually have extremely fine ideals. The husband wants to

—take care of his wife,

—aid in her emotional development,

—give her what she needs for her welfare and happiness,

—have the satisfaction of fathering children (in most cases),

—maintain a home where he may live in a pleasant and relaxed state,

—obtain and give happiness and warmth through physical affection,

—create an atmosphere in which others care about him, and

—create an atmosphere leading to self-actualization and maturity of himself and others (adapted from English and Pearson, 1963).

The new wife also desires these ideals to be realized and has a comparable list of her own. In spite of everybody's good intentions, most newlyweds do not find adjusting to marriage easy, even when they know each other well, are well-suited to each other, and come from stable homes.

Adjustment problems often begin on the honeymoon, which is frequently not well planned to accomplish its actual purpose: allowing the couple to become accustomed to their new roles and to each other. In many cases, the honeymoon is too filled with activity for the couple to get to know each other, too tiring for them to relax with each other, and too expensive for them to enjoy without worry.

During the first several months of marriage, many unanticipated difficulties may occur, until the couple finally work out reasonably healthy life patterns. Love and a willingness to make an effort can help produce a successful marriage and encourage personal growth.

Real love and a good marriage do not make two people as one. Rather, they make two people more distinctly two by letting them become better individuals than they were before. (A mathematical physicist in California)

You should not marry until your love is so strong you feel that you just *have to* get married. Marriage should never be based on "might as well" or "I think it's okay," but on "I feel I must." (A recent divorcee in Ohio)

I don't know if I really loved my husband when we married, although I thought I did at the time, but I let myself love him over the years, and I know I do now. Love must have a chance to grow, no matter what it is to begin with. (A teacher in Illinois)

Try to imagine yourself getting out of bed every morning, only half awake, and sitting down at the breakfast table, and across the table is this face, looking like hell. If you can still love that face, that's love. (A hospital executive in Texas)

The saddest thing in the world is to see someone get married with the idea of making over the other person. They are unhappy if they succeed and unhappy if they fail. (An Air Force sergeant in South Dakota)

How can you contribute to making your marriage successful? A few of the many possible ways follow:

Recognizing the needs of the other. Two people who have spent a great deal of time together under a variety of conditions should know each other very well. Yet the marriage relationship demands a much greater understanding. The two lives are so intertwined, so interdependent, that there is a constant necessity to be aware of each other's needs. In a good marriage, each party becomes increasingly sensitive to the needs of the other, until—after a time—each can understand his partner's feelings, even without being told.

Learning to communicate. Sharing thoughts and feelings is important in marriage. The strong, silent type may be romantic before marriage, but he can be a frustrating husband. Some men feel that expressing their fears and hopes is a sign of weakness, but the opposite is actually the case, since a man must feel secure in his masculinity in order to be able to express his feelings.

Communication is important on a day-to-day basis. When a problem arises, it is useful to be able to sit down and talk it out. A new husband who feels his wife is flirting too much may be reluctant to mention it directly, so he displaces his anger by sulking in the corner or criticizing his wife's dress. If he has an inkling of an idea why he does this, he will be even more embarrassed to talk about it. However, if he and his wife can discuss the problem later, it will suddenly become no problem at all. When a married couple lack the ability to communicate with each other, they lack an important quality in providing marital stability and satisfaction.

Respecting privacy. At the same time that communication is important, so is the opportunity for privacy. Married couples have the right to keep certain thoughts and feelings to themselves. A husband need not mention that he was unpopular back in high school; a wife may prefer to remain silent when a brief visit with an old boy friend rekindles some flame. While each should encourage the other to talk freely about feelings and ideas, each should also respect the need of the other for privacy. Married people not only have the right to psychological privacy, but to physical privacy as well. The opportunity to be alone upon occasion is very important to many people.

Maintaining individuality. Marriage, as stated before, should not make two people into one but should make them more distinctly two. Married couples tend to share similar values, attitudes, behavior patterns, and styles of living, but this is no reason to apply pressure when similarity does not occur. The husband or wife who wishes to make the other over in his own image should marry a mirror instead of a human being.

Learning to compromise. The importance of compromise is stated so often that it may actually have become exaggerated. Some compromise is necessary, but we often learn that a little discussion and thinking will allow both husband and wife to have what they wish. For example, Wife wants to visit their parents, and Husband argues that they just spent ten days with Wife's parents and he does not have the money to make the trip again; however, instead of compromising, Wife agrees to visit parents when Husband is out of town on a business trip. Both get what they wish.

Being faithful. Faithfulness neither begins nor ends with the sex act. Our society expects sexual faithfulness in marriage, and extramarital relations can easily be disastrous to the future of the couple.

Faithfulness is not only a matter of sex. Teasing and flirting may be harmless, or they may be a type of unfaithfulness. The man or woman who gives all his attention to work, children, clubs, or hobbies, and none to his spouse is also breaking the faith upon which the marriage was based. Forgetting or ignoring the human relationship in marriage can be as psychologically damaging as sexual infidelity.

Expecting too much. In countries where marriages are arranged, the participants do not expect a great deal of companionship and affection from the marriage. The husband may expect his wife to maintain the home, care for the children, uphold the family reputation, be careful with his money, be pleasant to him, give some physical affection, and respect his family. The wife expects to be cared for, given an occasional luxury, receive kindness, and be allowed some pleasures.

In the United States, expectations are much greater. We not only anticipate all the above, but much more. Both husband and wife expect the other to be social companion, share common interests and values, participate together with mutual friends, be sexually exciting, and be intellectually stimulating. Expectations, often including impossibly romantic notions, are often greater than can possibly be met. Although husbands and wives in arranged marriages may receive less, they also expect less. Thus, less difference exists between achievement and aspiration, and frustrations are fewer. This factor, often overlooked in discussion of marital success and failure, is undoubtedly a vitally important variable.

Student Marriages

Married college students, almost unheard of before World War II, are now extremely common. If the husband and wife are sufficiently mature and the situation is appropriate, student marriages can actually lead to greater self-actualization and greater academic achievement.

One particular danger of student marriages, especially if both husband and wife are young, is that the husband, who usually continues in college, may become more intellectually aware and demanding, while his wife is too busy with her work and her household to have time for reading or studying. Many wives of students make a special effort to find time for keeping up with their husbands, but others are in possible danger of realizing too late that their spouse has drifted away.

Marriage is probably the most rewarding and the most demanding relationship during adult life. Research has shown that successful marriages can, to an extent, be predicted from a knowledge of background factors, childhood experiences, personality, attitudes, and needs of each member of the couple. Marital role and marital role expectations also influence the happiness of marriage. An awareness of the importance of certain types of behavior during the marriage itself may lead to the increased satisfaction of security, love, and esteem needs.

Divorce

Statistics show that divorces increased steadily from the beginning of this century until a few years after the end of World War II; since then, the divorce rate has dropped back to what it was in the very early 1940's. We hear many reasons for the high rate of divorce, but a high divorce rate may be inevitable in a culture that feels marriage is primarily for the happiness of the two people involved rather than to please their families. If marriage is primarily for the happiness of the partners, then unhappiness would logically lead to unmarriage.

Several factors are related to divorce. For example, divorces are more common among less-educated people, among children of divorced parents, among religiously mixed marriages, among nonchurchgoers, for those with brief engagements, and for those who did not know each other very long before the marriage (Berelson and Steiner, 1964; Merrill, 1959). Divorces are especially common among couples married when still in their teens—about six times as common, according to the Purdue Opinion Panel (cited in the *Los Angeles Times*, May 25, 1961). The high proportion of teen-age brides who are pregnant undoubtedly contributes to the teen-age divorce rate; one investigator learned that nearly half of the high school brides were pregnant on their wedding day (Inselberg, 1961).

The real picture of divorce, however, is not given through statistics, but by observing the individuals involved. Divorce is a sign of failure, and most divorced people seem to feel that they have failed in one of life's most important tasks, a satisfactory marriage.

Not only the divorced couple, but their children, are punished for whatever mistakes were made. These children face three difficult problems: first, the months leading up to a divorce are usually months of tension and family disruption; second, the process of the divorce is often upsetting for the children; and, third, it is difficult for the children to live with only one parent or with a step-parent and see the remaining parent irregularly.

It has long been debated whether the child is better off with his parents divorced or with parents who are unhappily married. The dispute cannot be settled, except for individual cases. One child may be better off living with only one parent, because family arguments are hurting him deeply; another child has parents who conceal their unhappiness with each other, and he is probably better off if the marriage stays together.

Some never marry

Our society puts such a high value on marriage that we are often critical of those who do not marry. Some choose not to marry because they recognize they are unwilling to share their lives, or because they do not like any member of the opposite sex enough to live as man-and-wife. Others just do not find the right person at the right time.

While unmarried people certainly miss much of the enrichment a marriage can bring, they do gain in other ways. They can spend much more of their money upon themselves and have less financial concern regarding the future. They can do things and go places as they please, travel extensively if they want, without worrying about anyone else. Often they have warm relationships with relatives, married couples, or children and receive some of the enjoyment of marriage indirectly.

We often forget that certain people who do marry would have been better off to have avoided this relationship, but were pressured into it by well-meaning family and friends.

SUMMARY OF IMPORTANT IDEAS

1. Parents have always considered a proper marriage for their children as one of their most demanding responsibilities.

2. The purpose of courtship is to allow two people to get to know each other well enough to decide whether they wish to marry.

3. Parents are an inevitable factor to be considered in a future marriage.

4. Marriage across religious lines increases adjustment problems and the probability of divorce, but can still be successful.

5. Other problems in courtship include difficulty with friends, agreement on conventions, conflicting values, use of money, and affection and sex.

6. Healthy mutual love will help both members of the marriage to grow as individuals.

7. Marriage leads to the most important new relationships of adult years.

8. Husband and wife share some needs and values and hold other needs and values that complement each other; there is no evidence that opposites attract.

9. The success of a marriage is related to the success of the

marriage of the parents of the two people involved, to their happiness as children, and to other factors of their earlier years.

10. Self-concept and role are also related to marital success.

11. In marriage, husband and wife are encouraged to recognize each other's needs, learn to communicate with each other, respect each other's privacy, allow for individuality, learn to compromise, be faithful (and not just technically), and not demand too much of the other.

12. Student marriages have increased greatly since World War II.

13. Divorce rates seem high, but have remained roughly constant for about 25 years or more, except for the post-World War II period.

The mature years **11**

It seems a little unfair to spend five chapters discussing the first 25 years, and only one chapter discussing the subsequent 50 years. However, the principles of the previous chapters, including the chapters on perception, learning, and needs, do not change merely because a person is married and has a family. There are certain matters that are of particular concern in the middle and later years of life, and these are discussed here.

The early adult years are marked by new opportunities, new freedoms, and new responsibilities. The fight for emancipation from parents should now be over. Health is usually good; vocational skills have been recently acquired; social relationships may be enjoyed with fewer restrictions than ever before; and hopes for the future are high. Even the age 21, which technically begins the adult years, has a certain magic about it. You are now free in many ways—you can vote, order a drink, get married, or take a job without your parents' permission.

With these new freedoms come new responsibilities. The adult is expected to take full responsibility for his own behavior: he must organize his own time, learn how to be fully responsible for earning and spending money, seek advice when he needs it, and enter into a much more mature and demanding set of relationships. He is also fully responsible legally for his own actions and is expected to participate in the community and contribute to it.

The adult life cycle

The early adult years still involve much experimentation. The individual may experiment with his new emancipation from his parents, perhaps carrying freedom to excess one time, then being afraid to venture forth another. He tests out relationships with the opposite sex, but with marriage more likely to be the purpose than in earlier years. He tries different jobs, lives in different houses, participates in different activities. From the tremendous range of possible behavior patterns, he selects those which satisfy him the most.

As he moves into his thirties and forties, he gains a better idea of where he wants to go and where he is likely to be able to go. Although some people do make substantial changes in their life patterns after 30 or 35, most have settled into a type of routine that they will maintain thereafter, at least until retirement age.

Between 40 and 50 "should be the peak period in life, not only for financial and social success but also for authority and prestige" (Hurlock, 1959). During this period, the individual is still active, vigorous, and alert, and he has accumulated experience and knowledge. Identity, sex, emancipation, and finding a purpose in life are no longer such bothersome problems. They have been replaced, however, by the need to come to grips with the reality that time is not infinite, that what is going to be accomplished during the lifetime must be accomplished fairly soon, and that what is not accomplished within the decade of the fifties may never be accomplished.

The hopes a person feels in his twenties must, for the most part, be realized by the time he is in his fifties, or they will never be realized. For the individual, this decade demands a painful personal re-evaluation. Some of his friends have surpassed him and are much more successful than he; the expensive home he had hoped he would some day own may be as much a dream as ever; his children are not the geniuses he had always desired. Retirement is suddenly a matter of concern, and his health may no longer be so good. His level of aspiration must be modified in terms of the present reality.

However, maturation and personal growth do not cease when a person reaches 21; they continue throughout his life span. The long period from his mid-twenties to early fifties will be filled with a great deal of pleasure and satisfaction. There will be times when he will feel the great satisfaction of knowing that he has made effective use of his capabilities, that he has accomplished his goals on a work project or in preparing his children to meet the world or by giving enjoyment to others.

Even in later years, happiness, satisfaction, and self-actualization can continue. People then have much to look back upon and still have much to look ahead to. Some, of course, psychologically curl up and wait for death, but others use their later adult years to do the things they had always wanted to do, but for which they had never had the time. Their old age is rich and exciting, filled with warm, human relationships and stimulating activities.

Patterns of behavior across the life span

Behavior changes during the years from childhood through maturity, because at each stage of development new roles become appropriate. Nonetheless, certain consistent patterns do carry over from childhood into maturity. The aggressive child is likely to mature into a competitive adult; the intelligent child becomes an intelligent adult.

One interesting study traced a group of people from their infancy into their early adult years. The authors found that the need for achievement among children between six and ten predicted their actual achievement in their twenties; this was especially true for intellectual achievement. In the same study, teen-aged boys who did not date or show other typical masculine interests seemed to avoid contact with the opposite sex ten years later. Children who displayed no aggression turned into adults afraid to express aggressive feelings, and boys who were aggressive and dominant became competitive as adults (Kagan and Moss, 1962). Another study followed adults from their engagement until nearly 20 years later. The religious values and vocational interests of this group changed relatively little, although their attitudes toward marriage and child rearing did show change (Kelly, 1955).

Intelligence also shows considerable consistency over the years. Those who were more intelligent than average when they were young tend to remain above average in intelligence in their mature years (Bradway and Thompson, 1962). However, although an individual's intelligence remains constant *relative* to others of the same age, definite changes in intellectual functioning do occur over the years. After the rapid increase from infancy through childhood, the growth of intelligence slows down during the junior high school years. Then, in the late teens or early twenties, performance on *some types* of intellectual tasks ceases to change until the later years, when performance begins to decline (Bayley, 1955).

At one time it was believed that general intelligence does not improve beyond the early adolescent years, but recent research has suggested otherwise. Certain groups, such as those who attend college and who go into more intellectually demanding jobs, increase their IQ scores, and their intelligence does not drop until they are well advanced in years (Bayley and Oden, 1955).

In spite of general consistency in personality and intelligence, changes in the recognized patterns occur, especially—we would hypothesize—among those whose adult environment changes drastically or opens up increased opportunity for self-actualization.

> One successful young executive, a friend of the author's, spent his high school days as a member of a semidelinquent gang. The day they informed him they were going to hold up a garage, he refused to go along with them. The robbery was poorly planned, and all the boys were arrested. The author's friend panicked and enlisted in the navy, where he eventually earned his high school degree. Fortunately, his ability was observed by a shipmate, and he was encouraged to try college when his enlistment was up. Much to his own surprise, he was successful in college and enjoyed it very much.

The experience of this individual shows that opportunity for change in the life pattern is possible. However, of those arrested, none has yet been able to accomplish more than low-paying, unskilled jobs, and several have been repeat offenders.

Physical development and psychological reactions

Between early adulthood and old age, the body undergoes many slow changes. The hair thins out, especially for men, and the skin begins to develop wrinkles. Muscles tend to lose their tone, and an increase in weight is common. These changes, along with an increase in medical problems, usually do not make themselves felt until the person has approached or passed his middle forties; they occur to different people at different ages.

During the late forties, many women go through **menopause,** a period during which the menstrual flow becomes less and less frequent and eventually stops. Menopause signals the end of the woman's potential for child bearing.

The impact of menopause is more emotional than physical, although some women describe disturbing physical symptoms also. Women often feel that they must be able to conceive to be a true woman; when they lose this ability they feel they are also losing their femininity. Menopause is also a distinct and unavoidable sign of advancing age. These psychological problems, accentuated by physical discomfort, may produce feelings of depression and irritability.

The United States has been called a youth-centered society, because we place so much emphasis upon looking and behaving youthfully. Age means the end of this youth, of its health and energy and physical attractiveness, of its hopes and opportunities and status. And people resist the idea that they are growing old. Many men and women attack the most obvious symptoms of age through cosmetics, hair pieces, diets, and a variety of special treatments. Others participate in activities which appear out of keeping with their maturity level, such as the mother who insists upon being "one of the gang" at her fourteen-year-old's parties but refuses to spend time with her own age peers.

Although physical changes with age are rarely pleasing, people are certainly not equally bothered by them. Mature individuals who have built satisfying relationships and who have developed absorbing interests are likely to spend less time and energy worrying about physical changes. They are not so worried about looking youthful, nor so frightened of seeming older, since other, more exciting ventures take up their days; they find their work challenging and their family relationships rewarding; home, friends, and enjoyable leisure, perhaps combined with political work or artistic endeavors, keep them busy.

New opportunities—new responsibilities

Your life patterns change when you finish school and begin what you anticipate will be your career. Marriage and children produce another change in the life pattern. Although adolescent problems have hopefully disappeared by now, new problems have emerged. As an adult, however, your increased knowledge, understanding, and maturity should allow you to deal successfully with these problems. New opportunities and new responsibilities emerge through marriage and the family, financial considerations, the career, the mature sex role, participation in the community, and enjoyment of leisure.

Family responsibilities—family satisfactions

The chapter on courtship and marriage discussed the behavior patterns found in marriage and differentiated successful from unsuccessful marriages. Chapter 7 described various parent-child relationships and their results. At this point, we need add only a brief discussion.

Your parents are likely to be the most significant figures in your early development; your spouse and children will become vitally important to your adult years. Changes in your self-concept will depend to an appreciable extent on how these people look upon you and respond to you. The parent who is loved and respected by his family becomes a more complete person; the parent who is not loved or respected by his family becomes less of a person.

Having a marriage partner and children not only offers opportunities for growth but also adds demands and responsibilities. Your behavior, your health, your interpersonal relationships, your happiness now affect not only you but others. You can help others grow and mature effectively, or you can contribute to their having unfulfilled safety and love needs. How can you best help your family grow and make the most of their capacities?

Today's family, compared to the family of fifty years ago

—They live in cities and suburbs, not in small towns or on farms.

—They commute to work.

—They move frequently (one out of five Americans moved during the year 1955 *).

—They seldom live in the same home with grandparents; they often do not even live in the same community.

—They are less likely to have lost a parent by death, but more likely to have lived through parental divorce.

—Work is rarely a family affair.

—Education continues until the late teens or even longer.

—The mother is more likely to be working or involved in social, political, or service activities.

Thus, at the very time the members of the family become more dependent upon each other, due to being separated from family

*Caplan, 1964.

and childhood friends and community, the realities of our society force them apart because work and education no longer occur within the family.

The purpose of children

Do you want to have children? Why? For what purpose do you want children? At first, the idea of a purpose for children may seem absurd. We seldom think of children as having a purpose, since it seems natural to want children. Throughout history, however, children—especially male children—have had a very definite financial value: they were needed to help on the farm, to work in the family store, or to help support the family through some other form of work, and to take care of elderly and disabled parents and relatives.

Today, in the United States and in many other countries, children are needed neither to work for the family nor to care for the parents in their old age. As a matter of fact, having children is a tremendous expense and responsibility. Nonetheless, people continue to have children. Married couples without children are considered unfortunate, and those who do not wish children are looked upon as peculiar.

Many individuals feel that children can carry on the family name, and they receive great satisfaction when their children succeed. Having several children has even been called a status device, like having two Cadillacs or an expensive home. Some people desire children to gain the feeling that others are dependent upon them—we often gain self-esteem in knowing we are needed by someone else.

But the best reason for having children may very well be to enjoy them —enjoy watching them grow and enjoy helping them lead satisfying lives. Yet many foreigners observe that American parents do not really seem to love and enjoy their children. They remark that Americans worry about caring for their children, sending them to college, protecting them with insurance, and using good measures to protect their mental and physical health. But American parents just do not appear to others to enjoy their children. Does this relate to the often-heard comment that American parents push their children to grow up too fast? Why have so many foreigners felt this way? Do you feel that American parents are able to enjoy their children?

Some married couples do not want children. Without children they avoid responsibility and expense, and they can move around more easily. Some adults just do not especially like children. They feel children will be a nuisance and an inhibition, and they do not believe the benefits of parenthood are worth the problems. For them, parenthood will not be the enriching, maturing experience it can be for others.

Financial responsibilities

In our society, finances are important. The ways in which you get money and the ways in which you spend it influence much of your behavior. What you buy is determined not only by your income but also by your needs and self-concept, which affect both your expenditures and the conditions under which they are made.

> Jack Valdez and Marty Keene were both recently married and in the market for a refrigerator, which each needed within a week. Marty, after a little shopping, bought a refrigerator "on time," since he did not have the money to pay outright. The initial price of the refrigerator was $212, but he ended up paying $263 through extra charges for the time payments. Jack was more frugal. Through the newspaper advertisements, he picked up a used refrigerator for $50 from a person who was moving. Then he put $15 a month into a savings account at 4 percent interest. Ten months later, the $212 refrigerator was on sale for the special price of $172.95. Jack easily bought it for cash, then turned around and sold his old refrigerator for $45. By using a second-hand refrigerator for one year, Jack and his wife saved over $80.

Jack's approach seems to make sense, but it does not take into account Marty's self-concept. His self-esteem is based partly on his ability to buy things like a new refrigerator. Also, he feels that buying second-hand goods implies that he is not a good husband. He wants his wife to have "the best we can possibly afford." He knows his wife will entertain her friends in the breakfast nook, and he does not want them telling their husbands that he bought his wife a used appliance.

The same product is not worth the same amount to everyone. One couple gives up new clothing in order to take a trip; another family puts a substantial portion of its income into the bank instead of buying a new automobile; a third couple prefers to eat at home unless they can go to an expensive restaurant. The wife of an extremely wealthy hotel executive was asked by her husband whether she preferred a yacht or an original painting by the great artist Pablo Picasso. She chose the painting and hung it in the bedroom. What do you suppose motivated her? What would you select if you were offered $200,000 to spend on any *one* thing?

What financial responsibilities does a husband have? What about a wife? How much of our income should be put away against future old age, illness, or some catastrophe? What kinds of insurance should you carry? What is a good investment: land? stocks? government bonds?

Each of these questions can be answered only on an individual basis. How do you think you will answer them in ten years?

Even though the wealth of the average American has never been higher, more people and more businesses are going bankrupt (*Los Angeles Times*, February 3, 1966), largely because people are buying more through credit than their income justifies. In order to maintain an adequate level of protection for emergencies, the American family is advised to have enough savings to live on for six months, but very few families have this amount of money available. What sort of personality is a "money saver" likely to have? What about an "overspender"?

Opportunities through the career

During the adult years, career planning (discussed in Chapter 16) is of less concern than job satisfaction and vocational success. Work offers opportunities to fulfill many needs, including the need for self-actualization. It also adds responsibilities, since the world of work is a complex network in which each person depends upon others and, in turn, has others dependent upon him.

What does it mean to be successful on the job? Some desire the satisfaction of feeling that a job has been well done and that the results have some meaning. Others feel success comes from money or fame or prestige. Still others consider themselves successful if they can be creative or test out new ideas or be equal to some challenge. Success means different things to different people, depending upon their personal needs.

Figure 11–1. Qualities needed for advancement, according to college students*

Characteristic	Percentage of students believing important
Hard work	62%
Personality	57%
Know Right People	32%
Brains	31%
Luck	5%

*Goldsen et al., 1960.

Factors related to job success. What makes a person successful on a job? Some of the factors leading to success are fairly obvious: intelligence, education and training, human relations skills, appropriate personality, proper abilities, and effective career planning (see Chapter 16).

Figure 11–1 indicates the characteristics that college students believe will lead to advancement, which is certainly one type of success.

Personal and emotional stability are also related to job success. The work adjustment of a group of young employed people was found to be higher when their personality adjustment, tested some years earlier, was better (Havighurst et al., 1962), and anxiety seems to reduce work output (Hanes and Flippo, 1963). Various personality problems will affect job performance. The rigid person, although he might do well enough under normal conditions, may be unable to function in an unusual situation; an anxious person might communicate his worrying to others; a fearful person might be afraid to make a decision.

Whatever qualities a person has, there is rarely a substitute for hard work in achieving job success. Hard work does not necessarily mean physical labor, nor does it mean that every minute must be spent poring over the drawing board, recording numbers, reading books, or oiling machines. Hard work does mean doing the job completely, on schedule, as well as possible, and every time.

It is true that some of our work customs, such as the reluctance to fire a man who is supporting a family, protect certain incompetent and lazy workers. It is also true that occasionally the fellow who plays the angles seems to succeed. In the long run, however, diligent workers receive the rewards. Ironically enough, when they are rewarded for hard work by being promoted to a managerial position, they find themselves working still harder. Professional and managerial personnel have much less free time than plant workers and office clerks (Lehner and Kube, 1964). However, the professional and managerial people enjoy their work more (Hoppock, 1935) and feel they accomplish more and self-actualize more, which may explain their willingness to work longer hours.

Success in supervision. The role of the supervisor is more complex than many people realize. First of all, the supervisor must be able to perform many of the functions he supervises. A sales manager should be a reasonably good salesman; a charge nurse should have been a competent floor nurse. The supervisor must also make decisions and accept the blame when he is wrong. He must be able to get along with those whom he supervises and with those who supervise him. In addition, it is his task to communicate the messages of each group in the language of the other. For example, the superintendent of maintenance of a chain of banks may supervise 50 or 60 people; he must communicate their feelings about their work and explain highly technical maintenance matters to a vice-president, who may know little about maintenance and may have had limited contact with the maintenance crew.

According to one expert, supervisors should base their actions on five principles:

1. *Fair evaluation of work.* Supervisors should give appropriate praise and criticism, while taking care not to embarrass workers.

2. *Effective delegation of authority.* Supervisors must be able to know what tasks their subordinates can perform satisfactorily. Too many supervisors try to do too much themselves and do not know how to distribute work satisfactorily.

3. *Fair treatment for all.* All employees deserve equal treatment and need to be considered as worthy human beings.

4. *Availability to employees.* Supervisors should be available for employees to call upon them and discuss appropriate matters with them.

5. *Employee participation in decision making.* Employees often respond better when allowed to participate in decision making, even if they are used in a strictly advisory capacity. If the decision affects the employees, their reactions to the decision are important and their help may be valuable (Blum, 1956).

The same author also suggests that the supervisor avoid the following: (1) taking advantage of his superior position; (2) pretending he knows things when he does not, especially regarding the tasks at hand; (3) interfering with an employee's work or looking over his shoulder too much; (4) showing favoritism or discrimination; (5) criticizing employees in public; (6) spending too much time and effort on minor details; (7) giving orders that conflict with previous orders or with orders of other supervisors; (8) giving unnecessary orders (Blum, 1956).

Government and business organizations have learned that employees wish to feel themselves a part of the company and to feel respected, unique, and important. A series of studies conducted 40 years ago showed that industrial production increased when employees felt they were meaningful to the success of the company. Later studies showed that feeling a part of the company did even more to improve production than did financial rewards (Roethlisberger and Dickson, 1939).

These realizations created a new problem, as well as increased success, for supervisors. They needed to recognize that financial rewards and various threats are not necessarily effective in improving production or reducing absenteeism. Supervisors today are encouraged to be sensitive to the feelings, the frustrations, and the needs of those they supervise.

Although maintaining such sensitivity is not an easy task, it can pay rich rewards.

Being a supervisor carries prestige, opportunity for further advancement, and increased income, as well as more problems and more opportunities for satisfaction and self-actualization. Unfortunately, as many learn to their dismay, the qualifications for being a good supervisor differ from the qualifications for being a good worker.

The mature sex role

An individual's social roles not only change as he matures but differ considerably according to his sex. Boys, for example, are given much greater freedom than girls, even though girls mature more rapidly. Boys can misbehave, fight, get dirty—or even smoke or drink, cut school or miss church; although they may be criticized or punished, their treatment will be much more lenient than girls receive for the same offenses.

In our society and in most others, being a man is looked upon as more desirable than being a woman, and more American girls would prefer to have been boys than boys would prefer to have been girls (Brown, 1957). This sex preference stems from the greater freedom, the higher prestige, and the more exciting life (at least, so people think) of the man. Ours is a patriarchal and a patrilineal society, which means that the males dominate the females and make most decisions, and that the family name and material goods descend through the male.

Throughout the life span, the role of the woman is more restricted. She has less freedom to travel, to do things by herself, even to use the education she is now able to receive (given the choice between educating the son or the daughter, most families still would select the son). Even though the American woman is presently recognized as having the potential for equal maturity, competence, and stability, she is treated differently because of her sex role.

Some comments about the role of Arab women in the Middle East*

> —Before marriage, the Moslem girl is "expected to stay at home, to help with the housework and . . . the younger children, to obey her father, mother, brothers, and . . . older sisters."
> —In the very traditional families, the girl studies primarily household arts; she may even wear a cloak and veil; she has little voice in the selection of her husband, although she may refuse a marriage.

*Muhyi, 1959.

—The wife is not supposed to protest against anything her husband does.

—Most of the modern and better-educated girls disapprove of dancing or going to movies with boys.

A recent book entitled *The Feminine Mystique* (1963) struck at the heart of this issue. Author Betty Friedan reiterated that women are not really being treated as equal to men. Men, she felt, had persuaded women that self-actualization could be best attained through being a wife and mother, by learning to sew creative clothing for the children and cook exciting meals for "hubby." The author complained that women, in spite of more and more education, were wasting their training and intelligence on dull tasks; to keep women from competing with them on the job, men were trying to lull women into thinking that the home was really exciting, although these same men knew that this was not true. Miss Friedan urged women to get better training and education, to get interesting jobs, to make the most of their capacities and education.

Needless to say, the book caused a storm of controversy. Many women as well as men objected to the idea, claiming that Miss Friedan was out to break up homes. What she actually tried to do was alter the entire tradition of proper female sex-role behavior, and this is a fantastically difficult task. In simple terms, Miss Friedan seemed to be saying, "Women have brains, education, and needs for self-actualization; the life they lead at home is not sufficient to satisfy their needs for self-actualization; their brains and training qualify them for more exciting work; they deserve it." The book may have oversimplified the solution, but the problem is an important one: When the traditional sex role for women is no longer adequate to the needs they feel and express, what should be done?

Many women have complained that their world is surrounded by the walls of the kitchen and is inhabited by creatures three feet high with runny noses. They may exaggerate the excitement in the lives of their husbands, but there seems no doubt that many women have been frustrated by the activities they are forced into. Volunteer work, an evening college class, a lecture series, PTA work, an art class—these things are not enough for some women, who may be skilled teachers, secretaries, nurses, or beauticians. More than that, it is certainly not enough for those women who would have wished to be engineers, business executives, physicians, or electricians, but were kept out because of job prejudices against women.

Is a woman's first responsibility to herself or to her family? If it is to her family, does this mean she must remain in the home? "No!" shouts Miss Friedan, who goes on to claim that the woman is a better wife and

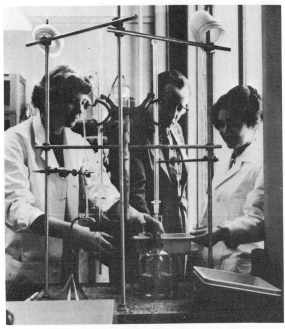

Figure 11–2. The job of secretary and receptionist can be very rewarding and is in keeping with the traditional female role. However, women can also achieve success in traditionally masculine fields such as natural science. Courtesy Antioch College News Bureau.

mother when she is self-actualizing through worthwhile work; she is more interesting, better company, and more satisfied with her self-concept. To evaluate Miss Friedan's contention, we can examine the role of the working wife.

The working wife

More and more women have joined the work force in our country, and this trend will undoubtedly continue. In 1964, 37 percent of all females aged ten and over worked—double the percentage working in 1900 (*Information Please Almanac*, 1966)—and one-third of all married women were working. Yet many married women who work are in conflict between wanting to work and wanting to spend their time in their homes.

There seem to be four major reasons why women work: first, to add money to the family bank account; second, because of needs that can best be satisfied by the feeling of accomplishment and self-actualization occurring through work; third, dislike of childcare (not necessarily of children) and of housework; fourth, pleasure from the activities and relationships that occur on the job but not at home.

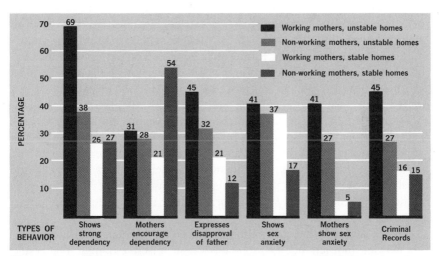

Figure 11–3. Effects of maternal employment and home stability upon boys (McCord, et al., 1963).

The woman who works to add money to the family bank account can do so, if there are no major child care expenses. However, working mothers often far overestimate the amount of money their work will add to the family because they underestimate the additional expenses: federal and local income tax, transportation (which sometimes includes a second car), cleaning help, lunches, clothing, cleaning and laundry, baby-sitting or nursery school, more frequent trips to the beauty parlor, not having time to shop at sales, and the extra recreation because "you're working so hard." One bank executive estimated that the average working wife with children has to earn three dollars to add one dollar to the family budget. To make matters worse, a married couple becomes accustomed to living on two incomes. If the wife should become pregnant, the loss of her income, even for a few months, could be disastrous.

If money is the only motive, the wife is likely to feel guilty at taking time from her children and her home. However, if she dislikes taking care of children all day, or if she has a need to do something with her talents, she may consider the income as a type of bonus. In such instances, and hopefully with the full support and understanding of her husband, working may well make her a better wife and mother than staying at home.

In one survey, half the men disapproved of working mothers, and over one-fourth of the women also disapproved (Goldsen et al., 1960).

Because the traditional male role requires that he support his wife financially, and because her working may imply that he is unable to do so, the husband of a working wife must have a healthy self-concept in order to make a good adjustment to his situation. He must be secure in his feelings of masculinity and not be fearful of criticism for his wife's working not to disturb him. Rather than actually competing with men for jobs, however, most women enter fields that are not dominated by men; less than 10 percent select business, law, medicine, or engineering for a desired future profession (Goldsen et al., 1960).

Some light has been shed upon the effect working mothers have upon their children, but the problem is far from settled. One study showed that year-old infants whose mothers did not work were more emotional and more active, but also more dependent upon their mothers (Caldwell and Hersher, 1964). Among very intelligent children, those with working mothers were more likely to perform below their capacities in school (Frankel, 1964).

A more sophisticated study took into account not only working versus nonworking mothers but stable homes versus unstable homes. The results indicate that the working mother in an unstable home had the most poorly adjusted children. However the children of working mothers who provided stable homes were not much different from those of nonworking mothers (McCord et al., 1963). There is also evidence that the mother's attitude toward working or being a housewife is most important; that is, mothers who want to be housewives and are housewives or who want to work and are working have good relationships with their children. Mothers at the office who would rather be at home and mothers at home who would rather be at the office have child-rearing problems (Yarrow et al., 1962).

The author would evaluate the working wife and mother as follows: the wife's working is appropriate (1) if the home is stable and the husband's self-concept is strong enough to avoid being greatly upset, (2) if the woman has psychological needs that can be met by working or if the family's financial position requires it, and (3) if she and her husband can compensate for the time spent away from the children and from each other by healthy love and attention when they are together.

Responsibilities and opportunities in the community

What responsibilities do you feel to your community? To your nation? To the world? You are a part of each of these; you expect each to offer you something. What do you wish to give in return? One great American, Horace Mann, believed that each person owes something to future generations. He stated, "Be ashamed to die until you have won some victory for humanity." Do you feel you have any responsibilities to win some victory for future generations?

The work and the responsibility of supporting our community is always divided unequally, with some people doing much more than others. Those willing to put forth the time and effort, however, may have the satisfaction of seeing the effects of their work.

A healthy personality wishes to participate actively in the democratic process. As an informed voter, he needs to know more than who belongs to what party or who is running for what congressional office. He also needs to know something about the men running for judge, for district attorney, and especially for the state legislature.

It is at the local level that you can be most influential. Few people can affect national or statewide elections, but you can have some impact upon nominees from your district to the state legislature. By joining and working for a political party, you can find ways to present your own ideas directly to the men who represent you.

Active participation in the political scene can be supported by intelligent reading. The daily newspaper offers an up-to-date picture of the world and the local community, along with editorial comments by a range of columnists. Supplementary reading in a variety of magazines is useful to obtain different points of view, and the truly curious reader will investigate sources that disagree with his views as well as those that substantiate his opinions.

Using community facilities. Every community offers a great deal in exchange for the money and energy its citizens supply. Some facilities, such as roads, schools, libraries, zoos, and police and fire protection, are supported by taxes. Entertainment and recreation are provided both by private business (movies, plays, bowling, golf, athletic contests, and concerts) and by public agencies (parks, tennis courts, museums, and swimming pools).

Local colleges offer educational opportunities, counseling, visiting speakers, and a variety of athletic and cultural programs. In addition, formal education need not stop when you have obtained your degree. People trained in technical fields in college may return afterwards for refresher courses, to investigate a new career, to add to their human relations skills, or to satisfy their curiosity about literature or history. Someone who has studied liberal arts may want to learn data processing, electronics, or typing. The range of educational opportunities after high school is vast, particularly in urban areas and college communities.

The world community. People can no longer shut themselves off from the rest of the world. The opposite ends of the earth are just a fraction of a second away by radio, a few hours by jet airplane, and—sad to say—not very far by intercontinental ballistic missiles. Your life may be deeply affected by a tribal feud in Iran, an impoverished economy in Indonesia, or a political fight in Iceland.

The healthy personality recognizes that he is a part of the world, and he wishes to have knowledge beyond the slogans of propagandists. This means that he needs to know something about the historical and cultural backgrounds of other nations, as well as of his own. He needs to try to understand how people around the world think and feel and develop self-concepts and aim at self-actualization. The reactions of a soldier in Laos, a politician in Gambia, or a farmer in France can be understood only in terms of *his* background, *his* culture, and *his* individual development.

How can you, as an individual, learn more about the world and contribute to the well-being of your country and to world peace? Reading, of course, is one way, but less academic approaches also exist. Foreign movies, for example, provide some insights; becoming friendly with people who were born and reared in other countries is an excellent source of information (your campus probably has many foreign students brought up in countries you know nothing about); traveling to and studying in other countries are, perhaps, the most effective approaches. Can you think of others?

Use of leisure

What do you like to do in your spare time? Sleep? Watch television? Tinker with an automobile? Listen to music? Read? Talk? Play cards? The amount of leisure time available to the working man has been increasing steadily over the years until, today, the average amount of leisure per work week is three times that of 1850 (Kaplan, 1960), and the future will most likely see a continued reduction in work hours and increase in leisure time. You may see, during your lifetime, a standard three-day weekend, a seven-hour day, a three-month vacation every ten years. If these occur, what will you do with your vastly increased leisure time?

Leisure can be used for relaxation or for exciting activities, but it is usually a change from the regular daily routine. A strenuous camping trip is just as truly leisure as a week of loafing around the house; surprisingly enough, a man who spends a week camping may return to work more refreshed than the man whose week was just a long, loafing weekend.

Some forms of leisure may actually be financially rewarding. The person who writes or takes photographs in his spare time may eventually earn money with his efforts; similarly, the person who fixes the car or sews for the children or paints the bedroom is saving money. If these tasks are enjoyable, they are leisure; if they are disliked, they are work.

Productive work as part of the American tradition can be traced back to our Puritan ancestors and the early days of Protestantism. Many Americans, perhaps without realizing it, look upon work as "good" and loafing as "bad." In casual conversation, you do not brag about how little you work, but about how hard you work. The emphasis upon productive work has become so much a part of the culture that you may find it difficult to loaf and relax without feeling you should be "doing something."

Yet leisure, either relaxing or exciting, can be just as fulfilling as work. As a matter of fact, people who use their leisure most effectively are likely to be able to work harder and get more done in the long run—and will probably live longer.

Educators are often very unhappy with the amount of time people watch television, the family television set being on an average of five hours a day, seven days a week, and even more than that in the winter (Bogart, 1962). Educators also point out that many programs are thoroughly enjoyed by first-graders, and yet are followed faithfully by their parents, which hardly speaks well for the maturity of the programming.

Television is relaxing. It requires neither thinking nor bodily activity. As such, it has a definite appeal to people who, regardless of how hard they work, want to be entertained without any effort. Watching television may help children from less-fortunate homes, by presenting them with good speech patterns and vocabulary, but it does little for the child or adult who has a stimulating home environment.

Claims are made that television reduces the time children would spend on more productive and stimulating activities, but the evidence does not fully bear this out. Watching television cuts most deeply into such activities as listening to the radio, going to movies, and reading comic books. In England, at least, it seemed to have little effect upon other activities; both book sales and library use, which dropped just after television began, increased as people ceased finding the novelty of the home screen exciting (Himmelweit, 1962).

Leisure activities are influenced by many factors, including the time available, facilities available, finances available, personality and needs, and interests (adapted from Lehner and Kube, 1964). People fortunate enough to have the initiative find ways to spend their leisure time enjoyably and with profit to themselves. Others are bored with their spare time and end up killing time in any way they can, and some—of course—use increased leisure time to get a second job.

The elderly

Patterns of behavior change during the later years of the adult life period, and the elderly person must adapt himself to new activities, new expectations, and new opportunities and limitations. Over the past few years, the interest in geriatrics (the treatment of the aged) and gerontology (the study of the aged) has increased greatly, until now a much better awareness exists concerning the elderly and their problems.

The proportion of the American population aged 65 or over has been steadily increasing. In 1900, under 5 percent of our population was in that age group, while over 10 percent will be within a very few years. In spite of this, Americans seem to fear becoming old and try to appear youthful. One famous Japanese author wrote "The sharpest difference between America and Japan is the truly inept manner of growing old demonstrated by the Americans and Europeans. . . . The sight of an old woman, decked in a sleeveless, short-skirted dress of a pink-flowered material, her face powdered a dead white, on the skating rink . . . is not objectionable, I suppose—but I . . . would not wish my grandmother to look like that" (Mishima, 1964).

In our society, the elderly often feel out of place. Homes are now constructed with family rooms, but not with a bedroom and bath for grandmother. Those who can afford it may buy a home in a community for the elderly, and spend the remainder of their lives surrounded by other older people, with occasional visits from their children and grandchildren.

Many who work professionally with the aged mention that those people seem to be avoided in our society. The responsibility felt by

American adults to respect and care for their elderly parents is believed to be less than that felt in many, probably most, countries. One nursing home director told the author that several of his elderly patients received no more than one or two visits a year from their children, even though the children were living and working within a short drive of his facility.

Changes in the aged

The elderly face many problems. Their changing physical appearance makes them less attractive in the eyes of the rest of society; they may begin to forget things quickly, even things told them a few minutes earlier; they become unaware of certain aspects of their grooming and dress; and personality and self-concept changes become evident. Just as the adolescent and the middle-aged person must learn new roles, the elderly also must learn new forms of behavior consistent with their age and situation.

Physical and intellectual changes. In old age, the bodily changes occur more rapidly. The senses of sight, hearing, taste, smell, touch, and balance become less sensitive. Fortunately in a way, the sense of pain also becomes less acute. Strength diminishes, and reaction time becomes longer, so that the responses of the elderly are sometimes slowed down (Birren, 1964).

The physical appearance changes in many ways. The skin becomes loose and wrinkled; the body shape changes; and hair continues to thin out and change in color to gray and white. Resistance to disease becomes less, and the bones become harder and more brittle.

Some types of intellectual abilities, e.g., those involving memory or perception, become less effectual in old age. Other capacities, such as knowledge and information, show little or no decrease. When severe decrements in intelligence do occur, they may result from physical illness rather than from normal aging (Birren, 1964).

Individual differences at this age are great, with some 80-year-olds still vigorous and some 60-year-olds showing definite signs of physical deterioration. The previous history of health, nutrition, and care affect the vitality of the elderly; their mental health and eagerness to live are also thought to be factors. Heredity and luck undoubtedly are also important. When death comes, it seems to be without pain in most cases, at least according to the words of the dying themselves (Osler, 1911).

Personality changes. The needs of the elderly are not met nearly so well as the needs of younger people. One psychologist (Kuhlen, 1963) has suggested five sources of frustration that restrict the satisfactions of both deficiency motives and growth motives.

(1) *An age status that idealizes youth.* Since youth is so admired, the aged often feel unwanted. Their self-esteem suffers, and they feel a frustration to which they respond in many of the ways described in Chapter 13.

(2) *Pressures of time and money that lead to restriction of interests and activities.* The elderly have limited earning potential and often live on pensions, social security, and gifts from their children. This forces them to be dependent upon the very individuals who, for years, had to depend upon them. The elderly, once having been independent, are likely to react even more negatively to this new dependency—perhaps felt as a type of regression—than the adolescent. At the same time, since they do not know how long they will live, they are forced to be cautious with their expenditures so that they can continue to support themselves.

The pressures of time operate differently for the aged. Since they recognize that the years ahead of them are limited, they may feel reluctant to begin any long-range projects. They can no longer look forward to new accomplishments. The hopes and plans that have not yet been fulfilled will probably never be fulfilled.

(3) *Physiological changes that demand attention.* Because of the increase in illness and the increased danger from accidents, the elderly become very much absorbed in their own physical problems. This restricts their opportunities to be concerned with other people and other things, and they may gain the reputation of being complainers.

(4) *Technological changes that outdate their skills.* The world is changing rapidly, and new inventions and processes occur constantly. Younger people can learn and become accustomed to these new ways, but older people have less opportunity and less motivation to do so.

(5) *The feeling that there is less chance to move out of the frustrating situation.* Change is more difficult for the elderly, and many of their unhappy life situations, these people realize, will never be changed. The elderly recognize that their physical and intellectual abilities are diminishing, and that they will not return (Kuhlen, 1963).

The elderly are also bothered by observing the death of their friends, which continually reminds them of their own death possibilities. All these factors lead some elderly to disengage or remove themselves psychologically and physically from certain activities and relationships (Cummings and Henry, 1961), both because of limited energy and because of the emotionally upsetting qualities of the activity or relationship.

Successful adjustment

The picture of the aged described above is certainly not a pleasing one. Some aspects of it, of course, are inevitable, in spite of advances of

Figure 11-4. Age need not be a barrier to activity, excitement, and self-actualization. These three men—a premier, a poet, and a performer—were all deeply involved in their work in their late seventies, and beyond. Courtesy Columbia Broadcasting System.

medical and social sciences and treatments. However, many elderly people remain very vital, productive, and active. What do you know about the lives of Albert Schweitzer, Herbert Hoover, Casey Stengel, Bernard Baruch, George Bernard Shaw, Grandma Moses, Amos Alonzo Stagg, Robert Frost, or George Washington Carver? Think of elderly people you know who lead enjoyable and productive lives: what qualities do they have that enable them to do this?

The elderly who do adjust better differ from the average older person in many ways. They gain satisfaction from their activities; they are able to accept the changes that come with age, rather than fighting these changes; they seek, instead of avoid, social relationships (Terman and Oden, 1959). People who have established healthy relationships with their children are more likely to enjoy these relationships in their later years.

Successful adjustment to old age is partly the result of proper planning. Men who plan for retirement and who want to retire remain happier and healthier, and they also are busier; those who do not plan or do not want to retire become bored easily (Thompson, 1958; Thompson and Streib, 1958).

When do you begin planning for old age? The answer is "Today." Financial planning begun during the early adult years will increase the chances of financial comfort during the later years. Physical health in later years is partly the result of diet, exercise, and other patterns begun today. Having interests and activities in the early adult years will mean a better chance of being interested in life in the later years. Such activities as travel, reading, music, certain types of mechanical work, painting, woodcraft, camping, and fishing can be begun in early years and easily carried over into later years.

People whose entire existence is centered exclusively around their family or their work find they have nothing with which to occupy themselves when their children are grown and independent and the retirement period begins. They feel useless and bored. The person who develops a variety of interests during the adult years can much more easily find enjoyable activities when he is elderly.

When death becomes imminent, only about 10 percent of the elderly will admit a fear of it, while another 30 percent express mixed feelings; the remainder state they are able to accept the inevitability of death (Jeffers, Nichols, and Eisdorfer, 1961). The way people face death is a reflection of the way they have adjusted earlier in their lives (Wolff, 1965).

Considerable attention has been given the aged recently. Community activity centers have been established; physicians, psychotherapists, and social workers have become more responsive to their psychological and

Figure 11-5. Even the elderly, restricted to wheel chairs, need not be past the point of enjoying life, if they can live in a well-run institution or with understanding relatives. Courtesy Orchard Gables Sanitarium. Photograph by Cliff Johnson.

medical needs; we recognize now that they are likely to wish to discuss the coming of death instead of avoiding it (Feifel, 1959); institutions for the elderly are becoming oriented toward keeping their patients active and involved in the world, rather than merely maintaining them as bed patients. Perhaps most important of all, there has been an increase in the demand that the elderly be able to live and to die in pleasant surroundings, with ample opportunity for activities and warm, human relationships, and in dignity.

SUMMARY OF IMPORTANT IDEAS

1. Maturity demands increasing responsibility, as well as offering new opportunity.

2. The life cycle provides an ever-changing pattern of demands, responsibilities, roles, activities, and problems.

3. Certain patterns do remain consistent from childhood into maturity.

4. The physical body undergoes many slow changes throughout the life span.

5. Marriage, children, and a home are characteristic of the years of maturity in Western culture.

6. Financial responsibilities and the opportunities and demands of the career are also characteristic of the years of maturity.

7. Success on the job, which may include success in a supervisory capacity, is a major source of concern during the adult years.

8. Differences between the male and the female sex roles are evident in all cultures; in the United States, the male role tends to be more prestigious.

9. Many people believe the sex role of the woman is unnecessarily restrictive.

10. The proportion of women, including married women, on the work force is much higher today than it was 50 years ago.

11. Numerous pros and cons of the issue of working wives and mothers are heard.

12. The mature individual has a responsibility to the community in which he lives, and—in turn—is offered many opportunities by that community.

13. People can no longer shut themselves off from the rest of the world.

14. Leisure can be used for relaxation or for exciting activities; the proportion of time available for leisure has increased steadily over the years.

15. The proportion of the American population over age 65 has increased steadily, until it is nearly twice that of 1900.

16. The elderly person has many difficulties, including that of lowered status, in adapting to his new role.

17. Many physical, intellectual, and personality changes occur in the later years.

III The development and effects of stress

Emotions and stress 12

Perhaps you just read Chapter 11; perhaps your instructor decided to follow another plan and asked you to read this chapter immediately following Chapter 5. Both approaches—or, indeed, several other approaches—do make sense. Thus, if you have just finished the material on human development, you may have noticed that inadequate parent-child relationships and poor marital adjustments were discussed, but the responses of the individual to these stress-provoking situations were not explored fully. If you have just finished reading Chapter 5, you have probably spent several weeks studying the human being under normal conditions, but not under stressful conditions. This chapter begins with a discussion of normal emotional responses, actually closely related to Chapters 4 and 5, then begins to view the operation of stress.

Human beings are capable of feeling and displaying a tremendous variety of **emotions,** from the greatest glee and happiness to the most miserable sorrow, from the heights of elation to the depths of depression, from extreme contentment to extreme agitation. If people felt no emotions, the world would be a much duller, although probably a more peaceful, place.

An emotion may be thought of as a feeling or a state of arousal that stirs an organism to observable action or to internal change, and that involves "sentiments." The similarity between emotion and motivation is obvious— they both evolved from the same Latin word meaning "to move." In addition, *emotional* feelings (joy, hatred, jealousy, fury) can serve as *motivation* for behavior.

Try to recall the last person who spoke to you. What emotions was he feeling at the time? How do you know? Determining whether a particular person is feeling a particular emotion at a particular time can be very difficult, perhaps impossible. However, we usually will accept the idea that an emotional state exists if one or more of the following criteria can be applied: (1) certain physiological changes have taken place which, by common agreement, indicate an emotional state; (2) the person reports that he is feeling one of the emotions; or (3) observers report that the person displays behavior commonly believed to be caused by an emotion. Although we assume that physiological changes underlie all emotional responses, it is rarely possible to investigate such an assumption; therefore, we must rely upon the report of the person himself or of an observer.

When an emotional state occurs, the body undergoes certain physiological changes. These include (1) a change in the electrical resistance of the skin surface, (2) change in breathing rate, (3) change in heart rate, (4) increase in muscular tension, (5) pounding, sickness, or "butterflies" in the stomach, (6) dryness in the mouth, and (7) changes in the brainwaves. Evidence exists that different emotions are related to different physiological change patterns (e.g., Ax, 1953). The changes may serve to motivate the organism into behavior or they may produce an emergency store of energy to facilitate such actions as fighting or running away.

Examples of emotions that motivate behavior are numerous. Mild fear of failure, for example, should cause a student to study harder; moderate anger may induce a policeman to run faster when chasing a suspect. Extreme emotional states have been known to allow amazing acts of strength and endurance, such as the instance reported several years ago of the small woman who lifted an automobile that had fallen on her son; normally, she probably had trouble lifting the tire. Given emergency conditions, however, her emotions not only motivated her to lift the car, but produced bodily changes that enabled her to lift the car.

Intense emotional feelings need not be effective in either motivating or facilitating behavior. Blushing or fainting result from physiological changes brought about by emotion, but are often far from facilitative when they occur; anger or fear can cause stuttering when verbal fluency is needed or "freezing" when quick action is needed. Strong feelings can also motivate impulsive behavior rather than appropriate behavior. The fear that leads to driving away from the scene of an accident, or the anger that causes an employee to shout his resignation at the boss are two examples.

Development and expression of emotions

The range of emotional behavior that any one person is capable of displaying is extremely great during maturity, or even during childhood, but observers report that young infants respond in similar fashion to all emotion-arousing stimuli. Thus, at birth, the only emotion shown is *excitement* or *arousal*. Before the infant is two months old, a pleasant state of excitement and an unpleasant state of excitement, often called delight and distress, can be distinguished. A few weeks later, anger, disgust, fear, and elation are identified, followed by most of the remaining emotions within the first 18 months (Bridges, 1932).

Both learning and maturation influence emotional development. Some emotional responses occur almost inevitably, with no opportunity for learning to take place. For example, an infant does not need to learn to smile when he is pleased—it happens inevitably—but he does need to learn to smile at the sight of his mother standing in the doorway with his bottle in her hand. He learns that this picture is soon to be followed by the opportunity to drink milk; using technical terms, we might describe his smile as a conditioned response to the stimulus of the pleasant scene. (See discussion of learning, page 66.)

Other emotional responses are learned. People learn to love their parents (and a few learn to dislike their parents); children learn to fear the dark, snakes, and the bully down the street. Later, fear may be aroused by the sight of a motorcycle policeman in the rearview mirror, by the news that an operation is needed, or by hearing some politician claim that war will begin within the year. Human emotions can be aroused by anticipation of the future or recollections of the past.

Expressing emotions

Sometimes it is simple to recognize the emotion another person is feeling. He may laugh or cry or show his feelings by the expression on his face. Judgment of the emotion felt is improved by knowing the entire situation, since facial expression alone can be misleading. In general, the more you know about the situation, the better you can judge what emotion is actually felt.

> Max Richards had been called up for his draft physical in the middle of his sophomore year at college. Because he was a little older than most sophomores and his district was short of eligible men, he was afraid he would be pulled out of college as two of his friends had been. He knew he would eventually have to serve in the army, but he was certainly not happy about it. At the examination, the physician declared Max 4F because of some minor physical problem. In a daze, Max dressed and, still shaking his head with bewilderment, walked out. As he left, a young private on duty saw him shaking his head and said, "Don't worry, bud; you can get an operation and be back here in six weeks."

People **project** their own feelings into a situation. The young private, who apparently enjoyed his army service, completely misinterpreted Max's headshaking, and projected his own feelings into the situation, assuming Max felt as he would have felt under similar circumstances.

In every society, people learn what emotions may properly be expressed under what conditions. Little boys are repeatedly told "Don't cry —don't be afraid—be a man," until they feel that being afraid and being masculine are contradictory. If this occurs, they are afraid to show any signs of fear and may also believe they have failed as men if they even feel fear. Sometimes such people make a great show of bravery, in order to prove to themselves that they are not afraid. One young man from the Union of South Africa joined a band of paid soldiers to fight in the Congo in 1964, because, as he expressed it, "I had to prove to myself that I was a man." Unfortunately, he lost his life doing it.

Children are discouraged not only from expressing fear, but also from expressing anger, especially anger toward adults. Children will commonly shout "I hate you!" at their parents, long before they have any accurate idea what "hate" means. If their display of anger is strictly punished, they learn not to express their anger directly; however, they cannot be stopped from feeling anger, which may then be expressed indirectly. Many emotional feelings occur that our society does not allow to be expressed directly.

Anger that cannot be directed toward parents can be redirected toward some handy object. After getting an undeserved scolding from his father, a student stormed out of the house, drove off in the family car, and—for the first time in the four years he had been driving—drove well over the speed limit and was ticketed. His anger was being **displaced** upon the automobile.

Many people who feel anger because of some frustration will take out their feelings on minorities, such as Negroes, Mexican-Americans, Indians, Jews, Catholics, or Southerners. This is known as displacing aggressions upon a scapegoat.

During the early 1930s, the fortunes of Germany were extremely low. The country had to repay massive debts for the war it had lost; the money system was so unstable that people did not know from one day to the next what prices would be; international esteem for the country was very low. Hitler, recognizing that the German people could not make effective use of their capabilities in the absence of national self-esteem, found a scapegoat in the Jews. Instead of directing their anger at

Figure 12–1. It is difficult to judge emotions from a photograph without knowledge of the situation. What were Marni's emotions at this moment? Was she happy? Frightened? Content? About to smile? About to cry? Photograph by Albert Kallis.

themselves for having lost World War I and for being unable to control their own economy, the Germans readily displaced their aggressions away from themselves and onto the Jews, who were thereby held responsible for all Germany's ill-fortune.

In major league baseball, when a team does not do well for a year or two, the owners often fire the manager. Although the team's inability to win may actually result from the unwilling-ness of the owners to buy good players and develop a good farm system, it is easier and cheaper to use the manager as a scapegoat.

When feelings of anger or fear are not expressed directly or displaced in some fashion, they may be repressed. Everyone has feelings he is unable to admit, even to himself (e.g., being so furious with parents as to, momentarily, wish to do them violence, or being fearful of not being truly successful on a future job), and these feelings become unconscious. However, even though you are not consciously aware of them, such feelings still influence behavior. Can you think of examples?

Different societies teach different forms of emotional expression. Affec-tion between an adult man and his father may be expressed by kissing and hugging in France, Italy, Israel, or Iran, but Americans usually just shake hands. In Japan, a son would rarely talk back in anger to his father, while such behavior is not uncommon in the United States. Englishmen have the reputation of showing their enthusiasm at athletic contests by clapping their hands, while Americans at a baseball game may shout, cheer, threaten the umpire, or even tear their programs and throw them onto the field; in Latin American countries, the response may be even more vio-lent.

Emotional restraint, while certainly necessary in many instances, can be carried too far. Americans are probably more likely to inhibit the expres-sion of their emotions than people in most countries. "Play it cool" is an attitude encouraged among many Americans of all ages. Many college students do not want to be involved in anything that arouses deep emo-tions and deep loyalties—even cheering at football games often results from razzle-dazzle cheerleaders rather than from deeply felt loyalty.

People who allow themselves to feel things deeply, instead of insisting upon playing it cool, find life more exciting. They are not dominated by deficiency motivation, which calls for the reduction of tensions, but by growth motivation, which enables them to be open to new experiences. They have sufficiently accounted for their physiological, safety, love, and esteem needs, to be able to become emotionally involved, even though it exposes them to the possibility of emotional pain and failure.

Examples of emotions: fear and anxiety

Two familiar emotional states are fear and **anxiety**. Feelings described as fear occur when a person responds to a present stimulus he can identify. He may feel fear if he stumbles across a rattlesnake, when he sees a snarling dog racing toward him, or when a drunk approaches him with threats of violence.

Anxiety, an emotional state closely related to fear, occurs when a person worries about what *might* happen in the future, or when he is fearful about some vague or unknown thing, the nature of which he cannot actually explain.

Watch airplane passengers when the plane begins to take off. Notice their variety of reactions, such as gripping their armrests, closing their eyes tightly, staring straight ahead. These are signs of normal anxiety, people anticipating future possibilities.

Figure 12–2. Is there any difficulty in deciding what emotion these two women are feeling? Would you have guessed that they are actresses? Courtesy Columbia Broadcasting System.

Some other examples of anxiety-provoking situations that are everyday occurrences:

> Your professor asks you to drop in to see him after class. You have no idea what he wants, but you did copy part of your homework directly from an encyclopedia.

> You have been driving about 20 miles an hour over the speed limit on a deserted country road, and you see automobile headlights flashing on and off in your mirror.

> About three weeks after applying for a job with a Chicago company, you find a note in your mailbox stating that the post office has a special delivery letter from Chicago for you. Unfortunately, today is Friday, and they are not open until Monday.

> You have just been informed that you will need an operation early next month. The operation is a routine one, resulting in complete success 97 percent of the time, and only one person in 200 dies as a result of the operation. But there is that 3 percent failure and that one death. . . .

What is it like to feel anxiety? When you feel anxious, you are strongly motivated to reduce this source of tension. Sometimes the reduction of anxiety is so rewarding that you would rather know the worst than remain uncertain. Doctors report that patients who have been anxious about whether they will need an operation are relieved when the decision is made, even when the decision is that the operation will be necessary. Anxiety tends to be deficiency-motivating rather than growth-motivating.

Sometimes it is difficult to relieve anxieties. Some people seem constantly anxious, to the point of disregarding the real world around them. The basis of their anxiety, then, arises from their own feelings of inadequacy, not from what is happening in their environment. You frequently meet students who are constantly anxious about their grades, even though they do well in all their classes. In one such instance, the student's anxiety resulted from his being compared to an older brother who was always at the top of his class; no performance of the younger brother could surpass that of the older, and parental praise was reserved for the older.

Tension-reducing behavior is very rewarding and a person may well repeat such behavior on later occasions when he feels anxiety. Thus, if a freshman's anxiety concerning dating is relieved by avoiding dates (and assuming this does not produce even greater problems), he is likely to continue to avoid dating, even if it means missing some fun and making up some strange excuses.

Since human beings have the ability to respond emotionally to what might happen in the future and since these responses are important motivators, the concept of anxiety is an important one in psychology. When fear, anxiety, or other emotions produced by stress lead to feelings of strain, we will use the term *tension* to describe the resulting condition.

Development of stress-aroused conditions

During the Korean War, prisoners of the Communists were exposed to a strange new method of breaking their resistance and their spirit. Instead of depending upon torture, starvation, and killing, the Chinese Communists created a situation so full of stress that many Americans were unable to behave effectively in the prison camps—claims have been made that some actually died, not from injuries or lack of food, but because the stress left them without the motivation to live (Schein, 1958).

The Chinese created stress through guilt by emphasizing the terrible things the United States had supposedly done to China. They created stress through anxiety by dividing the men into small groups and placing in many of these groups a prisoner who reported back to them; thus, the men never knew when they could speak freely. They created stress through **conflict** by promising special treatment to a group of prisoners, if one man in the group would "confess" to having been wrong in fighting Communism. They created stress through **frustration** by depriving the prisoners of adequate leadership by segregating the men from the noncoms, and sometimes removing a man from a group in which he began to show leadership.

Basic types of stress

Stress is a strong, unpleasant emotional force or pressure that produces feelings of tension or strain. It is motivating, rather than facilitating, and the resulting behavior is directed at the reduction of the stress and the resulting tension. The greater the stress, the stronger the motivation for its reduction. Stress can occur through frustration, conflict, anxiety, and guilt.

Frustration

Have you ever been caught in a major traffic jam while trying to get to a very important appointment on time? That would be an excellent example of frustration. When a person cannot reach the goal he desires, when the demands are greater than his ability, frustration occurs. Frustrations may be caused by personal inadequacies, natural conditions, or man-made conditions.

Personal inadequacy. Most girls are not going to win a beauty contest. No matter how intelligent or charming, no matter how clever in dressing and using makeup, they simply are not going to win. If such girls are really motivated to win a beauty contest, they are doomed to frustration.

Failing to win a beauty contest, fortunately, is not frustrating for many people, but other types of personal inadequacies are. Limited intelligence can keep a person from entering college; limited height can keep a competent soldier from being an officer; limited knowledge of English may cost a person the chance to get a good job. Limited social skills, limited business experience, limited funds, limited technical skills, limited strength, all these and many more can lead to mild or extreme frustrations.

Natural conditions. Conditions beyond your control can keep you from achieving a desired goal. A long period without rain will lead to limited food and water, destruction of farmland, and often, the death of animals; a fire started by lightning can destroy hundreds of acres of timberland and homes; fog can delay the return home of thousands of airline passengers. The difference in importance between a delayed flight and the destruction of homes is obvious; however, they both frustrate people.

Figure 12–3. A good example of frustration. The policemen are a barrier to the goal of the driver. Courtesy Columbia Broadcasting System.

Man-made conditions. Man is often his own worst enemy. Man creates wars and the resulting death, pain, and frustrations. Professors create frustrations for students, who, in turn, create frustrations for professors. Parents may provide great frustrations for children, who may not realize the frustrations they bring their parents.

Not all man-made frustrations are bad. The man-made law against my stealing your car may frustrate me, but it is very much in your interest. Restrictions on hitting a person when you get angry with him may be frustrating, but not to the person about to be hit. Some drivers are frustrated by speeding laws, but this is no reason to discard the laws.

Conflict

Conflict occurs when an individual is motivated by two or more needs, and the satisfaction of one causes the denial of the other. The old saying, "He has the tiger by the tail and can't let go," is a good example of a conflict.

Figure 12–4. An example of one man-made source of stress. Courtesy Antioch College News Bureau.

A conflict will occur only if the alternative goals are fairly equal in importance. Confronted with the choice between a delicious hamburger and a twenty-dollar bill, you would rarely be in conflict, no matter how much you loved hamburgers. However, if you had not eaten anything for two days and the hamburger was the only food available, a conflict might well exist.

There are four categories of conflict: **approach-approach, avoidance-avoidance, approach-avoidance,** and multiple approach-avoidance.

Approach-approach. Two desirable and mutually exclusive goals create an approach-approach conflict. Examples of an approach-approach conflict would be deciding between two good jobs, having to choose between buying a new suit and taking an exciting three-day trip, voting for a close friend or voting for someone else who is much more competent.

Avoidance-avoidance. Being forced to choose between two unpleasant alternatives leads to an avoidance-avoidance conflict. A few examples are getting a painful tooth pulled or having it continue to hurt, going on a date with a dull escort or staying home, studying a very difficult and tedious textbook or risking an F.

Approach-avoidance. Often one goal involves both pleasant and unpleasant alternatives. Getting a part-time job provides necessary spending money, but cuts into free time and social life; joining the navy for four years is patriotic and will enable you to visit exciting places, but it might do little for your career.

Multiple approach-avoidance. Most real situations involve a complex combination of pleasant and unpleasant factors, as exemplified in the following hypothetical case.

> George is faced with the following problem: he is presently a college student, but he does not enjoy college, nor is he doing especially well. If he leaves school, he will be drafted immediately, and he does not wish to go into the army. College will increase his lifetime income, give him a better understanding of the world, offer him enjoyable social activities, and may allow him to escape the draft altogether, since he is planning to marry his present steady when they are both 21. On the other hand, he is likely to flunk out, he is bored with his courses, and he can take over his father's hardware store whenever he wishes. In addition, he is not so certain he wants to marry this particular girl, although her father owns a chain of hardware stores and has no son to take into the business. Service would be an easy way to get away from his girl, but it will not help him in the hardware business; he hates marching and gets irritated when people give him orders.

George will have a difficult time making a decision. Settling conflicts becomes even more difficult because of the influence of unconscious motives. Part of George's motive for not wanting to get married is that the girl reminds him too much of his mother, who has made life miserable for his father by pushing him to be successful; taking orders in the army is too much like taking orders from his mother; working in a hardware store symbolizes the life his father led, which frightens George because he does not wish to live like his father. However, George is not aware of these feelings, even though they do influence his behavior.

A study of real-life conflict resulted from a disastrous series of tremendous explosions that rocked the town of Texas City. People were caught in the conflict between wanting to see what happened to their families and wanting to do what they could to stem the terrible destruction, between wanting to save their own lives and property and wanting to help others (Killian, 1952).

There is no good "trick" for settling conflicts. One possibility is to list all the pros and cons on a piece of paper; another is to toss a coin. A conflict between which of two movies to see can be settled by an impulsive decision, but a conflict between which of two colleges to attend demands thorough consideration.

Some people find making a decision to be very difficult. They cannot decide which movie to see, and so they end up missing the beginning; they cannot decide which job to accept and finally find both have been filled; they cannot decide where to vacation and then learn there are no more reservations. Such people may have weak self-concepts and may be very much frightened of making an error. They do not feel adequate in making decisions and are unwilling to accept the consequences of making the wrong decision.

Anxiety and guilt

Joseph McArthur had internalized his father's value that any form of disobedience of parental authority was evil. When he was 16, all his friends were actively dating, but Joe's father would not allow him to date or to attend house parties. One morning he felt so frustrated that—for the first time in his life— he argued with his father. The discussion became increasingly heated, until Joe finally yelled "Oh, drop dead!!" and stalked out of the house. That afternoon Mr. McArthur was killed in an automobile accident.

Joe felt that, somehow, the death was God's way of punishing him for his disobedience, even though he knew, logically, that this was impossible. He began to have frightening nightmares in which his father came back as a ghost to threaten to kill him in revenge. For weeks Joe was unable to sleep until thoroughly exhausted, because of a fear (which he again recognized as illogical) that he would die during his sleep. His guilt and his anxiety were slowly destroying his physical health and his emotional stability, until he finally sought help through a psychologist associated with his school.

Internalized values become very much a part of us, and when behavior violates these values, guilt and anxiety are common responses. Joe had internalized the value that disobedience was improper, and when it seemed to him that his disobedience and his hostile statement were related to his father's death, he felt very guilty. No matter how hard he tried to persuade himself that there was no cause-effect relationship between his outburst and his father's death, he continued to feel that his sin was going to be punished, and his dreams were an expression of the fear that the punishment would be his death. Guilt and anxiety worked simultaneously.

Frustration, conflict, anxiety, and guilt occur constantly in the lives of all people. Sometimes stress becomes too great, and the self-concept is inadequate to maintain itself in the face of this stress. Then, instead of being able to work toward utilizing his abilities to their fullest, the victim consumes his time and energy in dealing with the stress.

Specific stressful factors

Innumerable situations, incidents, relationships, and conditions are stressful. Those that affect children are not necessarily those that trouble college students, and those that disturb college students may differ from those that concern middle-aged people. Some types of situations, however, frequently appear stressful.

Family relationships. Even in emotionally stable family situations, stress frequently occurs. Frustration occurs when the parents need the car the evening of an important college dance; conflict is felt when the 17-year-old daughter wants to get married and her parents are violently opposed; guilt and anxiety result from trying to cover up for a night of cigarettes and liquor by coming home chewing a sweet-smelling gum.

Some families attempt to work out their conflicts and frustrations together, perhaps through sitting down and discussing the problem or working out a solution agreeable to all. Other parents put their foot down and demand complete and immediate obedience—which they may or may not get. The reactions of most families fall between these extreme positions.

Occasionally stress seems to affect a family all the time. Perhaps the parents fight with each other, placing the children in conflict; perhaps the father has such a great need to assert his own power that he constantly criticizes the children; perhaps the older brother has been so successful that other children are pushed to do as well, despite their interests and abilities.

> Jean, Mike, and Will Lambert ranged in age from 18 to 23. Their parents demanded that they be excellent students and also that they be socially active. The children had above average intelligence, but were not as brilliant as their parents assumed they were. Will, by studying very hard and not dating, got grades good enough to satisfy his mother, but was criticized by his father for being a sissy and an egghead. Mike was very popular, but did poorly in school. Jean, who was encouraged by her mother to be like Will, and by her father to be like Mike, was in such conflict that she did poorly in school and was too anxious over her low grades to be popular. When she began to show an interest in becoming a nurse, Mr. Lambert became angry because the pay was so low, and Mrs. Lambert was upset "because nurses have to do all those dirty jobs—like bedpans."
>
> The children left home as soon as they could, the boys both completing junior college, then entering the army, while Jean married a pleasant but dull man just before her nineteenth birthday. The parents then accused their children of being "hard-hearted and forgetting all about your parents, who love you so much and who did so much for you."

Love and affection. Important human relationships occur not only with parents, of course, but with a great variety of people. Marriage, going steady, dating, and good friendships between people of the same or opposite sex, all are sources of great satisfaction and great potential stress.

You become anxious (Does he really love me?) or guilty (I shouldn't have gone out on that late date) or frustrated (I love her so much, but she says I'm like a brother to her) or in conflict (I wish he'd ask me out, but I can't flirt too much when he's dating my best friend).

Some individuals refuse to risk the possible unhappy consequences of love and affection. In order to receive full satisfaction from a human relationship, you have to take a chance that the relationship will culminate in an unhappy separation. Any true affection means that you become dependent upon the other individual and upon the continuation of the relationship. In loving, you open yourself up to possible emotional pain, and—because of previous unhappy experiences or because of an inadequate self-concept—certain people are not willing to take this risk. They prefer giving little to a relationship, even if they get little in return, because they feel safer that way.

Opposing group standards. The ability to adhere to what you think is right when the entire group opposes your position is not only very difficult, but very stressful. Everyone has defied certain groups on minor matters—perhaps standing up for a friend the others were disparaging, perhaps expressing your admiration for a movie the others disliked, perhaps defending a political candidate no one else voted for—and each of these little acts caused a certain amount of stress.

Opposing group standards on important issues opens a person up to a variety of types of stress. He may endanger his status in the group; he may be threatened with property loss and even bodily injury or death; he may be isolated from all his friends. At the very least, he must face the conflict between remaining faithful to his values and making a major sacrifice.

Consider the stress and other forms of pressure that face the following:

> The student who is known to have reported the star quarterback for cheating.
>
> The coed who makes no secret of her belief that men are basically less intelligent than women and that she has no intention of ever becoming a slave to a man through marriage.
>
> The politician who exposes congressmen in his own party for having taken graft.
>
> A minister who advocates suicide as a proper act for an extremely elderly or painfully ill patient.

Sex-role demands. Every society has forms of behavior that are acceptable for members of one sex, but not for the other. In our culture, women take care of the home, while men produce the income; women are talkative, and men are silent; women like romance movies, and men prefer westerns. Men are expected to be taller, better educated, and more interested in "things" (as opposed to people).

Stress can occur when behavior contradicts the expected sex role. Men in college feel frustrated because they are not supporting themselves financially, while college women rarely feel guilty about having their families pay their way. The girl who telephones men and hints that they ask her out learns eventually that her behavior is considered improper. Both husband and wife may feel uncomfortable if the wife is more successful in her job than the husband is in his, and the discomfort is intensified if they are both in the same field.

Sex and hostile-aggressive behavior. Most Americans have internalized the values that sex behavior and **hostile-aggressive** behavior should not be expressed openly. Hitting someone when you get angry or "making a pass" when your sexual needs are aroused are certainly forbidden by custom and, often, by law. Even the thought of sexual or hostile-aggressive behavior may be felt improper (recall Joseph McArthur, page 269).

But, even though you cannot express these feelings, you continue to feel them, and the frustrations caused by not being able to respond to your feelings can be very stressful. After being teased by his younger sister for failing English, Jerry exclaimed, "I wanted to hit her so much I could feel my fist tingling."

When sexual or hostile-aggressive feelings are expressed in a socially or personally unacceptable fashion, guilt and anxiety ensue. If Jerry had hit his sister, his guilt and anxiety would have caused more stress than expressing his feelings would have settled.

Problems with authority figures. Ask any policeman, teacher, minister, or parent about the resentment some people have toward authority. We have all had to work toward being independent, and most adults have

Figure 12–5. What sort of trouble with authority figures does this character have? Courtesy Columbia Broadcasting System.

succeeded. However, some people find themselves unable to accept any authority or sign of not being independent. Many who fight authority the hardest have either had unpleasant experiences or are unable to feel secure in their independence. Lots of people have had an undeniably unhappy experience with someone in authority, but this is not an adequate basis for rejecting or resenting authority in general.

Academic and vocational success. Even though definitions of "success" might vary, most people consider academic and vocational success important. Pressures to succeed come from all around. The family, friends, the general community, and—usually—the self-concept, all encourage a high level of academic and vocational achievement. Frustratiohs are acutely felt by those who do not measure up to their own standards of success. Perhaps even more stressful are the fears and anxieties that "I may not make it." Such anxieties are likely to be stronger in the United States, which might be termed an achievement-oriented society, than in countries where greater importance is attached to success in having many children or in being recognized as a good wife and mother, a valiant warrior, or a cooperative member of the community.

Financial pressures. No matter how wealthy a person may appear, he usually does not have enough money to satisfy himself. As income and financial worth increase, the level of aspiration rises proportionately. Ask someone who has been working for ten years whether he could get along on what he was earning seven years ago. Then ask him whether he had fewer financial problems seven years ago or today. People all over the world envy the material possessions and financial opportunities of Americans, but the Americans themselves are rarely satisfied.

Money is a source of stress between husband and wife, parent and child, employer and employee, and—occasionally—college and student. Cheating, stealing, lying, and killing have often been the result of pressure to obtain money. Money may not be the root of all evil, but it is most certainly the root of some.

Although having money certainly causes conflict and anxiety, having very little money can lead to tremendous frustration, especially if the economically deprived individual sees others around him living much better. The misery of poverty is bearable until the impoverished suddenly decides that lots of people are much better off than he and that he deserves to have a better life than he has been living. This is an example of what has been called the law of **relative deprivation.**

Think of the stress caused by not having enough to eat, not being able to keep warm, not having the skills necessary for a job, not being able to live without worrying how you and your family will eat or where they will sleep tomorrow or next week, not being able to have occasional entertainment. In these instances, we are not discussing relative deprivation, but absolute poverty. Proportionately few Americans face this type of stress, but in some countries these hardships are frequently observed.

Health. As long as health is good, people seldom think about it. When health is poor or as people grow older, health worries increase. Poor health or physical defects or limitations can cause tremendous stress for those who suffer.

Death and bereavement. Although the idea of death is unpopular and many individuals attempt to deny its reality for them or for their loved ones, we all face an encounter with our own death and the death of others. The comment made to a friend of the author's by a fellow airplane passenger is especially indicative of the way many people feel about death; he began a statement by saying "If I should ever die . . ."

When someone you feel close to dies, you are sad because of the loss of friendship, companionship, and love, but sadness is not the only way to respond to grief. You may also feel guilty for the arguments you had, for not having been nicer than you were, or for having been neglectful. You may find that the image of the dead person is constantly in your mind's eye and that you continue to think of him, even when you wish to do other things. You may even show physical symptoms, such as loss of appetite, having an empty feeling in the stomach, or lacking your usual muscle power (Lindemann, 1944).

The mentally healthy response to the stress caused by bereavement is not simple. People who try not to show grief or who try to avoid thinking of the deceased person often take longer to be able to behave normally again. Crying and unhappiness are normal grief reactions, and tension is often caused by trying too hard to avoid displaying emotions (Lindemann, 1944). Once the grief is expressed, the person can begin to adjust to a life without the deceased and can begin to enter into new relationships.

Stress is inevitable in our daily living. Even young children meet frequent stress in their interactions with adults, with other children, and with their physical environment. Experience in meeting and dealing with this normal, day-to-day stress is not unhealthy for young children, assuming the stress is neither too heavy nor too frequent. As children learn to cope with mild stress, they gain in ability to cope with greater stress and are able to develop a self-concept as being competent and potentially independent.

A stable, secure childhood with loving, understanding parents seems to enable children to satisfy most of their deficiency motives and to build a sound self-concept. When stress does occur, such children are emotionally stronger and better able to call upon their resources to deal effectively with the stress. In the same fashion that a physically healthy person can recuperate from flu more rapidly than a physically ill person, the mentally healthy person can withstand emotional stress better than a mentally less-healthy person.

When you confront stress, whether it takes the form of frustration, conflict, guilt, or anxiety, you become uncomfortable and wish to reduce the effects of the stress. Stress, which arises from a great variety of situations in interaction with your own personality and needs, can also have a great variety of effects.

SUMMARY OF IMPORTANT IDEAS

1. Human beings are capable of feeling and displaying a tremendous range of emotions.

2. An emotion is a feeling or state of arousal that stirs an organism to observable action or to internal change and that involves "sentiments."

3. When an emotional state occurs, the body undergoes certain internal physiological changes; since these changes are usually difficult to observe, we often need to accept the report of the individual that he is feeling an emotion.

4. Emotions can be motivating; on occasion, emotions can reduce the effectiveness of behavior, but they are more likely to increase the effectiveness of behavior.

5. At birth, the only emotion expressed is excitement or arousal.

6. Some emotional responses occur almost inevitably; others occur as the result of learning.

7. It is difficult to determine by observation what a person is feeling; sometimes even the personal report of the individual is not an accurate report of his emotional state.

8. In every society, people learn what emotions may properly be expressed under what conditions.

9. Anger and other emotions may be displaced upon scapegoats.

10. Emotional restraint, while often necessary, can be carried too far.

11. Anxiety, an emotional state similar to fear, results from anticipation of the future or concern over some vague or unknown and unexplainable possibility.

12. Stressful conditions include conflict, frustration, anxiety, and guilt; it is inevitable in day-to-day living, but not all individuals have an equivalent ability to cope with stress.

13. Specific factors leading to stress include family relationships, love and affection, opposing group standards, sex role demands, sex and hostile-aggressive behavior, problems with authority figures, academic and vocational success, financial pressures, health problems, and death and bereavement.

Reactions to stress   **13**

You have just finished reading about the development of stress; the present chapter discusses the variety of responses stress elicits. Since every individual finds himself having to cope with stress throughout his life, many of the behavior patterns mentioned in this chapter may be familiar to you. You may even have noticed some of them in yourself, which is—of course—to be expected.

The architects who planned the Egyptian pyramids designed them with a strong, solid base, and the structures have withstood the punishment of many centuries. Men who design today's long-span bridges allow for some swaying in strong wind, because bridges with "bend" are less likely to break. If psychologists could design personalities as engineers and architects design structures, they would specify a strong, solid base, and enough flexibility for a little "bend" to prevent breaking.

The impact of stress upon human beings, just like the impact of stress upon buildings, is less if a firm base exists. In this case, the base would be the strength of the self-concept, which is directly related to the **stress tolerance** of a particular individual.

Flexibility, or adaptability, is also needed to withstand stress. Rigid people who are unable to modify their behavior in the face of stress are more likely to be harmed by the stress. In a violent storm, a thin bush with deep roots will neither break nor blow away, while a tall, rigid tree may break and a bush with shallow roots may be pulled out by the force of the storm. (A bush that is too flexible bends and twists in the slightest breeze, and no one ever knows its real form.)

The specific response to stress of any given individual depends upon his self-concept, stress tolerance (or frustration tolerance), and methods of adjustment, in addition to his previous experiences, the specific nature of the stress, and the immediate situation. Some major categories of response include bodily changes; rigidity, withdrawal, aggression, and disorganization; defense mechanisms; and new growth motivations.

Bodily changes in the face of stress

Every change in behavior involves a pattern of physiological changes. The brain, the **nervous system,** the **receptor** and **effector** organs, the voice box, and many other parts of the body must work together when you touch a hot stove, yell "Ouch!" and pull your hand away. More complicated forms of behavior involve more complex patterns of bodily change.

According to one theory, the body undergoes three stages of physiological change in response to stress. At the initial sign of stress, the *alarm reaction* occurs, at which point the body rapidly organizes itself to get ready to cope with the stress. The second stage, *resistance*, describes the continued attempt to cope with the problem. The final stage, *exhaustion*, comes after the body has used its resources in fighting the stress. Although this pattern of response, termed the **general-adaptation syndrome,** describes the physiological workings of the body, these workings in turn determine much observable human behavior (Selyé, 1956).

Psychosomatic problems

If the tension produced by stress continues for a long period of time, the resulting bodily changes will continue also. Unfortunately, these bodily changes, which initially protect the individual against stress, may have a harmful effect if extended too long and may actually contribute to such physical disorders as ulcers, asthma, and skin problems (recall the discussion of acne in Chapter 8).

These disorders are termed **psychosomatic**. They are real physical problems (not imaginary as some people think), but, instead of resulting from germs or a blow to the body, they result from physiological changes induced by stress. A psychosomatic headache is very painful; a psychosomatic asthma attack is extremely disruptive.

Ulcers, for example, may be caused by emotional tension that leads to an unusually heavy and long-term flow of chemical secretions produced by the body. Under normal circumstances, these chemicals are manufactured for only a short time, and the body's defenses can cope with them; under certain types of emotion (e.g., chronic resentment) or as the result of extremely intense emotions, the chemicals are produced over a longer period of time or in greater quantity, and the body cannot maintain its defenses. Eventually the chemicals overwhelm these defenses and cause sores, or ulcers, on the inner walls of the stomach (Wenger, Jones, and Jones, 1956).

Psychosomatic disorders, unlike faked disorders, are very real; unlike conversion reactions (discussed in the next chapter), they produce recognizable **organic** symptoms that may require medical treatment if they become incapacitating. Like other reactions to stress, these disorders appear both in mild and in severe forms.

One young college couple ran into a psychosomatic problem that finally ended their romance:

> Ed Bradford and Rita Alonzo met during tennis class, had their first date that evening, and were going steady by the end of the week. They clicked. After a few weeks of exciting romance, Rita became a little worried. She felt she was not ready for marriage, and Ed had begun to "hint around." She seriously considered breaking up with Ed but finally decided to continue to see him.

> On the way home from a party one night, Rita began to sneeze. Her eyes teared, her nose got extremely red and runny, and she sneezed and sneezed and sneezed. This, of course, spelled the end of the evening, and the usual parking period was called off.

Their next date ended the same way. The date after that, Ed was on guard, and arranged the evening so as to get to Rita's house early, supposedly to watch television. Rita's parents were there, and Rita showed no sign of a cold. Her parents usually went to bed about 11:00; at 10:45 Rita's eyes began to cloud, and she started to sniffle. By 11:00 her cold was going full blast. When Ed explained that he thought the cold was psychosomatic, Rita only laughed, but she soon began to recall other incidents in which colds kept her from situations she felt anxious about. Ed and Rita finally agreed to break off their relationship.*

Many other psychosomatic symptoms come to mind: the headache the night before a difficult examination, the nausea after seeing the mutilated victim of an automobile accident, the severe acne that develops during especially anxious periods. These, however, are not particularly damaging psychosomatic disorders, unlike ulcers or asthma, which build up over a long period of time and produce serious medical symptoms.

Other bodily reactions to stress

Psychosomatic disorders are not the only bodily reactions to stress. Fatigue and bedwetting are other frequently observed examples. Emotional tension over an extended period of time can be very tiring. Three hours of a difficult examination may be more fatiguing than three hours of physical labor; driving a dynamite truck is usually more tiring than driving the same truck loaded with wooden crates. The body mobilizes its energies to cope with stress, but the expended energies must be renewed through sleep or rest.

Fatigue and the resulting sleep can also be a form of escape. How often have you had the following type of experience?

8:00 P.M. You sit down to study. Tomorrow is an examination, and even though you are not fond of this textbook, you feel hopeful and almost enthusiastic.

9:00 P.M. You have read one chapter and now feel impossibly sleepy.

10:00 P.M. You cannot keep your eyes open any longer. You have read only a few pages during the past hour, and you remember little of these because of the brief naps you took

---

* A character in the musical comedy *Guys and Dolls* has a similar "psy-chosomatic" cold.

between sections. You decide to watch television, since you are not getting any real work done.

11:00 P.M. After an hour of television, during which you are not in the least sleepy, you return to your studies.

11:10 P.M. You decide that, since you are too sleepy to study, you might as well get a good night's sleep before the examination, so you go to bed.

1:00 A.M. You are still tossing and turning in bed. You have not been at all sleepy since you put your book down.

Fatigue has served to remove you from the unpleasant or stressful situation of studying a course you do not like or for an examination that causes you to feel anxious.

Bedwetting that continues beyond the age of five or six, or **enuresis** as it is technically called, is usually a reaction to stress rather than the result of muscular immaturity and is more common than generally supposed. One out of 40 young soldiers reported at least occasional bedwetting after the age of 18 (Thorne, 1944). Psychologists consider most bedwetting to be an indication of some emotional problem that may need to be resolved before the bedwetting ceases. However, devices are available that have used classical conditioning methods to cure bedwetting, by having the moisture trigger an electric connection that sets off a buzzer and wakens the child. Eventually he learns to wake up by himself in response to pressure upon the bladder, which is the stimulus that precedes the sound.

Rigidity, withdrawal, aggression, and disorganization

Stress not only produces **biochemical** changes, but also many overt behavioral changes. Some of the more familiar patterns of stress-induced behavior include rigidity, **withdrawal**, aggression, and disorganization.

Rigid behavior

People, like bridges and bushes, need some flexibility in the face of stress. They need to be able to re-evaluate their behavior and their beliefs, not at the slightest pressure, but when the situation is appropriate. Faced by stress, however, certain individuals become extremely rigid. When the situation causes them to feel anxious or confused, they fall back upon previous forms of behavior, rather than investigating new possibilities.

Some people appear to behave in a rigid fashion much of the time. They may see only black or white, rather than shades of gray; they may prefer a strong leader telling them what to do, rather than the freedom to decide their actions for themselves. The world of today is a fantastically complex place, and some of its problems seem almost impossible to solve, but these rigid individuals continue to believe in simple, clearcut solutions. One psychologist, in studying numerous groups, found that a sample of British Communists turned out the most rigid (Rokeach, 1960); other evidence exists that groups such as the Ku Klux Klan and the Black Muslims are also rigid, but even middle-of-the-roaders can be rigidly middle-of-the-road.

Because rigid people need something definite to cling to, they are called **intolerant of ambiguity.** Such individuals become unhappy when uncertain. They feel cheated by the psychology professor who cannot give them exact rules for "psyching out" their friends; they resent the artist whose painting can be interpreted in numerous ways; they become suspicious of the mechanic who cannot guarantee whether regular or premium gasoline is best for their car; they distrust the minister who feels that different religious views might be equally truthful; as students, they are miserable when given a term paper of indefinite length—they need to know how long it should be. And when they go on vacation, they need to know exactly where they are going, when they will arrive, how long they will be there, and what they will be doing. Complete flexibility, if such is possible, is not necessarily desirable, but in the long run, rigidity is not an adaptive response to stress.

Withdrawal

Withdrawal as a response to stress can be either physical or psychological. An example of the former would be the student who, facing an examination he expects to fail, does not show up; then he becomes afraid to see the professor again, and he eventually gets a failing grade for the course. The soldier who knows he will be disciplined for some minor matter may decide to pretend he is sick, or he may go AWOL.

Some people resort to alcohol to withdraw psychologically from stress. After a few drinks, the world seems to be a more pleasant place again. The self-concept, which might have suffered because of guilt or frustration due to failure, is temporarily adequate, and the threatening future looks rosy again. When the heavy drinker becomes sober, his problems return, so that being intoxicated becomes more rewarding than being sober, and drinking may become more frequent. Sadly enough, as you well know, heavy drinking does nothing to change the actual environment, but only temporarily changes the outlook upon the environment. To make matters worse, few people do anything to change their situation when they have been drinking; so their problems only become worse, which may lead to more drinking, and a circular frustration pattern of drinking → withdrawal → more drinking → more withdrawal is established.

Tranquilizers and sleep are two other ways of withdrawing temporarily from stress. Physicians may recommend tranquilizers to help a person feel better during a particularly tense situation; sleep is not only a type of retreat, but you may wake up feeling better equipped to deal with the problems. (In Russia, sleep is used as a form of psychotherapy.) Both types of withdrawal are useful, but both may be abused through overuse, and neither deal directly with the tension-inducing problem.

People can even use recreation, hobbies, television, schoolwork, sports, or their jobs as ways to withdraw from the demands of the world around them. Have you ever known anyone who withdrew into a world of "things," such as mechanical activities or books, in order to withdraw from the world of people?

Aggressive behavior

Stress, especially frustration, elicits feelings and expressions of anger and aggression. You may direct the aggression toward the cause of the frustration, toward another source (displacement), toward yourself, or you may attempt to ignore the feelings and not act upon them at all. Have you ever become so frustrated by pounding a nail crookedly that you smashed at it with your hammer, missing the nail but not necessarily your thumb? Have you ever forgotten that you parked your car in a tow-away zone, then "cussed yourself out" for being so stupid as you walked to the police parking lot to reclaim it?

Many types of riots have occurred in the history of the United States. Before the American Revolution and after passage of new British tax laws, "mobs organized by the (American) merchants rioted in the streets, attacked and pillaged the houses of the supporters of the (new tax) Act" (Hofstadter et al., 1957). In 1886, the famous Haymarket Riot in Chicago, a battle between union members and police, caused eleven deaths. In more recent years, rioting by Negroes has taken place in New York City, Los Angeles, Rochester, and elsewhere. Did you ever think of a riot as aggression resulting from frustration? Although it is difficult to predict the particular type of aggression that will result from frustration, you are fairly safe in predicting that some form of aggression will follow frustration.

Disorganized behavior

You may have heard the expression, "He got on his horse and went galloping off in all directions." The implication is that the person described is disorganized, a common reaction to stress. Frustrations, conflicts, and anxieties can become so great that an individual is no longer able to function effectively. He vacillates back and forth between one decision and another; he makes foolish errors on simple tasks; he forgets to do things that he normally never forgets. These are all forms of disorganization resulting from stress.

Figure 13–1. Her mother has just yelled at her for standing on the edge of the crib and rocking back and forth; notice the aggression in the girl's response to frustration. Photograph by Albert Kallis.

Rigidity, withdrawal, aggressive behavior, and disorganized behavior are all basic reactions to stress. These reactions may also be expressed through defense mechanisms.

Defense mechanisms

The need for self-esteem—and a resulting healthy self-concept—is very important. If you do not respect yourself unconsciously as well as consciously, your energies are expended in justifying your own behavior to yourself, and little effort can be channeled into developing your potential capabilities. When frustration, conflict, anxiety, or guilt threaten your self-concept, you tend to defend yourself and to try to retain your satisfying self-concept.

In his attempts to maintain and improve his self-concept, especially in the face of stress, each individual utilizes certain types of behavior, termed **defense mechanisms.** These mechanisms operate unconsciously and automatically, so that he is not aware he is using them (Coleman, 1964). For example, the fox unable to reach the grapes decided they were sour. He defended his self-concept against having to accept failure. If he had said to himself, "I'll pretend they are sour," he might have fooled others, but he would not have been able to fool himself and, thus, could not have defended his self-concept.

Probably the most basic of all defense mechanisms is **repression,** which was discussed in Chapter 2. Repression is a process that occurs when an individual is unable to recall or recognize something, because of unconscious needs to deny the awareness. The concept of repression is at the core of the psychoanalytic theory of personality, as described by Dr. Sigmund Freud.

> Sid Janson was an effective campus politician; he managed to win every time he ran for office, except the time he lost the election for vice-president of the senior class. Many years later, when he bumped into an old friend he had not seen since graduation, Sid's politicking career was brought up. "I wasn't too bad," Sid said, "I never lost an election." His friend mentioned that he had lost his campaign for vice-president of the senior class, but Sid shook his head. He was able to name six or seven offices he had won, including the treasurer of the German Club, but he could not recall losing any. A careful check of some old clippings in Sid's attic turned up the campaign he had lost.

If Sid could have recalled winning the relatively unimportant German Club office, it is unlikely that losing the senior class vice-presidency would be forgotten. Rather he had repressed this blow to his self-esteem.

Not only memories, but also ideas and feelings unacceptable to the self-concept are repressed. A child who is deeply resentful of some parental behavior may repress his resentment, since to recognize it would cause him to direct anger against the parent, an act unacceptable to his self-concept. The entire process, of course, is unconscious.

A conscious attempt at forgetting something is called **suppression.** When a favorite uncle of yours is very sick, you might try to forget about his illness by going to a movie; when you are very angry with your closest friend, you might decide to work your anger off through a hard game of tennis. In these instances, you are not fooling yourself, but you are making an effort to ignore the anxiety you feel and, perhaps, you may find it easier to hide your worry from your uncle when you visit, or your anger from your friend when you see him next (assuming, of course, you want to hide your feelings from them). Suppression, under the definition used in this book, is not a defense mechanism.

Many sorts of defense mechanisms have been observed. Some redirect responsibility from ourselves to other people or things; some allow us to withdraw either psychologically or emotionally; still others enable us to gain support for our self-concept by affiliating with those recognized as more capable. (The following discussion covers only a portion of the possible categories of defense mechanisms.)

Redirecting defense mechanisms

Sometimes a person seems to be trying to say, "Not me. I didn't do it. I couldn't. I'm not that type. It must have been two other guys." Of course, he does not actually make such statements, but his behavior implies that, unconsciously, he wants to redirect responsibility away from himself.

A very common redirection defense mechanism is **rationalization,** which is the attempt to make behavior or feelings seem rational, sensible, and consistent with the self-concept, when such is not actually the case.

Here are a list of common rationalizations for low examination grades. Remember that the students expressing these ideas actually believe their statements to be true.

> "There were too many tricky questions." (That may be true, but it never explains why the other students were not tricked.)

> "All the questions came from the one chapter I hadn't read." (This also may be true, but a careful check usually shows it is not.)

> "You never knew what the professor really wanted to know." (But the other students apparently did.)

> "I'm not interested in the course—the teacher is boring." (This may be true or it may be a rationalization by a student who is afraid he will fail.)

> "I didn't study." (Why? Is this a rationalization by a student who unconsciously felt he did not understand the course well enough? Was he afraid to try, because if he did try and then failed, he would have no excuse left?)

Each of these rationalizations explains failure in such a way as to protect the self-concept. It redirects the cause of failure to sources outside the self.

Projection is another way of redirecting responsibility. Two types of projection occur: first, you deny your own thoughts and feelings and attribute them to someone else; and second, you justify your own behavior by claiming that others feel the same way.

> A four-year-old had just been bawled out by his teacher for socking another child. "I had to do it," he sniffled. "Why?" asked the teacher. "Cause he wanted to hit me, so I hit him." "How do you know he wanted to hit you—he was playing with the blocks." "I just knew."
>
> In talking to his 16-year-old son, a father stated that "All men want money and power. Those are the only real goals in life."

The four-year-old is transparent in his use of projection (although nations have used the same defense mechanism for going to war), but the father's statement is less obvious as a projection. Whether or not he is correct, he is very probably projecting his own attitudes toward money and power onto "all men."

Sometimes people feel so guilty or anxious about their unconscious feelings and motives that they lean over backwards to deny them. They say, in essence, "I'm not the one you mean—look—I'm just the opposite." This is an example of **reaction formation.** The self-concept is protected by an exaggerated display of behavior indicating feelings opposite to those actually felt.

> Jay Laub was the most aggressive, girl-hungry fellow on campus. He had dates three or four nights a week and talked freely, although vaguely, about his supposedly active sex life. Still, he had a reputation among the girls as being easy to handle. His conscious self-concept was a reflection of his behavior: popular, aggressive, debonair. Unconsciously, however, Jay was afraid of girls, but he could not admit this to anyone, especially to himself. He was saying, unconsciously, "I'm the fastest, most popular, most aggressive guy around—it's obviously impossible even to consider that I'm afraid of girls." By the way, Jay was engaged five times but had not married by the time he was 36.

Movie and book censors, who always reserve the right for themselves to see or read what they want to forbid to others, may be using reaction formation. They seem to be saying, "Look how moral I am—I not only oppose seeing such terrible movies, but I keep other people from seeing them. Of course, I have to see them myself, but don't get me wrong—I don't really enjoy it."

Often people have feelings and needs, especially of an aggressive or sexual nature, which cannot be expressed directly. When you feel extreme anger toward authority figures, such as policemen, parents, or teachers, you are often frustrated in your attempts to show anger. Since in all likelihood you would be punished for expressing such feelings, you redirect the anger through the defense mechanism of **displacement**. Instead of expressing anger toward the person or thing responsible, you direct it at someone or something else. You cannot kick the teacher or yell at the traffic policeman; so you kick the wastebasket and yell at the clerk in the store—they are your scapegoats.

The rationalization, projection, reaction formation, or displacement occur without your realizing that anything other than objective perception and appropriate motives are behind your behavior.

Withdrawal mechanisms

Rather than face the threat to the self-concept and the resulting discomfort, people may withdraw. The withdrawal might be into **fantasy**, the defense mechanism used when people create their own world rather than face the conflicts, frustrations, and anxieties of the real world. Although the content of the fantasy is conscious, the ways in which the fantasy protects the self-concept are not conscious.

> John Malcolm has just been bawled out by a neighbor for playing his hi-fi too loud late at night. Slowly it is registering on John that this is the neighbor with three noisy dogs. Now he is fantasizing the retorts he should have made, and in his fantasy, he is making the neighbor feel very foolish.
>
> Portia Gregg has been hoping against hope that Brad Meinicker would ask her out, but Brad dated her roommate instead. When her roommate and Brad leave the dormitory, Portia fantasizes herself as Brad's date and mentally enacts the entire evening.

Fantasy is not the only type of withdrawal. Rather than withdraw into a dream world, you can withdraw into the past. When the present is too filled with anxiety and frustration, you can unconsciously retreat to the past.

An older child may demand to drink from a bottle and begin to wet his pants when his baby brother is born, although he had been weaned and toilet trained two years earlier. He is using the defense mechanism, **regression**, to return to an earlier form of behavior. In the face of frustration, adults will often regress to name calling, threats of violence, and other forms of childish behavior. When people long for the good old days, they are, in a way, expressing a desire to regress from the stress of the modern world.

People also withdraw from the emotional impact of frustration or anxiety through **intellectualization.** One student with a religious conflict undertook an intellectual study of religion and tried to bury his conflict in an intellectual explanation. Another student, whose fiancée broke off their engagement just three weeks before the scheduled wedding, developed a

Figure 13–2. Although this girl has shown nothing but love for her little brother, she has resumed thumbsucking since his birth. A good example of regression under stress. Photograph by Albert Kallis.

lengthy explanation for his ex-girl friend's behavior, using all sorts of psychological terms—he also tried to cover his emotional feelings with an intellectual explanation.

When a person is apathetic, we usually assume he is just not interested. However, **apathy** can be a defense mechanism unconsciously used when the frustrations or conflicts are too great. Removing oneself completely from the situation reduces the threat to the self-concept. "I don't really care if I make the team or not," protects the speaker's self-concept. If he does not make the team, his self-concept is not greatly damaged; if he does make the team, it is all to the good. Some students claim they are bored or apathetic about college when they are unconsciously trying to withdraw from a tension-provoking situation.

Affiliating mechanisms

Identification is the unconscious act of taking for oneself the attitudes, values, and behavior of a person or a group. As such, it is very important

Figure 13–3. Apathy and inactivity can be used as withdrawal defense mechanisms. Photograph by John G. Warford.

in the socialization process, and parents are often very much concerned about those with whom their children identify. A boy will identify with his father, and perhaps with a popular television hero as well. This adds to the boy's feelings of self-adequacy, because he feels, to some extent, that their abilities and positive traits are now his. The young child is expected to identify with the parent of the same sex, and behave like that person at least in regard to sex role. The concept "identification" is very similar to "internalization"* (see Chapter 6), which refers more specifically to values and attitudes.

You might also say "I identify as an American." Not only are you saying you are an American, but that you feel associated with your

Figure 13–4. A royal identification. Courtesy British Information Office.

country. Some people identify strongly with certain regions of the country; inhabitants of New York City, Texas, San Francisco, and Hawaii often have a strong regional identification. Some people also identify with a college (school spirit depends upon identification), with a church group, a social club, or an interest group. When you identify like this, the success of the group is felt as your success, and their failure is felt as your failure. The real baseball or football fan feels wonderful or miserable, depending upon whether his team wins or loses—his feelings could not be stronger if he were on the field playing.

*The term *introjection* has a meaning similar to *internalization.*

Defense mechanisms and "crutches"

We use most defense mechanisms to fool ourselves about ourselves. They function much like a psychological crutch to support an anxious self-concept. Like every crutch, they are necessary at certain times. You do not remove a person's crutch until he can walk without it; if you try to do so, he will either reject your offer or will fall and hurt himself.

To carry the analogy further, when a person on crutches reaches a certain point in his recovery, he can begin to walk for short distances without them. However, once again the doctor is faced with the same problem: premature removal of the crutch will cause the patient to fall and will perhaps worsen his condition.

If the doctor forces the patient to discard the crutch before the patient is ready, the patient may find a cane that is lying around the house; he may become angry and get another doctor; he may not use the crutch when the doctor is around, but continue to use it at other times. Sometimes, of course, the patient is nearly ready to walk without the crutch, and the encouragement from the physician is just what is needed to get him back on his feet, especially if the first couple of steps are firm and not painful.

The parallels between the physical crutch and the psychological crutch become more apparent through the experiences of Lorne Kunin.

> Lorne Kunin was a very mediocre artist, but every time his painting was not given an award or not exhibited, he claimed that "this proves how little people know about art." His fiancée tried to point out to him that he did not have enough artistic ability to become a successful painter and that he was constantly rationalizing his failures. At first Lorne was deeply hurt, but he soon decided that his fiancée was "just as stupid as the others," and he broke the engagement. After several years, Lorne became a successful businessman dealing in artists' supplies. He came to know many artists quite well, and he was considered an expert in his knowledge of art in the small city where he lived. With his business success and his expertise in art recognized, his self-concept became sufficiently strong, and he slowly accepted the idea that he could never have been a successful painter.

When Lorne was young, he needed the rationalization crutch to maintain his self-concept, and he totally rejected the help of those who tried to get him to discard it. At one point he tried to take a few steps without the crutch, but preferred getting rid of the "doctor," i.e., his fiancée. When time and other forms of success had improved his ability to function, he was able to maintain his self-concept without the crutch.

Professionals in psychology, psychiatry, and social work are extremely cautious in their attempts to get people to throw their crutches away, and they prefer to try to reduce the need for the crutch in other ways. Eventually, when the self-concept no longer needs defending, the use of the crutch ceases without resistance.

Defense mechanisms of many varieties occur in normal (and also non-normal) behavior. All share the qualities of occurring automatically, being used unconsciously, causing us to look good in our own eyes, and making our behavior appear consistent with our self-concept. These mechanisms serve an important purpose to the individual using them, and mental health goals are not served by premature attempts to persuade people not to use them.

Growth responses to stress

The previous discussion has implied that the effects of stress are always negative, but this is not necessarily the case. People have the capability of dealing with stress through positive action. Stress can lead to increased motivation to learn and to achieve, to new insights and more appropriate levels of aspiration, and to new approaches to old problems.

Increased motivation to learn and to achieve

Stress is often caused by lack of learning or lack of accomplishments, and the stressful situation motivates increased efforts and increased learning, which—in themselves—lead to increased self-esteem and opportunity to use available talents. If your frustration stems from being unable to dance, you can learn to dance; if you feel anxious about talking in groups because your vocabulary is limited, you can find numerous sources of help; if you feel guilty because you have not written your grandparents in nearly a year, you might write them.

Classroom exams provide stress that motivates learning; competition for the girl you are dating motivates increased attention from you; the possibility of promotion may motivate a higher level of achievement. In each of these instances, the resulting behavior may be deficiency motivated or growth motivated, depending upon the specifics of the situation and the individual.

New insights and new levels of aspiration

Colin was a very competent engineer who desired to move into a management position with his company. He received numerous salary increases, but never the supervisory job he wanted. Finally, the frustration of being passed over so often forced him to re-evaluate his own limitations, and he began to observe the way he treated his secretary and his assistant, the only two people working directly under his orders. Slowly he gained insight into the reasons for his not being promoted.

Sometimes the **insight** produced by stress might require a new **level of aspiration.** A politician is subjected to so much stress after losing the nomination for mayor three straight times that he decides to run for another, less-important post. A student who tackles an advanced mathematics course and does poorly decides to take a refresher course at a more elementary level. A salesman becomes frustrated because of boredom with his work and finally recognizes that he needs a different sort of challenge in his occupation.

If stress provides you with a better understanding of yourself or with a new, more appropriate level of aspiration, it has served a useful purpose.

New approaches to old problems

Stress often causes rigid behavior, in which the individual repeats previously unsuccessful acts.

You have misplaced your housekey, and your ride to campus is about to leave with or without you. You are looking frenziedly for the key. Where? In the same drawer you have already examined thoroughly and emptied out twice.

But the stress of the situation may force you to revise your morning habits, and you begin setting the alarm a little earlier, to allow for emergencies. In the same way, the physician is frustrated because of the innumerable encounters with patients suffering from an illness he cannot cure, and so he devotes some of his time and energy to finding a cure. A group of students is frustrated by the level of creativity in the movies, and they evolve new techniques in film-making.

Learning to live with stress

Sometimes there is nothing you can do about stress, e.g., you have an ill parent or the draft board is going to re-evaluate your deferment or you have had a recent traffic accident and the hearing is next Monday. Such stressful situations do occur, and you are powerless to affect them. Thus, all you can do is try to deal with your reactions to the stress. Perhaps talking to a professional counselor or close family friend or personal friend will help. Sometimes you can only try to ignore or live with the stress and put additional effort into the tasks the anxiety has disrupted.

SUMMARY OF IMPORTANT IDEAS

1. The degree of stress tolerance is related to the strength of the self-concept and the flexibility of the individual.

2. Physiological changes occur in response to stress.

3. A psychosomatic disorder is an organic change resulting from environmental or personal stress.

4. Other bodily reactions to stress include fatigue and bedwetting.

5. Other reactions to stress include rigid behavior and intolerance of ambiguity, withdrawal, aggressive behavior, and disorganized behavior.

6. Defense mechanisms are unconscious reactions that serve to protect the individual's self-concept and enable him to interpret his behavior as consistent with his values and self-concept.

7. Defense mechanisms may redirect responsibility (rationalization, projection, reaction formation, displacement), allow for withdrawal (fantasy, regression, intellectualization, apathy), and produce feelings of affiliation (identification).

8. Defense mechanisms often function as psychological crutches; there is a danger that they will be used longer than necessary, but removing them too quickly can result in falling.

9. Responses to stress may produce growth, e.g., increased motivation, new insights and new levels of aspiration, and new approaches to old problems; on other occasions, the individual needs to learn to live with the stress in his life.

The troubled personality **14**

When the stress becomes so great that the individual can no longer cope with it through the normal defense mechanisms and other response patterns described in Chapter 13, the result may be faulty or disturbed adjusting behavior. The degree of disturbance may become so great that the person requires professional care or even hospitalization; on the other hand, the disturbed behavior may be of such a nature that he can care for himself and continue a relatively normal life, although certain aspects of that life may appear strange or self-defeating.

What happens when the stress you face exceeds your level of stress tolerance? What happens when frustration, conflict, anxiety, or guilt become greater than your ability to handle them? What happens when defense mechanisms can no longer protect your self-concept from threatening attack?

People must find some way of adjusting to stress, and under the usual conditions of living, most individuals will make an adequate adjustment. Some, of course, will respond more effectively than others. However, when the demands of stress are greater than the individual can deal with, the result is often faulty or disturbed adjusting behavior. The degree to which behavior becomes faulty is determined by the degree of stress in the situation and the individual's personal background and resulting ability to cope with stress.

As the situation becomes more stressful, the faulty adjustment becomes more obvious, and the resulting behavior becomes more rigid, more irrational (from the view of the observer), more confused and disorganized, and less in touch with reality. If the stresses are moderately severe, the person will find great difficulty in being successful or happy in certain phases of his life but will be able to function in the day-to-day world. If the stresses are very severe, the person may need to be hospitalized both for self-protection and for care, since he can no longer care for himself or be responsible for some of his actions.

Why are some people able to withstand stress better than others? We believe that those who can satisfy their physiological, safety, love, and self-esteem motives are better able to withstand stress than those who cannot. They have established a strong and secure base, so that the world is not interpreted as threatening or disturbing. These people have come from homes in which the family relationships enabled them to feel loved and wanted, so that they could develop a concept of themselves as individuals of value and worth. They feel that they are likable because they have been liked; they feel respected because they have been shown respect; they feel secure because they have been given security. Since their needs are reasonably well satisfied and they have developed a healthy self-concept, they approach their problems realistically and the world appears a relatively friendly place.

We have talked so much about environmental stress as a cause of emotional disturbance that you may wish to ask, "Does our genetic inheritance have no effect at all?" The answer is necessarily incomplete— we really do not know. But many psychologists, including the author, would agree with one authority who says that genetic factors can have an influence in two ways. The first is that people have differing degrees of stress tolerance at birth, and the second is that inherited differences may influence the particular type of mental disturbance that occurs, *if* it occurs (Coleman, 1960). We would not state that a person has inherited a particular **mental illness,** but that he might have inherited a predisposition to that mental illness. Thus, if three different individuals were subjected to the exact same environment and exact same stress, one might develop an emotional disturbance of one type and severity, the second might develop a disturbance of another type and severity, and the third might show no signs of emotional disturbance whatsoever. However, keep in mind that the evidence for this point of view is still incomplete. (See page 97 for additional discussion about inherited factors in personality development.)

Who is normal?

Have you ever worried that you "weren't all there"? Did you ever do something "a little nutty"? Is it possible that you are not normal? What really is *normal* behavior?

The last question is not easy to answer. First, keep in mind that "normal" and "average" are different concepts. Average height, for adult American males, for example, is about five feet, ten inches, but normal height would probably range from about five feet, three inches to six feet, four inches; average grades may be a little above a straight C, but normal people receive grades of straight F and straight A, although both those extremes are unusual. The average person does not play chess, but chess players are certainly normal. Normality is, then, a wide range of possible behavior, not just an average.

Second, what is normal in one society or in one time period is not normal in another society or another time period. In 1750, it was normal to believe that witches could destroy your cattle by putting a curse on them; today, we would not consider such a belief to be normal for American college students. In Nepal, a country squeezed in between India and China, many citizens believe that smallpox is the "kiss of the gods," but that idea would not be considered normal in our country. So, to some extent, normal behavior depends upon the time and the place.

For the purposes of this book, we will use another definition and consider a normal person to be one who knows the difference between what is real and what is not, who does not use defense mechanisms to excess, who is able to get along satisfactorily outside of an institution, and whose day-to-day behavior is not dominated by *excessively* rigid, irrational, or self-defeating actions. Using this approach, a person may be far from average, yet still be normal.

Symptoms of the non-normal

There is no particular point at which a person moves from normal to non-normal. Certain types of behavior are, at least in our society, clearly normal; certain types are clearly non-normal; certain types are borderline. Consider a simple rationalization for not getting a job, as expressed by four different people.

> "I didn't get the job, even though I'm qualified, because I don't have a college degree." (Probably normal rationalization; perhaps true statement)

> "I didn't get the job, although I'm qualified, because the supervisor is afraid to hire someone smarter than he is." (Probably normal rationalization; probably not true statement)

> "I didn't get the job, although I'm well qualified, because the personnel director is part of a secret ring of scientists who are trying to get control of the company, and they know I will expose them." (Most probably no longer normal; most probably not true statement; person may be mentally ill)

> "I didn't get the job because the president of the company is under the control of the Devil who has eaten away his brain and now wants to take over the plant to control the world." (No comment necessary)

Many deeply disturbed people behave normally most of the time; almost all normal people have some mannerisms or ideas or behavior that might be considered non-normal. The sniffles share certain symptoms with pneumonia; a student after drinking a bottle of beer shares certain characteristics with an alcoholic. Yet no one would claim that the sniffles *is* pneumonia, or that behavior after one drink *is* alcoholism.

Emotional disturbance is not an all-or-none happening, but a matter of degree. The following are examples of some symptoms of emotional disturbance that are often found in normal people but may occur in exaggerated form in very deeply disturbed individuals:

> *Depression*—feeling that everything is going wrong, that nothing matters.

> *Inappropriate worry and fear*—constantly worried or afraid about one thing or another, far out of proportion to the actual cause; chronic anxiety.

> *Suspicion*—inability to trust others, feeling that others are deceitful.

Inadequate emotional control—crying, being frightened, getting angry far out of proportion to actual stimuli.

Overly strict emotional control—not showing emotions, even when appropriate circumstances occur.

Fantasy—daydreaming so much that little gets done.

Rigidity—difficulty in behaving or thinking in new ways, tendency to follow rituals in behavior.

Organic symptoms—fatigue, illnesses, and ailments that occur without medical basis.

Hostility—undue readiness to fight, argue, or verbally attack others.

Ineffectiveness—inability to make decisions, dislike of taking responsibility for own behavior, behaving in immature fashion.

Unhappiness and tension—seeing the world as a difficult, tense place.

Inadequate interpersonal relations—contacts with other people marked by hostility, arguments, tension, suspicion, overdependence, and other signs of inadequacy.

Everyone exhibits behavior patterns like those described above from time to time, and exaggerated worry about them may be labeled **symptomitis,** a common disorder of college students, especially those in medicine, nursing, and psychology.

> Webley R. Confused had a classical case of symptomitis during his freshman year. When his psychology professor talked about rationalization, Webley knew he himself rationalized all the time; when he heard about sibling rivalry, he recalled how much he disliked his brothers; the study of religious values reminded him that he had a religious conflict. When the professor lectured on mental illness, Webley panicked—he had every symptom the professor described, and the more he heard, the worse they became.

People who overestimate the importance of some insignificant example of unusual behavior are creating unnecessary stress. People who underestimate the importance of consistently unusual behavior are ignoring a potentially real problem.

The final evaluation should be left to professionally trained people. Very few untrained people consider themselves competent to diagnose cancer, to construct a skyscraper, or to program a computer. Unfortunately, many untrained people feel competent to diagnose and even treat serious emotional problems. Trying to determine who has received adequate training is a more difficult matter. Teachers, ministers, lawyers, policemen, and physicians are constantly placed in the position of being asked to help people with emotional problems. How should they respond in such situations? When should they decide that they have exhausted their own competence and suggest the individual ask for professional psychiatric help? The validity of advice rendered through newspaper and magazine columns appears especially open to question. It is implausible that even the most sophisticated individual can learn enough about the writer of a brief letter to offer valuable advice to the letter-writer. These columns probably do no harm, as long as they are read for fun.

But most important of all: "I don't know exactly why, but people always seem to come to me with their problems. I guess I'm that sort of person." When did you last hear someone say something like that? When did you last say something like that? What are your responsibilities when people bring their problems to you? How should you respond?

Severe emotional disturbances

Symptoms described on pages 300–301 occur in exaggerated form in emotionally disturbed people. In the severely disturbed, depression may become so great that the individual does nothing but feel sorry for himself or berate himself for his own inadequacies; the emotional control can be so inadequate that there seems no relationship between the emotion expressed and the actual circumstances; the rigidity is often so great that the person must follow carefully arranged rituals or risk being extremely upset and partially incapacitated. He may even lose contact with reality and become actually incapacitated.

The emotionally disturbed, like everyone else, are trying to find methods to cope with the stress in their environment. However, because of the interaction between their own unique, often faulty, personality structure and the intense stress that occurs, their method of coping with the stress does not enable them to live a satisfactory life. Rather than consider them abnormal people, you might think of them as people under abnormal stress. Keep in mind that the stress is abnormal *for them* because of their background and personality—it might impress you as being rather mild stress, if you do not understand their personal background and feelings.

Some facts and figures on mental illness in the United States *

—At least one person in ten has some form of mental or emotional illness that needs psychiatric treatment.

—There are more people in hospitals with mental illness at any one time than with all other diseases combined.

—In 1964, 1,100,000 persons received treatment in either a mental hospital or a psychiatric ward of a general hospital.

—On any one day, about 760,000 persons are under psychiatric care either in these hospitals or under the direct jurisdiction of these hospitals.

—Each year about 600,000 persons are admitted for psychiatric treatment to one of these hospitals.

—*With good care and treatment,* seven out of ten patients admitted to mental hospitals can leave "partially or totally" recovered.

—Approximately 860,000 children and adults are served by the 1880 public and private out-patient clinics in the United States; many of these clinics are part-time, and most have long waiting lists.

—About $1,853,000,000 is spent annually on the care and treatment of patients in government-supported mental hospitals and related facilities (not including private facilities).

—An estimated $5,000,000,000 is lost to industry because of absenteeism caused by emotional disturbances and mental illness; approximately $2,000,000,000 is lost in purchasing power by people hospitalized.

* From *Facts about mental illness,* 1965 fact sheet, issued by the National Association for Mental Health.

The two major classifications of severe emotional disturbances are the **neuroses** and the **psychoses.** Both neurotics and psychotics may display exaggerated forms of behavior patterns described on page 300–301 Neurosis is considered a relatively mild personality disturbance that usually does not incapacitate the individual nor demand his hospitalization; psychosis is a very severe personality disturbance that may necessitate hospitalization. The differences between neurotic behavior and psychotic behavior are not always clear-cut, but the following may serve as an acceptable guide:

1. Psychosis is more severe and implies greater personality disorganization.
2. Psychotics are often dangerous to themselves or others and may destroy property; neurotics rarely are dangerous in these ways.
3. Psychotics usually need hospitalization both for care and for protection; neurotics can usually get along without special care and without hospitalization.
4. Psychotics rarely recognize that they are emotionally ill, while neu-

rotics often are aware of their symptoms, although they still cannot change their neurotic behavior.

5. Psychotics may show intellectual deterioration, while neurotics can function at or near their normal intellectual level.
6. Psychotics are out of touch with reality in some way; neurotics can differentiate reality from the nonreal, although they are unable to control the aspects of their own behavior affected by their neuroses.
7. Neurotics are much more likely to respond to psychotherapy than are psychotics.
8. Psychotics often exhibit **delusions** and **hallucinations,** while neurotics do not.

A delusion is a false belief, e.g., the belief that "people over there are talking about you," or that you are the ruler of the universe, or that you are being slowly eaten up by invisible insects. Hallucinations are perceptions that occur without external stimuli, e.g., hearing voices inside your head or tasting poison in your food. The following case provides examples both of delusions and of hallucinations:

> Jackson Wade was an intense young engineering student who worked hard at his studies and rarely socialized. He had been brought up on a small farm, and had developed amazing physical strength which he displayed only through being undisputed Indian wrestling champion of the freshman class. The day after the Thanksgiving holiday, Mrs. Wade telephoned the college vice-president to warn him that Jackson had told his younger brother that the vice-president had been plotting to have him expelled from college, and that it would be necessary to kill the vice-president to prevent his putting the expulsion into effect.
>
> Jackson drove back to campus with a shotgun and a rifle on the back seat of the car. Somehow he managed to elude the three-man police force in the town where the college was located, and he returned to his dormitory parking lot but slept in his car for two nights. On the third day, two of his friends noticed him in the car but were not aware either of his condition or of his threats. They asked him to accompany them to breakfast, which Jackson did without protest. On the way, they had to pass the police station, and Jackson walked in and asked the officer in charge to help him. He explained that his voices had initially commanded him to kill the vice-president, but later new and stronger voices insisted that he confess his intended crime to the police.

The delusion in this instance was Jackson's false belief that the vice-president was plotting to have him expelled from college; the hallucinations were the "voices" that commanded him first to murder the official and, later, to give himself up instead. Check the factors differentiating neurosis from psychosis to determine how many of them described Jackson. Was he neurotic or psychotic at the time described above?

Now that the broad outlines of neuroses and psychoses have been presented, we can focus upon the recognized categories and their usual symptoms. Please try to remember, however, that real people do not always fall into the neat pigeonholes described below. Not only do many individuals display symptoms from more than one category, but symptoms do not remain static—severely disturbed people change their behavior patterns just as normal people do.

Neurosis

Neurotics, or psychoneurotics, are those individuals who exhibit relatively mild personality disturbance in the way they handle stress. Although they can get along without hospitalization or constant supervision, they display certain behavior that marks them as neurotic.

An estimated one American in twenty exhibits at least mildly disruptive neurotic tendencies (Cattell and Scheier, 1961), and evidence indicates that neurosis is found more frequently among the wealthy than among the poor (Hollingshead, 1958). The classifications of neurotic behavior include **anxiety reactions, conversion reactions, dissociative reactions, phobic reactions, obsessive-compulsive reactions,** and **depressive reactions.**

Anxiety reaction. Anxiety is a fear of something vague, uncertain, or nonexistent. A person suffering an anxiety reaction feels great fear or anxiety, often for extended periods of time, with no apparent immediate cause. Bodily changes, such as rapid heart beat and extreme perspiring, often accompany these feelings of anxiety.

Conversion reaction. A psychosomatic illness is a real physical illness caused by emotional stress. Malingering refers to purposely faking some type of medical problem. Conversion reaction, which can be confused with the other two, describes sensory or motor functioning that is defective without apparent physical damage. Unlike psychosomatic problems, no bodily changes are found; unlike malingering, no conscious faking is involved.

The term **hysterical** is used in connection with conversion reactions. A person is said to have hysterical blindness when he cannot see, but no damage has occurred to his eyes, brain, or nervous system. Medical treatment is often useless, because no physical problem is involved. In spite of a lack of actual organic symptoms, however, the hysterical symptoms appear to be real and do share certain characteristics with normal medical problems.

A woman of 50, plastered heavily with make-up in a useless effort to look 30, attended one of the author's lectures. During the question period, she told the following story: "About three years ago, I woke up one morning to find I just couldn't straighten my back. At first I thought I had slept in a draft and that a hot bath would help, but it didn't. Then I began to become afraid, and I called my physician. He took all sorts of X rays and did other tests and finally told me that he couldn't find anything wrong. Well, that really got me—here I couldn't straighten up and this idiot doctor couldn't figure out why, so I really told him off. I had seven weeks' sick leave coming from my company, and I phoned a friend whose brother was a doctor and would verify that I couldn't work. After about six weeks, I was getting pretty sick of being at home, when a friend dropped in one Sunday. I told him what had been happening, and he just looked at me and laughed. He said, 'That's the poorest excuse for staying home I've ever seen, you faker. *Stand up straight!*' When he yelled at me, I got so startled that I guess I stood up straight, and I haven't had any trouble since."

It later turned out that the woman's hysterical paralysis began on the anniversary of the death of her father, who had a severe spinal condition in his last few years.

Dissociative reactions. There are several types of dissociative reactions. The **multiple personality,** a very rare occurrence in real life, seems popular in fiction. This condition refers to one person who exhibits two or more distinctly different personalities. *Dr. Jekyll and Mr. Hyde,* a short novel by Robert Louis Stevenson and later a movie, describes a multiple personality, although the shift between Jekyll and Hyde is produced by a chemical potion.

Several years ago, a book (later turned into a film) appeared describing a true instance of multiple personality. The title was *Three Faces of Eve,* by Thigpen and Cleckley (1957). The original Eve was a quiet, sweet woman with few bad habits, while the second Eve was a fun-loving, sexy creature who hated the first Eve. Later, a third Eve emerged who, with the aid of a psychiatrist, managed to eliminate the other two Eves and turn the woman back into one personality again. The different personalities had different values, different handwriting, different IQs, and different ways of talking. Finally a fourth Eve emerged with mature values, eventually becoming the only Eve.

Another dissociative reaction is **amnesia,** also very popular with writers of fiction. Amnesia is the total or partial blocking of memories concerning certain past events or periods of time, usually assumed to result from emotional stress working through the mechanism of repression. When this memory blocking occurs over an extended period of time, the condition is termed a **fugue state;** some fugue victims will actually begin a new life with a new identity, although such cases are rare.

Phobic reactions. From time to time, a person will exhibit a dread or morbid fear of some object, some person, or some situation. This morbid fear or phobia is much stronger than the situation normally calls for. Perhaps you occasionally feel a little uncomfortable in a small elevator, but the person with claustrophobia (fear of enclosed places) might perspire, shake, or even faint in the elevator. Whatever produces the phobic reaction is often interpreted as a symbolic substitute for the real cause of fear and anxiety.

Obsessive-compulsive behavior. In the very famous sleep-walking scene in Shakespeare's *Macbeth*, Lady Macbeth, some time after Macbeth had killed the king, wanders through the halls of the castle muttering, "Out, out, damned spot." She is attempting, symbolically, to rub her hands clean of the blood of the king whose murder she encouraged, but she cannot do so. Lady Macbeth is obsessed with the idea she has the king's blood still upon her and feels compelled to continue rubbing and cleaning her hands. The obsession is the idea, and the compulsion is the hand rubbing. Obsessions and compulsions are usually considered "a single . . . behavior pattern" (English and English, 1958).

In obsessive-compulsive behavior, a person's thinking is dominated by a feeling, an image, or an idea—he is obsessed by it. The compulsive behavior is an attempt to cope with the obsession through some ritualistic act, which seems to be a symbolic attempt to ward off the "evil." The compulsive behavior often seems irrational not only to observers but to the person himself.

> Rocky Prater, an excellent student in high school, went to college only because of pressure from his older brother. Unfortunately, he signed up for an inappropriate major and got into several courses he hated, so that the entire school day seemed difficult and dull. Shortly before mid-terms, Rocky developed an obsession that he had not set his alarm clock. He would lean out of bed to check, but it was always set. Sometimes he would wake up in the middle of the night with the terrible feeling that the alarm was not set, but it always was. Still he compulsively continued to go through this alarm-checking ritual every night at least once and often more frequently.
>
> Finally his counselor helped him realize that his obsession was based on his unconscious desire to sleep through his morning classes, and that the compulsion was his unconscious method of

counteracting these unrecognized feelings. Only then did his
obsessive-compulsive behavior fade away.

Rocky was certainly not seriously neurotic, in spite of his exhibiting
this particular obsessive-compulsive behavior pattern. As a matter of fact,
his specific symptom is not unusual in college students. This is, however,
an excellent example of a normal person's having one non-normal pattern
of behavior which interferes only slightly with day-to-day effectiveness.
What other examples of obsessive-compulsive behavior have you observed?

Depressive reaction. Some people have the constant feeling that nothing is going the way it should, that life has little fun or pleasure, and that
the future appears bleak. If a person maintains such attitudes far in excess
of what the conditions justify, his symptoms are those of a neurotic
depressive.

Psychosis

By and large, human beings can deal with stress well enough to avoid
becoming psychologically incapacitated. Occasionally they use neurotic
defenses to cope with the stress in their lives. Sometimes, however, for
reasons not fully understood, the person under stress will not use neurotic defenses, but will respond by losing touch with reality, i.e., by
becoming psychotic.

Unlike neurotics, the estimated one million people (Coleman, 1964)
who become psychotic for reasons other than organic causes are found
more frequently among the lower social classes and among the elderly
(Hollingshead, 1958).

Psychoses may be either **organic** (physical) or **functional** (environmental). Organic psychoses are produced directly by bodily changes.
Some examples are general paresis (caused by syphilis), brain tumor,
brain injury, and certain forms of glandular disturbance. When an elderly
person becomes mentally ill with no previous history of extreme emotional problems he often suffers from **senile psychosis,** which seems to be
at least partially the result of organic changes.

Functional psychoses occur when the stress in the environment becomes greater than the person can tolerate. The real world becomes too
painful, and the person must retreat to a world he can create for himself.
This does not imply, by any means, that mentally ill people are happy.
The general opinion of expatients and professionals working with the
mentally ill is that they are extremely unhappy; fearful and anxious;
suspicious; and for the most part, unable to enjoy work, human relation-

ships, or anything else, no matter how they might appear to a casual observer.

Although psychotics often require hospitalization, some of them are able to function normally enough to remain outside an institution; their psychosis affects only a portion of their lives. In one instance, an otherwise normal 72-year-old man accused his 68-year-old wife of running around with their granddaughter's husband. Another example involved a young man who was observed to be mumbling to himself as he worked. A few questions disclosed that he was talking to his ancestors. Other than

Figure 14–1. College students participating in Project Weekend, an educational service project of the Mental Health Association of Los Angeles County, converse with patients on a ward of a local state mental hospital. Courtesy Mental Health Association of Los Angeles County.

this unusual practice and his inability to enter into even the most casual human relationship (he was unable to look at anyone's face when conversing), he displayed no obvious signs of mental illness, and he maintained his job for many years.

Even though the functional psychoses are initiated by environmental stress, all thinking—and therefore all mental illness—involves physiological changes. Thus, the environmental stress in some fashion creates a form of biochemical change that results in behavior classified as functional psychosis.

At the same time, the organic psychoses affect people who have already lived many years, and the specific symptoms generated by an organic illness depend not only upon the disorder itself, but upon the unique history of the individual. An understanding both of biochemical and of environmental factors is necessary for a full understanding of today's knowledge of mental illness.

Although people do not fit neatly into categories, the following classification system has been widely used to describe psychotics:

Schizophrenic reactions. **Schizophrenia** is the most common form of psychosis. Several types of schizophrenia have been described, although overlap among them often occurs and differences are not always clear in real cases.

The **simple schizophrenic** shows a loss of interests, loss of ambition, emotional indifference, and withdrawal from social relations (Coleman, 1964). Situations that would arouse deep emotional feeling in a normal person receive only a casual shrug. This schizophrenic copes with stress by withdrawal from most of the world but often remains sufficiently intact to avoid hospitalization.

Perhaps the most dramatic form of mental illness is the **paranoid schizophrenic.** He has bizarre delusions (false beliefs) and frequent hallucinations (false perceptions). His behavior is often extremely unusual, and he will almost inevitably come to the attention of the medical authorities.

> Barney Hauser was from a very strict, devoutly religious family and had been brought up with a strong sense of the horrible price a person paid for sin, whether actually committed or committed through fantasy. During his senior year in high school, his parents decided to obtain a divorce. Shortly after they separated, Barney had a dream which recurred frequently in later weeks. In the dream, Barney was told that he was a re-creation of Jesus Christ, and that "the Son of God would be thrown out of the House of God."
>
> At first he told no one, since he knew people would laugh at him or think that he was crazy. As the dream was repeated again and again, he came to believe it was true, and he thought of a way to test the dream's truth. In the poorest section of his city was an old church called the "House of God." Since this was the phrase that turned up in his dream, Barney visited the minister of this church to ask his advice. The minister quickly realized how disturbed Barney was and asked him to leave, but

Barney refused and began to pound on the desk in his excitement. The noise brought some men from the store next door, and they held Barney while the minister called the police. Barney was taken from the church to the nearest psychiatric hospital. However, the entire occurrence only confirmed his dream: the Son of God (Barney Hauser) was being thrown out of the House of God.

Barney remained in the mental hospital about a year, but was released in 1963 and, as of this writing, has not needed further treatment. Since his release, he has entered college, where his performance has been adequate, and he is beginning to establish friendships. Barney's experience shows how hallucinations (the voice in his dreams) and delusions (the belief he was the re-creation of Jesus) form a mentally ill pattern of behavior.

A person is considered to have paranoid delusions when he feels people are always talking about him, plotting against him, trying to kill him, or ready to ask him to conquer the universe. A person is having hallucinations when he hears someone call him a traitor, tastes poison in his food, smells poison gases, or has some little demons nipping his heels. One navy veteran integrated his latest work assignment with his paranoid pattern when he believed he was receiving radar signals from Mars that controlled his thinking and forced him to think "strange thoughts."

The **catatonic schizophrenic** may spend days, weeks, or longer in an apparent stupor. If his hands are placed upon his head, they may remain there for hours (try it for a few minutes); he needs to be dressed, bathed, and fed. In spite of his apparent withdrawal, the catatonic is often very much aware of what is going on, and his passive behavior occasionally changes into violence, probably accompanied by hallucinations and delusions.

Confused, immature, and often silly, the **hebephrenic schizophrenic** has strange ideas and responds inappropriately to emotional situations. He uses words incorrectly and sometimes makes up his own. The hebephrenic frequently regresses to childish behavior.

Several other classifications of schizophrenic behavior have also been described. These are the childhood schizophrenic (some young children show psychotic symptoms, particularly involving extensive fantasy behavior); the chronic undifferentiated schizophrenic (in certain cases, a variety of schizophrenic symptoms may be observed, often at a mild level); the acute undifferentiated schizophrenic (similar to the previous type, except that the symptoms come suddenly and may disappear or change suddenly); the schizo-affective schizophrenic (such individuals show considerable depression or elation, along with their other schizophrenic symptoms); and the residual schizophrenic (those who have recovered sufficiently to leave the institution but who still exhibit mild schizo-phrenic symptoms).

Affective reactions. The second major grouping of psychotic charac-teristics refers to patients whose major disruption is in mood. They may exhibit extreme depression or extreme elation, often accompanied by delusions and hallucinations. Some patients alternate between a depressed state and an elated or **manic** state. In between the two psychotic condi-tions such a patient may function normally in the community for months or even years. This is termed **manic-depressive psychosis, circular type.**

Most manic-depressive patients, however, display only manic or only depressed symptoms. The manic is, in varying degrees, joyful, boisterous, and excited; he claims that everything in the world is just wonderful. He talks rapidly and constantly and is very optimistic, although these atti-tudes may be interpreted as camouflage for low self-esteem.

The depressed patient is just the opposite. If he is inactive, sad, pessi-mistic, and prone to delusions about being dead or rotting away, he is referred to as a **retarded depressive.** If, on the other hand, his depression involves a great deal of activity, rapid walking, and talking about how terrible he is, the symptoms describe an **agitated depressive** (White, 1964). Both groups display considerable self-hatred and frequently dis-cuss suicide.

Two other types of affective disorders may be briefly mentioned. The **psychotic depressive** and the **involutional psychotic** both exhibit depressed behavior. The former is similar to the depressed condition of the manic-depressive disorders, although the symptoms seem to be more directly the result of the immediate environment. The latter is a disturbance that typically occurs around the age of 45 to 55 for women and 50 to 60 for men and often involves agitation, anxiety over approaching old age and loss of vitality, and feelings of guilt and hopelessness.

Paranoid reactions. **Paranoid** (as opposed to paranoid schizophrenic) symptoms include the development of a system of delusions that are consistent, seem to make good sense, and are often persuasive to others. The delusion often centers around persecution or grandeur, but the rest of the individual's behavior seems relatively normal. Some paranoids have hallucinations but do not discuss them, because they know they will not be believed.

The two classifications of paranoid reactions are paranoia and the paranoid state. They differ only in that the latter is a little more confused, less seemingly logical, and more likely to be temporary.

> Peter Beschwan, a competent engineer, was fired from his job
> with a missile research company. The reason for his being fired

was a book outlining a new theory of aerodynamics that he had written and had published at his own expense. When the company's senior engineers read the book, they expressed great doubt that Peter had any idea of what he was talking about, and they felt his statement that his theory "outshone both Einstein and Newton" was—to say the least—a little far-fetched. When Peter learned that he was being fired, he immediately sent a letter to the company president in New York City, and, when he received a brief, unsatisfactory answer, he wrote protests to several top state officials, including the attorney-general and the governor. His letters were so well written and made so much sense to anyone who could not understand the technical problems under consideration that one state legislator demanded that a legislative committee investigate the missile company for incompetence in the use of tax funds for research. At that point, Peter wrote a follow-up letter to the legislator, thanking him for his interest. He then added that the suicide of a well-known nightclub singer was actually murder. She had spoken up for him after her performance one evening, and Peter's employer had ordered her killed.

In every other respect, Peter remained a competent, well-functioning individual. He had no hallucinations, got along well with his fellow-employees on his new job, was a good husband and father, and lived a sensible and rather conservative life. As long as the topic of his book and his old job are avoided, you would never know he had any psychotic symptoms; even if he did tell you about his troubles, you might be inclined to believe him—at least until he told you about the nightclub singer.

Everyone must cope with stress, and you inevitably find that, at various times and in various ways, your life is made less pleasant and less successful as a result of stress. Most people are able to develop adequate methods for dealing with the stress they encounter. It is only when the individual is unable to handle the stress that he employs neurotic defenses or finds the real world so emotionally painful that he must retreat from it with psychotic symptoms.

Personality disorders

Instead of exhibiting neurotic or psychotic symptoms, some people handle disruptive stress by heavy use of alcohol or narcotics, through sexual deviation, by suicide, by gambling, or by criminal behavior. The particular form or forms employed are influenced by the person's attitudes, values, self-concept, and previous psycho-social and, perhaps, medical history, as well as the characteristics of the immediate situation. (Criminal behavior will not be discussed in this book, because it receives such thorough coverage in other classes.)

Alcoholism and drug addiction

"One drink is too many and one hundred is not enough." That expression, which is a basic belief of members of Alcoholics Anonymous, states the major problem of the true **alcoholic** (many very heavy drinkers are not true alcoholics). Once he begins, the alcoholic cannot stop.

Although many people turn to liquor during times of stress, only a portion of these become addicted to it. These find they *must* have a drink —and another and another. Once they become alcoholic, they eventually lose their jobs, their friends, and their money. Even if the initial stress has disappeared, the alcoholism and the tragedy it brings produces its own stressful problems. One competent authority estimates the United States has 5,000,000 people with life adjustments seriously impaired by alcohol (Coleman, 1964).

In comparison, the 60,000 **drug addicts** seem like a very small group. Yet, even more than alcohol, some narcotics create a tremendous craving that can be satisfied only by more narcotics. Drugs, like alcohol, temporarily produce a wonderful feeling of well-being, but the same stressful world is there when the drug wears off. The world under the influence of drugs seems so much more pleasant that the desire to escape the real world plus the habit-forming effects of the drug motivate another try.

Often, a person insists that he will have no trouble kicking the drug habit when he is ready. The evidence does not bear this out. Those individuals who become addicted to drugs (not all drugs, of course, are addicting) find it overwhelmingly difficult to overcome their obsessive desire for more. Since most drug addicts do not have the funds to pay the high prices demanded by drug peddlers, they often turn to crime and prostitution for the money needed to satisfy their addiction.

Treatment both for alcoholics and for drug addicts has included psychotherapy, medication in a hospital setting, vocational rehabilitation, and membership in such organizations as Alcoholics Anonymous, Addicts Anonymous, and Synanon. Alcoholics seem more amenable to treatment than addicts, and Alcoholics Anonymous, with hundreds of chapters around the country, has had conspicuous success in helping alcoholics remain sober. AA's program includes social activities, regular meetings with explanations from members about how the organization has helped them remain sober, and—as one member phrased it—"a willingness to sit up all night and hold the hand of any member who has either had too much or thinks he will." Synanon is a large house—the original one is in

Santa Monica, California—where narcotic addicts live together and try to help each other in a relatively normal social setting, in order to overcome their addictions.

Sexual deviation

Many forms of sexual deviation occur in our society, the best known probably being **homosexuality**. Both male and female homosexuals prefer sexual relationships with their own sex, rather than with the opposite sex. Homosexuality is found among some lower forms of animals, and is reported in societies throughout the world, some of which are highly tolerant of such behavior (Ford and Beach, 1951).

Several stereotypes concerning homosexuals are totally lacking in evidence. For example, there is no good evidence that homosexuality is determined genetically or that it results from an imbalance of biochemicals, although there are some data that suggest such a possibility (Kallmann, 1953; Spectrum, 1960). Also, it is a mistaken notion that the effeminate man and the masculine woman are homosexual, while the masculine-appearing men and the highly feminine women are not; physical appearance and mannerisms can be very deceiving on this score. A third incorrect stereotype is that homosexuals have found a method of adjusting to the world which makes them happier than most heterosexuals.

Both laws and social values are strongly opposed to homosexual behavior in America today. As a result, both male and female homosexuals are fearful of police interference with their activities and, simultaneously, feel a sense of guilt for having participated in homosexual acts. Even a normal attraction, without sexual implications, to someone of your own sex may produce such guilt that an adult man finds it difficult to kiss his own father or embrace his own brother, although such affection is displayed freely in many nations of the world.

Suicide

In the United States, suicide is an illegal act and is also considered by many as an act against God. However, in some countries, killing oneself is considered appropriate under certain circumstances. Recently, suicide has been interpreted as a sign of extreme stress and, in most instances, mental illness. Although the person who fails in his suicide attempt is liable to criminal prosecution, he is more likely to receive psychiatric help in our country today. That suicide *may* result from emotional disturbance is evident; that all suicides *must* be caused by emotional disturbance is far from established.

According to folklore, people who threaten suicide will not actually kill themselves. This is completely untrue. A suicide threat or attempt is definite basis for concern and, perhaps, psychological treatment. Many people who threaten or attempt suicide may not really wish to die; they may be calling for help, using the suicide threat or attempt as a way to attract attention. One recent theory suggests that suicide occurs when people feel helpless and hopeless, and the suicide effort is their way of getting others to recognize their plight and rescue them from helplessness and hopelessness (Kobler and Stotland, 1964). Even unsuccessful suicide attempts may be injurious to health, and there is no way of knowing in advance whether the attempt will be successful or not.

A great deal of attention has recently focused on the problem of suicide, which ranks about twenty-fifth in causes of death in the United States and fourth among those of student age (United States Public Health Service; *Los Angeles Times*, May 17, 1966). One major effort to reduce suicides has been the establishment of Suicide Prevention Bureaus, patterned after that in Los Angeles. These agencies encourage potential suicides to contact them to discuss their difficulties before making the attempt; they also offer psychotherapy to people who have failed in their efforts. They are answering the cry for help (Farberow and Shneidman, 1961).

Compulsive gambling

The attitudes of Americans toward gambling are amazingly contradictory. You may find, for example, that horse racing is legal in your state, but that you cannot legally play poker for money on your front porch; bookies may be prosecuted by state law, but they are supposed to purchase a federal license nonetheless; one church condemns gambling, while another raises money by sponsoring Bingo games. Gambling laws are inconsistent from state to state or even from town to town and are very difficult to enforce.

Gambling is common in many colleges, and the stakes range from penny-ante to several dollars a chip or a point. As stakes go higher, the game attracts people who have developed an elaborate system of cheating. One university student, who worked his way through college by gambling, admitted that he was proficient at stacking the deck, slipping in marked cards, cutting as he wished, and using other tricks. "Hell, no, I don't feel sorry for those guys. They're a greedy bunch anyhow, or they wouldn't be gambling. If I find out that some guy is really broke or comes from a poor home or something, I make sure he breaks even or wins a little." A professional gambler once remarked to the author, "When I was a kid (about 1915), gambling depended upon skill. Now it's just a matter of who cheats best."

A study of gamblers shows them to be rebellious and unconventional people who describe themselves as "hating regulations." The problem gambler, however, like the problem drinker, is the *compulsive gambler*— the man who *must* gamble. He may or may not enjoy gambling, but he cannot stop. There are an estimated 6,000,000 compulsive gamblers in the United States, and they lose an estimated $20 billion a year (Rosten, 1961). For comparison, the entire cost of *all* education in the United States is only about $28 billion a year (*Statistical Abstracts*, 1965).

To show the power of the gambling compulsion, the following story is often told:

> Joe Doakes, a compulsive gambler, comes into a new town for a sales convention. As soon as business is over, he asks a taxi driver where he can find a game. "There's only one game in this town, Mister, and that's at Sharkey's Bar, but I'll warn you—it's as crooked as they come." Joe thanks the driver and gets out of the taxi. The next morning, he bumps into the driver again. "What did you do last night, Mister? Catch a movie?" "No, I thought I'd try the game at Sharkey's—I lost about $400." "But I told you it was crooked." "Yeah, but it was the only game in town."

Help for the troubled personality

Neurotics, psychotics, and individuals with personality disorders often wish to receive help in dealing with their difficulties. Their friends and relatives may wish to encourage them to seek help. And even people without severe or obvious problems may wish help in handling the stress they face, so that less of their time and energy is expended on the stress and more can be directed toward being themselves and using their capacities.

Just like the best treatment for medical and dental problems, the best treatment for psychological problems is prevention. There is good reason to believe that better parent-child relationships, fewer unhappy homes, and less poverty would all lead to fewer emotional problems and personality disorders.

However, we do not really know the best way to achieve these goals. More than that, we do not know why some people from apparently good homes and healthy family situations still become neurotic or alcoholic, while others brought up in seemingly inadequate homes turn out to be well adjusted and able to self-actualize. Psychologists and others have been able to suggest certain principles of mental health that would reduce the proportion of troubled personalities, but much work remains both in determining effective methods of prevention and in persuading people to apply them.

Help for disturbed people ranges from tranquilizers to psychotherapy to hospitalization. Each approach has its place, depending upon the individual and the circumstances.

When a person seeks help for an emotional problem, he is trying to unlearn attitudes and feelings that took years to be learned. These are very much a part of him. They form part of his self-concept, are built into his defense mechanisms, and have greatly influenced his internalized values and social relationships. Thus, although a brief period of psychological help may make a person feel better and behave more effectively,

Figure 14–2. The brig *Euphemia* was California's first mental hospital. It also housed convicts. Courtesy California Department of Mental Hygiene.

any deep-seated problem may necessitate longer treatment. Fortunately, it does not always take a long time to be able to improve day-to-day behavior through psychological help. Help is available through mental hospitals, psychotherapy, and other sources.

Mental hospitals

The emotionally disturbed person must learn new ways of looking upon himself, upon others, and upon the world in general. Sometimes he can do this in a mental hospital, where many of the stresses of everyday living are removed (although, unfortunately, others are added). The use of hospitals for disturbed people is relatively new. Up until 175 years ago, psychotics and others lived under conditions as bad as the worst prisons of the time. Before that, they had been tortured and killed for being witches and helpers of the devil.

Conditions in mental hospitals in the United States slowly became better over the years, but even today many are overcrowded and under-staffed. Now the use of such institutions is entering a new phase. More and more patients are being helped on a part-time basis. These patients may spend evenings or weekends in the hospital but work at regular jobs during the day, or they may live at home but come to a **halfway house** during the day (Wechsler, 1960). More and more effort is being made to help patients continue their normal pattern of living as much as possible.

Figure 14–3. One ward at an overcrowded mental hospital. Courtesy California Department of Mental Hygiene.

Psychotherapy

Psychotherapy is the process through which a person trained in psychological treatment techniques applies these techniques, using personal consultation, to help another learn to handle his problems more effectively. Psychotherapy is not limited to emotionally disturbed individuals but is frequently used by normal people with normal problems who feel the help will be valuable. Although most psychotherapy involves one therapist and one client or patient, group psychotherapy has been shown to be effective also.

Usually a person in psychotherapy will talk about himself and his feelings, while the psychotherapist listens and tries to help the client understand himself, his attitudes, and his feelings. Many psychotherapeutic theories exist, and psychotherapists argue over which is best. However, the approaches have a great deal in common.

(1) Each theory makes use of a therapist who shows interest, trust, and respect for the client. The therapist may or may not offer obvious encouragement, but the mere fact that he listens carefully and responds with understanding and patience is reassuring.

(2) Each theory includes the opportunity for the client to express his feelings. In the therapy situation, the client can usually discuss his most personal fears, desires, hates, and his most embarrassing and guilt-producing behavior and fantasies. Once they are expressed by the client and accepted by the therapist, the client often feels less anxious and his self-concept achieves a new sense of adequacy. We cannot express all these feelings to those we love, nor to a casual stranger, but we can do so to a person who shows he is interested in us and respects us.

(3) Each theory makes some use of the client's increasing his insight into his own feelings and motives. Although insight itself is no guarantee of improved self-concept, insight in combination with the opportunity for self-expression and a healthy client-therapist relationship seems to be helpful. If the therapist tries to force the client to understand himself too quickly, the client may quit therapy—he will feel the therapist does not really understand him. Insight must come gradually.

(4) Each theory attempts to create new forms of behavior, new attitudes, and new self-concepts. These are aimed at enabling the person to function more effectively in society *and* to recognize himself as an adequate and worthwhile individual.

The individual schools of therapy, in spite of sharing many basic characteristics, also differ in many respects. Some emphasize the need for lengthy treatment, while others try to provide treatment in a brief period of time. Some require that the therapist keep his own values divorced from his therapy, while others enable the therapist to include his values. Some insist that the individual remain responsible for the pacing and the direction of the therapy, while others give the therapist more freedom to control the therapy. Some include the use of psychological tests, while others reject this device. Some assume sex to be the usual source of difficulty, while others emphasize the self-concept, the encounter with death, personal identity and meaning, or inappropriate conditioned responses.

Psychotherapy does not always lead to marked improvement. Sometimes little or no apparent change occurs, although improvement may have a delayed reaction. Fortunately, many people are helped greatly.

Psychotherapy should not be thought fun for the client, even though its long-range effects are good. We all use defense mechanisms to fool ourselves. Psychotherapy may force people to see themselves as they really are, and even though the therapist does his best to make insight a positive experience, self-recognition is often very painful. One young man, for example, recognized in therapy that he had delighted in tormenting his father. Unfortunately, his father was dead, and since he could not apologize, he felt very guilty. Several therapy sessions were spent trying to ease these guilt feelings, but these sessions were only partially successful.

Other methods

Psychotherapy may be used for all forms of emotional and social problems, but since it is expensive and time-consuming and since there are not nearly enough trained therapists to fulfill the demand, other forms of treatment are frequently used.

One common way of reducing anxiety is to take **tranquilizers.** These pills do not solve any problems, but they help you to feel better. Unfortunately, many people find it too easy to depend upon tranquilizers, and they never face up to their real problems.

Other treatment methods include occupational therapy, music therapy, recreation therapy, and art therapy, all of which give the patient a form of activity and an opportunity to express himself. Drugs and hypnosis are occasionally used, with varying degrees of success. More drastic methods include brain surgery (not used much now for functional psychoses) and shock treatments, both of which cause behavior changes through physiological changes.

Help for the college student

The odds are high that you or one of your close friends or relatives will someday be placed in a mental hospital. Of all people living in the United States today, an estimated one-in-ten to one-in-twenty will someday occupy a bed in a mental hospital or halfway house. Many others will need some sort of help outside of institutions. Thus, help for the troubled personality is of immediate concern to the college student.

Colleges themselves offer a variety of counseling facilities, some providing short-term and occasionally long-term psychotherapy for students. Help for study difficulties or vocational problems is usually available, either through the counseling center or through a faculty member.

Free or low-cost community facilities are often at hand, although they may require a lengthy waiting period. Someone on the college faculty or administration can usually help a student locate an appropriate community facility or provide the name of a competent psychotherapist. If help is not available at his own school, a student can contact another college or university in the area to get such information or ask a local physician or minister for a referral. The Yellow Pages of the telephone book usually carry a list of psychologists and psychiatrists, but not all these are necessarily qualified. Since many "psychoquacks" masquerade as qualified psychotherapists, a person seeking help should make certain he is using the proper channels.

Sometimes an attempt to obtain help meets with frustration. You get yourself all ready to talk with someone and then find that all appointments are booked for ten days. Or you finally decide to get low-cost psychotherapy and learn that your community has no facilities. It is best to be persistent. Once you have taken the first step, make certain you get the help you desire.

SUMMARY OF IMPORTANT IDEAS

1. When the demands of stress are greater than the individual can deal with, the result is often faulty or disturbed adjusting behavior; as the situation becomes more stressful, the faulty adjustment becomes more obvious, and the resulting behavior becomes more confused and disorganized, more rigid, and more (apparently) irrational.

2. Normal behavior falls within a wide range of possibilities; normal and average are different concepts.

3. Normal behavior varies as a result of the culture.

4. Many deeply disturbed people behave normally most of the time; almost all normal people have some mannerisms or ideas or behavior that might be considered non-normal.

5. Emotionally disturbed people can be considered as people under abnormal stress, although the stress may not seem abnormal to the outside observer.

6. The two major classifications of severe emotional disturbance are the neuroses and the psychoses; among the many differences between the two are the following: the neuroses are milder, less likely to require hospitalization, and more amenable to psychotherapy and other forms of treatment than are the psychoses.

7. Among the symptoms of neuroses are extreme anxiety, defective sensory or motor functioning without organic cause, disso-

ciative reactions, extreme fears or phobias, obsessive-compulsive behavior, and chronic depression.

8. Among the symptoms of psychoses are hallucinations, delusions, inappropriate emotional responses, withdrawal from social relationships, feelings of persecution and other paranoid feelings, physical immobility, regression to earlier stages of development, extreme depression, and extreme elation.

9. Psychosis may be caused by functional (environmental) or organic (bodily) factors.

10. Some people handle disruptive stress by heavy use of alcohol or narcotics, sexual deviation, suicide, compulsive gambling, or criminal behavior.

11. Alcoholism occurs when "one drink is too many and a hundred is not enough."

12. Drug addiction often leads to criminal acts to obtain the funds to purchase more narcotics.

13. The best-known form of sexual deviation is undoubtedly homosexuality.

14. The causes of suicide and attempted suicide include extreme stress, emotional disturbance, helplessness, and hopelessness.

15. Gambling, although illegal in many communities, is very common; Gamblers Anonymous serves compulsive gamblers, as Alcoholics Anonymous helps compulsive drinkers.

16. Mental hospitals and various forms of therapy are commonly utilized; psychotherapy is frequently preferred, and schools of psychotherapy have many concepts in common, in spite of their differences.

17. Like everyone else, the college student frequently needs some form of professional psychological help for emotional problems.

IV *Man and his society*

Career planning and the world of work 15

This chapter represents a substantial break with the materials of the previous few chapters. Until now, the emphasis has been upon the individual; here we shift the focus to the social environment. Your sociology class may have dealt with the same topics, but in a different way. The first chapter in this section involves careers and work. Once again, you will read about personality, needs, and self-actualization, but in the context of career planning. An individual human being— the unique result of perception, learning, needs, early and later development, emotions and stresses, and sometimes even highly disruptive life circumstances—now is approached as part of a social environment.

What career field are you planning to enter? Why? How much do you know about this field? Do you know what is required to enter the field? The nature of the work? The working conditions? The opportunities for advancement? In what ways will the work satisfy your needs? We can assume it will earn you enough money to pay for food and shelter, but will it help you satisfy your security or self-esteem needs? Will it offer you the possibility for self-actualization?

Answers to these questions cannot be given on the spot, but such answers are very important to career planning and subsequent satisfactions during the adult years. After all, for better than two-thirds of your lifetime, for more than one-third of your waking hours, you will be engaged in activities related to producing income. Except for the retired and the housewife (whose working hours may be longer than her husband's), almost all adults work for financial return. Your career and your subsequent success and satisfaction are highly significant in many ways. Inevitably, your job determines your income and, thus, affects what you buy and your level of living. Your job also is a measure of your status and that of your family, a status only partially related to income. Thus, a teen-ager complained to "Dear Abby" that her parents pressured her to break up with her boy friend only because his father was a garbage collector, although the incomes of the two families seemed comparable (*Los Angeles Times*, December 31, 1965).

Your job reflects your educational level, your past achievements and future prospects, your values and attitudes, your self-concept, and—at least for some people—your means of personal growth and self-actualization.

Job success and **job satisfaction** (although related, they are not the same thing) can support an already healthy self-concept or help bolster low self-esteem. They can lead to great satisfaction, the feeling of accomplishment, and self-actualization. Lack of job success and low job satisfaction can have just the opposite effects.

Because the importance of work is generally recognized, most college students have already given considerable thought to their careers before their freshman year, and some have already worked out a thoughtful, sensible career plan.

Too often, however, their vocational planning is unrealistic in light of their abilities, interests, and personality. A girl who played the lead in the high school play is confident she will be a movie star; a boy wants to be a lawyer because he enjoys arguing; another wants to study personnel management because he likes people; and invariably several students have had stories rejected by *Playboy, Saturday Evening Post,* and *McCall's.*

Frequently the student's vocational plans result from family pressures to enter a career that satisfies the parents but may be unrelated to the student's goals and values. Sometimes a student plans an unrealistic career because parents, teachers, and friends demand his decision before he is actually ready to make one. Those who can make a proper vocational choice before beginning college are fortunate, but students who are pressured to make their decision too quickly will regret their hurry in later years.

Some of the major sources of confusion regarding vocational fields include the requirements for entering the field (e.g., education, skills, health, union membership); potential income (a large majority of college students anticipated an unrealistically high income after ten years of work; Goldsen et al., 1960); the amount of work and time necessary for success and advancement; and the availability of openings at the managerial and professional levels for which the individual is qualified (there are ample openings today, but few people can meet management demands). Effective career planning demands a knowledge both of yourself and of the nature of jobs and the job market.

Personal characteristics in career planning

How well do you know yourself? What should you know about yourself when you begin your career planning? Does it matter whether you are aggressive or shy, adept with your hands or clumsy, interested more in earning money or more in helping others? Of course it does. Some of the more important personal characteristics in career planning include interests, needs, values, personality, abilities, education, environmental pressures, and **demographic** characteristics such as age, health, and citizenship.

Interest, needs, values, and personality characteristics

If you are interested in your work, if the tasks you perform help satisfy your needs, if the purpose and methods of your organization are consistent with your values, if your personality characteristics are appropriate for the work, then you are very likely to be successful on the job. You will readily spend extra time on the job, and the time will pass quickly. You will not have the feeling, when you get up in the morning, "Nuts, another day of work. I'll sure be glad when this is over."

Unfortunately, not everyone is interested in his work or satisfied with what he does or with the organization for which he works. His work bores him. He spends each day looking forward to going home; each week, looking forward to the weekend; each year, living for vacation.

Why do certain people end up in a career they dislike? Perhaps because they lacked the training or competence to do what they wanted; or else they misjudged their own interests and personal attributes; some may have wrongly estimated the degree to which they valued money or status or working conditions; others have simply yielded to the demands of family and friends. There are inevitably those who never really planned their careers, but suddenly found themselves in the middle of a career before they ever stopped to figure it out.

Each individual has a unique pattern of interests, needs, values, and personality characteristics. Any one pattern is appropriate for certain careers but not for others. Police applicants, for example, have higher

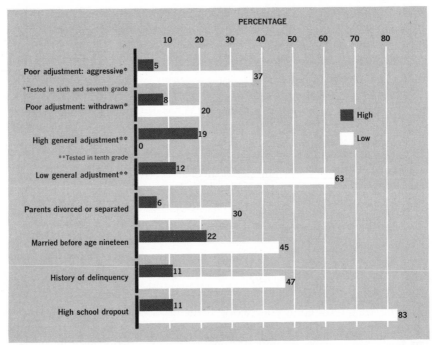

Figure 15-1. Comparison of high and low work-adjustment groups (Havighurst et al., 1962).

than average needs for achievement, dominance, and exhibitionism; they are also very masculine, but not especially interested in independence (Matarazzo et al., 1964).

One recent investigation tried to determine what basic factors relate to career choice. The authors found that a person's selection of a vocational field depends largely on the degree of importance he places upon the following: (1) having a good self-concept (desire to be popular, emotionally stable, influential); (2) being personally comfortable; (3) enjoying artistic and creative tasks; (4) desiring prestige; (5) enjoying scientific and technical tasks; (6) being able to help others and to become personally mature. Students majoring in business placed above average value on personal comfort; clergymen stressed the value of helping others; both nurses and secretaries indicated above average value on both personal comfort and helping others (Astin and Nichols, 1964). How much importance do you attribute to each of these six values?

The "high" in Figure 15–1 refers to being considered in the top quarter in work adjustment at about age nineteen; the "low" refers to being considered in the bottom eighth in work adjustment at the same age. Note that personality tests as early as sixth grade can predict, to some extent, job success seven or eight years later. However, it is well to remain aware that, in spite of the obvious trends, there were successful individuals in each grouping (Havighurst et al., 1962).

Abilities

As the result of the dynamic interplay between heredity and environment, each person develops a unique pattern of **abilities** and potential abilities. Since different careers emphasize different ability patterns, an effective career plan tries to match the abilities of the individual to the requirements of the field. Both automobile salesmen and bank managers need to have good verbal ability, but the automobile salesman should have a different type of persuasive ability. A carpenter and a nurse both require a minimum level of ability with numbers, but the carpenter needs the ability to look at a blueprint and turn the plan into reality, while the nurse must be able to deal with ill patients.

How successful are you in maintaining good relationships with other people? Almost every job depends to some extent upon this ability, and some—like salesman, social worker, minister, union organizer—depend greatly on human relations ability. However, even skill in human relations has many facets, and much more than the ability and interest in getting along with people must be considered for career planning. The following hypothetical case combines several actual occurrences:

> Evelyn Darcieux came to the counselor's office to discuss her career plans. "I don't have much idea of what I want to do, except I want to work with people." The counselor grinned a little. "Okay, if that's all you care about. You could be a

Figure 15–2. The demand for technical skills requires both workers and teachers. Courtesy Parks Job Corps Center, Litton Industries.

missionary in Africa, or a policewoman on the narcotics squad, or a lifeguard, or a nursery school teacher. All these jobs involve the ability to work with people." Evelyn laughed, and the counselor continued, "Of course, the most important thing is to decide what kind of relationship you want with what kind of people. Very few of us have the ability to get along with all people under all conditions. Do you want to be in charge of people or work under people? Do you think you have the ability to persuade others or to learn to see through others when they try to persuade you? Do you have the ability to make decisions, and risk being unpopular? Or do you prefer to carry through someone else's decision? Does your ability extend to all age groups equally? To normal or to emotionally disturbed people or to lawbreakers? Do you prefer a few people at a time or many? The same people every day or new people all the time?" Evelyn cut in as the counselor paused a moment, "I see— let me think about it."

When she returned a week later, she had given the matter much thought. "I think I know what I want, although, of course, I might change later. But I think I want to work with adults, normal people. I'd like to work with the same people, rather than different ones, and I want to be in charge of people, even if I do become unpopular. Also I'd prefer to have close relationships with a few people, rather than more casual relationships with a large number."

Can you suggest some vocations which would meet Evelyn's criteria? Each individual has job-related abilities, but—like Evelyn—many people need help in relating their abilities to vocational fields.

Education and training

Although many organizations give some on-the-job training, schools and colleges are responsible for teaching most job skills. Traditionally colleges and universities trained managerial and professional personnel, while high school marked the end for everyone else. Today the junior colleges supply not only a stream of students to four-year institutions, but another stream directly into the job market. Careers in such fields as engineering, teaching, forestry, library science, or city planning require four years or more of college. Other careers are open both to junior college and to four-year college graduates, with sometimes one and sometimes the other being favored. Such careers include: insurance salesman, police officer, freelance writer, X-ray technician, dental assistant, auto mechanic, electrician, stenographer, nurse, printer, stock broker, office manager, commercial artist, and television repairman.

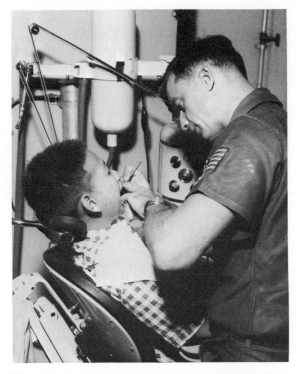

Figure 15–3. What kind of relationship with what kind of people do you want on your future job? This Air Force sergeant is in Vietnam as a dental technician. Courtesy United States Air Force.

Environmental pressures

Although many people do ·not realize it, career planning is strongly influenced by several sources of environmental pressures, including family and friends. These pressures often operate unconsciously because they stem from values the student has internalized before entering college.

> The son of a soldier killed in the Korean War has internalized the value that a professional army career is dignified and worthy.

> A young girl watches her mother wait table in a restaurant and internalizes her mother's beliefs that office work is far preferable.

> A young father spends hours, together with his son, working happily to keep the family car clean, efficient, and comfortable. The son grows up feeling that being an auto mechanic would be getting paid for having fun.

Pressures, of course, may be more obvious, such as the father who offered his son a new sports car if he decided to study accounting, or the girl whose parents would not finance her college if she majored in journalism.

Friends can also influence vocational choice. A person whose friends are all entering college is reluctant to admit that he has no intention of going. If everybody in a group of college women expects to become a career girl, their one friend who is interested only in marriage and a home may feel inadequate.

Demographic characteristics

In certain vocational fields, success depends not only on ability, or even ability plus luck plus pull. Other factors, often having little or nothing to do with ability, are related to getting jobs and must be considered in career planning. These include sex, age, race, religion, and nationality.

Sex. In the United States, certain vocational fields are looked upon as being largely or strictly for men; these include engineering, medicine*, physics, construction work, radio announcing, and many factory jobs. Other careers, such as elementary school teaching, nursing, and many secretarial jobs, are thought most appropriate for women.

A person can, of course, enter a career traditionally associated with the opposite sex, although he may face discrimination both in receiving training and in getting jobs. Nonetheless, anyone who feels he will receive important satisfactions from such a career has the opportunity to prepare for it; in spite of difficulties, openings are available.

Age. Some positions are closed to those who are too young, while others are closed to those too old. Even looking too young may be a problem. A competent personnel interviewer had difficulty getting a job, because, although he was 26 years old, he looked much younger, and the personnel director felt that prospective workers would take him for a teen-ager and be resentful. Looking older is an advantage for young people, while looking young may be an advantage for those in the latter half of their working careers.

Race, religion, and nationality. Members of certain groups find work unusually difficult to obtain, even when they have the necessary qualifications. The Negro American is undoubtedly the most severely punished by job discrimination, although Americans of Mexican, Italian, Greek, and Asian ancestry also meet frequent hiring and promotion problems; Jews, Catholics, and the American Indian have similarly suffered from job discrimination.

*In Russia, over half the physicians are women.

A large portion of the difficulties faced by the Negro, like those faced by women, result from their long history of being considered inferior. Because of economic and cultural deprivation, many Negroes do not fully comprehend that education and training can lead them to good jobs and income. Of course, they have been told, but being told and comprehending are different matters. Since, for numerous environmental reasons, many Negroes are in the lower social classes, the statement of one author regarding social class applies particularly well.

> Occupational choice is much more restricted in the lower classes . . . because of fewer opportunities for education and training, lowered expectations, ignorance of alternatives, need for early income, probably a greater stress on immediate gratification of desires, the lack of informed and sympathetic adult advice, and the greater operation of chance (Berelson and Steiner, 1964).

However, even the Negro with high competence has trouble getting a job. "We'd like to hire you as a salesman, but our customers are all white." "I'm sure you're a good engineer, but a lot of our employees might not understand." "Your experience as a nurse is fine, but our patients might not like it." "You can't get a job here without a union card and you can't get a union card without someone sponsoring you, and I don't know anyone in the union who would sponsor you."

These are representative of the statements made when Negroes apply for jobs. A Negro student, then, must answer three questions: (1) If he is interested in a career that seems closed to Negroes, should he train for that position or for another position that might be easier to get—or both? (2) If he cannot find a job appropriate for his abilities and training in his own community, should he look elsewhere, take a lesser job, or fight for what he feels he deserves? (3) If he is offered a reasonable position by a company with an apparent policy of never promoting Negroes, should he accept it with the idea of proving himself or take a lesser job with more future promise? How would you decide such dilemmas?

Members of discriminated-against minority groups also face another difficult problem: if they are turned down for a job, they may never be certain whether their minority status was the basis, or whether the job was taken by a more competent individual. Thus, they lose an opportunity for self-evaluation and gain an opportunity for rationalization. More recently, many major companies have begun recruiting qualified Negroes for higher-level positions, and the Job Corps is providing excellent training for members of *all* racial groups who left school too soon to receive job skills.

And so forth . . . . Other individual characteristics also enter into career planning. These include physical health and stamina, appearance and size, sensory acuity such as good vision and hearing, citizenship, criminal record, driver's license, and present marital status. By and large, you can evaluate the relevance of these additional characteristics to your career choices; then you can determine how you qualify for each.

To plan a career, an individual should know about himself and about the variety of career possibilities. He needs to consider his own unique pattern of background, personality, and abilities and to relate these to what various vocational fields offer and what they require.

Job considerations in career planning

So far the discussion has emphasized the qualities of the job-holder, but careful consideration of the characteristics of the job and the job market is also essential. Do you have a clear picture of the career field you intend to enter? What are its requirements? What does it offer you? Some of the more important considerations in evaluating a career field include the job market, job requirements, job description, working conditions, advancement opportunities, income and other material benefits, the social status of the job, and the opportunity for personal growth and satisfaction. (Figure 15—5 shows how one large group of college students evaluated the important aspects of their future careers.) Keep in mind that you may be well suited for more than one vocational field. How would you prepare under such circumstances?

Getting the job

Even a good career plan loses some value if a student does not know how to look for a job. Many unnecessary frustrations may be eliminated by a carefully planned and conducted job search.

1. Begin to search for a position eight to ten weeks before graduation.
2. Use all available sources: classified advertisements, government job listings, friends and relatives, college and other placement bureaus.
3. Apply to several organizations.
4. Be prepared to wait—personnel decisions may take several weeks.
5. Have references all lined up.

6. Have a well-executed biographical outline mimeographed—
these can be left with references, enclosed in letters to prospective employers, used to supplement application forms,
sent to friends to "keep an eye out for me."

7. For job interviews, dress appropriately, be relaxed, and do
not try too hard to impress the interviewer; honesty is the
best policy.

The job market

Our country is a dynamically changing nation. Entire vocational fields
are born and disappear each decade. Automation is eliminating certain
careers while creating new ones. The funeral director, the kindergarten
teacher, the commercial artist, the policeman, and the receptionist are all
likely to be around for a while. But miners, railroad firemen, dock
workers, and certain types of white-collar workers are going the way of
the blacksmith.

Nor are all job fields equally crowded. At any given time, certain
career areas have an overabundance of qualified people, while other fields
are suffering a shortage. Also the job market in your community may
differ from the job market 100 or 1,000 miles away. And because of the
changing nature of the job market, training and education beyond high

Figure 15–4. Computers are part of the world of tomorrow. Courtesy California State College at Los Angeles.

school become important in providing career flexibility, so that you can
move easily from one job field to a related one. Without a doubt, your
career plan is made more effective by careful consideration of the job
market, both present and future, both local and national.

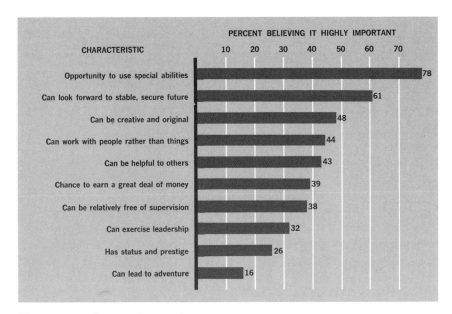

Figure 15–5. Career characteristics considered important by college students (Goldsen et al., 1960).

Job requirements

Different vocations, of course, have different requirements. Experience, education, human relations ability, and good written and spoken English are merely a few of the many types of demands that must be met to succeed in certain vocational fields.

Job requirements must be known before any career plan can be established. Many students talk casually about becoming dentists or atomic physicists only to learn to their dismay that these careers demand seven or eight years or more of college. Others decide to become electricians or television stagehands and do not find out soon enough that they must enter a highly selective union.

Standards in many vocational fields are being upgraded. Fifty years ago, teachers and social workers did not even need a high school diploma in many states; today most such positions demand a minimum of a college degree. The nurse, pharmacist, funeral director, librarian, and military officer have all seen their fields tighten requirements for entrance. Some states now demand that barbers, policemen, and real estate salesmen all pass written examinations.

Earlier it was stated that career planning demanded an awareness of personal characteristics. Job requirements are the other side of the coin, and the career plan should attempt to match personal characteristics with job requirements. (You may prefer to consider job requirements as pertaining not only to getting the position, but also to success and satisfaction on the job.)

Job description

What, precisely, will you be doing on your eventual job? Strangely enough, many students do not bother to investigate carefully. It sounds romantic to be an FBI agent, but what does he do on a typical day? Some girls think nurses spend all their time helping kindly old women and unhappy little children, but what do nurses actually do? The work of an airplane pilot or a reporter may seem exciting, but what do they really do?

Exactly what tasks do the potential jobs in your career field call for? Will you sell to people? Buy from people? Give orders? Take orders? Make decisions? Carry out decisions of others? Use a pencil? A lathe? A

"IBM. Good morning."

Figure 15–6. Automation is a threat to many types of jobs, but there is no substitute for a pleasant receptionist. (Well, almost none.) Courtesy Ed Fisher.

typewriter? Be subject to stress? To time pressures? Sit behind a desk? Work outside? Travel around the country? Around the city? After all, the things you do from day to day will be a controlling element in your enjoyment of your career. Too often people allow the **image** of their job field to blind them to the importance of the daily routines.

Working conditions

Health, safety, cleanliness, comfort, having a private office and a personal secretary, being indoors or outdoors, these working conditions are inevitable considerations in career planning.

The forest ranger spends much time alone; the skilled automobile mechanic gets greasy; the beautician handles chemicals; the riveter works under noisy conditions (so does the nursery school teacher); the stockbroker wears a business suit and sits all day in an office.

Literally hundreds of potential factors are involved in working conditions, ranging from the hours, the shift, and the travel requirements to the dirt, the temperature, and the smells.

Advancement opportunities

Advancement can come within a vocation or by changing to a related vocation, within a company or by changing companies. The plumber opens a plumbing equipment shop and becomes a businessman; then he sells his business and is appointed vice-president of a company manufacturing plumbing equipment. Another plumber becomes increasingly successful, takes on several helpers, yet remains a plumber himself. Both have advanced.

However, certain careers offer only limited advancement. To make matters worse, some positions look good at first and offer a fairly good salary; then, after several years, the employee realizes that he cannot advance and that he would have to take a severe salary cut if he changed jobs.

These dead-end jobs are very frustrating, because a look into the future reflects back an image of the present. To contemplate many more years of disagreeable work is hardly a pleasant thought, but—fortunately—additional education or training often enables a person to advance within his own company or to move to a better position elsewhere.

Income and other benefits

Some people have a great need for money, while others get along well on a moderate amount. One element of career planning is the evaluation of how the individual's needs would be satisfied by his probable income in various fields. Although such information is available, many students overestimate their own future income potential.

Salary is not the only form of payment. Various fringe benefits, including vacations and extra pay for overtime, cost large employers an estimated 27 percent of their payroll and are increasing twice as quickly as base salaries (Zollitsch, 1964). The value of fringe benefits varies greatly from field to field and from job to job.

Social status of the job

When people are asked to rank jobs according to status, they do so with remarkable consistency (Deeg and Paterson, 1947), and the average rankings today are not much different from those of 30 years ago. One of the main reasons students attend college is to be able to get a "better" job, with "better" referring to social status as much as to income.

> Gene Machover had been working as a wholesale milk delivery man for twelve years. Unlike the door-to-door delivery man, who usually carries only two or three bottles at a time, Gene had to carry two or three dozen at a time. Considering his lack of job skills, the pay was good, but two things bothered Gene: (1) his income was remaining fairly constant and promotion was unlikely, since administrative positions were usually given college graduates; and (2) his back was beginning to bother him. He began to look for a new career field and soon found a position representing a canned-goods producer. His job was to visit food markets to see that his company's products were well displayed, to introduce new products, and to take care of complaints. His initial income dropped by 30 percent, but Gene anticipated he could make that up over the years to come. In addition, he proudly listed other advantages: he drove a company car; he did not have to wake up at 4:30 in the morning; he could stay clean all day; he had no heavy lifting. And his wife took pride in hanging white shirts on the clothes line instead of his uniform shirts.

Gene improved his working conditions, his advancement opportunities, and his job status, even though his income dropped temporarily and became less secure. Evidence exists that higher-status positions lead to feelings of greater personal satisfaction (Hoppock, 1935).

Opportunity for job satisfaction, personal growth, and self-actualization

In final analysis the purpose of career planning is to help the individual become as satisfied as possible with his career and his various jobs. If his choice of career is appropriate, the individual's work experience should provide him with personal growth and the opportunity for self-actualization.

Job satisfaction is important not only to the worker but also to his employer, since employees who find their jobs satisfying tend to do better work (Herzberg et al., 1957). Although exceptions do occur, research has shown that accidents are fewer, absenteeism is less, and performance is better when employee attitudes toward work are good (Brayfield and Crockett, 1955).

After careful research, two psychologists (Zander and Quinn, 1962) concluded that job satisfaction depends upon seven major factors: (1) an opportunity for self-actualization; (2) a supervisor who takes a personal interest in his employees; (3) a clear understanding of the task to be done; (4) high pay *relative* to those on similar jobs and the feeling that the work is recognized; (5) supervisors and fellow workers who support your decisions and complaints; (6) a job with higher status; and (7) participation in the process of making decisions regarding your own work.

Notice how many of the above factors involve relationships with fellow workers and with supervisors, especially in terms of being respected and being treated as a mature, competent human being.

When the job offers the opportunity for self-actualization, job satisfaction is greatly increased. Work is far more satisfying when the individual is able to use his present talents and develop new ones, when he feels he has done a good job that benefits others and that they appreciate, when self-expression can take place, when a challenge exists, and when the nature of the work is felt to reflect the individual's "real" self.

When the person feels he is no longer improving, no longer learning, no longer finding new ways to do things, he begins to mark time. The working day becomes a time to be gotten through as quickly and easily as possible, and important satisfactions come primarily from sources outside of work.

Many of us think that a person must achieve something big in order to feel he is self-actualizing. The following is an example of just the opposite:

> Elton Baintree* had a very small role in a Broadway show starring Helen Hayes. Although well into his fifties at the time, Mr. Baintree had never known an actress he had admired more than Miss Hayes. His great joy from merely sharing the stage with such a fine actress undoubtedly outshone the satisfaction

---

*Elton Baintree is not the correct name of the actor. However, the remainder of the anecdote is as accurate as my memory for an incident that occurred over 20 years ago. The meeting with this exciting man made a great impact upon me at the time, and I still carry his enthusiasm with me.

some of the more important actors received from what, to them, was just another acting job. On one occasion, Miss Hayes told him that his two lines (he had only three in the entire show) brightened up the final moments of the second act. These words were a great treasure for Mr. Baintree.

Mr. Baintree worked with his three lines and few minutes of action to give more meaning to his role. He put more effort into his small part than many actors put into leads. Few people recalled him after leaving the theater, but Elton Baintree gained a tremendous amount of satisfaction and personal growth from his work in this play. Unfortunately, not many people have Mr. Baintree's gift for seeing a small part as having meaning in terms of a larger production, nor do many have the ability to strive constantly for growth and improvement.

Self-actualization is possible in any career. Like Elton Baintree, each individual has the option of turning a small role into something meaning-ful, or else he can just go through the motions and do an adequate job. Some people can achieve great personal growth through being an artist or a writer; others will find maximum self-actualization by being a landscape gardener, a government official, a housewife, or an insurance salesman.

Each person is unique, with a unique set of abilities, interests, and other characteristics. Thus each person must find self-actualization through work in his own way. Planning for the career that seems to offer the greatest possibilities for self-actualization is a difficult but fruitful task.

Early work experience

College students usually have little or no job experience in the voca-tional field they enter, but many opportunities are available for part-time and summer positions which relate directly or indirectly to future jobs. Even delivering newspapers, jerking sodas, or baby-sitting provide experi-ence in earning and handling money, taking responsibility and initiative, and dealing with a variety of personalities. Almost half the high school students report some paid employment during a given year (Harris, 1961), and well over half the boys between 14 and 18 worked, many of them 20 hours a week and more (Boys' Clubs of America, 1960).

During college, jobs directly related to future careers may be available. The secretarial or business major may find office work; future nurses may work as hospital aides or volunteers; summer camp work and Sunday School teaching are valuable experience for a variety of vocations.

Having had some work experience, or even a regular volunteer posi-tion, has at least three advantages: (1) employers are more likely to select

Figure 15–7. This student has tentatively selected forestry for a career. What sorts of working conditions would he seem to like? Courtesy Antioch College and Ohio Agricultural Experiment Station.

a person with even brief experience over those with none; (2) supervisors can give valuable recommendations; and (3) having worked, the student has a much better idea of what to expect in the future.

The combination of work experience and classroom learning is more valuable than either without the other. Not only is the experience useful, but it is a way to test your future possibilities in a field.

> A college business major worked part-time and summers in a large department store. After three years of this, he decided he hated department stores in particular and merchandising in general, but his father persuaded him that his income potential was very high in merchandising, so he continued his major. After graduation he took a job with a large chain department store, but was neither successful nor happy. Eventually he drifted into personnel work, where his performance was somewhat better.

Military service

Experience in the military can be both vocationally and academically profitable, or it can simply be marking time. The armed services encourage personnel to take courses on the base and at nearby colleges. In addition, of course, many military jobs provide valuable work experience. A medical technology major serves in the army medics; a hotel management major orders food for navy mess; a future public relations man is assigned to an information and education unit. For these men, the years of military service provided meaningful vocational experience.

Creating a job

Do you have the initiative, creativity, and motivation to develop your own job? Not only is this financially rewarding, but it offers an exciting challenge and is also most impressive to future employers.

> Mel Michale attended a small Ohio college where all the students lived in dormitories. Although a college coffee shop was open until nearly midnight, many of the students did not like to leave their studies to walk over, especially in snowy weather. Mel started delivering small pies, sandwiches, and coffee to the dorms, and soon had a steady demand for his services.

By learning what products or services are desired in a community, you may be able to establish a thriving business. It demands careful planning and often consumes more time than you expected, but both the financial rewards and the personal satisfaction are great.

Sources of information

For effective career planning, the student must have information both about himself and about the various vocational fields. Information sources for the latter are readily available, but learning about yourself is much more difficult and gives rise to some interesting problems.

Information concerning vocational fields

Many publications describe jobs and career fields. The college counselor or public library may have files of occupational information, including books, pamphlets, and even films discussing various careers. These sources give the income potential, educational requirements, advancement opportunities, work description, and much more information relevant to specific careers. Much occupational information, however, paints an unduly attractive picture of the specified career and underestimates its disadvantages.

"You'd make a good corporation president, cabinet member, attorney general or Supreme Court justice."

Figure 15–8. Sometimes students need help in understanding the meaning of their vocational-aptitude test results. Courtesy Ed Fisher.

Good sources of occupational information include people presently in the relevant field, people who have recently left that field, and college counselors, who usually have a large fund of information through their personal experience.

Sources of information concerning job availability

Newspaper "want ads." Most newspapers have extensive listings of available jobs. By reading these for several months before the time for applying a person can gain insight into the type of position he might wish. One warning is necessary: certain help-wanted ads, especially those recruiting commission salesmen, may exaggerate the earning potential or misrepresent the actual work to be done; following these up may be a waste of time. *Employment agencies.* The United States Employment Service has branches in all major cities in the country. The USES makes job arrangements without cost, and frequently maintains extensive job listings. Private agencies, however, will charge a fee either to the employer or the employee. Reputable agencies only make this charge, however, if the person actually takes the job. Since the better private agencies often get job listings not available to the USES, their services are useful. It is far better to pay an agency 10% of the first year's salary, than to remain unemployed four weeks longer than necessary or accept an inferior position.

Government Civil Service listings. The proportion of city, county, state, and federal government jobs has been increasing steadily over the years. Some of these positions require competitive written examinations, while others do not. Lists of job availabilities, job requirements, and examination dates are easily obtained through the proper authorities.

Personal contacts. An amazingly high proportion of jobs are gotten through personal contacts. You hear of a friend who has been promoted, and the company needs to fill his position; your father's old Army friend is assistant manager of a furniture store, and you are interested in retailing and fulfill the job requirements.

Personal initiative. To send a direct letter to the personnel director of an organization or to make a personal call are very appropriate methods of job-hunting.

Information concerning the student

Learning about yourself is more difficult for several reasons. First, psychologists can measure some human characteristics with reasonable accuracy, but they have not been as successful in measuring personality attributes such as motivation to succeed on the job or ability to make sound decisions. Second, people often resist accepting their limitations or admitting their inadequacies. Third, people tend to interpret information about themselves so that they are placed in a favorable light. Fourth, even when a great deal of information is available, it is not always known how this information about the individual relates to vocational fields.

Many colleges provide counseling facilities, where trained personnel can aid you in understanding yourself. In addition, the instructor of this course can probably give you help or will refer you to someone who can. Whether self-evaluation is done through a counseling center or in class, the individual will have to take into account his interests, his aptitudes and previous achievements, and his needs and personality.

Evaluating interests. You can do many things to evaluate your own interests. You can examine your activities: what do you enjoy doing? how do you spend your time? what do you do well? You can also evaluate your high school and college courses and activities in the same way.

Two tests of interest are widely used. One, the Kuder Preference

Record, is familiar to many students as the test that asks you to select which of three activities you like most and which you like least. The second major interest test, the Strong Vocational Interest Blank, gives students letter grades, according to how closely their interests compare with successful men in different career fields.

Evaluating aptitudes and achievement. An **aptitude** is *the capacity to become competent,* assuming adequate training. Students often confuse interest tests with aptitude tests. Although they are related, they are far from identical. A politician may have a great interest in painting, but little potential competence. A housewife may have a great aptitude for public speaking, but little interest.

Aptitude is also confused with **achievement.** Aptitude refers to the *potential* capacity to do something; achievement refers to the *present* ability to do something. Numerous aptitude and achievement tests, some quite good, are available to counselors.

Evaluating needs and personality. Counselors use a combination of tests and interviews to help a student evaluate his personality and needs. The validity of personality tests is less than the validity of aptitude and interest tests, and less is known about how or why certain personality attributes fit a person for specific job fields. As a result, some counselors limit or even omit personality tests in vocational counseling.

Most students attempt to understand themselves, and a few pride themselves that they actually do see themselves fairly and objectively. Psychologists and other counselors, however, would be skeptical of such a claim. You, as an individual, can make some judgments regarding your needs and personality from how others react to you and from your previous experiences, but even this approach is severely limited in predicting future vocational success.

Preparing for a future career is certainly one of the major purposes in college education in America today. Colleges provide training in skills necessary for jobs and increase understanding and appreciation of others, of ourselves, and of the world around us, all of which may indirectly affect future job performance. Careers can be planned haphazardly, they can be virtually the result of a string of accidents, or they can be planned in a thoughtful, organized way. The characteristics both of the individual and of the career field must be considered in such planning.

SUMMARY OF IMPORTANT IDEAS

1. Other than housewives, the disabled, and the retired, almost all adults work for financial return.

2. Choice of career and the subsequent success and satisfaction are highly significant in many ways.

3. Job success and job satisfaction are important to the adequacy of the self-concept and the enjoyment of life.

4. Students and others often lack the necessary information and understanding for career planning.

5. For an effective career plan, the individual should be able to evaluate his interests, needs, values, personality, and ability; he should also be aware of how his educational level, age, health, and other characteristics affect his career potential.

6. In addition to having self-awareness, the individual planning his career needs to be informed regarding the characteristics of the job and of the job market.

7. Different job fields offer differing opportunities and have differing requirements.

8. Vocational selection necessitates an awareness of the day-to-day demands of the job, i.e., the job characteristics, as well as such factors as income and fringe benefits, working conditions, advancement opportunities, and the opportunity for satisfaction and personal growth.

9. Work experience, even experience in summer and part-time jobs, is useful in career planning.

10. Military service can be both vocationally and academically profitable.

11. Numerous sources of information are available regarding jobs, e.g., booklets, people in the field, college instructors, college occupational information files, and films.

12. Numerous sources of information about the student are available through counseling, testing, and self-evaluation.

The individual and his groups 16

In earlier chapters, the emphasis was upon the individual and the family; in Chapter 15, attention shifted to the vocational group. The present chapter moves the focus to other groups with which an individual identifies or associates. This material is one major aspect of most courses in social psychology.

Man is a social being. He has developed an extremely complex network of groups, ranging from the small, face-to-face group like the family, to the large, impersonal group, like the political party or religious denomination.

Could you get along without groups? Obviously not. Your food, clothing, transportation, social life and entertainment, education, religious observances, and safety are possible only because of groups. Consider each of the motives in Maslow's hierarchy of motives: (1) the physiological need of hunger is satisfied, in our society, because numerous groups grow, process, transport, distribute, and sell food; (2) safety needs are met through such groups as the family, the police force, the courts, and the military; (3) love needs are gratified through friendship and family groups; (4) esteem needs often receive satisfaction through the family group, social groups, work groups; and (5) self-actualization for many of us occurs through accomplishments in a group setting.

The groups you belong to have a major influence upon your self-concept. People identify the success and failure of their groups as their own success and failure. When an American wins an Olympic medal, when a graduate of your college is elected assemblyman, when a girl from your home town is elected Miss America, you feel a sense of pride from belonging to the same group. Similarly, you feel embarrassed when a fraternity brother is arrested for hit-and-run driving or a member of your church is accused of bribery.

Group loyalties can be amazingly strong. People will sacrifice their lives for their family or their country. Smaller, face-to-face groups seem to command even stronger loyalties than larger, less-personal groups. The Chinese Communists, recognizing this, did their best to breed suspicion within their Korean War prisoners' groups (Schein, 1958). During the Second World War, both American and German soldiers felt as much or even more loyalty to their own units than to the country as a whole (Shils, 1950; Shils and Janowitz, 1948). Workers will often do less than their best if their best exceeds the expected performance set informally by their work group (Roethlisberger and Dickson, 1939).

Although most people find great satisfaction from being with a variety of groups, some people prefer only occasional group contact. Healthy needs may keep an individual from groups, e.g., he feels that he works better alone or that his leisure-time interests can be pursued better without others around; his needs for solitude, however, may be unhealthy ones, e.g., the feeling that he is socially inadequate. Whether you are a joiner or a loner, you are still part of some groups, and these groups do have an influence upon you.

In 1965, *Newsweek* surveyed hundreds of college students at more than

50 colleges to see how students felt about the world, their colleges, their future, and themselves. One of the questions asked was, "How much confidence do you have in these institutions?" Figure 16–1 shows the percentage of students that indicated a "great deal" of trust in the institution mentioned.

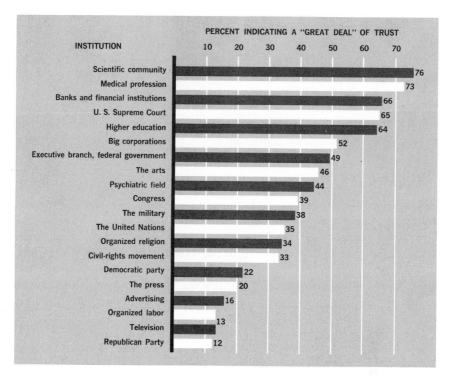

Figure 16–1. How students view the world around them. (*Newsweek*, 1965).

And one final introductory comment: it is important to keep in mind that groups are made up of individuals, each of whom behaves in ways discussed in earlier chapters.

Group pressures on group members

Because groups are so important in satisfying needs and because a person does build extensive group loyalties, he becomes dependent upon groups and is deeply concerned about how their members feel about him. As a result, individuals often receive considerable pressure to conform to group demands, a pressure made very difficult to resist by an understandable reluctance to risk being forced out of the group or losing status in the group. Even the disapproval of other group members is carefully avoided.

In extreme situations, the punishment for disobeying the demands of the group may be death or complete isolation. Usually this is unnecessary because people do not violate the standards of groups they join, since the act of joining implies acceptance of the values of the group (when joining is not voluntary, the situation may differ). The longer they remain members, the more—on the whole—people internalize the values of the group as their own. The American Medical Association, for example, wields a great deal of power, and almost all physicians must join. However, most of them prefer to join, not because of pressure but because the AMA represents their interests and satisfies many important needs. Labor unions function in the same way. Some doctors and some union members prefer not to join, and few would agree with every action taken by their organization, but they do find themselves basically in agreement.

Conformity

Conformity occurs when a person's actions or judgments are determined by the pressures of a group, rather than by his own values. Instances of conformity would include the freshman who forces himself to smoke only because others do; or the fraternity member who makes derogatory remarks about Italians without believing them himself, because his "brothers" do; or the students who changed their evaluations of people judged from photographs when they were told how other students rated the pictures (Goldberg, 1954).

Use of the term "conformity" presents a problem, because people tend to apply it to behavior when they disapprove, and to say "he was persuaded" or "he saw the light," when they approve. Thursday's newspaper will editorialize that students conform too much; Friday's edition will complain that students do not do what they are told. The real complaint is not that students conform, but that they do not conform to the desires of the newspaper.

Another problem occurs in using "conformity" to describe the behavior of the **other-directed** person. As the name implies, this person has such a strong need for approval by one or more of the groups with which he associates that he accepts their values as being his values without any critical evaluation or any concern with his own long-range value system (Riesman et al., 1955). As a child, the other-directed individual internalized one important value from his parents and society: gain the approval and acceptance of the group. Therefore, his conscience is the group attitudes of the moment, not his own personal commitments. But is the other-directed person conforming? On the one hand, he is behaving according to the demands of the group; on the other hand, he firmly believes that this is the proper way to behave.

Acting in opposition to the demands of the group can produce a high level of worry or anxiety. Recall the study of the students who were asked to judge the length of a line, when the psychologist arranged to have the other members of the judging group purposely make an incorrect judgment (see page 55). Those who "called them as they saw them" indicated higher anxiety as measured by physiological changes in the body (Bogdonoff et al., 1961). In one demonstration, a subject who disagreed with the group on every occasion was dripping with perspiration by the end of the session, even though he was completely correct. Remaining independent is neither psychologically, socially, nor physiologically easy, but it can be very satisfying.

Conformity obstructs self-actualization, because the conformist is not expressing his own feelings or doing what he feels is correct. Rather, he responds to the pressures of the social environment. The anticonformist, who is rebelling against society, is not self-actualizing either; like the conformist, he is merely responding to the social pressures, even though his response is negative instead of positive. The true individualist is neither rebelling nor giving in, but is acting according to his own values. He is being himself and is able to develop his talents without fear that society does not admire or pay those talents sufficiently. But how do you, the observer, decide who is an individualist and who is a conformist or anticonformist?

Many sincere people believe they have the right to decide what forms of individualism are allowable in the thinking, speaking, reading, and viewing of others. Through censorship and various forms of group pressure, they attempt to control what can be said and written. There is a point, we would probably all agree, at which irresponsibility can occur, but we would have trouble agreeing about where that point is. Do you believe, for example, that strong group pressure should be brought to bear to restrict the freedom of speech of Americans? What if they use this freedom of speech to advocate Communism? Revolution? Slavery? Murder? Or, to use a less serious example, what sort of group pressure should exist in the area of student dress in class? Should students be allowed to come to class barefoot? With shorts? With no clothes at all? How do you decide where group pressure should take over? What freedoms are you willing to give others?

Many people we consider heroes today were violently criticized during their lives for not conforming. The best-known of these is undoubtedly

"Damned radicals!"

Figure 16–2. New ideas are often disturbing to the group. Courtesy Ed Fisher.

Christ, who was severely punished for not conforming. Others who lived more recently include Henry David Thoreau, Voltaire, Samuel Gompers, Henrik Ibsen, Mark Twain, Martin Luther, and Patrick Henry.

Recent research on obedience to authority has led to some relevant and extremely thought-provoking results. In one study, the subject was directed by the experimenter to administer electric shocks to another person as punishment for making incorrect responses on a simple learning task. Each time the other person, who was supposedly strapped in a chair behind closed doors, made a wrong response, the subject was ordered to increase the intensity of the shock. This continued until the person being shocked began to shriek and beg to have the project stopped, but the experimenter demanded that the subject continue. In about half the cases, and with a variety of types of subjects, the shocks were continued in spite of evidence that they were causing great pain and were perhaps having dangerous effects. The subjects appeared to be continuing (although they showed great hesitancy and unhappiness) largely because they were being ordered to do so—and they were obedient.

In actuality, the person supposedly being shocked was an actor, and his entire role was faked. However, none of the subjects realized this, and many seemed willing, although tense and fearful, to extend the series of shocks as long as the experimenter ordered (Milgrim, 1965). What are the implications in this study for the future possibility of countries being taken over by dictators? What does this study suggest about the Nazi regime in Germany and Adolph Eichmann's plea at his war-crime trial in Israel?

Obedience to an individual and conformity to a group have much in common. Those whose needs for security, love, or esteem are inadequately met are probably more likely to give in to others or to accept uncritically the ideas of others. To be a true individualist is to accept ideas upon what *you* feel is adequate basis and to think and behave as you feel proper. You will take what others think into consideration but will not let it become the major basis for your own thoughts and behavior.

The effects of group membership, of course, vary depending upon the particular group. Since almost everyone is influenced by **social-class** group identification and by **ethnic** group identification, we will explore these in more detail.

Effects of social-class group membership

In a democracy that emphasizes equality, as in the United States, the idea of social class is unpopular. After all, social class implies that there is a recognized hierarchy in which people are ranked according to respect and status. What does this do to the idea that everyone is created equal and that no one is better than anyone else?

The answer is simple: social class is not a moral judgment but a description of how a person acts and how others react to him. In moving up in social class, you find an increase in income, education, influence, and status, among other things. This certainly suggests that people in the higher-social-class groups are more fortunate or better *off* than others, but not that they are better than others.

Would you be pleased if your sister married a physician? What if she married a union carpenter? Or a bartender who just won $100,000 in a guessing contest? How hard would you try to avoid a fist fight? Would you prefer to fight with words? Your answers will be based on values that are partly the result of social-class associations. No answer is right or wrong, except in relation to values.

A person's social class is evaluated primarily by his attitudes, values, and manners (Krech et al., 1962). Other factors include the use of language, formal education, job status, income, neighborhood, and even child-rearing techniques, as well as family background. Although we divide people into social-class groups (a very common division is upper class, middle class, working class, and lower class), these groups are not separated by distinct boundaries, but are on a continuum. Nor do people *always* behave as a "typical person" of that class is expected to behave; most exhibit nontypical behavior at times.

Not only are social-class values and behavior directly affected by a person's friendship group, but his friendship group is inevitably affected

Figure 16–3. How is social class represented in this picture? Courtesy Columbia Broadcasting System.

by his social values. Most friendships, especially dating friendships, are between people of the same or similar social-class background (Hollingshead, 1949). The reasons are many. First, people of the same social class tend to share the same interests and values; second, they are likely to be at or aspiring to, the same level on their jobs; third, they live in the same neighborhoods and, therefore, attend the same schools; fourth, many people feel that a friendship with a person lower on the scale is not a good idea; fifth, they may also feel that people higher on the scale are snobbish.

As one interesting example of how social-class association affects behavior, note Figure 16–4. A comparison of middle-class and upper-middle-class with working-class mothers indicated that child-rearing practices differentiate the two groups. Obedience and neatness are considered more

Figure 16–4. Child-rearing methods among middle-class and working-class parents.*

Belief	Preferred by working class	Preferred by middle class
Children should be toilet trained casually.		x
Children should not play "Doctor" and other games involving nudity. Modesty is important.	x	
Masturbation and sex play with other children must be avoided.	x	
Children should be neat and clean.	x	
Spanking and other physical punishments are effective discipline methods.	x	
Threats of withdrawing love are used in disciplining children.		x
Children must obey their parents.	x	
Children must be considerate of others.		x
Children should never talk back or show aggression toward parents.	x	
Children should not fight back or defend themselves against other children.		x
Both fathers and mothers should show children affection, including physical affection.		x
Children should be dependable and use self-control.		x
Children should be curious about things.		x
Parents should exert pressure for children to do as well as possible in school.	x	
Parents should exert pressure for children to complete all the schooling they are capable of.		x

*This chart has been abstracted from: Kohn, 1959; Maccoby et al., 1955; and Sears et al., 1957.

important by working-class parents; dependability and self-control are stressed more by middle-class mothers. Which group do you feel uses more effective punishment? Which group do you feel uses more correct practices?

Another characteristic distinguishing social-class groupings is the attitude toward physical aggression. Actual physical fighting is more common among lower-class children and adults, while the middle class expresses aggressive feelings through words or other less direct methods. Does this mean that middle-class people are cowardly? Does it mean that lower-class people, who want to settle matters right away, rather than wait and cool down (Schneider and Lysgaard, 1953), are tough?

Educational and vocational goals

Nowhere is the importance of social-class values better exemplified than in the pursuit of educational and vocational goals. Even the use of education as a means of achieving goals is a value acceptable primarily to the working class, middle class, and upper class. Lower-social-class people seldom consider education as proper *for themselves.* They may dream about being famous doctors or astronauts, but they rarely contemplate ways to achieve these goals.

To draw a parallel, you might feel that you could write a good movie script. You tell others how you feel, and you think a lot about it, but you never *do* anything about it. The whole business is just a hazy dream. It never occurs to you that books have been published about writing movie scripts or that courses are available in some colleges; you know you need an agent, but you do not know how to try to get one; you know nothing about the instructions to the cameraman. So it all remains a dream, until you are about 50, when you begin to tell people, "Oh, I could have written a movie script if I had wanted to, but I never had the time." Many children from the lower social class have the same hazy dream about college, because they understand very little about college and just assume that college is for other people. Insistence upon academic success is common in upper-, middle-, and working-class homes, but is expressed less frequently by lower-class parents. Since these parents, often through conditions beyond their control, did not advance far in school, they are less familiar with the purpose or the methods of formal education, and they are less effective in encouraging their children to succeed in school. They may even be a little suspicious of it, feeling that children, especially girls, who get extensive education, will come to consider themselves superior to their parents.

Although lower-class children are much more likely to come from financially poorer homes, the family income has less to do with their social-class values than the ideas expressed by their parents and other friends and relatives. Many poor families sincerely encourage their children to do well in school, and these parents do all they can to help their children succeed. Often immigrant parents bring with them a tradition of admiration for education, and their children internalize these values and succeed in school and in work, although the parents always remain poor.

Social class is self-perpetuating from generation to generation. For example, lower-social-class parents do not encourage education, but education is the best way for young people today to move up in social class. Since lower-class children, for a variety of reasons, do not do as well in school, they are not eligible for good jobs; thus their incomes are restricted, they live in a lower-class neighborhood, and they marry and have children who mature into the same pattern.

To accentuate the problem, lower-class people are less likely to internalize the value that immediate satisfactions should be sacrificed for long-range satisfactions (Gross, 1958). College education means sacrificing immediate income for a long-range better job; saving in the bank means sacrificing immediate pleasures for a nicer home or investment or retirement security in the future; working extra hours on the job means having less fun now, but increasing chances of promotion. The college education, savings in the bank or investments, working extra hours are all ways to move up the social-class ladder, but lower-class people do not recognize these acts as relevant, and they frequently ignore them.

School dropouts very definitely reflect social-class differences; middle- and upper-class children rarely drop out of school. Not only do their parents encourage them more, but the teachers are also middle class and understand them and appreciate their problems more (Ausubel, 1954). The middle-class teacher and the middle-class student speak the same language. Also, lower-class parents are more concerned with salary, while middle-class parents emphasize the enjoyment received from the work (Hyman, 1953). Thus, lower-class children are more likely to want to see an immediate relationship between their schoolwork and their anticipated future job, which often does not appear to require an academic background. Middle- and upper-class children see more relationship between their future job success and job satisfaction and such courses as English or history. The lower-class children, not finding any meaning in education for them, tend to drop out of school.

Yet, in spite of this picture, some lower-social-class children break the pattern, get a good education or training, and obtain a job which is generally regarded as a working-class or middle-class position. These have received help and encouragement from a teacher, a minister, a parent, a family friend; maybe they found something exciting in a book they read, or perhaps military service opened up a new world to them. In 1963, college students all over the country began to volunteer to spend a couple of hours a week tutoring children who came from culturally deprived backgrounds; a year later, the federal government began to set up training programs for school dropouts to learn job skills. The present trend is, most definitely, to recognize the problems of lower-social-class people and to try to alleviate them. However, in achieving this, the values of lower-social-class people seem to undergo change. Do you see any moral or psychological problem in one group's trying to change the values of another group?

Of course, you might say: "These people are lucky—they aren't worried about education or jobs. They're happy, maybe even better off than I am. Leave them alone." Or you might say: "There's nothing wrong with these people—they're just lazy; they want to be poor and avoid responsibility; if they don't have the initiative to do something about themselves, I don't want to bother helping them." The author disagrees with both these points of view, but they should be discussed and understood.

Social-class mobility

The social-class structure is not permanently fixed. People constantly move up and down. Marriage, of course, offers one way to change social-class association, although merely marrying a person of another social class will not be sufficient; one's values and behavior must also change. Today, increased educational opportunities have enabled a great upward movement in social class.

The person with **social-class mobility** has two types of problems: first, he is entering into social relationships with people whose values and manners he may not fully understand and who might have low regard for his background; second, he is leaving an old group of friends whose resentment of his desertion might induce feelings of guilt. Many college students have had the experience of meeting an old high school friend, who now seems to live in a totally different world. Some old friends seem to have made no progress since high school, while others have advanced tremendously.

The socially mobile person must adapt himself to the different manners, speech patterns, and values he encounters. Those who make the transition most successfully have begun to internalize the values of the new group even before they have moved into it (Krech et al., 1962). Those socially mobile individuals who have difficulty internalizing these values often feel uncomfortable when in the company of their new friends. To make matters worse, their children frequently take on the values of the new group very quickly and feel resentful that their parents are not truly of the group.

The person moving down the social scale seems less happy and adjusted with his new role than does the person moving up (Douvan and Adelson, 1958); he even shows more racial prejudice (Adorno et al., 1950). Even those moving up, however, may be tense and uncomfortable trying to adjust to values and manners that are new to them, and they risk being labeled social climbers, snobs, or simply "not one of us." Although many people move along the social-class scale with little or no problem, others pay a psychological penalty.

People usually internalize the values and behavior of parents, friends, family members, and neighbors. To some extent, these values are shared by others who, as a result, are assigned a particular status or class position by the community. Such values as vocational and educational goals and such behavior as methods of expressing aggressive feelings are indications of the class with which you identify. Social class should not imply a moral "good" or "bad" but a place in the status system of the community.

Effects of ethnic-group membership

Numerous religious, racial, linguistic, and national-origin groups live in the United States. The term *ethnic* is applied to a group whose members share one or more of these qualities. What ethnic groups do you belong to? Catholic? American of Irish ancestry? Negro? Jewish? American Indian? American of Mexican ancestry? American of Armenian ancestry?

Ethnic-group membership affects personality in two major ways: first, different ethnic groups maintain somewhat different values, which are communicated to each new generation (we find that divorce, suicide, and crime rates, for example, differ greatly from ethnic group to ethnic group; Kalish, 1966); and, second, people are evaluated partly in light of how their ethnic-group affiliations are perceived.

The self-concept, which depends so greatly upon how you feel others look upon you, is inevitably influenced by how you feel others look upon the ethnic group to which you belong. If you associate yourself with an ethnic group commonly regarded as inferior and inadequate, your self-concept and resulting behavior cannot help but be affected. Perception of an ethnic group is often reflected in everyday expressions ("jew" him down), in laws (American Indians living on the reservations cannot vote), in fiction and movies (how often do popular books or films show an American of Mexican ancestry as the handsome hero who wins the beautiful girl?), or in customs (most cities and towns have districts that exclude certain ethnic-group members as residents, without regard to their other characteristics). Under these circumstances, members of the particular group often internalize these attitudes as part of their self-concept.

Membership in an ethnic minority-group may affect an individual's personality in six ways, according to one source: (1) possible reduction in normal and casual contacts and communication with members of other groups; (2) increased importance of his own ethnic-group membership;

(3) increased effort for acceptance by majority group; (4) development of hostile and stereotyped attitudes toward other groups; (5) possible negative effect upon self-esteem and self-concept; and (6) increased acceptance of violence if directed at majority group (Berelson and Steiner, 1964).

The role of the Negro American

Of all the ethnic groups in the United States today, the Negro American appears to be the most harshly treated because of his ethnic-group status. Consider some of the problems he meets:

—Certain jobs are closed to him, regardless of his ability and training.

—Certain social relationships are not easily available to him.

—He is not always permitted to rent or purchase a home that fits his family's needs and finances.

—He has evidence that he may not receive equal treatment before the law.

—In some communities he lives in fear of violence, which he dares not return.

—He has had to go to court to demand equal voting rights and equal educational opportunity.

—Hospitals may provide less-adequate facilities.

—Restaurants, hotels, and motels frequently offer him inferior service or reject him altogether (consider his problems on a long automobile trip).

—The educational system reminds him that his origins were in slavery, forgetting that the ancestors of most non-Negroes were poor, illiterate peasants 300 years ago.

Can you think of other problems faced by Negroes? How would you deal with these problems? What prejudices do *you* face because of your ethnic background?

Negro children gain an awareness of their ethnic identification and, to some extent, ethnic role when they are as young as three or four (Clark and Clark, 1958). Many Negro parents admit having difficulty explaining to their children what it means to be a Negro American (Pettigrew, 1964), and their children find disturbing contradictions in what happens to them each day. They learn that their uncle, while waiting for a bus in a Los Angeles suburb, was told by a policeman to "get out of town before sunset, if you know what's good for you"; they learn that their cousin in

Alabama was not allowed to register to vote in 1964 because he could not answer some questions on the American constitution that stumped even learned university professors; they enter a small restaurant for a hamburger with their parents, while visiting in Indiana, and are told they will not be served.

So many things occur just because they are Negroes that young Negro children may develop resentment of being Negro. This resentment necessarily means that they resent themselves. However, people who resent themselves are unhappy people and have lower self-esteem. Some Negroes respond to the situation by withdrawing; they do not exert a maximum effort and seem to be saying, "If they don't think I'm any good, they must be right. So I'm no good, and I won't work very hard at trying."

Others do increase their efforts, but often with the frustration that being a Negro means they must work harder to get the same things as a comparable non-Negro. Still other Negroes direct their feelings of resentment right back at the non-Negroes. In the process, many innocent non-Negroes are hurt, just as many innocent Negroes are hurt by the prejudice of the non-Negroes. Negro resentment may be expressed when a Negro store clerk is unnecessarily rude to a non-Negro customer; it may be expressed when five Negro boys beat up an elderly non-Negro in a New York subway; it may be expressed when a Negro sailor loafs so that non-Negroes must do more work.

Many non-Negroes feel hurt by such behavior. "After all, I don't care if a Negro moves next door to me or goes to my kids' school—why does the colored mailman get nasty with me?" But the Negro who is expressing his resentment, or displacing his aggression, is usually not concerned with checking into the ethnic attitudes of all the non-Negroes he meets. He may feel that the men who burned Negro churches and displayed other forms of anti-Negro violence did not bother checking into the attitudes of the people they attacked. Both Negroes and whites are prone to stereotyping.

The family of the Negro also suffers. The Negro male is hired less frequently than non-Negroes of equal qualifications and is fired with less reason, thus making it very difficult for him to keep a job.

> The assistant personnel director of a large manufacturing plant (part, incidentally, of one of the 30 largest companies in the country) told the author how his supervisor got around the restrictions of seniority in laying off workers during personnel cutbacks. In sections where Negroes had more seniority than non-Negroes, the latter would be shifted to other sections, leaving the Negroes with the least seniority. The Negroes

would then be laid off, and, after a safe period of time, the non-Negroes would be transferred back. The unions either did not notice or chose not to say anything. This took place in 1954. Would it be likely to happen today?

The Negro woman, on the other hand, can usually get employment, although not necessarily well-paid employment, and is not likely to lose her position. Thus, the usual roles are reversed, and the woman is the stable breadwinner in the Negro home. This circumstance has two signifi-

Figure 16–5. For the first time, in 1965, a Negro played a sustaining lead role as a hero on a network television show. Courtesy National Broadcasting Company.

cant, deleterious results: first, the male children do not as often have a man in the home whose behavior they could internalize to learn the proper male role; and, second, the Negro male, unable to live up to what is expected of him in the male role, feels inadequate and may not try as hard as necessary, again increasing the difficulty of the Negro male child in learning proper male behavior patterns. This family situation leads to an increased number of broken homes, which again accentuates problems of sex-role development and other family problems.

Even the Negro as seen on television, in movies, and in books and newspapers perpetuates the stereotype. Up until very recently, Negroes were very rarely pictured in advertisements for general consumption. Although many Western cowboy heroes and villains were Negro (Durham and Jones, 1965), this is never indicated on the screen, where Negroes usually play servants and uneducated people. How often do you see middle-class Negroes appear as movie or television characters?

Interestingly, Negroes who are proud of their own ethnic status are also more satisfied with the behavior of non-Negroes (Noel, 1964). The Negro who dislikes whites is also likely to be less proud of being Negro. Perhaps their resentment of themselves is redirected as resentment of others.

The Negro role and intelligence

A logical concern is whether the Negro's role affects his intelligence. The initial answer is "Yes, non-Negroes do receive higher average scores on IQ tests, although a substantial proportion of Negroes have much higher intelligence than the average non-Negro." To complicate the picture more, Negroes in the Northern states have about the same average IQ as non-Negroes in the Southern states (see Anastasi, 1958), and IQ scores go up among Southern Negro children when they move to Northern cities (Lee, 1951).

Many social factors contribute to the lower IQ scores of Negroes, a major one being the lesser educational opportunities they receive. Since Negroes tend to come from poorer homes, they receive less academic encouragement in their homes and hear inferior English, on the whole; they also find more pressure to get a job as soon as possible, since the family income is often low. Each new generation is penalized for the inadequate opportunities of the previous generation. In addition, the self-concept of the Negro is so affected by what he hears around him that he can quite easily internalize the value that he is not intellectually competent and, therefore, he may not bother trying.

Other evidence also supports the idea that his limited environment has caused the lower level of Negro achievement. For example, his degree of Caucasian ancestry does not affect his IQ scores, although—if racial superiority were genetically inherited—the Negro with 75 percent Caucasian ancestry would be more intelligent than the Negro with only 5 percent Caucasian background (Witty and Jenkins, 1936).

Evaluating the evidence, psychologists, sociologists, and anthropologists have overwhelmingly concluded that—to the best of their present knowledge—racial differences in intelligence occur because of environmental differences, and, when equal opportunities are given, racial IQ differences will disappear.

The Negro middle class

Part of the evidence for the previous statement is the rapidly growing Negro middle class, whose values and manners are similar in almost every way to non-Negroes of the same class (Parker and Kleiner, 1964). Unlike the Negroes described earlier, the fathers do support the family and the sons do not have difficulty learning masculine behavior patterns. They dislike violence as much as their Caucasian equivalent (remember that attitudes toward physical fighting are due to social class, not race), and they value education greatly.

The Negro schoolteacher shares as little with the Negro domestic as the white schoolteacher shares with the white domestic. Middle-class Negroes want to move into integrated areas because the neighborhoods are often prettier and less crowded, and the schools are usually better. They are willing and anxious to contribute to the continued attractiveness of the neighborhood and the standards of the schools. Essentially, they are seeking the basic suburban living standard and rarely wish their children to date non-Negroes (Hughes and Watts, 1964). As a matter of fact, Negroes are little if any more enthusiastic about inter-racial marriages than are Caucasians.

Since middle-class Negroes share so many values with middle-class whites, they wish to become a part of middle-class America (Pettigrew, 1964). Instead, the middle-class whites often try to force them to identify with lower-class Negroes, demanding that race and not social class should be the major basis for association. Thus, the middle-class Negro is caught in a conflict: on the one hand, his values and ideas and social-class role make him a natural companion to the non-Negro of the same social class; on the other hand, his ethnic identification and the demands of many whites pressure him to associate primarily with other Negroes.

Some people feel that the middle-class or even the poor Negro has so many advantages over the Russians or the Chinese that he should not complain. However, Negroes do not develop their self-concept and self-esteem in comparison with Russians or Chinese, but with other Americans.

The past ten years have seen greatly increased opportunities for Negroes, resulting from changes in laws and changes in people. The next decade will probably see a continuation of this pattern, along with a continuation of the occasional violence of the past few years. Resistance to social change is always great, and violence is no newcomer in the conflict between those desiring change and those preferring things as is.

Other ethnic groups share some problems with the Negro, and also have unique problems of their own. A discussion of the related topic of prejudice is given in the next chapter.

Leadership roles

Almost every group distinguishes between the role (or roles) of **leader** and of follower. The leader ". . . by his actions modifies, directs, or controls the attitudes and actions of one or more followers" (English and English, 1958). Leadership, thus, stems from the influence one individual has upon others.

Using this definition, have you ever been a leader? What did you do to become a leader? From the definition, it is obvious that everyone exerts leadership on some occasions, while a few people seem to be leaders under a variety of circumstances.

Different situations call for different leaders. Each group has its unique membership, goals, organizational structure, and immediate circumstances. The qualities needed to influence one group are not necessarily the qualities to influence another group, or even to influence the same group at a different time. The man who makes an excellent chief of police may be unable to lead a group of Sunday School children; a school principal might do well as a leader under normal conditions but fail miserably under stress. The more similar two situations are, the more likely a leader in one situation is to become a leader in the other.

A leader must be able to satisfy the needs of his group, but groups are not always stable in terms of membership, immediate circumstances, or needs and goals. Therefore, the demands a group makes upon its leader change constantly; if one leader cannot keep up with the changes, his influence will diminish and the members will seek another leader. Although leaders certainly do influence groups, people often underestimate the necessity for leaders to be responsive to the needs of the group.

Types of leaders

Arguments over who is really the leader of a particular group are often impossible to resolve, unless recognition is given the possibility that more than one person at a time may function as a leader. Consider the following types of leaders and the hypothetical situation created to show how several different people can be leaders simultaneously, without conflict.

369

1. *Popular leader*—selected by voting or expressed approval of group members.
2. *Appointed leader*—group has little or no voice in selecting leader, e.g., a work group or a military group.
3. *Emergent leader*—as the group operates, a member becomes leader because group members turn to him for leadership.
4. *Subject-matter-expert leader*—someone with expert knowledge on an important topic will exert considerable influence, although often only for a brief time.
5. *Figurehead leader*—someone who does not play the role of leader, but is presented to the public as a leader, perhaps for public relations purposes.

> A group of students wished to organize a new political party on campus. After looking around, they selected Gordon Baines as their chairman, not because he was competent, but because he was a star athlete and was well liked by everyone. He was a figurehead leader. The new political party quickly realized that Tim Malley was the most able member, but he had a bad temper and irritated people. Without ever officially saying so, they turned to Tim for advice and usually followed his plans; Tim controlled the group as an emergent leader, but had no title. Fred Balzer was elected vice-president because everyone in the group liked him, and he became the popular leader. Pete Jablockski, who had been student body president two years earlier, agreed to lend his advice in running the election campaign, thus becoming a subject-matter-expert leader. However, Pete had already graduated, so Tom Rice was appointed chairman of the Campaign Committee, which decided that Fred Balzer was their most likely candidate for student body president.

Qualities of leaders

Although leadership roles change as the situation changes, a person who is leader under one set of conditions has a better-than-average chance of becoming a leader in another situation. After all, leadership roles, even of different groups, do share certain elements with each other. Many qualities have been found with greater frequency in people identified as leaders than in those identified as nonleaders (Gibb, 1954), even though no two leadership situations demand the exact same qualities.

Leaders, for example, have outdone their followers in

—physical health (Izard and Manhold, 1954),
—intelligence (Stodgill, 1948),
—grades and ability to communicate (Gowan, 1955),

—awareness of who in the group is popular and who is not (Bugental and Lehner, 1958),

—numerous personality measures, such as good adjustment, self-confidence, dominance, sociability, cheerfulness, sense of humor (Mann, 1959), and responsibility and tactfulness (Tarnopol, 1958).

Most important, leaders must have certain qualities that advance the purposes of the group. Physical attractiveness would be more likely to be found among leaders of college sororities than among female business executives; one sort of skill and daring will contribute to leadership of a delinquent gang, while different sorts will produce a military leader or a business leader.

Leadership methods

Successful leaders must appeal to the needs of their followers in order to get things done. By and large, the leader who tries to take the membership in directions it opposes will either lose his leadership position, be unsuccessful, or cause the disintegration of his group. Some leaders have obtained their position by anticipating what the group's needs will be and finding a way of helping them achieve their goals. Many political leaders owe their success to anticipating what the voters will want in the future and taking a stand on those issues.

We often talk about three kinds of leadership: democratic, authoritarian, and laissez-faire. The democratic method allows each member of the group to express his ideas, and the democratic leader tries to be friendly and to respect all the members. The **authoritarian** leader attempts to run things strictly, without giving his followers much voice in how things are to be done. The **laissez-faire** leader is casual and easygoing, and lets things run themselves.

When groups of boys under the democratic, authoritarian, and laissez-faire methods were compared, the democratically led boys appeared to be the friendliest, the most independent of the leader, and the least discontented. Nonetheless, some of the boys appeared to prefer a nondemocratically led group (Lippett and White, 1958). Democratic leadership produced the sort of behavior we in the United States consider important, but people in some other countries, as well as some Americans, might consider obedience to be more important than independence, and would prefer a nondemocratic group experience.

Effective group discussion

In some instances, a group is formed to make a decision, provide advice, or perform a task by general agreement rather than by voting or through the power of a leader. For example, an advertising agency has just picked up a new account, and the director has assigned the account executive, the staff artist, the staff copy editor, a representative of the manufacturer, an accountant, and a package design expert to plan advertising strategy. The committee is instructed to work together and obtain general agreement for all major decisions. A member of this group who is adept at functioning in such discussions may exert considerable influence over the rest of the individuals, and may be very helpful in guiding the way to a **group decision,** without haggling or hurt feelings.

A few guidelines to effective behavior in discussion groups

1. Present information and ideas to the group, but do not try to impose them upon the group. The more you argue, the more you force others to argue back, until they will refuse to be budged.

2. Avoid dealing in personalities or playing politics. You are not trying to win a point, but to find a solution.

3. Consider the ideas of others carefully.

4. Let the group move along. Once your ideas have been aired, let a decision be reached; once a decision has been reached, let the group move on.

5. Be brief and to the point.

6. Keep the group on the topic. It is amazing how frequently a group discussion becomes involved with irrelevant points.

7. Remain alert to those who are not participating. The silent ones may be agreeing or they may merely be unable to get a word in edgewise. Make certain everyone has a chance to say what he feels.

8. Help the group understand its goals and help them move toward those goals. Try to define the issues, if they need defining; when the time is right, suggest moving to a decision instead of endless talk.

9. Try to summarize the progress from time to time. This will draw attention to how much has been accomplished and will also startle a few people who were under the impression that something entirely different had been agreed upon.

10. Try to clarify the meaning of others, if there is any doubt. "What you are saying is . . ." or "Is this what you really mean: . . . ?"

11. Reconcile differences instead of arguing them out. This may result in a compromise or a totally new idea.

The process of group decision making is often slow and frustrating, but it has been successful for several reasons. First, more often than not, group decisions turn out to be better than decisions made by one person (Argyle, 1957). Second, a group decision means that the entire group has participated in the decision and, therefore, has given it at least passive acceptance. Third, members are more likely to abide by a group decision and not attempt to make it ineffectual at a later time. Being allowed to discuss an issue openly appears more persuasive, assuming ample evidence is available, than a well-planned lecture would be (Lewin, 1958). Fourth,

Figure 16–6. An important student-government committee meeting. Courtesy Antioch College News Bureau.

an effective group discussion allows for the interplay of ideas, so that each person can build on the contributions of others, and the group often ends up with a decision that no one individual would have arrived at by himself.

Group discussions are not influenced equally by all members. One important type of discussion group, the jury, is more influenced by men and by those in higher-prestige jobs (Strodtbeck et al., 1958). Nor is participation equally distributed: those who talk more in groups also have more education, higher income, more frequent attendance, and more memberships in other groups (McGinnies and Vaughan, 1957).

Whether a group is directed by a formally designated leader, an emergent leader, or no leader at all, each member is able to perform the leadership role at times and to make important contributions to the progress of the group.

SUMMARY OF IMPORTANT IDEAS

1. Man has developed an extremely complex network of groups, ranging from small, face-to-face groups to large impersonal groups.

2. Groups have an important influence upon the personality and self-concept of those who belong; the amount of influence varies greatly as the result of the particular individual and particular group.

3. Group loyalties can be extremely strong.

4. Although most people find satisfaction from being with a variety of groups, some people prefer only occasional group contact.

5. Because groups are so important and loyalties are so strong, it is easy to become dependent upon groups and upon the ways in which other members feel; pressure for conformity to group values is common.

6. Conformity occurs when a person's actions or judgments are determined by the pressures of a group, rather than by his own values.

7. Many people respond submissively to authority, even when authority demands disapproved behavior.

8. Social-class identification is important in determining behavior; a person's social class may be evaluated by his income, his ancestors, his job, or his education, but psychologists and many others tend to feel that the most important criteria are attitudes, values, and manners.

9. Educational and vocational goals are related to social-class identification.

10. Social-class identification tends to be self-perpetuating, although people can become socially mobile through marriage, education, vocational achievement, fame, and changes in attitudes and values.

11. Socially mobile persons face some problems of acceptance in the new group, as well as conflict over leaving an old group.

12. Ethnic-group membership affects personality in two key ways: by influencing attitudes and values through internalization, and by producing an evaluation of the individual as a reflection of his ethnic group.

13. The Negro American appears to be the most harshly treated because of this ethnic-group status.

14. Partly because of job availability, the sex roles of the Negro

man and woman are not consistent with general American sex roles; this affects not only the individuals directly involved, but the opportunity for their children to observe acceptable sex-role behavior at home and in the community.

15. The consensus of professional opinion among psychologists is that no inherited differences in intelligence exist between races.

16. The Negro middle-class citizen is similar in almost every way to non-Negroes of comparable social-class standing.

17. Leadership is the result of influence one individual has upon another.

18. Different situations call for different leadership qualities.

19. Democratic leadership is the most successful leadership approach in the United States, all else being equal.

20. Effectiveness in small group discussion is an important skill.

The importance of values 17

This look at values and attitudes may remind you of closely related materials in the discussion of human needs, of the development of the sex role, or of the process of internalizing feelings of guilt. The emphasis in the discussion presented here is upon values as related to the group identifications that lead to the formation of these values. Although the focus upon values has been largely fostered by social psychologists, the topic is coming under scrutiny by psychologists with a variety of interests.

What do you value? Life? Happiness? Freedom? Health? Money? Fun? Achievement? Travel? How much do you value each of these things? Do you value fun more than money in the bank? Do you value freedom more than security? Do you value your religious beliefs enough to give up your life for them? Do you value a college degree enough to postpone purchasing a new automobile for two years?

Values are **beliefs** regarding what are desirable and undesirable goals and ways of reaching those goals (after English and English, 1958). When you value something highly, you are strongly motivated by it. If you place a high value on money or new cars or grades, you will be strongly motivated to gain these goals. Understanding the nature and development of values is very important to the understanding of human behavior.

Values, like needs, may be consciously or unconsciously held. People recognize their conscious values and can think about them and discuss them with others, but they will also have values that influence their behavior but of which they have no conscious awareness. A person may place great value on being thought good-looking without being aware that he has such a value; he might even deny that he values good looks, but it would show through in his behavior, the way he dresses, the way he always asks whether others think he is good-looking, the way he worries about the slightest mark on his face.

Values often conflict with each other. A soldier places a high value upon patriotism and being a hero, but he also desires to stay alive. A student esteems honesty, but he also desires the friendship of his roommate who wants to copy from his exam paper. A coed seeks popularity, but also seeks good grades, which take so much time.

Values shape behavior in many ways. The man who places a high value on earning money will behave differently from the man who places a high value upon being of service to other men. These two men will probably enter different vocational fields, vote for different political candidates, join different clubs, and try to teach their children different values.

People also seek friends whose values are similar to theirs. The college student who is satisfied with a C average usually makes friends among others with similar values; the political liberal or conservative becomes friendly more easily with others of similar political beliefs; the accounting major tends to have relatively more friends interested in business than in teaching. (There are many exceptions, but the tendency to select friends with similar values still exists.)

Sometimes a person is not even aware that he does join groups and make friends where his values are generally accepted. Some of you are proud of having "all sorts of people" for friends. However, if you stop to think, you will usually find that most (not necessarily all) of your friends share many values with you. You are likely to have relatively similar values regarding such subjects as moral and immoral behavior, religion, politics, school, money, the meaning of freedom, the purpose of work, and the place of athletics on campus.

For evidence of the way values help determine friendship, notice the seating at your college cafeteria. At one table will be those who value athletics; another table will be filled with girls from the most popular clubs; at a third table will be seated students with artistic interests; the science majors will fill a fourth table.

Some basic values

The best-known test of values is undoubtedly the Study of Values, constructed by Professors Allport, Vernon, and Lindzey (1960). This questionnaire investigates the relative importance of six categories of values which the test's designers felt were the most basic human values.

Theoretical—values the discovery of truth; critical, rational, intellectual; oriented toward the sciences or philosophy; systematic.

Economic—values the useful and the practical; emphasis upon money and material goods; similar to stereotype of businessman.

Aesthetic—values form and grace; artistic.

Social—values social relationships, particularly giving to people from a psychological (not necessarily financial) point of view.

Political—values power and influence (not necessarily in politics).

Religious—values unity; mystic, wants to understand the meaning of the world.

Values are not isolated but occur in patterns, often called **value systems**. For example, students who favor the principles of the Bill of Rights in the United States Constitution also show less prejudice toward minority groups (Robin and Story, 1964). What other values would you guess these students held?

How values are formed

Parents and other significant figures probably have the greatest influence upon the formation of values and attitudes. First, they reward the attitudes and values they like, leaving the others unrewarded or perhaps punished; second, they provide models that their children consciously and unconsciously copy; and third, they live in such a way that the children, as they develop their self-concept by internalizing what their parents think of them, also internalize the parental values regarding education, God, humanity, or work. Since the child hears his parents' ideas and relatively little else in his first few years, he internalizes these without much conflict.

Figure 17–1. How much value do you put on money? Here is the way pure gold is handled at the New York Federal Reserve Bank. Courtesy Columbia Broadcasting System.

Even in later years, children maintain much the same values as their parents. With few exceptions, studies have shown that children's values and attitudes resemble those of their parents, for example, in politics, in economics, in religion, and in other areas (e.g., Hyman, 1959; Newcomb and Svehla, 1937).

Of course, children's values are not exact duplicates of their parents' values. A value that parents maintain with relatively little enthusiasm may not be internalized by their children at all. Occasionally, adolescents and young adults will rebel aggressively against their parents' views, although this rebellion frequently disappears as they leave home, marry, and achieve a sense of emancipation from their parents. From time to time, a child develops such an intense dislike for his parents or their values that he will discard parental values permanently.

Values are also influenced by the self-concept and by needs (which are, of course, greatly influenced by parents). People maintain values that are consistent with their self-concept and expressive of their personality characteristics. People who are rigid and inflexible tend to value cleanliness and orderliness, rather than casualness and informality. People who are anxious and fearful may prefer a strong, perhaps dictatorial, leader they feel will protect them. If you conceive of yourself as studious and serious, you will likely place a high value on these characteristics.

Parents and the home are not the only influences upon values. As children mature, other forces, including direct experiences, friends, the school, the community, the vocational field, and church associations, begin to have an effect.

Direct experiences

Strangely, direct experiences are probably less important in affecting values than are the ideas internalized through parents, friends, and groups. If you have internalized the belief that prayers are answered or football players are stupid, an unanswered prayer or a bright football player will rarely change your mind. You merely admit that one prayer was not answered, or one football player was not dumb. If, on the other hand, a particular prayer is answered or a particular football player is stupid, you accept this as evidence for your position.

People often find it so important to maintain their values that they do so, even in the face of great evidence. A devoutly religious student commented to an agnostic friend, "You don't really take your own experiences into consideration. If Jesus ever did appear to you in a real vision, you would probably put yourself in a mental hospital rather than admit He truly existed." The agnostic admitted the student was correct.

This, of course, is not to say that personal experiences never change values.

> "One summer I joined the staff of a summer day camp in Gates Mills, a very wealthy community close to where I lived. I had been raised in an average sort of home, and I felt that these rich kids would give me a lot of trouble—I just *knew* that they would be snobs. To make matters worse, most of the other counselors were also from wealthy homes. Much to my surprise, this was the best bunch of kids I ever worked with. They were creative, interested in camp, bright, and reasonably well behaved without being goody-goody. Of course, a similar camp in another wealthy community might have been altogether different, but I certainly changed my attitude about children from wealthy homes."

The friendship group

You tend to make friends with people having certain values and interests similar to yours. Once you have become friends, however, pressure occurs for you to accept other values of the group. Thus an amateur actor joins the college dramatic club because he enjoys theater and likes to be with others who also value acting and the arts. At this school, however, the college dramatic club also places high value upon good grades and upon drinking beer. Belonging to the club and admiring certain of their values, the amateur actor finds subtle pressure to get good grades and to learn to drink beer. If he is highly motivated to succeed in the club, he is quite likely to begin to drink beer and to work for higher grades. Even if he does neither, he is not likely to brag about low grades or to disapprove of beer drinkers.

The values of the friends you select interact dynamically with your own personality and values to affect your value system, as you simultaneously influence theirs. Parents, recognizing this, encourage their children to develop friendships with playmates having values the parents approve.

Education

The process of formal education affects values in many ways. Your values are influenced by the books you read, the teachers you listen to, and the other students you meet. You learn about the values of other countries and of earlier periods in your own country. You study the values of the men who began the American Revolution, the French Revolution, the Russian Revolution, and the many South American and Asian revolutions. You learn from teachers who place a high value on being creative, from those who stress memorization, and from those emphasizing proper manners and good behavior.

The first year in college is often disturbing because you are told so many things that appear to contradict not only what you learned in high school, but also other things you are learning in college. You are told that human behavior is caused by climate, body chemistry, love, hunger, traditions, society, money, religion—the professors cannot seem to get together. Are these professors actually disagreeing?

Temporary confusion regarding certain values may not be bad. Since students usually find that they form new values, often similar to the old ones but usually more carefully thought out, this confusion may be part of the path to maturity and self-understanding. The person who has never been confused has never had to think through what he believes with care.

> "I never realized how much I was an American and a capitalist until I spent a year in another country. Having to live with new values made me examine my own values very carefully. I had seen the Statue of Liberty many times before, but on the trip home I cried when I saw the 'Lady.'"

"When I finished high school, I had pretty strong religious convictions—I figured I knew what was right, and no one was going to change me. By the middle of my second semester in college, what with philosophy and psychology and history courses and all, I doubted everything—I didn't know what was 'truth' any more. Somehow—I really don't know exactly how—about a year after I finished college, I realized I knew what I believed again. I still had occasional doubts, but these didn't bother me any more. My views weren't that much different from when I was in high school, but now I knew why I believed what I did."

The two students making the statements paraphrased above were involved in situations in which doubt and confusion led to growth and maturity.

The community

Every society has developed, through its unique circumstances of history and geography, its own values. Even two towns or two cities located an hour's drive apart may emphasize different values: people in one will work hard to provide money for an art museum, while residents of the other will work just as hard to raise funds for a ball park.

Values held by the general community need not be rigid. A variety of types of behavior may be allowed. Our society, for example, considers college success to be a positive value, yet many in our country do not feel college is worthwhile. They are not put in jail or whipped, although they are punished in milder ways. Others in the community may criticize them, and they are likely to be turned down for jobs that demand some college.

The penalty for violating certain other values, however, is severe. In Texas in 1950, a white man bragged to the author that he slammed a bus window down on the hand of a Negro man who disobeyed the values of that community by sitting in the front section of the bus. In Russia today, church-going Christians suffer from job discrimination. In Pasadena, California, a high school teacher was dismissed when he rejected the principal's demand that he shave off his beard.

Values that occur in one place and at one time, however, will differ from values held at other places and during other times. In Pasadena, Christians do not suffer job discrimination; in Russia, a teacher can grow a beard; in Texas *today* a Negro can ride in front of the bus. As the world changes, values change. Consider the effects that some of the following changes have had upon the values of the people of college age today:

—The proportion of Americans attending college has increased tremendously.

—A steadily rising proportion of the population is over age 65.

—Consumer credit has been very easy to get.

—Artists and writers can earn a living.

—Urban centers have suddenly increased representation in state legislatures.

Figure 17–2. These two scenes were photographed within a few miles of each other in Brazil. How would the values of the inhabitants of the two types of buildings differ? Courtesy Columbia Broadcasting System.

—The work week is getting shorter and shorter.

—Ethnic groups, such as Americans of Mexican ancestry and Negroes, are increasingly likely to vote in elections.

All of these things, and many, many more, contribute to changes in the attitudes and values of the community although basic values of an individual change only very slowly. The conditions of the community today are different from those faced by the parents of today's college student when they first looked for work. These parents faced a depression and labor unrest, or a war and military service with a good possibility of going into combat. Today, while the tensions have not disappeared, they result from different problems, and these problems produce some of the changes in the community's values.

A serious student of human behavior will wish to learn the historical origins of the values of the general community and of the subgroups within this general community. How did unions begin, how did they rise in power, and what are they like today? What is the recent history of the American Indian, and what is his life like today? What was the beginning of free education, and how has this affected our country? Understanding such historical problems will help you understand the values and feelings of the older union member, the American Indian, and the schoolteacher who is extremely dedicated to free education. In the same way, to understand the values of people in other countries, you need to understand their history and traditions.

It is impossible to live in a community (the word "community" may be used to refer to either a village, a city or a part of a city, or a country *in this case*) without being influenced by the values of that community. If the values of the parents are similar to those of the general community,

Figure 17–3. Technology is valued all over the world. Argentine industrialists visit an industrial-arts laboratory at an American college. Courtesy California State College at Los Angeles.

the children are more likely to internalize these values than if only a minority of the community members agree with the parents (Berelson and Steiner, 1964). Although parents cannot shield their children from the general community values, they can make an effort to provide their children with their own values before the children have much community contact. Parents who do not wish their children to smoke or drink, for example, cannot wait until the children are 16 before teaching them about tobacco and alcohol. Such values should be learned at a much earlier age, if the children are to ignore the general community attitudes.

Vocation

Your vocation also influences your values and attitudes. You may be influenced by those with whom you work, or by your supervisors, or by the management philosophy or union philosophy prevailing at your company.

In addition, the type of work itself influences attitudes. A policeman spends so much time with the least pleasant elements in society that he may develop the belief that people cannot be trusted. A minister, partly because of the respect people have for his position, is much more likely to see people at their best—even the same people that the policeman sees at their worst. Thus, the type of work you do and the work relationships you enter into help form some of your values.

Of course, both the policeman and the minister bring their previous experiences and personalities to the situation. Each may have entered his vocational field to help people, but each has elected a different way of going about this job. The very values that encourage one person to become a representative of the law and another, the representative of God, will also affect the ways in which each looks upon others and interprets their behavior. Your needs and your attitudes draw you to certain types of work; the work influences the nature of your contacts with people, which is, in turn, interpreted through your unique personality; your attitudes and values are affected accordingly.

Thus, although parents and other significant figures are considered the primary influences upon values and attitudes, personal experiences, friends, educational experiences, the community, vocational contacts, and religious associations also contribute.

How values change

Values and attitudes, like other elements in personality, undergo continual change, even though these changes are often slight and occur slowly.

As your roles and self-concept change, your values change also. The adolescent may value popularity with his own group, while the adult values being liked by the boss. The worker places greater value on his union, until he becomes a supervisor, at which time his values emphasize the success of the company. The professor who now values hard work, as a student valued "living it up." A freshman girl does not place much value upon avoiding a fellow with a "fast" reputation, but the same girl, when *her* daughter wants to date in the "fast" crowd, finds she has a strongly negative attitude.

Changing the values of others

It seems logical that a good sound argument would be sufficient to change someone's values. That is, assuming you had tremendous logic and a pile of evidence on *your* side—you should be able to convince any normal person that you were correct and that his values were wrong. Try it. It does not work very often.

Values and beliefs are closely related to needs and motives and are often learned very early in life. Attacking them with logic merely forces the other person to try to defend them with logic. Soon, he is so deeply involved in justifying his views that he finds arguments he had never considered before. Often the best way to make certain a person *never* changes his values is to argue vociferously against them. The stronger his needs to hold these values, the more difficult it is to change them. Attacking strongly held values can cause them to be still more firmly maintained (Kelley and Volkart, 1952), often with the support of defense mechanisms.

However, values and attitudes can be changed. The professions of advertising and public relations are devoted to changing people's attitudes and their resulting behavior. Salesmen, teachers, ministers, and clinical psychologists also find that much of their working time is spent changing attitudes and values, including people's attitudes toward themselves, i.e., their self-concepts.

Occasionally one dramatic event can alter an attitude or value. An English professor was drowning; he swore to return to belief in his religion if he lived. He did live and became a devoutly religious man thereafter. More commonly, however, values change slowly, as the result of many things, and people who wish to persuade others must take this into account.

Thus, advertisers establish continuous campaigns, not just an occasional advertisement; psychotherapists meet continually with their patients, not just once; ministers have learned that the overnight convert usually becomes a backslider (in spite of the occasional convert as described above).

Since values are closely related to needs, the self-concept, and other personality characteristics, value change can be produced by changing the needs or the self-concept. Although this is difficult, it can occur. One commercial firm used this principle when they learned that housewives were reluctant to buy instant coffee because they held the attitude that using instant coffee was a sign of laziness, and they had the need to have the self-concept of hard-working women (Haire, 1950). The advertisers were then able to change their approach from emphasizing the convenience of instant coffee to emphasizing its taste and aroma, thus playing up to the needs of the housewife. Similarly, politicians attempt to persuade people that their election will satisfy the needs of the voters, i.e., for better schools, lower taxes, better military protection, less air and water pollution—whatever the voter perceives as his own needs. In the same fashion, the values children hold regarding school may improve if the children overcome fear of school or feelings of inadequacy in school.

> A seven-year-old boy, the son of immigrant parents who spoke little English, had great difficulty doing second grade reading. The parents agreed to have him repeat the first half of the second grade, which enabled him to be a better reader than his classmates, instead of near the bottom of the class. His need to avoid school and his self-concept of inadequacy both faded, and his attitude toward school changed from strongly negative to mildly positive, even though he was bothered by being left back.

The success of attempts to change attitudes and values is partly the result of the personalities of those under pressure to change. At one interracial summer camp, some of the campers became more prejudiced by the end of their camp experience, while others became less prejudiced. Compared to the latter, those who became more prejudiced were more aggressive and more afraid of punishment, yet they also felt more picked on (Mussen, 1950). The same camp environment and the same Negro friends led to better attitudes toward Negroes among some non-Negro children, and more negative attitudes among other white children, depending upon their previous personality and values.

Personality is related to value change in another way. Since people appear to have the need to believe a consistency exists between their values and their behavior, if something occurs that changes their behavior, they are also inclined to change their values accordingly. Thus, two groups of people were paid to lie about some relatively unimportant matter to their friends; one group was paid $20 each, and the second group was paid only $1 each. A later inquiry found that those paid the smaller amount of money had changed their attitudes somewhat about the matter concerning which they lied; they had—to some extent—come to believe what they had said. The other group did not change much at all. Apparently the higher-paid individuals could justify the lie by having received so much money, but the group that told a falsehood for so little money had behaved inconsistently—they could not justify having lied, so they altered their values to reduce the significance of the lie (Festinger, 1957). Perhaps you have had a similar experience. Have you ever purchased something you could not really afford and then tried to convince yourself that you had made a wise purchase? This helps salesmen immeasurably, since people who buy things tend to justify their purchasing behavior and are not likely to return the goods, even if they did not get a good buy. Another example would be deciding which of two movies you wished to see: once the decision was made, your values would be interpreted in such a way that the choice you made was supported.

> In college, Jack Trevor prided himself on wanting to be of service to humanity, particularly by using his writing talents to improve the conditions of the economically impoverished. After graduation, he found he could not make a living through free-lance writing, so he took a job with a men's magazine that published stories emphasizing murder, lust, and crime. Five years later, he had become editor of the magazine and was earning a substantial income. However, his values had changed. When he first began with the organization, he claimed he would only stay long enough to "get me started, because this magazine really puts out trash." Now that he seemed to have given up his mission to help the poor, he justified his behavior by stating that the magazine was important because many poor people read it and received great enjoyment from it; therefore, he was really providing an important and useful service to the poor. His values and attitudes had changed in order to become consistent with his actual behavior.

Persuasion and propaganda. Both education and **propaganda** are aimed at changing values and at getting across new information. The differences between education and propaganda are fewer than many people think, since propaganda may be educational and education may include propaganda. Propaganda to persuade people to give to the National Heart Association may include a lot of educational material; education in a psychology class may include some propaganda regarding the professor's viewpoint.

However, education and propaganda have different purposes. The purpose of education is to provide information and understanding, then allow the student to make up his own mind. It is directed toward increasing personal growth. Propaganda is concerned solely with changing values, attitudes, and behavior *in a particular direction,* and any learning involved is only incidental. Propagandists may purposely distort the material they present, while educators are supposed to be as objective as possible.

Some propaganda terms

Appeal to Authority. The claim that a particular authority favors the behavior considered. An expert, a respected textbook, or a prestigious person are all considered authorities.

Bandwagon Effect. The attempt to persuade people by claiming that everybody is doing it.

Big Lie. An obvious lie which is told so often that people begin to believe it. Some people, for example, will feel that "where there's smoke, there's fire."

Guilt by Association. The suggestion that a person has done something wrong because he has had some association with another person who has done something wrong. "Dr. Carr was seen with Mr. Holt, who is known to be a Fascist." They might have attended the same college and have been seen in different parts of the room at an alumni meeting.

Image. The picture held by the public, or segments of the public, regarding a person or a product. The common image of the United States in Communist China is "Imperialist" and "Colonialist."

Plain Folks. The attempt to persuade people by causing them to believe that the attitude or behavior is similar to that of "just ordinary people." The implication is that the *opposing* views are held by snobs.

Snob Appeal. The attempt to persuade people by causing them to believe that the attitude or behavior is similar to that of the wealthy or the famous.

Transfer. The opposite of guilt by association, *transfer* is the suggestion that a person is good because he is associated with something good.

To a large extent, whether you believe something is education or propaganda depends upon how you feel about the issues. The Democratic candidate for Congress insists that the newspaper articles he writes are educational, but his Republican opponent claims that they are mostly propaganda. The Democrat believes that what he is writing is true and gives his readers a better understanding. The Republican believes that his opponent has omitted important facts and misinterpreted important events. Strangely, both men are being sincere. Is there propaganda in this book? How is it brought in? Is it also educational?

The effective propagandist remains aware of certain basic principles of persuasion, including the following:

> He always takes into account the specific audience he is reaching. A television commercial to sell used cars is different from one selling new cars. The politician running for office in a financially poor area emphasizes different issues from one campaigning in a wealthy area; they even tell different jokes and use different vocabularies.

> He keeps in mind that group loyalties are important. The politician joins many clubs and tries to get representatives from different racial, religious, social-class, and age groups working for him.

> He must consider how to present the issues. Should he try the emotional or soft-sell approach? Should he attack his opposition directly or not? Should he assume that the audience understands the issues, or should he try to explain the issues?

> He must remember to work upon the needs of the audience. Are they motivated by security or prestige or sex appeal or income? Both advertisers and politicians are highly skilled at recognizing the needs of the people they are trying to reach.

The factors that produce changes in attitudes and values are very complex and differ from person to person and from time to time. Short-term changes, especially on issues that are not considered very important, may occur without too much difficulty. However, it is much more difficult to produce long-term changes, changes in values considered important, or changes in values that are part of a value system and related to the needs of the person.

The meaning of prejudice

To be **prejudiced** is to make a "pre-judgment" or to make a judgment or hold an attitude before all the necessary information is available. Being prejudiced also implies that the attitude or feeling is held with some degree of emotion and is not readily altered.

Everyone holds prejudices that lead either to favorable or unfavorable reactions toward people, things, and ideas. You may be prejudiced against a western on television without even seeing the show. You may be prejudiced against women who lisp or in favor of men who smoke pipes.

Although everyone has prejudices, this is not to say that any particular prejudice is either natural or inevitable. As with any attitude, belief, or value, prejudices are learned largely through interaction with significant figures and tend to fit in with personality needs and the self-concept. Also, like other values, they are difficult to change. They resist logic because they satisfy needs that may be more important than logic, or because they were so effectively internalized that they are stronger than logic. Research has shown that people have trouble with simple problems in logic, if their prejudices become involved (Sells, 1936).

Prejudice, discrimination, and segregation

Prejudice is an attitude. **Discrimination** is a form of behavior that usually arises from prejudice. Discrimination refers to treating people unequally. The prejudice against women leads to discrimination against hiring women for certain jobs. Prejudice against adolescents leads to discrimination against them by some adults. Prejudice favoring well-behaved students leads teachers to discriminate in their favor by giving them better grades than they deserve. What groups do you discriminate for or against? Why?

Discrimination not only arises from prejudice, but—in turn—increases prejudice. As children grow up observing women being discriminated against, they tend to internalize the value that women really are inferior, thus leading to prejudice. Prejudices and discrimination have dynamic interaction.

You may recall that the term *discrimination* occurred with a slightly different meaning in the earlier discussion on learning, in Chapter 4. The original meaning of discrimination is "to distinguish" or "to recognize a difference between." It is obviously necessary for a child to learn to discriminate *between* his mother and his teacher, or between the street and the sidewalk. However, *discrimination* is also used in the sense of discrimination *for* or *against*. The real problem of discrimination in the area of racial prejudice is that it is not used appropriately. For example, instead of discriminating between Jews or Negroes who have good qualities and those who have poor qualities, some people lump all Jews or all Negroes together *indiscriminately*, and then endow all members of these groups with the characteristics of the worst members of each group. Proper discrimination is vital in gaining a realistic view of the world, but discriminating *for* or *against*, when based on previous biases, reduces the ability to see the world realistically. Do you know of people who are not sufficiently discriminating among teen-agers?

Since attitudes and values, when deeply felt, resist change, it is almost impossible to alter already-formed prejudices by passing laws. *However,* laws can affect discriminatory behavior which, in turn, will help create situations in which prejudices may be more easily changed and in which prejudices will not be so effectively passed on from generation to generation. Would you keep women from voting? Your great-grandparents did, but laws were eventually passed that gave women the vote and other forms of legal equality. There is a definite tendency to accept *what is* as being *what is right*. Few Americans wanted women to vote 70 years ago, yet few Americans would deny women the right to vote today.

When prejudice and discrimination become severe, **segregation** often results. Segregation is the act of isolating members of certain groups. At various times in history, the Jews were segregated in Europe and were not allowed to live anywhere except in small, overcrowded ghettos.

Groups may segregate themselves. They try to live near others whom they consider similar. This similarity may be based upon race, religion, national origin, or social class. In some parts of the country, communities have been established where the elderly live segregated from people of other age groups.

Self-segregation or "clannishness" may result from a dislike for others. It may also be caused by **in-group** preference, which occurs when members of a particular group feel more comfortable with others in their group and feel uncomfortable with those who are not members of their group. The elderly, living in segregated cities, are not prejudiced against younger people, but they may feel more comfortable and more accepted in a community of the elderly. Americans of Armenian origin often live close to each other, not because they dislike non-Armenians, but because they want to share traditions and customs with each other, and because they are more comfortable with each other. When segregation results from prejudice, it cannot be considered the result of in-group preference. (To observe a good example of in-group preference, notice how faculty chaperones stick together at student dances.)

Examples of ethnic-group prejudice, discrimination, and segregation.

When is prejudice against ethnic groups appropriate? How about discrimination? Segregation? What rights do you have to avoid members of groups if you wish? Would it be right for your club to blackball someone because his ancestors were born in Africa? In Greece? In Sweden? If you do not wish a member of a particular group to live near you, what action is justified? Economic pressure? Social avoidance? Threatening telephone calls? Damaging his property? Physical violence? What are the financial costs of discrimination? What are the psychological costs to the victim and to the discriminator?

The Irish immigrants who settled in New England and New York during and shortly after the potato famine of 1840 were the object of much prejudice and discrimination. They were accused of being drunks, of fighting, of ignoring laws, of neglecting education, of being involved in improper sex acts, of being traitors to the United States (*Newsweek*, 1964). They could get jobs only as maids and unskilled laborers, and many employers refused to hire Irish at all. Even intelligent people were convinced that the Irish were just not capable of receiving an education or holding a responsible position.

As a result, the Irish clung together, rarely went on for further education, and developed self-concepts somewhat similar to what they were told about themselves. Their frustrations eventually burst through during the 1870s with a group called the Molly Maguires. The Mollies "struck back with incredible savagery, total terror—murdering, dynamiting, burning, pulling out tongues and slicing off ears" (*Newsweek*, 1964). Of course, such behavior only increased the hatred and fear others had of the Irish.

Over the years, the Irish changed this image people had of them. As time passed, their position improved financially, educationally, and politically. Today, the picture of the Irishman is substantially different. He is still seen as a strong person who will not back away from a fight, but he now is the hero, rather than the villain. The self-concept of the Irish has changed also, and the term "shanty Irish," common even 40 years ago, is rarely heard today. Then, in 1960, a man of Irish descent was elected president of the United States. However, for nearly a century, the Irish in the United States suffered prejudice and discrimination. The cost in money, in human suffering, and in progress for the country as a whole was tremendous.

A second example of the wastefulness of prejudice is the feelings expressed toward the Americans of German ancestry during World War I, and toward the Americans of Japanese ancestry during World War II. In 1918, Americans of German background were subjected to many forms of name-calling and hatred. They were accused of being sympathetic with the Germans who were fighting the Americans at that time, and many eventually had to change their names to avoid prejudice and discrimination.

In 1942, Americans of Japanese ancestry met with an even more obvious form of prejudice and discrimination. It was more obvious for two reasons: first, it came directly and officially from the United States government, and second, although almost all Americans of Japanese ancestry were affected, almost none of German ancestry were similarly affected.

The Japanese-Americans were removed from their homes on the West

Coast and placed in what amounted to prison camps scattered around the country. They were often pressured into selling their property, usually at a fraction of its true value, giving up their businesses, and living under worse conditions than we often demanded of enemy prisoners. As one Nisei social worker stated, "I lived in the stable next to Sea Biscuit's for two months. Of course, they had only put one horse in that stable, but they put four Japanese into it." This action was later proved illegal, but the wartime hysteria allowed people's prejudices and hates to come into full play. It is ironic that the 442nd Division, made up primarily of Japanese-Americans, suffered an extremely high casualty rate and earned one of the highest proportions of awards of any American military unit in World War II.

Once again, the cost of prejudice in money and in human misery was overwhelming, and—in looking back—few, if any, reputable Americans felt the Japanese Relocation Centers achieved anything to help the war effort.

Today, people of Irish, of German, of Japanese ancestry are all much more accepted in our country. The 20-year-old grandson of Irish immigrants is very much like the 20-year-old grandson of German or Japanese immigrants. A few differences remain in attitudes and values, but they are alike in many more ways than they are different.

Many groups have suffered from prejudice and discrimination in the past or the present in the United States, yet prejudice is probably less now than it was earlier in our history. The following are just a few examples of discriminated-against groups drawn from our history: union members, Americans of Mexican ancestry, policemen, Negroes, Roman Catholics, Masons, Southern whites, Jews, soldiers, Socialists, poor people, American Indians, atheists, wealthy people, actors, Americans of Greek ancestry, Mormons.

Prejudice against racial and religious groups is not limited to the United States. Citizens of countries highly critical of prejudices in the United States display strong prejudices themselves, although usually not as violent or as well-publicized as American ethnic prejudices.

England, for example, has recently been the scene of considerable prejudice and discrimination against nonwhite people from the West Indies, Pakistan, and elsewhere. The tiny South American country British Guiana has been in turmoil for several years because of fierce prejudices of the residents of African and of Asian background against each other. In India, the Untouchables are still subjected to discrimination, although laws officially forbid it. Communist Russia has shown prejudices against the Jews, and Canadians of French origin claim that British-Canadians discriminate against them.

The fact that prejudice exists in different countries cannot be used as an excuse by other countries. Prejudice against ethnic groups, no matter where it occurs, is learned, and no evidence exists that this learning is in the least inevitable.

Nor does prejudice result from one simple cause; it is brought about by a combination of several. Consider the problems of Theresa Guerra:

> Theresa was brought up by affectionate, loving parents, who, nonetheless, accepted the values of their homeland, Mexico, as to the proper role for a woman: getting married and having children. Since Theresa had little contact with children outside the Mexican-American community, she never questioned her future role. Also, since neither parent was especially concerned about having their daughter educated beyond ninth grade (in their village in Mexico, women rarely had gone beyond the sixth grade), they gave Theresa no encouragement in her school achievement. Little English was spoken in the home, and English-language books and magazines were never available. Because she was one of eight children, Theresa received relatively little time and attention from her parents, both of whom worked.
>
> However, one of her high school teachers felt that she did have the potential for college. Unfortunately, when she spoke to the assistant principal, he checked Theresa's IQ scores (administered when she barely spoke English) and claimed that she "wasn't too bright—just like the rest of *them*." The teacher then spoke to the school counselor, but he did not wish to be bothered with anyone who could not go on to college, and he insisted that girls from "that kind of background were hopeless."
>
> The teacher persevered and decided to wait for the PTA open house to talk with Mr. and Mrs. Guerra. However, the Guerras both worked hard all day, and had little energy or interest to visit the school when they did not really care if their daughter continued or not. Finally, in frustration, the teacher telephoned Mrs. Guerra to ask her to make an appointment. Mrs. Guerra was doubly embarrassed: she was reluctant to admit that she worked in a bar and she was ashamed to meet with a well-dressed, well-spoken "Anglo," when her own dress and speech were so inadequate. Although she was pleased by the attention Theresa was receiving, she was afraid to ask her husband for help, since she was positive he would get angry with her for suggesting their daughter should go to college when none of their sons seemed to have such an inclination.
>
> Mrs. Guerra made one appointment and did not arrive; she made another one and called in to break it. She then said she would call the teacher for a third appointment, but never did.

The teacher finally decided that, perhaps, the assistant principal and the school counselor were correct in their appraisal of Mexican-Americans.

Prejudice, personality, and needs. Certain personality characteristics and needs are more associated with highly prejudiced individuals than with others. People who are rigid and not open to new ideas or ways of thinking, for example, tend to be more prejudiced than average (Rokeach, 1960). Prejudiced individuals also demand an extremely high level of neatness, cleanliness, and sex morality, insisting upon very severe punishment for those who do not live up to their standards. Such people also like things to be clear and obvious, and they dislike art or writing or even ideas they cannot understand. They frequently insist that all problems should have simple, neat answers (Allport, 1954).

Human beings have a need for self-esteem, and ethnic prejudices can sometimes help to maintain this need. Thus, the individual who looks upon himself as highly competent, but is unable to get a job he feels is worthy of him, may complain that "The Jews are trying to destroy the job market," or "The Mexican-Americans will work cheap, so there's no place for me." Either claim explains his inability to be hired in such a way that he retains his self-esteem.

Prejudices against ethnic groups are found throughout the world and throughout history, although they are learned and are far from inevitable. The cost of prejudice and discrimination, both in money and in misery, is extensive. Prejudice can be produced by any one or several of many factors, and the specific prejudices fit into the general value system of the person holding the prejudice.

SUMMARY OF IMPORTANT IDEAS

1. Values are beliefs about what constitutes worthwhile and nonworthwhile goals and methods of reaching those goals.

2. Values may be consciously or unconsciously held and may conflict with each other.

3. Values shape behavior in many ways, e.g., through vocational selection, choice of friends, and leisure activities.

4. Values are formed through the internalization of parents' values and those of other significant figures, through reward and punishment, and through imitation of parents.

5. In spite of the importance of the values of parents, children's values are not exact duplicates of them.

6. Values are also influenced by personality, personal experi-

ences, the friendship group and other groups, education, the community, and the job field.

7. Values can change, although the changes occur slowly.

8. Changing the values of others is a very difficult task.

9. Propaganda and education differ in purpose, but not necessarily in content.

10. Prejudices, or "pre-judgments," may be positive or negative.

11. Prejudice is an attitude; discrimination is a form of behavior that often results from prejudice; segregation is a physical separation that often results from prejudice and discrimination.

12. Prejudices are learned, and although everyone has prejudices, there is no evidence that any particular prejudice is "normal" or inevitable.

13. Ethnic prejudices exist all over the world but differ in intensity, in content, and in victim.

14. No one factor can explain all types of prejudice.

Religious values and group memberships   18

This chapter has been included for two major reasons. First, because everyone has had some form of personal experience with them, religious groups and religious values provide a framework for the study of groups and values in general. Second, the author feels that religious groups and religious values are underestimated as forces both in this country and in the world in general. Before evaluating the author's assertion, read the numerous definitional approaches to the term "religious" so that you can interpret the term in its broadest sense.

No discussion of social behavior would be complete without a consideration of the role of religion, which has been so vitally important throughout the history of humanity. Religion has influenced human behavior both through the effects of religious beliefs and through the effects of religious group memberships.

To find a universally agreed-upon definition of religion is impossible, nor is it the purpose of a psychology book to become immersed in theological debate. However, a few brief comments are in order. The definition of religion most commonly accepted by Americans would undoubtedly resemble that in *Webster's Intercollegiate Dictionary* (Fifth edition): "The service and adoration of God or a god, as expressed in forms of worship." Or, "An awareness or conviction of the existence of a supreme being, arousing reverence, love, gratitude, the will to obey and serve, and the like." Other types of definitions are also possible; for example, religion might be considered as man's relationship to other men, man's method of explaining the unknown, man's ultimate concern (that is, whatever man is primarily concerned with or whatever he would be willing to die for), or man's ethical and moral guidelines.

Each of you has a set of values and beliefs that affects your feelings about and behavior toward a supreme being, your relationships with people, your definition of your ultimate concern, and your method of explaining the unknown. These values may emphasize the sacred, such as a strong belief in an all-good, all-powerful God, in afterlife, and in the effectiveness of church ritual and prayer. They may emphasize secular values, such as improving relationships among men, helping achieve peace, and improving physical and emotional health. The values may be strictly followed or frequently violated, relatively stable or in a state of change, carefully thought about or learned from parents and never questioned. They may motivate you to join a religious group or to remain apart from any religious group, to mature and use your capabilities or to become narrow and limit your thinking. However your religious values affect you, you do have values related to religious matters, although you may not be particularly aware of them.

The concern of this chapter, of course, is not to evaluate the validity of religious values or the adequacy of religious groups, but to discuss such psychological matters as the development of religious values, the religious beliefs and problems of college students, and the relationship between religion and mental health.

Development of religious beliefs

People learn religious beliefs and values, as they learn all beliefs and values, primarily through interaction with significant figures, although the school, the general community, and the mass media also have an effect. The unique personality of the individual is another obvious influence upon the set of values each person evolves.

Religious development in childhood
and adolescence

Young children usually internalize the religious values of their parents and other significant figures in their environment. They almost always

Figure 18–1. One might argue that the Ku Klux Klan is a religion for some people since all other values are forsaken for the values of the Klan. The costumes, the cross, the flag, and the hoods of this initiation ritual are obviously based upon religious symbols. Courtesy Columbia Broadcasting System.

attend the church selected for them by their parents, usually without much question. Children tend to look upon God as a person and accept literal interpretations of what they are told: one girl who had been told "God is in you" was afraid He would leave when she had her tonsils removed. Prayer is frequently looked upon as a method of wishing for things, since children are too young to understand the concept of prayer as communication with God. "God is viewed like an absent-minded magician" (cited in Smith, 1961).

In adolescence, questioning of certain aspects of religion begins. This questioning may also involve criticism, although criticism tends to be leveled at ceremonies and rituals, rather than at the basic beliefs. Undoubtedly many adolescents (and many adults) never see religion as being more than rituals and ceremonies. Doubting and questioning do not necessarily indicate loss of faith and may actually be a sign of maturity, since childish concepts of God may need revision (Hurlock, 1959).

A recent study of religious experiences of ninth-graders had interesting results. When asked, "When do you feel closest to God?" most of the respondents referred to some activity related to the church, and many reported having had this feeling a time when they were alone. The personal experiences which made them feel "especially close to God" occurred most frequently when the student or a close friend or relative narrowly escaped death or injury; the second most common situation was again when the student was alone (Elkind and Elkind, 1962). The importance of privacy and solitude in the religious feelings of these students is significant.

"Well, you were the one who said we shouldn't force religion on them—that they'd find it for themselves."

Figure 18–2. Children usually internalize their parents' religious values. Of course, first they must know what these values are. Courtesy Ed Fisher.

Toward the end of high school and during the years immediately following, young people increase their religious criticisms and doubts (Kuhlen and Arnold, 1944). Although this is often interpreted as a period of antireligious feelings and even atheism or agnosticism, such claims are not borne out by research. Young people in the 16-to-25 age range are rarely atheistic or agnostic, unless their parents are. Their criticisms of religion probably stem from a combination of two factors: first, they are seeking to understand their religious values better and must test them in discussion, even argument, with others; and second, they are made un-happy by some of the behavior they observe in people who are, or claim to be, religious. Also, in attacking religion, they are indirectly attacking the authority of their parents, who represent the religious views in question. Numerous studies have shown that 90 percent or more of the adolescents surveyed believe in God and that a large proportion also accept the ideas of a Christian afterlife, of the value of prayer, and of the need for ritual and ceremony (e.g., Kuhlen and Arnold, 1944).

The changes in adolescent religious attitudes that do occur with age seem to be the following: (1) from a literal interpretation of the Bible to a symbolic interpretation; (2) from an almost complete acceptance of religious rituals, prayers, and ceremonies, to some doubt; (3) from a strong belief that only "my" religion is correct to a feeling that all religions have something to offer; (4) from a virtually total belief in the existence of God to some questioning (e.g., Kuhlen and Arnold, 1944).

Church attendance in adolescence typically drops off. Whereas part of this may be due to increased doubting, most of the decrease probably results from reduced family demands for attendance. Many parents insist that their young children go to church, but are more lenient with their teen-agers.

Development in youth, maturity, and old age

The man who is 20 years old today has lived through a world quite different from that of the person who was 20 years old in 1947 or the person who will be 20 in 1981. It would be strange if they had identical values concerning religion. Parents of the present generation of college students should not expect their children to agree with them any more than the next generation will agree with this one. Yet people accept the religious values of their parents to a higher degree than they accept most other types of values (Fisher, 1948). When a shift does occur, it is usually away from the traditional beliefs.

Once the person is married and away from his parents' home, antag-onisms to parental values often fade away. By the time his own children begin to arrive, and especially when they reach Sunday School age, he is likely to join a church again. Thus, from age 35 on, religious activity and traditional beliefs increase (Argyle, 1959). Religious conflicts tend to disappear during these middle years and church attendance is high.

As people move from middle age to old age, they state that religion becomes more important to them and that they hold their religious beliefs more firmly, although their church attendance and church activities diminish (Moberg, 1965). This apparent inconsistency is caused by health problems and transportation difficulties as well as by the orientation of most church programs toward satisfying the needs of children, adolescents, and young adults rather than the elderly.

Many religious viewpoints, including atheism, exist in the United States. Such diverse religious groups as the Roman Catholic, Orthodox Jewish, Ethical Culture, Christian Science, Southern Baptist, Advent Christian, Episcopalian, Buddhist, and Pentecostal, represent a fantastic variety of religious values. The mature individual can evolve a set of religious beliefs, perhaps closely related to a particular denomination or perhaps not, which he has thought through and found appropriate. His behavior and his values will not be the result of habit or fear, or deficiency motives, but of belief and conviction. If he is primarily growth-motivated, these values will help him grow and use his capabilities and will not involve him in persecutions, prejudices, or attempts to silence those who disagree with him. The mature person remains open to new ideas and to possible change, without altering his beliefs every time he finds a new friend or takes another philosophy course.

Religious beliefs of college students

The religious beliefs of college students vary greatly from school to school. In some colleges, almost all students attend church, while only a small fraction will go to church at other schools. All in all, about one in four college students attends church every week, and about one in four does not attend at all during his college years. Attendance increases after graduation (Jacob, 1957).

A recent major investigation of college student religious attitudes included 4,600 male students, primarily in East Coast colleges. Although this group is certainly not completely typical of the country (for example, mostly nonchurch schools were included), their responses are worth considering.

Half these students accepted the traditional view of God, while fewer than 20 percent discarded the idea of God, and most of this latter group said they believed in man, in science, or in natural law. Over one in four believed in "a power greater than myself which some people call God and some people call Nature." Just 1 percent claimed to be actual atheists. The two major motives for seeking religion were belief in God, and desire for personal adjustment and dealing with the problems of life and getting along with others (Goldsen et al., 1960).

Those students who practiced their religion were more likely to feel that cheating is wrong but were also more likely to agree with the statement, "If everyone else cheats, why shouldn't I?" They were also less likely to be nonconformists and were less likely to believe others should be allowed to express nonconforming ideas. Religious students in this study were slightly less tolerant of Negroes than were less-religious students (Goldsen et al., 1960).

Results of two more recent surveys support the above data, with some qualifications. *Newsweek's* campus poll indicated that three out of four college students believed in God, but that "in many cases the belief was highly tenuous." Also, almost 40 percent of all students interviewed felt that their college experiences had caused them to question their faith (*Newsweek*, 1965). An earlier study (Gallup and Hill, 1961) showed two out of three college students displaying a "very firm" belief in God and only about 7 percent disbelieving in God's existence.

Putting the above studies together with other information, a picture emerges of religious values among college students. By and large, they believe very firmly in the traditional God, but—when they do not—they are either uncertain or have accepted science, man, or nature as their "ultimate concern." In later years, many of them will slowly move back to the values they internalized in their earlier years and will undoubtedly join some church group, probably the same one their parents belong to or one slightly less traditional in its views. A small portion will retain agnostic or atheistic beliefs into maturity and throughout their lives.

Some major religious problems of college students

Religious conflicts occur throughout mature life, but the period between the middle teens and the middle twenties is often considered the most difficult, perhaps because so many people begin to consider the more complex problems of life at this point. Among the problems college students commonly confront are the science-versus-religion controversy, learning about other religions, considering the purpose of life, and defining the place of religious freedom.

Science and religion. Scientific and technical achievements have become so important in our world today that some people claim they have been made a substitute for religion. In addition, *certain* scientific findings appear to conflict with *certain* beliefs held by *some* religious groups. For example, the scientific assumption that the world is millions of years old conflicts with the belief that it is only a few thousand years old; the scientific approach to mental illness conflicts with the idea that disturbed people are inhabited by devils, an idea still maintained by a few clergymen, although rejected by the overwhelming majority.

Nonetheless, the vast proportion of scientific findings do not conflict with the religious beliefs of any group, and many religious denominations find nothing in science to conflict with their teachings. However, scientific thinking and religious thinking each demand different sorts of faith:

scientific thinking demands a faith in the scientific method and the potential ability of man to comprehend the universe (see pages 5–6), and traditional religious thinking demands faith in an unseen supreme being.

Students are taught to think scientifically, to demand to see results, to insist upon observing variables, to be able to predict what will happen if compound *A* is added to compound *J*. Such learning may cause them to distrust thinking that does not operate scientifically and to cast aside

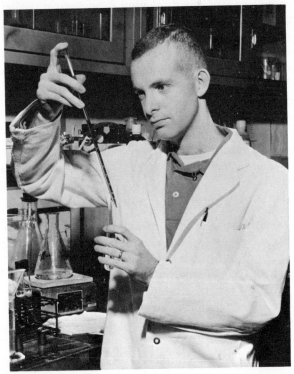

Figure 18–3. How will this student's interest in science affect his religious values? Courtesy Antioch College News Bureau.

traditional religious beliefs, because they cannot be tested scientifically. Thus, the beliefs of science and religion do not conflict, but the methods do. These same students, however, recognize that not all decisions require scientific proof, e.g., political beliefs or the choice of a date for Saturday night.

Many students feel they must choose between science and religion. Such a choice seems unnecessary, since the scientific method can be used for scientific and technical matters, and a completely different approach can be used for religious matters.

Some students, of course, are looking for ammunition with which they can attack their parents' authority, and they find that antireligious arguments are very useful. On other occasions, students become upset when the professor appears to disagree with their religious values, and they become overly critical of everything the professor says.

> Mary Casey, a very bright girl with deep religious convictions, was failing Introduction to Psychology at the state college she attended. She visited the professor at his office and explained that her belief in free will seemed to conflict with the psychological idea that human behavior results from heredity and environment. "I've gotten so I don't trust anything you say—I think perhaps it's all sinful." The instructor pointed out that the existence of soul and free will could easily be included in his explanation, if she wished. He had not stated that heredity and environment were the only possible causes of behavior, but that they were the only causes of behavior *which psychologists could measure* with their present methods. He added that, even though his views and Mary's were not the same, she could learn his ideas without changing hers.

The frustrations and irritations of attending a class in which the textbook or professor appeared to disagree with the student's values have caused student unhappiness and even academic failure. Often the extent of real disagreement is exaggerated, but even when a major difference exists, a truly devout student is unlikely to alter his own views. (See Chapter 17 regarding the changing of values.)

Learning about the religions of others. Many students receive little or no religious training before college; others receive good training in their own religion but learn nothing of other philosophies or customs. In either instance, college life can be upsetting, partially because courses discuss numerous religious ideas and partially because contact with students of other religious backgrounds is inevitable.

> John Holdren grew up in a small town where people believed the theory of evolution to be the work of the Devil. The state constitution restricted the way evolution could be taught, and all his childhood was spent with people of similar religious values. "I even felt a little brave when my Boy Scout troop visited a Catholic church once a year."

> Will Gilberg was raised in a section of a large city where almost all his neighbors were Jewish, and well over 80 percent of his high school was Jewish. He had never had a non-Jewish close friend.

> When John and Will were assigned as roommates at college, they liked each other, but with reservations. John was as-

tounded that anyone in America could deny the divinity of Jesus without being struck dead on the spot, and Will was dismayed that anyone in America could deny the truth of evolution. John began to worry that Will would not go to heaven, and Will began to worry that John was really anti-Semitic; John's religion taught him that drinking was sinful, and Will's religion included wine in its ceremonies.

Both took a philosophy course taught by a visiting professor from India. Since they had both always taken their own religious views for granted, learning how Christianity and Judaism looked to a scholar from Asia was very disconcerting. John firmly believed that Jesus walked on water; Will firmly believed that Moses parted the Red Sea; yet both were shaken when they realized how strange such miracles sounded to a person from a totally different culture.

New ideas from professors, from reading, and from other students left both boys confused about the "rightness" of their own values and the "wrongness" of the values of the other. All in all, their first year of college, in spite of offering them considerable growth in maturity and understanding, was extremely stressful.

The purpose of life. College students are sometimes disturbed by the question: "What is the purpose of life?" Students have heard the explanations of others—that the purpose of life is to serve God, or to serve fellow men, or to enjoy life, or to be successful, or to serve country. But many students come to doubt that any of these purposes is *the* purpose for life, yet they cannot find an adequate substitute.

These students may go through a period of confusion and even depression. Life has no purpose; life seems vacant and meaningless. By reading, talking, and thinking, they begin to formulate what they feel to be the purpose in life. This formulation is not static, and is likely to continue to develop and change during their mature years, but the confusion and depression that they may have felt as students will probably not recur.

The place of religious freedom. When asked directly how they felt about religious freedom, over 90 percent of the students surveyed expressed their belief in "unrestricted freedom to practice one's own religion." However, nearly one in four felt that religions preaching "unwholesome ideas" should be suppressed, a direct contradiction of the first belief; another 17 percent were uncertain (Goldsen et al., 1960).

Not only students, but adults of all ages are similarly uncertain about how much religious freedom they wish to allow. When asked directly, they always favor religious freedom. However, notice above that fully 40 percent of these students were opposed to allowing "unwholesome" religious ideas to be expressed. Thus, they did not truly favor complete religious freedom, but only freedom for those religions that did not make them unhappy. Are there any religions whose freedom you might not approve?

The degree to which any college student finds religious conflicts upsetting undoubtedly relates to the general emotional stability of the student. Students with normal mental health will be able to deal with the problems discussed above with little or no emotional upset, while students with a history of emotional instability will find that religious conflicts intensify their other problems.

Religion and healthy adjustment

Like other values, religious values can offer opportunities for growth and increased self-esteem and stability, or they can lead to intense conflict and may limit the possibilities for growth motivation. Similarly, the church group may be warm, friendly, and emotionally satisfying, or cold, demanding, and emotionally punishing. Among the most important elements of religion in its relationship to healthy adjustment are faith, rituals, guilt, and church affiliation.

Faith, values, and healthy adjustment

An individual can have faith in any one of many religious value systems (or some combination of several). He may have faith that God exists or that no God exists, that the soul goes to heaven or hell after death or that neither the soul nor heaven or hell are real, that prayers are answered or that prayers are a waste of time. He may place more faith in science or technology than in the traditional religious values. When you view the behavior of peoples throughout the world, you can see that some undoubtedly have more faith in Communism or money or power than in a personal God.

Faith implies acceptance of a system of religious beliefs based upon what the individual feels is sufficient evidence or authority. It can be supported by logic, but it does not depend upon logic. You have faith when you say, "I don't know exactly why, but I feel that my concept of a supreme being is correct—it just has to be—I just know it is." Or you might have faith in the accuracy of a particular authority, such as the Bible, your parents, a minister, a philosopher, or a friend. Perhaps you believe you have come to your religious values through a process of reasoning; in that case, you have faith in your ability to understand religious ideas with your own reason.

A person cannot consciously decide to have faith. Faith can occur in many ways, but not through your saying, "I think I'd better get faith." Faith is a set of beliefs and values and is acquired just as other values are acquired.

Religious faith affects behavior in ways many people never consider. For example, if you believe life on earth is only a "vale of tears" before entering the life after death, you may be less concerned with poverty or education: after all, being poor or uneducated is not so important, because it is temporary, and only the life after death is permanent. If, on the other hand, you have faith that all life ends at death, then the life on this earth becomes very important, since it is the only existence you will ever know.

In order to be faithful to their religious values, people have faced many hardships and even death. Anyone rejecting the religious values of the great majority of his culture faces prejudice and persecution. Basic needs, such as hunger and safety, often go unsatisfied in order to maintain religious values.

The specific religious values are probably no more important to healthy adjustment than the degree to which the values are consistent with the person's daily behavior and acceptable in the surrounding society. As mentioned elsewhere (page 272), opposing the standards of the group increases stress; also behaving inconsistently with the self-concept can produce conflict and guilt. The person, for example, who firmly believes that cursing is wrong, yet curses anyway, will feel a conflict between his values and his behavior. He may eventually change his behavior or he may alter his values or he may justify swearing in some fashion, but he will be motivated to reduce the tension-producing feeling of conflict.

A few people maintain religious values that are helpful neither for healthy adjustment nor self-actualization. They may interpret their religion, often incorrectly, as unforgiving; they may have an "evil" thought and feel they have committed a terrible wrong; or they may feel their values require that all who disagree are inferior and should be eliminated, with violence if necessary. Those faiths that are unforgiving, that demand an impossible level of "pure thinking," or that encourage disrespect or violence are not conducive to healthy emotional development in a democratic country such as the United States.

Rituals

Rituals are important or meaningless, depending upon your religious feelings and your previous experiences with those rituals. Certain rituals are beautiful and add richness to life—many non-Catholics, for example, can enjoy the color and excitement in a Roman Catholic high mass. Other rituals, such as the Catholic ritual of kneeling before entering and leaving the church pew, may be very meaningful to a Catholic, but have little significance to a non-Catholic.

High school and college students are often searching for religious values and are very much aware of inconsistencies. They are looking for meaning in religion and criticize rituals that seem impractical or so automatic that they appear meaningless. Also, students live in the present and often have little patience for the past, while rituals usually have evolved over years, perhaps centuries, and have meanings that are often traditional rather than contemporary.

Figure 18–4. Not all rituals are in the church. Here is the British Navy ritual of piping aboard a famous person or a high ranking officer. Courtesy Columbia Broadcasting System.

Rituals become very familiar and may be comforting and satisfying, particularly in times of stress. They frequently occur in a group setting and give those who participate a feeling of belonging to the group and a way of expressing their associations. On the other hand, a ritual can become a meaningless chore or habit that people continue to perform because of some vaguely felt belief that ignoring it will bring bad luck. When neglecting this type of ritual causes guilt and anxiety, the ritual is not only meaningless but potentially harmful emotionally.

Guilt and relief from guilt

Religious beliefs can contribute both to increased feelings of guilt and anxiety and to decreased feelings of guilt and anxiety. Religion creates guilt when it is interpreted as overly demanding and overly punishing. When a young child fears he will go to hell because he sneaked a candy bar from the drugstore, and when he wakes up shrieking from a nightmare of burning in hell, the guilt has progressed too far. When a college student cannot sleep at night because he fears he will be punished by God for harboring some slight religious doubt, anxiety has progressed too far. Religion sets up standards for behavior and feelings, but most religious leaders are aware that not all people can live up to these standards at all times.

Since people often find they cannot live up to religious standards, they feel the need for being forgiven. This can occur through prayer, through contemplation, and through such devices as the confessional. Not only can these methods be used to reduce the guilt and anxiety brought about

"I don't believe in it any more, either, but I think it's a beautiful old cultural ritual which should be preserved."

Figure 18–5. College students are often impatient with religious rituals—especially those they perceive as hypocritical. Courtesy Ed Fisher.

by religious standards, but they can occasionally reduce guilt that originated in ways having little or nothing to do with religion.

> Martin Marcus and his brother did not get along as children, and, unlike most brothers, had even more difficulty as adults. Suddenly, when he was only 31, Martin's brother was killed in an airplane crash. Martin had so often thought about how good it would be to get his brother out of the way, that, in a sense, he

felt responsible for the death. Martin finally undertook a lengthy period of prayer and contemplation, in the hope that he could gain a feeling of having been forgiven.

Martin's guilty feelings resulted from having wished that terrible things would happen to his brother, since he certainly had nothing to do with the actual death. Martin could not apologize and be forgiven; his brother was dead and could not forgive him. Nor could Martin admit to anyone else why he felt as he did. What if he had not believed in God? Then, in some fashion, he would have had to arrive at the belief that "my brother would have forgiven me, had he actually understood."

Religious beliefs exert a great influence upon behavior through inducing and reducing guilt and anxiety. Do you think that the feeling of having been forgiven can go so far in reducing guilt as to allow irresponsibility?

Church affiliation

Motivation for church attendance varies. Some people go to church because they think it looks good to friends and neighbors; others have been persuaded that it aids peace of mind; still others attend with the vague feeling that they can "stay on the good side of God, just in case there is a God." Other motives include business contacts, social contacts, seeing who else is going, and looking the minister over.

Nonetheless, most church attendance is probably motivated by a sincere desire to join with a community of others to express deeply felt spiritual beliefs. In this large, seemingly impersonal world, many feel alone and vulnerable. Church membership not only gives spiritual satisfaction, but also provides the important feeling of belonging to a group that has similar beliefs and performs similar rituals.

For some, unfortunately, church affiliation leads to such extreme loyalties that other churches and their members are looked down upon or discriminated against. There are people who believe certain religious views mark a person as inferior or immoral. Such thinking may make it difficult to maintain healthy adjustment in a world where so many religious views are presented and where the present trend is to come religiously closer together through the ecumenical movement.

What about the nonbeliever?

"People who don't believe in God are lucky—they can do anything they please, and they don't have to worry about being punished."

"People who don't believe in God are in a miserable state—they must always be scared that something terrible will happen to them when they die."

413

The difference in behavior between believers and nonbelievers is much less than many people think. Nonbelievers neither do anything they please nor are they scared something terrible will happen. The nonbeliever is not without problems, since he is taking an unpopular position, and he may be criticized for his views. However, there is no evidence that his emotional health or self-actualization suffers for not believing in God.

As a matter of fact, although evidence does establish the churchgoer as drinking and smoking less than the nonchurchgoer (an expected relationship), the churchgoer does not seem to be more honest (Goldsen et al., 1960), less racially prejudiced (Allport and Kramer, 1946), or more concerned with the value of human life and of mankind (Kirkpatrick, 1949). It may well be the consistency with which a belief is held, rather than the belief itself, that determines emotionally healthy behavior. Those who attended church irregularly were more fearful of death than either regular churchgoers or those who never attended (Kalish, 1963).

The nonbeliever usually has faith in something, perhaps other people or science. He may reject religious rituals, but receive some of the richness of such rituals through enjoyment of art or music; his guilt cannot be relieved through confession or prayer, but he also avoids certain sources of guilt; although he does not belong to a church group, he may belong to professional or vocational groups. For some people, then, religious affiliation leads to more healthy adjustment; other people satisfy their psychological needs in other ways.

SUMMARY OF THE IMPORTANT IDEAS

1. There are many possible definitions of religion: "the service and adoration of God or a god, as expressed in forms of worship," or man's relationship to other men, or man's method of explaining the unknown, or man's ultimate concern.

2. Young children usually internalize the religious values of their parents and other significant figures; they rarely resist their parents' requests regarding prayer, church attendance, or ritual adherence.

3. Adolescents feel close to God in situations involving privacy and solitude.

4. Religious values of adolescents change somewhat with age; the changes involve a diminishing acceptance of the Bible in literal terms, some doubts concerning rituals and prayers, more tolerance for other beliefs, and a very slight bit of questioning the existence of God.

5. Religious values and activities continue to change after adolescence; in middle age, religious conflict seems to disappear; in old age, beliefs are held more firmly, although religious activities diminish.

6. Most college students believe in God, although some define their belief as being in "a power greater than myself that some people call God and some people call Nature."

7. College students face certain religious problems including the possibility of conflict between science and religion, confusion occurring when learning the religious beliefs of others, determining the purpose of life, and deciding upon the place of religious freedom.

8. Religion affects mental health both through religious values and through religious group membership; either may lead to better emotional health or may precipitate mental health problems.

9. The degree to which a person leads his life consistent with his religious values probably contributes to mental health also.

10. Religious rituals are important or meaningless, depending upon the individual's feelings, previous experience, and the context in which the ritual is conducted; college students often attack rituals because rituals seem to lack contemporary meaning.

11. Religious values may increase guilt feelings and may also allow reduction in guilt feelings.

12. Motivation for church affiliation varies from person to person.

13. Those who do not believe in the more commonly accepted explanations of God and other religious matters, receive comparable satisfactions in other ways.

V The healthy personality

The healthy personality **19**

The healthy personality has been discussed throughout the book. Every chapter has had something to say about it, but it seemed proper to end this text with final comments upon healthy adjustment and self-actualization. The author has continually tried to emphasize normal and healthy human behavior, as opposed to the abnormal and unhealthy, although he recognizes many readers get a kick out of studying peculiar behavior. Nonetheless, most readers are normal, and most have the potential for a healthy and self-actualizing personality. Therefore, the final chapter will discuss a few additional ramifications of the positive aspects of human beings.

What constitutes a mentally and emotionally **healthy personality**? Is it the absence of the severe problems discussed in Chapter 14? Is it being average? Is it being like most of the people around you? Do you have a "healthy personality"?

When you speak of a person who is physically healthy, you do not mean merely that he is not ill or handicapped, nor do you mean his health is average, nor that he is like most of the people around him. Being healthy is a positive concept—you think not just of the absence of trouble, but of the presence of vitality, strength, and endurance.

In the same way, the healthy personality should be defined in terms of positive qualities. You are not healthy merely because you have avoided neurotic, psychotic, or criminal behavior; you should also be motivated by needs for self-actualization, you should be able to enter into mutually rewarding friendship and love relationships, and you should be able to deal creatively with the environment.

Self-actualization and the healthy personality

Behavior of the psychologically healthy person results primarily from growth motives, rather than deficiency motives. He has done a reasonably good job of satisfying his more basic needs and is able to turn his attention toward satisfying his need for personal growth. Dr. Abraham Maslow, in studying healthy, self-actualizing personalities, decided that they differed from other people in thirteen basic ways (cited in Maslow, 1962).* (You may wish to review the earlier discussion of self-actualization in Chapter 2.)

1. *Superior perception of reality.* The healthy personality does not have such strong prejudices or fears or rigidities that he must reinterpret the world to suit himself. People who constantly blame communists or capitalists for all that troubles the world are not perceiving reality. This implies that healthy personalities have less need for defense mechanisms.

2. *Increased acceptance of self, of others, and of nature.* Some people do not like themselves. They are overly critical and unforgiving regarding themselves. They do not think that they are worthwhile people. In addition, they are unduly critical and unforgiving of others, and may also feel that people in general are just no good. The healthy personality recognizes that he and all other people have limitations, but that people are worthwhile and should be accepted as worthy individuals. This does not mean that healthy personalities are not self-critical, but that they

---

*The headings are directly from Professor Maslow, but the explanations are the responsibility of the author of this book, as he interprets Dr. Maslow.

enjoy a basic self-confidence, with the criticisms directed at producing some changes, rather than leading to a deadening depression.

A Buddhist legend clarifies the healthy personality*

Once the Enlightened One came upon a couple of young boys having a fist fight. One of them was on the ground, with the other sitting on him. When they saw Lord Buddha approaching, they both jumped up and stood apologetically before him. Lord Buddha asked the winner what caused him to knock his friend down. "He called me a liar," the boy said.

"Are you a liar?" asked Lord Buddha.

"No, sir," was the reply.

"Then why did you fight?" asked the Enlightened One. "You know, you are the best one to decide whether you really lied or not. If you did lie, you should thank your friend for bringing it to your attention. If you had not lied, you know that your friend was mistaken. In either case, there seems to be no cause for such temper. You certainly do not knock a person down when he greets you by calling you a handsome and wonderful fellow, do you? You either thank him, or tell him he is mistaken, but you do not hit him."

In this legend, Buddha shows that the healthy personality has enough self-acceptance not to be bothered when an accusation is untrue, and has enough acceptance of others not to become angry when a friend makes an error.

*From Chatterjee, M. N., *Society in the Making*. Ann Arbor: Edwards Brothers, Inc., 1942, p. 30.

---

3. *Increased spontaneity.* Healthy personalities can be relaxed and spontaneous. They need not worry unnecessarily about what others think, and, thus, they can behave more naturally. "Spontaneity" does not mean that they violate the rights of others or that they enjoy shocking others, but that they *can* act impulsively and emotionally.

4. *Increase in problem centering.* Since self-actualizing persons are not overly concerned with personal problems and satisfying status needs, they have the energy and the desire to deal with the particular problems or activities that strike them as challenging.

5. *Increase in detachment and desire for privacy.* These days, there is so much emphasis upon getting along with others, that we often neglect the importance of privacy. The self-actualizing person enjoys privacy and the opportunity to be concerned with his own thoughts and ideas.

6. *Increased* autonomy *and resistance to being dominated by the culture.* The healthy personality can remain independent of the pressures around him. Self-actualizing people can evaluate the world they live in, without being blinded by the fact that they are living in it. They remain faithful to their own values and are not susceptible to the pressures of propaganda.

7. *Greater freshness of appreciation and richness of emotional reaction.* Self-actualizing people are not bored with life and do not need to run after new thrills. They can enjoy new experiences and see new elements in "the same old thing." They can find stimulation and pleasure in a conversation, a playing baby, or an old piece of driftwood.

8. *Higher frequency of all-absorbing experiences.* From time to time, some of us have an experience that is so enthralling, so exciting, so absorbing, that we virtually lose track of time and place. We are "taken out of ourselves," and the experience is a very wonderful one. Self-actualizing people report this occurrence more often.

9. *Increased feelings of brotherhood to man.* The phrase "brotherhood of man" is often used without real meaning. The healthy personality truly understands this concept. It is not just that he has friends, but that he feels he is a part of all mankind. Whatever happens to any man happens to all men, and, thus, happens to him.

10. *Good relationships with others.* Those with healthy personalities are able to have a few very close, meaningful relationships, although they are not necessarily popular with a large group.

11. *More democratic beliefs.* Healthy personalities accept people for what they are, not for the labels (such as race, religion, or vocation) attached to them. They believe every human being is entitled to dignity and esteem.

12. *Greatly increased creativity.* Several of the previously described characteristics explain the creative abilities of the healthy personality. He is not overly involved with his own problems; he can respond spontaneously; he is relatively free from domination by his surroundings. Therefore, he can see new relationships and consider new ideas without being hampered by the prejudices and rigidity of less-healthy personalities.

13. *More subtle sense of humor, which lacks hostility.* Self-actualizers find more humor in the world, but the humor is not at the expense of someone else. They do not find it funny when someone else is embarrassed or criticized. They enjoy laughing with people, but not at people,

and they do not look upon personal misfortune as a cause for laughter. (This final factor is not listed with the others, but appears elsewhere in Maslow's writing.)

Additional characteristics of the healthy personality

Professor Maslow described the characteristics he observed through his research. They, by no means, exhaust the list of possible characteristics of self-actualizing individuals. The author will suggest a few more.

Figure 19–1. Can you see a type of beauty in this misshapen tree? Photo by John G. Warford.

14. *The ability to make decisions, to accept responsibility for decisions, and to face the consequences of decisions.* Too often people do not wish to make decisions, because decisions involve responsibility. Inevitably, some decisions will be wrong, but the healthy personality can make decisions when called upon. Since he is problem centered, his decisions should be—on the whole—based on objective evaluation, rather than his own personal needs or anxieties.

15. *Increased goal-directedness.* The self-actualizer is working toward goals, rather than just "living" without any idea of what he wishes to do or why. His goals may not be those which please others—they may even be considered foolish—and he may not achieve all his goals, but his behavior is not random or aimless.

16. *High integrity.* Integrity means being honest, not merely to the letter of the laws of honesty and decency, but to the spirit. A healthy personality not only has integrity for himself, but can accept others as having integrity.

17. *Appropriate flexibility.* Times occur when people must be able to change their attitudes and ways of thinking. Flexibility, or lack of rigidity, does not mean bowing to the slightest pressures; it does mean being willing to consider change when the circumstances have changed or the information available has changed.

18. *High social consciousness.* Although the healthy personality is often detached and values privacy, he does not shut himself off from the world. He is willing to take a position on an issue, even though his position may be unpopular.

19. *High social awareness.* Healthy personalities are aware of the effects they have upon others. They respond to others as "complete and whole individuals" (Maslow, 1962). To the healthy personality, other people are not objects or tools, but full human beings.

20. *High ability to give and to receive.* We all need to be able to give to others, both materially and in terms of our time, our energies, and our interest and concern. Since the healthy personality recognizes the importance of giving, he realizes the importance of being a gracious receiver. To give without being able to receive is as degrading to others as receiving without thought of giving.

21. *Increased insight.* People are limited in the degree to which they can understand themselves, but the healthy personality finds that less interferes with his self-understanding, because he feels secure and accepted. He observes how others react to him, when he succeeds and when he fails, when he seems motivated and when he is unmoved. Thus, he can increase his self-understanding.

The healthy, self-actualizing person is certainly not perfect. What is stated above are not characteristics that every self-actualizing person lives up to, but characteristics more descriptive of these individuals than of others. You may think of other qualities that have been omitted, or you may feel that some of the characteristics listed have been overestimated in importance.

Friendship and the healthy personality

All people have the potential to enter into warm and mutually rewarding friendships. The value of friendship is widely recognized, and most college students state they would rather have a few close friends than a large circle of casual acquaintances.

The healthy personality can both give to and receive from friendship—friendship is not a one-way street. You find that your friendship bolsters your self-concept by helping you recognize that others can like and respect you, and also that you are able to give another the liking and respect that bolsters *his* self-concept and helps him become a more complete person.

Deep and sincere friendships are very satisfying, but they also present the possibility of loss. When you like someone, you place trust in him and become dependent upon him in certain ways. If he disapproves of your behavior, you are more than normally upset; if he ignores you, moves away, or even dies, you may feel you have been cheated, even though you may recognize how unfair such a feeling is. You have invested a part of yourself in him just as you invest money in a bank, and you count on some sort of return. If you get nothing in return, or worse, if the investment is destroyed, the emotional pain can be great. In any form of friendship, and especially in love and marriage, people take a chance on being hurt. In order to gain from a relationship, you must risk something. The healthy personality has sufficient feelings of self-adequacy that he can take this risk; on the other hand, a person whose ability to handle stress is already reaching its limit may find too much anxiety in risking a close friendship, and he is unable to give, or even to receive, in a close relationship.

Some people have been so badly hurt by others that they are unable to trust people enough to build friendship. Foster children, for example, who are moved from home to home, are often unable to trust others; in their experience, each time they allow themselves to like a new foster family, they are moved to another home.

Building healthy friendships

Good friendships are based on many factors. Friends tend to be of the same racial, religious, social, and age groups; they tend to have similar intelligence and get similar grades; they tend to live or work near each other.

In addition to having similar background characteristics, friends also have similar needs, interests, reading habits, morals, and scores on personality tests (Ausubel, 1954; Banta and Hetherington, 1963; Izard, 1963). These factors enable people to satisfy each other's needs and to communicate with each other with understanding, an ability just as important in healthy friendships as in good marriages. Thus, in friendships, as in all healthy human relationships, the parties resemble each other in certain ways and are complementary in satisfying each other's needs in other ways.

Healthy friendships are built upon the satisfaction of healthy needs. They are also built upon many other factors. Dr. Carl Rogers, a well-known and highly respected psychologist, mentions some of the things he has learned through his many years of experience.

> *It does not help, in the long run, to act like someone I am not.**
>
> To pretend to be someone or to know something or to feel in some way that is not true to yourself builds neither friendship, trust, nor your own self-concept.
>
> *I find I am more effective when I can listen acceptingly to myself, and can be myself.*
>
> People should try to understand how they really feel about others and not condemn themselves if these feelings are not what they "should be." If you are bored or irritated with people, you should recognize how you feel and not be self-critical.
>
> *I have found it of enormous value when I can permit myself to understand another person.*
>
> Instead of trying to judge the words or behavior of another person critically, it is more valuable to try to understand why he does what he does.
>
> *I have found it enriching to open channels through which others can communicate their feelings to me.*
>
> People are often reluctant to discuss their real feelings for fear they will be laughed at or criticized. It is appropriate to allow them to express their feelings to you, even if you disagree with them.
>
> *I have found it highly rewarding when I can accept another person.*
>
> It is not easy to accept another person for himself, without basing your acceptance on his race or his money or his beliefs or

*The italicized statements are either directly quoted or slightly altered from Dr. Rogers's original statements.

his age. Yet accepting others along with their feelings and attitudes and values—even if they are in disagreement with yours—is rewarding.

The more I am aware of myself and others, the less I wish to rush in to "fix things."

In relationships with other individuals, you gain more by being yourself and trying to understand and accept others, rather than trying to change others over (Rogers, 1961).

Healthy friendships are based upon the satisfaction of healthy needs. They are a source of satisfaction to both parties and help both parties to become more complete and individual. Although friendships do place some restrictions upon behavior, the over-all result of a good friendship is to enable both individuals to feel liked, respected, and able to have more freedom rather than less.

The healthy personality and love

Many similarities exist between a healthy friendship and a healthy love relationship. The latter is, by and large, an extension of the former, although love can exist without friendship.

The healthy personality is capable of giving love and is able to affect others so that they love him. He is neither afraid nor ashamed of giving and receiving sincere love and affection. Love, in the sense we use the term here, is not limited to relationships between mature adults of opposite sexes. Love can occur between virtually any two people. But love need not be "between." A human being may love another without reciprocation. In a way, he can also love objects, such as an expressive painting, a familiar house, or—at least among some people—an automobile; he can love concepts that have great meaning to him, such as his God, his country, his "way of life"; and he can love people who do not return the love, such as his month-old son, a recent political or religious figure he has never met, or his mother who died as he was born.

Love should help both the person giving and the person receiving to grow and to be better able to become what they wish to become. Although love, like friendship, has obvious hazards in that it opens the giver to the possibilities both of rejection by the loved one and of loss of the loved one, it should be enriching.

Consider the variety of situations to which the term "love" can be—without any doubt—properly applied:

A parent and his child may love each other, regardless of the age of either one; the love may continue long after one of them has died. Under certain conditions an individual might feel love for a parent of whom he has little or no memory.

A husband and wife may retain a very deep love for each other throughout their lives. And, like the parent-child relationship, after one of the couple dies, the surviving spouse may continue to love the deceased mate, even though he or she loves another person and remarries. There is no principle of human behavior that prevents a person from loving both living and deceased spouses.

When a man and woman, not married to each other, develop a friendship deep enough to call love, but without overtones of sex or romance, they are very fortunate. Sadly enough, complications can arise in such a relationship, especially if either is married to someone else and if the relationship encourages jealousy from those not included. Nonetheless, such relationships can and do occur.

An individual may feel love for nonparental significant figures, such as a grandmother, a maid, or even a teacher. Children who spend a long period in a hospital might direct such feelings toward a doctor or a nurse. You can undoubtedly think of other circumstances which would lead to a similar sort of love.

The word "love" is sometimes used to describe the overwhelming feeling of need created by physical attraction and great dependency without strong affection. (Recall the experiences of Evan Mann on page 207.) Is this a proper use of the term?

The greatly admired psychologist Erich Fromm differentiates mature and immature love. In mature love, you remain very much an individual and retain every bit of personal dignity and integrity; mature love enables an individual to break through the unpleasant sense of loneliness and isolation that so many people feel. Immature love requires that the other person offer love first (like the parent offering love to the infant) and that love be based on needs for the loved one. Mature love follows the principle "I am loved because I love," and "I need you because I love you," not "I love because I am loved," or "I love you because I need you" (Fromm, 1956).

Unhealthy expressions of love

What is often called "love" can tear down an individual's self-concept instead of building it up; it can produce constant fear, anxiety, and pain; it can lead to deficiency motivation instead of growth motivation. These things occur when love is rejected or in danger of being rejected, when it is too demanding, or when it is based upon psychologically unhealthy needs. Such love would appear inconsistent with the healthy personality (we might even question whether the word "love" is properly applied to such cases, but this is not the occasion to begin a semantic argument), and you might wish to consider the following cases in this context.

Bob Frand was very much attached to his mother, and he lived with her until she died, shortly after his thirty-first birthday. Up until that time he had dated frequently, but had never been involved with any girl for more than a few weeks. However, he was greatly upset by his mother's death and sought comfort with a woman at work, an attractive, very understanding 45-year-old widow whose husband had died only a few months earlier. They began to see each other casually, until the woman decided to move to Florida, where a married daughter was living. At that point, Bob declared his love for her and, in a whirlwind romance, persuaded her to marry him. Once married, Bob immediately manipulated their relationship so that his wife did the same things for him that his mother had done, and he pouted and fussed like a child when the new Mrs. Frand tried to have him play the normal male role in the home. Bob had no interest in sex relationships, although he spoke very vaguely of having children "someday." When his wife decided to spend two weeks with her daughter and grandchildren, Bob complained bitterly that she did not love him. Then, the day before she was scheduled to leave, he began to vomit and complained of terrible headaches. His wife canceled her trip. She never learned that Bob's mother became so concerned over his slightest sniffle that he could completely dominate her by pretending illness or, as in this case, developing a psychosomatic condition.

Joe Calvin came to Los Angeles with a high school diploma, an amazing memory, and tremendous motivation to get rich and be able to forget his poverty-stricken, rural Texas background. Maria Kent came to Los Angeles with a college degree, a great sensitivity to the arts, and a desire to make good on her own without the help of her family's money and status. They met, were strongly attracted to each other, and married. But the mild disagreements they had had before their marriage flared into a constant state of bickering and arguing after their marriage. Maria admired Joe's energy and ambition, but she resented his lack of sympathy for the arts and his lack of patience for others from similarly poor backgrounds who could not be successful. Joe liked the idea of having a wife who dressed well, knew the right people, and enjoyed art, but he resented the way she nagged him to go to museums and concerts with her and to give more money to charities for the poor, which Joe felt was just money thrown away.

Joe came more and more to remind Maria of all that she disliked in her father, and in her irritation she began to criticize him for his manners, his speech errors, and his lack of education; she was particularly hostile when Joe's well-educated business associates and friends were with them. Maria would shift the conversation to a new painter or a well-known book they had all read in college, and force Joe to admit his ignorance. Joe reciprocated by withdrawing from Maria into his work. He explained to her that her clothes and other money demands forced him to expand his business and devote more time to it. He emphasized how little she knew about practical matters.

As Joe withdrew into work, Maria withdrew into the community art league, the literary guild, and a relief organization for American Indians. Tired of waiting until 9:00 for Joe to come home from work, Maria volunteered for evening activities, leaving Joe to return to an empty house and a few cans stacked by the sink. Joe so hated the empty house that he began to have his dinners downtown, and came home only after several after-dinner drinks. At that point, Maria announced that she had accepted a job offer working with American Indians that would require her to be away from home several days at a time.

Neither the Frands nor the Calvins were happy in their marriages. In the former, the unhealthy needs that caused Bob to marry in the first place made him dependent upon his wife, yet very demanding upon her. The Calvins' problem is much different: here are two basically adequate people who are unable to communicate with each other; each frustrates the other and each frustration leads to a new aggressive response which, in turn, leads to a new frustration. Slowly each is tearing the other down, leaving a less adequate person who is, obviously, less able to respond to his spouse's needs. Would you apply the term "love" to the Frand marriage? How about the Calvin marriage?

Love is an enriching, enhancing experience when it is mutual, when it involves healthy, growth motives, when the people involved can communicate with each other, and when it produces healthy interdependency, but not overdependency. When love is not mutually rewarding, it is possible that the term is being incorrectly applied.

Creativity and the healthy personality

Friendship and love have been studied by psychologists for many years, but the attention directed at creativity is recent. Being creative, we now realize, is not the same thing as being intelligent, and people with extremely high IQ scores may show little creativity, while those with average intelligence exhibit highly creative behavior at times.

Creativeness is defined as "ability to find new solutions to a problem or new modes of artistic expression" (English and English, 1958).

A businessman may be creative in finding a way to enter a previously untouched market, while an artist who turns out one basic type of

Figure 19-2. In the heart of the Watts section of Los Angeles stand these towers—the work of one man—created from pipes and bottles and stones and odds and ends. Do you feel that the Watts Towers are an example of healthy creativity? Courtesy Columbia Broadcasting System.

painting with many slight variations is not creative, although he may be a competent craftsman. A housewife who creates her own recipes for homemade soups and breads is more creative than an author who writes only "formula stuff."

There is a real danger in discussing who is or what is creative, since psychologists are far from agreeing among themselves on how to judge creativity. What do you think is meant by "creative?" Following is a list of individuals the author considers to be creative. Do you agree? Whom would you add? Whom would you eliminate? Why?

Some representative creative people

George Washington Carver (scientist)
Charlie Chaplin (actor)
Charles Darwin (scientist)
Walt Disney (artist-businessman)
Thomas Edison (inventor)
Albert Einstein (scientist)
Henry Ford (businessman)
Benjamin Franklin (inventor, writer, political figure)
Sigmund Freud (psychiatrist)
Mahatma Gandhi (political figure)
James Joyce (author)
Gustav Mahler (composer)
Horace Mann (educator)
Karl Marx (political theorist)
Pablo Picasso (artist)
Ayn Rand (author-philosopher)
Knute Rockne (football coach)

> You may not approve of what each of these individuals did with their creative abilities, but—for the moment—consider the creative nature of their accomplishments.

Recent research has compared highly creative students with highly intelligent (but not especially creative) students. The former were less well-liked by their teachers, placed more importance on sense of humor, and were more likely to choose unusual vocations. Perhaps of more importance, the highly creative were much less interested in working toward what most of us consider to be success; they preferred to wander off in their own directions, doing what they wished (Getzels and Jackson, 1962).

Other studies have shown highly creative people to be (1) less rigid and less likely to want "everything in its place and a place for everything"; (2) better able to enjoy new ways of doing things and less dependent upon rigid routine; (3) more flexible in their thinking; (4) less motivated to be just like everyone else; and (5) more accepting of their own "irrational" impulses (Berelson and Steiner, 1964). The similarity between these characteristics of the creative personality and Dr. Maslow's description of the self-actualizing personality is striking.

Every society has many pressures against creativity and in favor of conformity. Creative people do things differently, and people who do things differently are often a bit frightening to the others. Sometimes creative people have ideas that seem to oppose the accepted way of thinking and living. Sigmund Freud and James Joyce are examples of men who have been attacked for their creative ideas. Modern art has also been widely attacked by people who make no attempt to understand it.

To differentiate the truly creative from the merely clever or the actually crackpot is not always easy. However, some people are so fearful of new ideas and new ways of doing things that they accuse all change as being dangerous or peculiar.

As an example of how disturbing new and different ideas can be, an incident involving a student nurse and her supervisor is most appropriate.

> The student had been dating a young doctor known for being critical of the methods used by the nursing supervisor, who had been very slow to take advantage of new ideas. When the student asked her supervisor why she did not try some of the newer approaches, the older woman sputtered, "Is that what that young doctor told you? Why don't you stand on your own two feet and do as *I* tell you?"

Have you wondered why the topic of creativity is discussed here rather than with materials on thinking or on intelligence? The author believes that creativity is a healthy way of dealing with the environment, and that being creative is one indication of a healthy personality. However, many creative people have led miserably unhappy lives and certainly appeared to be anything but healthy personalities. The author still feels that their creativeness was a healthy way for them to express their unhappiness and frustrations. That is, being creative does not mean that a person is inevitably emotionally healthy, but that—for his own individual situation—he has found one of the most effective ways possible to deal with his environment and to satisfy his need for self-actualization.

FINAL COMMENTS

What enables one person to have a healthy personality, while another individual is less fortunate? The entire book has been an attempt to answer this question. Part of the answer is "pure luck." The healthy personality is more fortunate in picking his parents. Because of his genes, he is physically healthy and lacks deformities; his mother maintained a good diet and followed medical advice, and he was a healthy baby at birth. In addition, his parents offered him love, security, stability, need satisfaction, and the opportunity to grow and mature properly.

But what of the person with a less fortunate beginning? Is the individual from a broken home or someone who acquired a physical handicap also able to become a healthy personality? The answer is most certainly "yes." These individuals may have more difficulty in becoming healthy personalities, but the goal is still possible. Even the person who has suffered severe emotional upset at one time in his life may later become an effective and healthy personality. Growth-motivated behavior and the possibility of self-actualizing experiences are potentially available to everyone.

The healthy personality is able to handle the stresses he encounters and can do an adequate job of satisfying his physiological, safety, love, and esteem needs. He can meet the environment rather than being over-whelmed by it. He can enjoy life and not interfere with the opportunities of others to enjoy life. He can feel anger, sadness, or even jealousy, and can express these feelings under appropriate circumstances, without being dominated by his anger, his sadness, or his jealousy. Also he can recognize that he is not a helpless pawn at the mercy of a master chess player, but that he is an independent individual with worth, abilities, feelings, and the desire to lead an enjoyable, productive, eventful, self-actualizing life.

This chapter has been written as though the healthy personality is a person, but this is obviously not the case. The healthy personality is an abstract concept. It is a goal, something that people can attempt to achieve. Even those individuals who could never be described as healthy personalities can receive enjoyment from life, be productive, enter into rewarding human relationships, and handle much of the stress they face.

Thus, each individual has some healthy personality characteristics and is deficient in other characteristics. Each individual has the potential within him to increase the ways in which he can be described as a healthy personality. Each individual can devote at least a portion of his attention to self-actualization, rewarding friendships, mutually satisfying love relationships, and creativity.

SUMMARY OF IMPORTANT IDEAS

1. The healthy personality refers to positive qualities, not just the absence of negative qualities.

2. Behavior of the healthy personality results primarily from growth motives, rather than deficiency motives.

3. The healthy personality can both give to and receive from friends.

4. The healthy personality can enter into a mutually satisfying love relationship, without anxiety over the possibility of loss of the loved person.

5. Both friendship and love relationships should lead to growth, although unhealthy expressions of love and friendship do occur.

6. The healthy personality is free to be creative.

7. Although those individuals with more security and love in their homes have advantages in being healthy personalities, physically—and even emotionally—handicapped people can compensate for their difficulties and become healthy personalities.

8. The healthy personality is not without stress but has learned to handle the stress he encounters.

9. The healthy personality is actually an abstract concept, rather than a real human being.

Appendixes

Appendix I   College orientation

College success depends upon more than attending classes and studying for examinations. It requires that you integrate your learning into something meaningful to you and related to your personal and vocational life. College administrators and faculty members, aware of this, provide many resources to help students achieve these goals. These resources include the setting up of a major, so that your courses can be taken in proper sequence and made personally and vocationally meaningful; a variety of campus activities to enrich student life in ways that the classroom cannot do; and many sources of information and counseling to help you make your own decisions concerning your future. As a result, it is hoped, each student will become aware of his own capabilities and of the skills and understanding necessary to develop these capabilities.

Planning your college program

Did you know what your major would be before you entered college? Have you changed your mind? Regardless of how you answered these questions, you will find many other college students like yourself. College not only provides courses for growth in understanding, information, and skills; it also encourages personal growth and maturity through self-evaluation and sometimes painful reappraisals. The important thing to remember in planning your college program is that the courses make sense to you and lead to the goals that allow you the greatest use of your capacities. Thus, both vocational and personal considerations must be taken into account.

In deciding on a major, you might ask yourself the following questions:

1. Will this field help me become the sort of person I wish to become?

2. Will it provide the satisfactions I especially desire?

3. Will it be sufficiently challenging to provide the stimulation for self-actualization?

4. Will it provide a sense of accomplishment?

5. Will it help me reach my vocational goals?

6. Will it enable me to develop the talents I think I possess?

7. Will I be able to learn what I want to learn?

8. Will I enjoy the courses I must take and be able to take the courses I want to take?

9. Will I be able to take courses with the faculty members I want to get to know?

Are there any questions you would wish to add?

Selecting your courses

You have only limited freedom in deciding which particular courses to take. You must, for example, satisfy any general requirements set by the college for all students; second, you must satisfy all field requirements established by the professors in your major department; third, you may need to satisfy certain options allowed for your major, which gives you some leeway; fourth, you may select from a great variety of courses to complete your graduation credits.

You will be further limited if you wish to transfer to a similar program at a similar college or to a much different program at a much different sort of college. In either case, you will need to consider the demands of the college you wish to enter and the demands of the college you are now attending.

Since the courses required by your major, your minor (if you have one), and your general program account for most of the units needed for graduation, you will have only a limited number of free-elective courses. What criteria can you set up to determine which free electives to take? One guideline, which some students follow carefully, is the "will-it-help-me-make-a-buck" criterion. Each possible elective is evaluated by its potential contribution to future income, and the student registers for the courses that pay off the most financially.

The author does not favor this approach. The time you spend in college may be your best opportunity to sample the tremendous store of knowledge and understanding available through higher education. Your free electives offer you the chance to investigate a topic about which you have always been curious or to take a course with a highly regarded professor or to fill what you consider to be a gap in your educational background.

Did you enjoy art classes in high school? Try a course in figure drawing. Do you find pleasure in reading poetry to a friend? Register for a literature course. Do you feel you need to know more about fixing automobiles? Sign up for an introduction to auto mechanics. Do you hope to travel? Take a cultural and political geography course. Do you think you might run for political office some day? Try a course or two in political science. Have you thought about increasing your enjoyment of leisure? Try photography or cooking or creative writing or stage design. Do you want a real intellectual challenge? Consider advanced courses in philosophy or math or history or science. The possibilities are limited only by your time and your energy.

A great deal of discussion is heard about whether a student should take more courses in his specialty or whether he should experiment more. A survey of college graduates showed that about one-third wished they had specialized more and one-fifth felt they had specialized too much (Havemann and West, 1952). Thus, the degree of specialization desired seems to be a matter of individual taste.

Selecting your instructors

Most of you have come to college to learn; it is axiomatic that you learn the most from the best instructors, whether they are "hard" or "easy," whether they are "nice guys" or "old grouches." You may have trouble evaluating professors, since the most common source of information is other students, who have well-known biases. Sometimes one professor will strongly recommend another, but faculty members are reluctant to show partiality. If you use student evaluations, learn why your informant feels as he does: the business law instructor is liked by Jack Gerson because he knows his field, but disliked by Ed Meadows because he is frequently sarcastic. The sophisticated student will check on faculty through several different sources, learning not only whether they are liked, but—more important—*why* they are liked and *for what classes* they are liked.

The college catalogue

Although most students probably read their college catalogue before entering college, they too often ignore it once they begin to take classes. This neglect is unfortunate, since the catalogue contains not only descriptions of courses and requirements for majors but also such information as the history of the school, available scholarships and loans, the academic background of the faculty members, graduation requirements, and a host of rules and regulations. Consider a few of the questions covered in the catalogue.

1. What courses are required to graduate in your major? How many units are required in the major? In a minor? In general education courses?

2. What happens if a new catalogue appears during your second year on campus and changes the requirements? Which set of rules do you operate under?

3. If a college regulation works a particular hardship upon you, what can you do about it? For example, if your college requires three credits of Speech, but you completed a similar two-credit course at another college, can you arrange to meet the present obligation? What system of petitions does your college have?

4. What is the meaning of "probation" at your school? How long can you remain on probation? How do you get off probation?

5. What does the grade *Incomplete* signify? How long do you have in which to make it up? What happens if you do not make it up? It is amazing how often students wait until the last minute to make up an Incomplete, only to find out the professor is on leave, or that he is no longer willing to administer an examination that should have been taken ten months earlier, or that he has taken a job elsewhere.

6. If you have a special project closely related to your college program, is there any way you can get faculty supervision for the project and receive academic credit?

7. Your campus has an outstanding professor who is an excellent lecturer, but you do not wish to take his course for credit. Can you arrange to listen to his lectures?

8. How do you compute your grade-point ratio? What would the grade-point ratio be for the following, assuming A equaled four points: English, A (3 credits); Psychology, B (3 credits); Physical Education, B (1 credit); Shop, C (3 credits); Government, C (3 credits); Chorus, C (1 credit)? The answer is upside-down at the bottom of this page.

2.71

9. Can you get credit for any course by taking an examination instead of the course itself?

10. How much time do you have to drop a course without risking a failing grade? What is the deadline to drop courses that you are passing?

11. If you fail a course, then take it over and get a C, how do you compute your grade-point ratio?

12. How can you arrange to take a course at another college during the summer and transfer the credits back to your own college?

13. What courses require prerequisites and how important is it to have had the prerequisites before registering for a course?

Campus activities

The academic program is assumed to be the most important part of college life. However, American colleges usually provide extensive activity programs, some with little or no relationship to specific course work. Since your future growth and satisfactions will certainly not come completely through your vocation, your on-campus growth and satisfaction need not come solely through classroom experience.

Colleges provide a wide assortment of social, athletic, creative, and political activities that contribute to the learning process. The value of these activities has been essentially accepted by faculty and administrators, although concern exists when students begin to ignore their classwork because they become so involved with activities.

In the 20 years between 1930 and 1950, several studies indicated that students who participated in activities also received better grades (e.g., Stright, 1947; Gustad, 1952), earned more money after graduation (Jepsen, 1951), and were better adjusted (Stone, 1951). However, more recent research suggests that this situation might have changed (Kalish and Bartos, 1960). Since Sputnik startled American educators into placing greater emphasis upon academic work, many of the better students no longer have the interest or the time to participate in school activities.

The effects of this recent trend, which has been observed both in high schools and in colleges, are still unknown. However, it does seem unfortunate that the most talented students no longer contribute to the activity program as they once did.

Social organizations and social activities

Although many types of campus organizations include a social program along with their other activities, most campuses have social clubs that

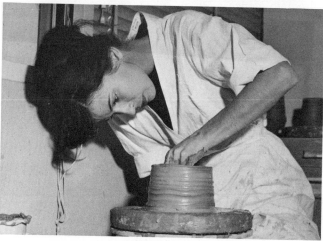

Figure Ap–I–1. Both athletics and the creative arts have a place on college campuses. Courtesy California State College at Los Angeles.

promote social affairs for their own members and, on occasion, for the entire student body.

These social clubs, especially if they have the status of fraternities and sororities, are simultaneously much admired and much disliked. The negative responses are based upon the clubs' selection practices, which emphasize racial, religious, and social-class factors; snobbery in restricting dating and other social relationships; numerous instances of organized cheating and violation of college regulations; and demands for conformity. Those favoring the clubs cite their efforts in building school spirit and school loyalty, their participation in student government, their promotion of sincere friendships among members, and their value in providing contacts and experiences that will be useful after graduation.

Social activities, however, are not limited to members of organized groups. Colleges provide a variety of social programs, ranging from Saturday-evening formals to coffee shop bull sessions. Social life has a definite place on campus; it breaks the routine of study, provides relaxation and enjoyment, and has educational value itself since students are responsible for much of the planning, organizing, and actual work.

Dangers in an exaggerated social life occur both for club members and for nonmembers. Social life can become too time consuming and energy consuming for anyone who lets it. Even the seemingly harmless coffee break may stretch into a two-hour bull session.

Athletics

Is the college athlete *the* "Big Man on Campus"? Or is he "just a slob who gets paid to play football"? Both interpretations are heard on our college campuses. One psychologist did learn that athletes (in high school, however) tended to become leaders during flight training with the United States Air Force (Krumboltz et al., 1959). We can all point to certain well-known figures, such as Supreme Court Justice Byron White, who were once athletes. Some psychologists do believe that team sports "build character" and are "a great leveler in a democracy" (McKinney, 1960).

In spite of this and additional support, we do not actually know whether intercollegiate competitive sports have a beneficial effect upon the participants. Certainly the pressures to win are sufficiently great at some colleges that all else becomes secondary, including studies. The author was told by one of his students that he had seen a nationally famous football player rifling the drawer of a professor's desk to look at the next day's examination—the player had bribed the janitor to let him into the office. (The student, by the way, was also on the football team and was amused rather than disturbed by the incident, which had occurred several years earlier.) This is, of course, an isolated incident, but it

Figure Ap–I–2. College offers the opportunity to develop your capability to play whatever sports you enjoy and can easily continue after you leave college. Courtesy Antioch College News Bureau. Photograph by Axel Bahnsen.

does show the pressures under which college athletes are placed by their extremely demanding schedule.

In addition to the handful of athletes who participate in intercollegiate competition, many colleges encourage all students to join in intramurals and informal athletic activities as much as possible. The opportunity for exercise is good for students who spend most of their day sitting in the classroom, the library, and the snack bar. Also, since exercise is recommended for the postcollege years, college is an excellent time to develop your capability to play whatever sports you enjoy and can easily continue after you leave college. Some examples that fit these criteria include tennis, volleyball, handball, golf, archery, swimming, and bowling. (After all, how many of you will have access to the people and the facilities for football, baseball, or basketball after you leave college?)

At the very least, athletics provide a source of achievement, an opportunity to let off steam, good exercise, an expression of teamwork and cooperation, and a competitive challenge. Both the participant and the observer can profit, although the former receives much more than the latter. When athletics are at their finest, they approach the heroic. When they are corrupt, they corrupt the entire campus.

The arts

Many schools offer their students the opportunity to participate in dramatics, music, art, dance, photography, debate, and both creative and journalistic writing. As with athletics, the training is available to those

few with professional hopes and to the many who wish to express themselves and gain satisfaction through a leisure activity.

The United States is presently going through what some have termed a
"culture boom." Hundreds of communities have established amateur theater groups; dozens of big and small cities have their own orchestras; art
exhibits are seen everywhere; and hundreds of magazines offer authors of
fiction, nonfiction, and poetry the chance to be published. College is an
excellent place to begin to develop your own talents in one or more of
these activities that can lead to so much leisure-time satisfaction and
pleasure in the years following college.

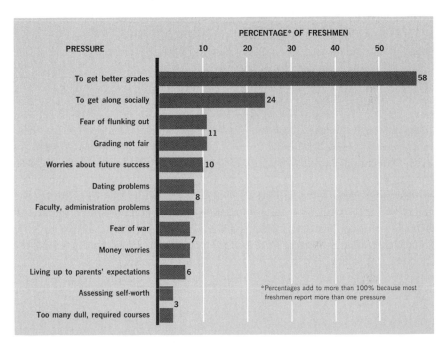

Figure Ap–I–3. Problems college freshmen feel depress them most. Courtesy
the *Harris Survey* by Louis Harris, published in the *Los Angeles Times*,
March 18, 1965.

Student politics: on campus and off

Student politics fall into two distinct and almost unrelated categories:
student government and off-campus politics. Each offers excitement and
experience—and hazards.

Student government provides a training for future community leaders.
Students receive valuable experience in administration, making decisions,

influencing others, learning their own capacities and limitations, and—to some extent—learning the complexities of political action. Some campuses have dozens, perhaps hundreds, of opportunities to participate in student-government committee-work each year.

Unfortunately, most students ignore their governing body except for a flurry of excitement around election time. The similarity to the national disinterest in government is obvious and distressing. Although some student apathy undoubtedly results from the student government's power being so limited, the greater part probably stems from plain indifference.

Off-campus politics is another matter entirely. From the end of World War II until recently, students were frequently criticized for not paying enough attention to the nation and the world. A few students, especially those associated with politically liberal organizations, were active, but most were not. Then, with the rising campus popularity of the conservative movement in national politics, campus political involvement shifted somewhat to the conservative. Many colleges that had previously seen only the liberal viewpoint now were faced with the conflict and the excitement of opposing views.

About the same time the conservative student groups were taking shape, the civil rights organizations caught the imagination of students, and many participated in demonstrations at their own campus, while others traveled to communities in Southern states and worked for Negro rights there. Hundreds of students were imprisoned, pounded by water from high-pressure hoses, verbally abused, physically beaten, and at least four were killed for their efforts. Only time will allow the proper perspective to evaluate these student activities, but even the most casual observer has noticed the spirit and the excitement brought about by these actions. Nonetheless, in spite of the arousal of a segment of the student population, most college students, like most of their parents, avoid any political involvement except voting and criticizing.

Why do you suppose this disinterest occurs? Are the students afraid to be associated with certain movements? Are they too involved in their own small world of classes, dates, and part-time jobs? Do they feel so set apart from the world or so powerless to do anything that activity seems a meaningless gesture? Are they "playing it cool," emotionally uninvolved? Do they prefer to let others do the work for them? These are some of the explanations offered—what is your feeling?

A variety of campus activities, in addition to those mentioned, are conducted at many schools. Some examples are a social and educational club in which foreign and American students can meet; an organization to help tutor children from culturally deprived areas; preprofessional clubs for students with interest in nursing, teaching, psychology, or business management; clubs affiliated with different religious groups; and national and international groups like Phi Beta Kappa, National Student Association, and World University Service.

Campus activities allow a change in routine, lead to personal growth through leisure opportunities, give some students the chance to excel, and encourage artistic and creative endeavor. Also, some learning is directly related to later job demands, especially in human relations and leadership.

Challenges to success and sources of help

Although students are expected to be much more independent in college than they were in high school, college authorities recognize that student personal and academic growth may be limited by numerous factors. Among the most common of these are academic problems, social and emotional problems, financial difficulties, and health problems. These, of course, are not isolated areas, but interact with each other. What is originally a financial problem might lead to a health problem, which, in turn, produces an achievement problem that subsequently aggravates the health problem.

Fortunately, many colleges are well equipped with sources of help for the various problems. These sources include counseling facilities, faculty advisers, the library, and medical counsel.

The area of academic achievement

The definition of "college success" differs from person to person. Whereas one student thinks success is equivalent to "getting through my freshman year," another demands an A average as the measure of success. Most students, however, would agree that having a grade-point average low enough to be put on probation is definitely not success.

Sometimes low grades lead to irrational, self-defeating behavior; the student blames everyone but himself, and he becomes bitter. Or he may feel inadequate and decide to give up. On the other hand, low grades affect some students like a cold shower on a sleepy person—the shock jolts them back to reality.

If, as one group of college women stated, adjusting to college-level work is the biggest problem in college (Will, 1957), what can be done by the student whose grades fall below an appropriate level? The answer: many things. First, he can check with his instructors to try to learn where he is having trouble:

> An analysis of errors on a multiple-choice sociology examination turned up evidence that the student was not paying close enough attention in class.
>
> Observation of a student's textbook showed that he was underlining too much.

A brief discussion with a student whose parents were born in Mexico indicated that her knowledge of American slang and idioms was limited, and she did not fully understand the class lectures and discussion.

In each instance, the course instructor was able to help the student track down the source of difficulty and make plans to overcome it.

Second, when the instructors cannot help, the college counselor often can. Low grades can result from inadequate high school background, poor study methods, physical illness, insufficient motivation—or lack of the necessary academic aptitude. College counselors, through tests and interviews, can usually determine the basis for low grades.

Third, if nothing seems to work, the student must re-evaluate his college goals. Perhaps he needs to shift from one major to another or from one college to another. Perhaps the answer is to leave college and enter business school or a hospital training-program for nurses. In some instances, it might be better to take a job or enlist in the armed forces, with the idea of returning to college at a later time with a more realistic and mature set of goals.

However, any drastic action should be taken only when all other possibilities have been eliminated, that is, when the student is studying as hard as he can, when he has eliminated poor study methods, when he believes that personal or health or emotional problems are not producing his difficulties, and when he is certain that neither outside work nor social obligations are robbing him of needed time.

Social and emotional problems

Life is not divided into neat, isolated compartments. Whatever affects one phase of living also affects other phases. When a marriage is unhappy, more than the family life of the couple is disturbed: their job effectiveness may be reduced; their children may become anxious; even their physical health may be disrupted. In the same way, academic success and failure do not stand in isolation. An unhappy family situation, an unfaithful fiancée, or an undue amount of suspicion can all reduce study effectiveness and deprive the student of his maximum opportunity for effective use of his abilities.

Mike Minton's childhood had been secure and happy, but his father died when Mike was twelve, and his mother eventually married a man of modest means with children of his own. The insurance money left by Mike's father gradually went to pay living expenses, although it had originally been earmarked for Mike's college. In the meantime, the relationship between Mike's mother and her new husband had deteriorated, and sometimes their arguments became so violent that blows were exchanged. At this point, Mike began his freshman year as a dormitory student at a junior college about four hours' drive from home. Because of his limited funds, he had to work 30 hours a week to support himself. Letters from home were far from happy, and the combination of physical fatigue from his heavy load of work-plus-study and his anxiety regarding the situation at home caused Mike to flunk out of college by the end of the second semester.

In studies comparing underachieving students with overachieving students, personal problems are consistently shown to affect academic performance. The underachiever, for example, tends to lack confidence and to be somewhat depressed; he shows signs of maladjustment more openly, thus indicating that he lacks control; he is less likely to have a good relationship with his parents and is less likely to like his instructors; with other people, he tends to be withdrawn, disinterested, apathetic, and dependent; he is also more likely to resent authority figures. The low-achieving student may also be uncertain about his goals in college, or else he tends to set goals for himself that are beyond his level of ability (Taylor, 1964). This is not to say that these personal problems inevitably cause college problems, nor that college problems inevitably produce personality problems; all we can say is that students who are not living up to their potential in college tend to be the same ones who have difficulties in nonacademic areas. Since personal problems imply that the individual has not adequately satisfied needs lower on the hierarchy, he is unable to make the most of the capacities he does have.

Financial problems

The man with all the money he wants is a rarity anywhere in the world. In college, students with financial difficulties often seem to outnumber those without such difficulties. For some, the only financial limitation is the inability to buy a ninth suit of clothes, an expensive bottle of perfume, or a new automobile. Nonetheless, certain students find that their success, even their ability to remain in college, is threatened by money problems.

Student funds come from two major sources: family funds and personal earnings. (Of course, students pay only a portion of the cost of their education, the rest being borne by the taxpayers or donors.) Recent estimates are that over half of American college students earn a large part or all of their college expenses (Gallup and Hill, 1961).

To intensify the problem, college students like to be independent, and their independence is curtailed when they are supported by funds from home. In order to be independent, some students will reject family offers of support, and will take part-time jobs. Occasionally, unfortunately, the work-plus-study load is more than the student can take, and he either must quit work, leave school, or risk physical illness.

Students whose living costs are greater than their available funds plus earnings from part-time work have several alternatives:

1. Scholarships and grants are available for students with good academic records or with a background of participation in campus activities. Obtaining a scholarship of $50 to $100 is often easy, if that amount of money is vital to remaining in school.

2. Today's generation of college students has an unprecedented opportunity to obtain low-interest loans. The federal government has allotted hundreds of thousands of dollars for student loans, to be given through individual colleges. State and local governments, as well as banks and the college authorities themselves, have made other funds available.

3. A compromise measure is to work full time and attend classes on a part-time basis. Although postponing eventual completion of college, such a procedure is usually better than carrying a full academic load while trying to hold a full-time job.

4. Often overlooked is the possibility of reducing expenses, which may be simpler than increasing earnings. In today's wealthy society, people feel entitled to luxuries. However, certain items can be readily eliminated from the budget if necessary. Have you ever made out a budget, then kept a day-to-day expenditure log, to see how to cut your expenses?

5. On some campuses, a work-study program provides supervised jobs offering both income and college credits. The jobs are usually expected to be relevant to the student's major or his vocational goals, and a job-evaluation paper may be required along with successful performance on the job.

Since students are often unaware of all the potential sources of financial help, those who face extremely restricted financial support are usually encouraged to make an appointment at the campus scholarship and loan office, with a college counselor, or with whoever else might be appropriate.

Physical health problems

Students are more likely to neglect their physical health than their automobiles, their appearance, or their social activities. Fatigue and poor diet are common on college campuses. Physical problems inevitably reduce study efficiency. Although more obvious physical problems, such as a high fever or stomach cramps, usually receive attention, many students ignore the need to maintain a good day-to-day program of physical care.

Most readers of this book will take a course that discusses physical health and hygiene in considerable depth, so we will restrict the discussion here to a brief outline of the requirements of a good personal health program, an anecdote involving the author and a college hallmate, and a discussion of tobacco and alcohol.

A brief outline of a personal health program—and an anecdote. Physicians are agreed that preventive medicine and good personal health care would reduce the rates of illness and death by a considerable degree. What are some of the health procedures they suggest?

1. Maintain an effective and well-balanced diet. No one is harmed by missing one meal or spending one day stuffing himself with milk shakes and hot dogs, but some students make a career of such diets, while others take great pride in avoiding vegetables, indulging in excessive sweets and soft drinks, and keeping breakfast down to the barest minimum.

Figure Ap–I–4. Exercise is an important part of a health program. Courtesy Columbia Broadcasting System.

2. Getting adequate exercise. Once the required courses in physical education cease, a large percentage of students obtain their exercise in walking to and from the parking lot. This pattern remains the same for the rest of their lives.

3. Get sufficient sleep. Sleep needs differ from person to person, but students tend to pride themselves on how little sleep they had the night before. During exam week, some students resemble zombies more than people, and zombies are not very good at taking exams.

4. Have regular medical and dental examinations. Dentists usually suggest two visits a year, while physicians recommend annual checkups after age 30 or 35, and one thorough check every two years before then.

5. Take care of minor medical and dental problems before they become major ones. A good night's sleep and a day in bed may prevent a cold from turning into something more serious; cleaning a bad scratch with soap and water can avoid infection; reporting a vague ache or dizziness or nausea may give the doctor a clue to what would otherwise become a serious illness.

6. Avoid medication without the approval of a physician, and do not make excessive use of alcohol, tobacco, or such drugs as the numerous pills that guarantee to keep you awake.

A good friend of the author's learned about the effects of extreme fatigue when he and the author were taking freshman economics together.

> The economics midterm was scheduled for 10:10 Wednesday morning, and Ralph Zeff closeted himself in a study room at six the evening before to begin reading the semester's assignments, which his active social life had prevented previously. Sixteen hours, three packs of cigarettes, twelve cups of black coffee, and five stay-awake pills later, Ralph walked into the classroom, satisfied with his all-night job of cramming. When I left the exam, about ten minutes before the bell, I had to walk past Ralph's chair. I noticed his head was resting on his left hand, which was also being used as an eye-shield. Since I had already turned my paper in, I looked to check Ralph's answers, and I was startled to notice only about one-third of the questions had been completed. At that point I pulled his arm away from his forehead, and he woke up with a snort that caused everyone in the room to snicker. P.S., he flunked the exam.

Alcohol and tobacco. In spite of religious, family, legal, and medical attacks, drinking and smoking are very popular throughout our country, including our colleges and universities. The moral aspects of drinking and smoking, assuming they are not done in such a way as to be offensive to others, are matters each of you must interpret in view of your own personal beliefs. Medical and psychological evaluation, however, may be made here.

In recent years, careful compilation of statistics has shown that smokers have a briefer life expectancy than nonsmokers, even when comparing people living under comparable air pollution conditions and functioning under comparable degrees of stress.

Alcohol can be consumed in moderation with no permanent damage although it may cause temporary loss of judgment, of visual ability, and of inhibitions (all very dangerous to automobile drivers). After sufficient time has elapsed, the alcohol is absorbed into the body, and normal behavior will recur. Because inhibitions are reduced, however, some people feel freer in their sex behavior after several drinks, although the actual capacity to enjoy sex is reduced (Leuba, 1961). Chronic heavy drinking, of course, can lead to inability to perform effectively in class, on the job, or in social situations.

Smoking and drinking are two symbols of the adult world forbidden to children and adolescents. Thus, the adolescent who takes a beer or a cigarette is also partaking of a symbol of the society into which he desires entrance. His self-concept may be bolstered by the change in his picture of himself.

"I've quit smoking."

Figure Ap–I–5. The relationship between smoking and cancer has caused many people to stop. Courtesy Ed Fisher.

Smokers and drinkers seem to differ in several ways from abstainers. Heavy drinkers in college, for example, turned out to be less ambitious, less effective in planning and organizing, and less certain of their goals. On the other hand, they seemed as stable as nondrinkers, and actually were less likely to conform (Kukuk, 1960). College graduates who smoke heavily were more likely to become businessmen and executives, while light smokers turned to teaching, law, and journalism (Seltzer, 1964).

The pros and cons of smoking and drinking make a good topic for class discussion, but underlying such a discussion must be one major question: are the satisfactions received from smoking and drinking worth the risk of permanent health damage (for tobacco) and temporary reduction in judgment (for alcohol)?

Special groups and special adjustments

Compared to the college of 50 years ago, the college of today has more older students, more married students, more working students, and more foreign students. Each of these groups has its own special challenges to success.

Older students. Most tax-supported colleges and junior colleges have a substantial number of students in their thirties and older. At some colleges, one-fourth or more of the students are 30 years old or older. The needs motivating these students to return to school include such practical desires as receiving more rapid promotions, higher income, and more flexibility in shifting to a new job field; other motives include the desire to understand more of the world, to receive better insight into oneself, and to experiment with new areas of knowledge. If this author's observations are accurate, older students are more aware of the significance of self-actualization. Many of them have left well-paying jobs to return to college; others add college courses to their normal workload at the sacrifice of leisure. These students have come to college precisely because their present situation does not allow them the opportunity to use their capacities, and, often in spite of good incomes, they are frustrated by the lack of creative, challenging opportunities.

Married students. Married students, whether 19 or 49, share the problem of having responsibilities outside the classroom. They may be responsible for supporting a family, for caring for a house and children, and for providing affection and attention for one or more people. The demands upon them, especially for those who combine work and college, are great, and academic success often depends upon the cooperation of the spouse. In spite of such problems, faculty members often believe married people make above-average students.

Working students. The combination of work and study can actually improve study effectiveness, *if* the combination does not demand too much time and too much energy. Full-time students can work up to about twelve hours a week without harming their studies, but beyond that their grades go down (McKinney, 1960). The actual work-plus-study load a person can successfully carry varies greatly from individual to individual.

A study conducted just after World War II showed that nearly one-fourth of all male college graduates and about one-tenth of female graduates had put themselves completely through college with their own earnings; only one in six men and less than half the women were financed 100 percent by their parents. However, working during college showed little relationship either to grades or to participation in college activities (Havemann and West, 1952). Today, an even higher proportion of students earn part or all of their college expenses.

International students.   An estimated 74,000 international students were studying in the United States in 1965 (estimate of International Institute of Education). Some foreign students are supported by their governments or the United States government, while others are financed by their parents, the college they are attending, or themselves. They come from the familiar countries: Germany, France, Japan, and Italy, as well as from little-known lands like Nepal, Sudan, Gabon, Kuwait, Cambodia, and Surinam.

Too often, these foreign students, not knowing how they will be treated by American students, spend a great deal of time with each other and do not get to know the country in which they are studying. Foreign students are often a much better source of information on some matters than are textbooks or professors. At the same time, they need the opportunity to learn about the United States, so that they may take back to their own countries a friendly and realistic interpretation.

Foreign students have major adjustment problems when they begin their studies in the United States, and they again must make an adjustment when they return to their own countries. One typical pattern is to feel excited and elated upon arriving in the United States; to become increasingly frustrated and unhappy after the initial enthusiasm wears off and the problems of adjusting to an alien culture make themselves felt; to learn to deal with these frustrations and enjoy the educational experience; to return to the home country and find change in themselves so that they no longer fit as well into their home countries; and to learn to deal with this second set of frustrations and readjust to their own countries (Gullahorn and Gullahorn, 1963).

Sources of help

Extensive facilities are available on some college campuses to help students cope with their problems and make the most of their capabilities; other schools have almost nothing. College students have stated time and time again that they are interested in discussing their problems with someone, but the same students often neglect the opportunities when offered. Over 40 percent of the residents of a woman's dormitory at one university expressed a desire to meet with a counselor of some sort (Will, 1957); at another large state college, over 80 percent of the entering freshmen signed up for noncredit, voluntary freshman orientation discussion groups, which met weekly.

Those students who do seek help seem to benefit from it. Counseled students get better grades, participate more in activities, and appear better adjusted than a group similar except for counseling (Gustad, 1951). Before counseling began, one study showed, counseled students received lower grades than noncounseled students of equal ability; after counseling, both groups were getting the same grades, suggesting that the counseling definitely helped (Ivey, 1962).

Two cautions need to be sounded: first, counseling is not magic, and some students profit little or not at all from counseling; and, second, students should consider help provided by the college other than direct counseling.

Occasionally, someone expresses the view that getting help is for weak people, and that strong people go it alone. Such an attitude wins neither wars nor college degrees. Actually, the strong person is willing to accept help when it is needed, since the help is aimed at getting him to help himself to use his capacities better. Of course, becoming too dependent upon a counselor or teacher, so that no decision can be made without seeking his advice, is a sign neither of growing strength nor of successful counseling.

The reason for seeking counsel may range from wanting the answer to a simple question about course requirements to wishing help in dealing with a highly disturbing emotional problem. Although colleges do not provide all the facilities an individual might need, someone will at least be able to refer the questioner to the proper facility.

Faculty adviser. At most colleges, each student is either assigned to a faculty adviser or encouraged to request such an assignment, usually with someone in his major field of concentration. The primary task of the faculty adviser is to counsel the student concerning the academic program, the selection of courses, the interpretation of rules and regulations, and vocational and personal goals.

In addition, the faculty adviser—and most other faculty members as well—are willing to listen to a student's problems, either personal or academic, and to try to be of help. However, the mere fact that someone is a professor (or doctor or lawyer or teacher) does not automatically make him competent to deal with such problems. Knowing that, many faculty members will refer students to other campus facilities or, occasionally, to off-campus agencies.

Counseling centers. Most colleges have some sort of counseling center where students can discuss virtually any kind of problem with someone trained in counseling. The counselor may be a clinical psychologist or psychiatrist who is especially qualified to discuss more disturbing personal and emotional problems, or he may be a specialist in student personnel work and more interested in study problems, vocational problems, or academic planning. Counselors will use a combination of discussion, information, and psychological tests in their sessions.

College counseling centers perform two major functions. First, counseling may give necessary information: Can I shift majors without losing credit? Can I get credit for military service? Are jobs available for people like me after I get my degree here? What courses outside my major would help me become a good short-story writer?

Second, counseling helps the student understand himself better. He learns about his abilities and interests through tests, about his qualifications for certain job fields through occupational information, and about his own personality and motivation through discussion with the counselor. Sometimes counseling requires consideration of personality problems more properly the province of a clinical psychologist or psychiatrist; under such circumstances, the counselor may continue to see the student regularly over a period of time, or he may refer the student to another individual or to an agency in the community.

This very brief description of counseling may make it appear simple; it is not. Learning about ourselves is much more difficult than it might seem. Everyone has weaknesses he does not wish to expose to others; sometimes, you are not even able to see past these "blind spots" yourself.

> Don Griggs had decided, during a stint in the Army Medical Corps, that he wanted to be a surgeon. He knew that high school science courses had given him trouble, but he felt he could make it up in college. By the end of his first year in college, he had a C average in his nonscience courses and a D average in his science courses; the low grades put him on probation. When he went for counseling, he learned that his aptitude tests showed him to be very weak in science. He even admitted to the counselor that he did not like science courses, but he insisted that he wanted to go to medical school. After two difficult years in college, Don reenlisted in the Medical Corps.

Almost all the evidence in Don's case pointed to his not being successful as a medical student, but he refused to believe the evidence or to change his thinking about himself. Of course, instances do occur where the evidence is wrong, but Don's case was not among them. Even though Don did not learn as much about himself as the counselor had hoped, he did have an opportunity to discuss the army as a career; therefore, the counseling experience did give him some increased self-understanding and some additional information about military careers. He eventually found the armed forces offered the best opportunities for working in a medical and surgical setting, without having been to medical school.

College medical facilities. Most campus medical facilities offer a variety of services, ranging from nosedrops to emergency service for broken legs. Some colleges, especially those with dormitories, usually include extensive medical care and even hospitalization on campus. The dispensary may also give immunization injections, supply consultation for weight problems, and offer many sorts of medical advice.

Library. One of the best sources of counsel and information, and one of the most neglected, is the college library. Here is the wisdom of the centuries (admittedly, along with a great deal of ignorance), and a staff of trained professionals, often specialists, to help you locate what you wish. Do you have a religious conflict? What did St. Augustine say? What would Albert Schweitzer or Paul Tillich think? Are you confused about your major? Here are biographies of famous men and women in your future vocation; here also is a collection of information about job opportunities. Are you having trouble filling out your income tax? Here are books on how to do it.

Other resources. A variety of individuals affiliated with colleges can supply advice or other forms of help. These include the college pastor or other religious advisers, residence hall advisers, the veterans' adviser, the foreign-student adviser, and the job placement counselor. At the same time, individual faculty members themselves have information and contacts; after all, business and government leaders frequently come to professors for advice.

In general, college campuses provide innumerable resources for those needing help, but, unlike high school, help rarely comes looking for the student. In college, the student must take the initiative.

A final word

This appendix has covered some of the topics discussed in a college orientation course, but others have been ignored on the assumption that they are already well known to you. For example, we have said nothing about the importance of learning where things are located on your campus, about knowing the history and traditions of your college, about the value of school spirit, or about the specific majors available on various campuses.

Perhaps the most important point is one mentioned in Chapter 9: a college is a community of scholars who come together to share their learning and to try to learn more. The more you participate in this community, the more you will gain, the greater maturity you will develop, and the greater feeling of accomplishment and satisfaction you will have.

SUMMARY OF THE IMPORTANT IDEAS

1. Success in college depends upon more than attending classes and studying for examinations; it depends upon integrating learning into something meaningful and relating it to other facets of life.

2. The student must decide what his major field of study will be; sometimes he must select a minor.

3. He must select his courses, and hopefully, he will be able to select effective teachers.

4. Campus activities are available at most colleges; they may supplement course work, may relate to future vocational goals, or may seem totally unrelated to either but lead to personal enjoyment, personal growth, or pure relaxation.

5. Campus activities include social life and social clubs, spectator and participant athletics, the arts, and both on-campus and off-campus politics.

6. Challenges to college success come from the areas of academic achievement, social and emotional problems, financial problems, and physical health problems.

7. A program of good physical health practices can be worked out.

8. Although alcohol seems to have only a temporary effect, if taken in moderation, tobacco appears to have a permanent and harmful effect.

9. Older students, married and working students, and international students have their own special problem areas.

10. Most campuses supply numerous sources of help for students, including faculty advisers and counseling centers.

Appendix II   Study methods

At various points in the book, suggestions for improved study methods have been mentioned; these have included learning applied to study, the SQ3R method of studying textbooks, and the importance of having goals for study effectiveness. In this final appendix section, we have outlined some additional methods for improving study effectiveness. For those who have had study methods courses, the following pages will serve as a review; for those who have not had such a course, these pages will provide some concrete suggestions. However, since your present course is not study methods, but human behavior, the author does not feel it appropriate to present a full treatment of the topic here.

This appendix will cover time schedules (to supplement the materials on pages 186–188), note-taking, notebooks, textbook reading (to supplement the materials on page 82), and examinations.*

Time schedules

Several things must be kept in mind when making out a time schedule, in addition to the caution: "Be realistic."

(1) *Balance.* A balance of academic work, social life, campus activities, and outside work is desirable. Too much of any one of these can make your college years a chore.

(2) *Health.* Without physical health, a student cannot achieve any

---

*Appendix II has been adapted from *Making the Most of College*, by Richard A. Kalish, © 1959 by Wadsworth Publishing Company.

goals. Consideration, then, must be given to adequate time for meals, rest and sleep, and some exercise.

(3) *Time intervals.* The length of time a student can study will depend upon many factors, including the type of work the course demands, the student's level of ability in that course, and the time of day and fatigue level when the study occurs. Some students study more effectively in the morning or afternoon, while others are night owls. If you are fascinated by accounting, but dislike psychology, you may be able to study accounting for 90 minutes at a stretch but find psychology becomes very boring after 50 minutes.

(4) *Breaks.* Each student must determine his own ability to work without becoming fatigued, so that breaks may be scheduled most advantageously. Short breaks, five to ten minutes per hour, are long enough to have the desired effect of reducing the feeling of monotony, without letting the student get too involved with other matters and without wasting time.

Some students, of course, carry such a heavy load that the above comments are irrelevant. One student in this category was a 30-year-old man who had a wife and two children and who held down a full-time job while carrying almost a full-time course load. Thanks to a cooperative family and an excellent ability to organize his time, he was able to continue like this for five years until getting his degree. Many who have attempted such a schedule have found it impossible.

Steps in constructing a study schedule

First, using a schedule like that shown on page 467, fill in all hours that cannot be changed, such as class and laboratory hours, transportation to and from campus, and eating and sleeping times. You might wish to make a preliminary schedule on scratch paper during the week as you observe how you can actually spend your time.

Second, using a different-colored pencil, schedule your flexible commitments during the remaining hours. Estimate the number of study hours each course is likely to demand, and schedule them accordingly. Also schedule time spent on campus activities, social life, and work. In doing this, consider the following suggestions:

> Specify the particular course you will study, rather than marking "Study" on the schedule.
>
> Allow from 50 to 90 minutes for studying each course at any one time interval. Less than 50 minutes is usually inefficient; more than 90 minutes can be boring or fatiguing.

Figure about ten minutes break per study hour. During this time, get out of your chair and move around a bit, perhaps have some coffee or return the telephone call that came while you were studying.

Make effective use of in-between hours, such as the hour from the end of your 9:00 A.M. class to the beginning of your 11:00 A.M. class.

Try to schedule study time for a class that has just ended or is just about to begin.

Allow three to five minutes before and after each class to review lecture notes and textbook notes relevant to that class.

Allow about 20 minutes between the end of the studying in the evening and going to bed; this is to help you unwind.

Leave a couple of free hours on Sunday to review all the work from the past week.

Make use of free minutes. Waiting for the bus, sitting in the barbershop, waiting for a late appointment all provide a few minutes during which certain types of study are possible. These moments are useful for memorizing foreign language vocabulary, silently rehearsing a speech, or proofreading a composition.

Give yourself the luxury of at least one full evening a week without any attempts to study.

Third, once the schedule is made up, carry it with you for a week and look at it from time to time to see how well you are following it. When it is impractical to follow, make changes, but allow sufficient time to accomplish the required study for each course. Of course, flexibility is necessary, since unexpected personal and academic events constantly occur. In such cases, make certain that for each hour that is changed from "Study" to "Meet airplane" or "Type term paper," you change another hour back to "Study," at least for that week.

Fourth, keep one copy of the final schedule near your study desk and carry another copy with you for immediate reference. Remember that the schedule belongs to you; you do not belong to it.

The importance of a study schedule cannot be exaggerated. There is little difficulty in constructing one, but there may be considerable difficulty in adhering to it. The schedule shown here is that of the hypothetical Tom Frosh. It shows what an average student who finds himself busy can do to accomplish everything necessary and still have time left over.

A typical study schedule

Tom is a freshman who reads quickly but absorbs scientific concepts slowly. Last semester he took a course in effective study methods. This semester he has worked out a schedule for himself. He is taking basic courses in psychology, accounting, sociology, and philosophy (for three credits each); he is taking a stiff laboratory chemistry course (for four credits); he is also taking speech and physical education (one credit each). He plays intramural softball, lives on campus and works for his dinners, and hates to have studies "hanging over his head" on weekends. If necessary, he will spend weekend time studying for examinations or doing term papers. You can see that, in spite of a very full course load, intramurals, and five hours of work a week, Tom will usually have most of his weekends free, and he has at least one hour a day to relax, read, watch television, or nap.

Lecture notes

Both the form and the content of lecture notes are important, although the content is the more vital. In order to increase the value of the content, it is necessary to listen and evaluate critically, rather than to attempt to scribble down every word of the lecture. It is usually best to determine the important elements of the lecture and to try to grasp the organization (true—some professors seem to have no organization to their lectures, but most do), then include the important facts and the lecture organization into your notes. These notes, it is often observed, should be in the student's own words, rather than verbatim from the lecture, except in such matters as definitions. The form in which notes are taken is also important. The form a student uses provides organization to his notes.

The paragraph form *

Form of taking notes—form is important—provides organization; major points, minor points, relationships, details. Paragraph form—easiest, poorest, write until idea changes, then begin new paragraph. Sentence form—more difficult than paragraph form, better, series of numbered statements. Standard outline form— best for organization, most difficult; uses Roman numerals, letters, numbers, indentation to show organization. Notes for your guidance. Dash outline form—also like standard outline form, but uses dashes instead of symbols; good organization, simple. Preferable: standard outline form and dash outline form. May combine.

As you can readily observe, this form shows organization by the use of punctuation. However, good organization is extremely difficult to de-

---

*The decision to use short phrases for certain sample forms and sentences for others was made arbitrarily.

Figure Ap II–1. Time schedule*

Hour	Mon.	Tues.	Wed.	Thurs.	Fri.	Sat.	Sun.
7:00	Breakfast				→	Sleep	Sleep
8:00	Psychology	STudy Accounting	Psychology	STudy Accounting	Psychology	Breakfast	
9:00	STudy Psychology	Accounting	STudy Psychology	Accounting	STudy Psychology	Accounting	Breakfast
10:00	Philosophy	Chemistry	Philosophy	Chemistry	Philosophy	Chemistry	Church
11:00	SPeech	STudy Chemistry	SPeech	STudy Chemistry	Prepare SPeech	STudy Chemistry	
12:00	Lunch						→
1:00	Sociology	Chemistry Lab	Sociology	WORK ON Chem Lab RePORT	Sociology	Recreation	Recreation
2:00	Physical Education		Physical Education		DO Accounting Problems		
3:00	STudy Philosophy	Softball	STudy Philosophy	Softball			
4:00	STudy Psychology		STudy Accounting				
5:00	Relax				→		Dinner
6:00	Dinner				→		Review
7:00	WonK				→	Relax	
8:00	STudy Philosophy	STudy Psychology	STudy Philosophy	STudy Philosophy	Recreation	Recreation	Look oven sPeech
9:00	STudy Sociology	watch Television	STudy Sociology	STudy Sociology			STudy Sociology
10:00	STudy Chemistry		STudy Accounting	STudy Chemistry			MaKe-uP
11:00	Sleep				→		Sleep

Name ___Tom Frosh___

*The hours for recreation are underlined with dots; they are flexible and can easily be changed. The hours for study are underlined with dashes; they are flexible and can be exchanged with other flexible hours. The hours that cannot be altered are underlined with a solid line; they are fixed hours. The hours not underlined may be exchanged, but exchange would cause considerable inconvenience.

velop. Also, reading over notes which are written in a solid paragraph tends to become tiring.

The sentence form

1. The form of taking notes is important.
2. It provides organization by showing major points, minor points, their relationship to each other, and details.
3. The paragraph form is the easiest to use and the poorest.
4. For the paragraph form you write as a paragraph until the idea changes.
5. The sentence form, a little more difficult and a little better, is a series of numbered statements.
6. The standard outline form is the best for organization and the most difficult to follow.
7. It uses Roman numerals, letters, numbers, and various types of indentation.
8. Remember that notes are for your guidance only.
9. The dash outline form is also a variation of the standard outline form, but uses dashes instead of symbols.
10. It has organization, and avoids the confusion of the standard outline system.
11. The standard outline form and the dash system are best, although you may prefer to combine forms.

The sentence form uses no organization to speak of, but it is a little easier to read than the paragraph form.

Standard outline form

    I. Form of taking notes
       A. Form is important
       B. Form provides organization
          1. Major points
          2. Minor points
          3. Relationships between them
          4. Details
   II. Comparison of forms
       A. Paragraph form
          1. Easiest
          2. Poorest
       B. Sentence form
          1. More difficult
          2. Better
       C. Standard outline form

        1. Best for organization
        2. Most difficult
     D. Dash outline form
        1. Like standard
        2. With dashes
          a. No complex symbols
          b. Good organization
  III. Preferable: standard or dash or a combination

This form shows good organization. Major points fit under minor points, and the method of indenting emphasizes this process.

Dash outline form

—Form of taking notes
  —important because provides organization
    —major points, minor points, relationships between them, details
  —Paragraph form
    —easiest, but poorest
    —write until idea changes; begin new paragraph
  —Sentence form
    —more difficult, but better
    —series of numbered statements
  —Standard outline form
    —best for organization, but most difficult
    —uses Roman numerals, letters, numbers, indentation
  —notes are for your guidance
  —Dash outline form
    —like standard, but uses dashes
    —has good organization
  —best: standard or dash
    —may combine forms

This form is similar to the Standard outline form, but omits the complex system of symbols. While it gains in simplicity, it does lose a little in organization by depending solely upon indention for form.

Samples of good and poor lecture notes

Figures Ap II–2A and Ap II–2B are based on the following material:

Excerpt from a classroom lecture. It really does make a difference how far a student sits from the professor in a class. There are students who always come in late and sit far away from the professor. These tend to be the students who do not do very well. Of course, because they come in late, the professor feels that they probably aren't interested. Yet I had one student, a girl—she was editor of the campus newspaper and very active on campus. She came in late to one of my classes and would sit far in the back; sometimes, although not often, she would cut class. She received excellent grades in my class and in every other class. I wondered about this until I learned that she studied diligently and compensated for coming late. And in spite of sitting far in the back, she paid close attention to what was going on in class. As a matter of fact, she sat in the back just to prove it could be done, because she didn't believe what I said about sitting in front.

As I recall, it was largely because of her that I ran a little experiment in class. Of course, it wasn't a real experiment in technical terms, but I did it just for fun and to see what would happen. The day after the examination, I passed a piece of paper around the class—I didn't have required seating in the class and there was plenty of room for students to spread out in the classroom—and asked the students to write their names according to a seating plan. Then I divided the class into three groups: the first group consisted of the forty students sitting in the first four rows; Group B consisted of twenty students sitting in the next three rows; Group C was made up of the remaining twenty students—they spread out for at least eight to ten rows.

Sure enough, just as I figured—the first group averaged the grade of low $B-$; the last group, those in the back, averaged a low $C-$; the middle group averaged a little above a straight C. I think that proved my point.

I'd say several factors influenced this: (1) better students tend to seek out positions in the front of the class; (2) students sitting farther back have more distractions, more moving heads in front of them, more opportunity to look outside the window or through open doors. I remember one student who became fascinated by a couple holding hands outside of class. He couldn't keep his eyes off them—kept looking through the window and paid no attention to class. Later I found out it was his best friend and a former girl friend—oh, well. Another reason is that students who sit in the back are often under the misapprehension that they can write letters, sleep, or daydream without being noticed. At any rate, you should try to avoid sitting in the back of a classroom, especially if the room is large. I'd say any seat in the front half is all right.

Notebooks

Good notebooks, like many other study aids, show much individual variation. Approaches successful for some people may be unsuccessful for

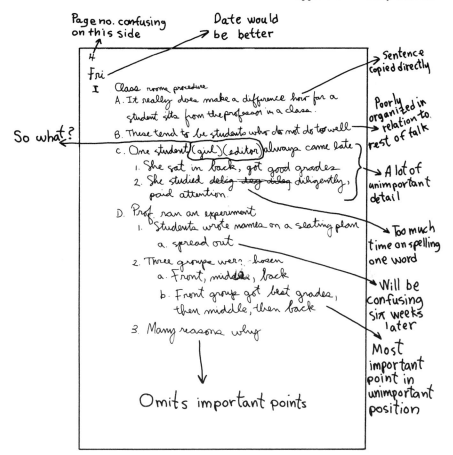

Figure Ap II–2A. This outline shows many obvious errors, although it does cover much that is important. Organization is poor; important points are missed. It will be difficult to read and understand this material eight or ten weeks later.

others. The suggestions listed below have been found useful by many students. Before evaluating their effectiveness, it is preferable to use them for six to eight weeks, so that they have become part of the study habit pattern.

—Use a standard-sized 8½″ x 11″ notebook.

—Do not use a clipboard, small shorthand notebook (unless you are a skilled stenographer), ruled pad, or loose sheets of paper.

—Place your name, address, and telephone number inside each notebook. (Not a bad idea to do the same with your textbooks.)

—Enter the date each class period.

—Number each page.

—Reserve the first two pages for assignments; then begin lecture notes; halfway through the notebook, or section of the notebook, fold down one sheet of paper; begin reading notes there.

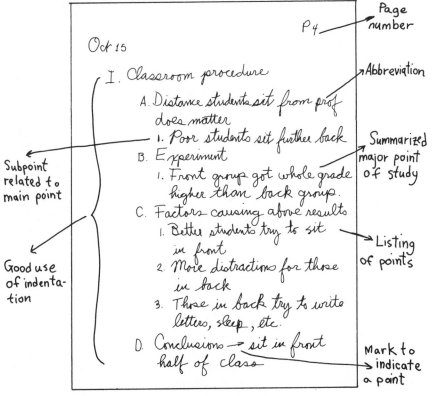

Figure Ap II–2B. A good set of lecture notes.

—Keep each course separated from other courses, either through different notebooks or with dividers.

—Take notes in pen, preferably fountain pen, and keep a ballpoint handy for emergency.

—Use one side of the page only; the other side can be used for "necessary doodling," assignments, later additions, notes to yourself, and lecture note summaries.

—Use your own words.

—Use emphasis marks to indicate material that seems especially important.

—After each class period, summarize the notes for that day on the unused side of the page, i.e., opposite your notes.

Studying textbooks

The excellent approach to studying textbooks, SQ3R, has been described on page 82. At this point, we will merely add a few suggestions on how to mark textbooks. The sample below shows how one person applied SQ3R and marginal notations to a history text.

Sample of SQ3R applied to textbook pages

Material from an actual history textbook* has been used to show you how to apply SQ3R and the suggested notations. You might feel other information from the text is more important, but this is the approach of one person.

IV. THE "ERA OF GOOD FEELINGS"

The Election of 1816. The "Era of Good Feelings" was in **name to remember** fact an interlude of acrimonious local factionalism between the War of 1812 and the beginnings of Jacksonian Democracy. It received its name simply because the absence of a **word to look up later** two-party system and a passing moment of harmony caused **important paragraph** a magazine editor to use a phrase that has intrigued subsequent historians.

In the election of 1816, when the rest of the country almost unanimously went Republican, many New England Federalists still clung to their old party. To broaden their appeal in the campaign, they nominated Rufus King, a New **name to remember** Yorker who had originally opposed the War of 1812 but later had pleased the patriots by favoring its vigorous prosecution. A more important battle than the election itself was the fight among Republican leaders over their own standard-bearer. William H. Crawford of Georgia had the support of the old Randolph states' rights contingent, but **name to remember** Madison succeeded in persuading party leaders to nominate his Secretary of State, the Virginian, James Monroe.

*From Richard Hofstadter, William Miller, and Daniel Aaron, *The United States: The History of a Republic*, Prentice-Hall, Inc., 1957, pp. 183–186. Reprinted by permission.

Monroe found the election as easy to win as the nomination, and received 183 electoral votes to 34 for King. The Federalist candidate, the last in history, carried only Massachusetts, Connecticut, and Delaware.

Monroe appointed a strong cabinet, of which the ablest member was a New Englander, John Quincy Adams, whose presence as Secretary of State put the conduct of foreign affairs in the hands of a skilled diplomat and appeased the feelings of many New Englanders. At the very beginning of his administration, Monroe made a journey through the northeastern states that was topped by an extremely cordial reception in New England. After this trip, Boston's *Columbian Sentinel* published an article entitled "Era of Good Feelings," in which it noted with pleasure "all the circumstances . . . during the late Presidential Jubilee . . . which attended the demonstration of good feelings." By 1816, the Republicans under Madison had shown so much concern for manufactures and the tariff, for an army and a navy, even for chartering a national bank, that the old issues no longer stood in the way of reconciliation. It seemed as though Virginia and Massachusetts had made peace at last; and indeed, Monroe was re-elected in 1820 with only a single vote (from New Hampshire) cast against him in the entire electoral college.

The Postwar Economic Boom. While manufacturers struggled to maintain themselves against foreign competition, most of the country enjoyed a brief but heartening period of prosperity. England's textile manufacturing boom, reflected in her massive exports to the United States, brought with it an enormous demand for southern cotton for her tireless machines. The end of the war also revived the European market for southern tobacco. Poor European harvests in 1816 and 1817 added to the demand for western corn, wheat, pork, and beef. With these agricultural staples Americans were able to pay for their record imports of manufactures right after the peace.

This combination of factors drew thousands to the West and Southwest. Between 1810 and 1820, Indiana grew 500 per cent, Illinois 268 per cent, Missouri 237 per cent, and Mississippi 87 per cent. By 1820, Ohio had become more populous than Massachusetts, and the entire West, with about 2,200,000 settlers, had more people than New England. As always in American history, a boom in agriculture brought a boom in land speculation. Spurring on the speculative boom were the 300 or more state and "private" banks that were established after the First Bank of the United States went out of existence in 1811. By 1817, state and private banks had issued $100 million in paper money, much of it unnegotiable even in neighboring communities. Although these "facility notes," as they were called, helped newcomers get started and oldsters to expand, often enough they served only to create an obligation on which the banker could foreclose simply by withholding further "facilities" at his pleasure. "What," asked the journalist Hezekiah Niles, "is to be the end of such a business?—Mammoth fortunes for the *wise*, wretched poverty -for the *foolish*. . . . SPECULATION in a Coach, HONESTY in the Jail."

The Second Bank and the End of the Boom. By 1817, the Second Bank of the United States, chartered the year before, entered the business picture. Back in 1814, financiers like John Jacob Astor and Stephen Girard, who had lent large amounts to the government to aid the war effort, had begun agitating for a new United States bank to mobilize the financial resources of the country. But in 1815, though the government had been forced the previous year to suspend payments in specie, a bill for a new bank which passed Congress was struck down by Madison's veto. By 1816, the postwar boom began to make itself felt. Since heavy agricultural exports had failed to match the value of imported goods, scarce specie was drained from the country to pay the balances owed abroad. Most of the gold that remained was in demand to finance land speculation. Thus the government found it increasingly difficult to get acceptable currency for its daily and seasonal needs. Early in 1816, therefore, Secretary of the Treasury Alexander Dallas tailored a bank bill to the requirements of Congress and the President. In April, it passed over the opposition of New England, where the state banks were well-managed and it was not needed. It had the firm backing of Calhoun and Clay.

Like the first national bank, the Second Bank of the United States was chartered for 20 years as the sole depository for government funds. Its capital, reflecting the

[margin annotations: "names to remember", "name to remember", "Facts to remember"]

growth of the country, was placed at $35 million, three and a half times the amount set for the earlier bank. Of this sum, the government was to subscribe one-fifth, or $7 million. Of the remainder, $7 million was to be subscribed in specie and $21 million in the form of securities of the United States. Five of the Bank's 25 directors were to be appointed by the president of the United States; the rest by American stockholders. Foreign stockholders were to have no voice in the Bank's affairs. The Second Bank had the right to establish branches in different parts of the country. Foreseeing competition, however, influential local bankers had persuaded the politicians to write into some western state constitutions provisions against "foreign banks" doing business within their borders.

fact to remember

Ill-managed from the first in the places where it could do business, the new B.U.S. proceeded to justify local fears by outdoing even the state banks in the lavishness of its loans. These were extended in the form of notes that were more acceptable than the notes issued by the local banks. In retaliation, the injured bankers got their states to try to tax out of existence both the branches and the notes of "the monster." In the summer of 1818, the B.U.S. was at last ready with deflationary measures to control the boom. But these measures only made it unpopular with both the people and the local bankers. The sudden contraction of credit prevented many people from keeping up payments on their speculative debts, and before the year 1819 was out, the whole boom collapsed.

Confused check later ?

Actually, the economic collapse was worldwide. The revival of European harvests after the Napoleonic wars and the weakening of the postwar textile boom combined to create a glut both of wheat and cotton in world markets. But the depression was most severe in the United States and most devastating in the West.

Fact to remember

The crisis prompted a number of states to abolish the useless and degrading punishment of imprisonment for debt and to pass liberal bankruptcy laws and laws easing the settlement of contracts. Congress also came to the aid of the West with a new land act in 1820 making it possible for a settler to buy an 80-acre homestead for $100 in cash. The next year it added a Relief Act to assist those people whom earlier credit provisions had got into trouble.

The Role of the Supreme Court. Against this background of local self-assertion, expanding commerce and invention, internal depression, and quarrels between debtors and creditors, John Marshall issued a series of historic Supreme Court decisions. A veteran of the Revolutionary wars and of Federalist diplomacy, Marshall had been one of the early and outspoken advocates of the Federal Constitution in Virginia, and after the death of Washington he remained the greatest exponent of Federalism in his state. He was not deeply learned in the law, but he had a dominating personality and a command of persuasive logic. As Chief Justice, he imposed his stamp on the Court and usually imposed his will on the form of its decisions. We have already observed how, appointed in 1801 by John Adams, he laid the basis in *Marbury* v. *Madison* (1803) for the Court's power to declare acts of Congress unconstitutional (see p. 156) and how, in *Fletcher* v. *Peck* (1810), he upheld the obligation of contracts against state interference (see p. 159). In a series of subsequent decisions—often the subject of much controversy—he greatly expanded the authority of the Court and the powers of the federal government, limited the scope of action by the states, and defended the sanctity of private contracts against legislative interference.

    In 1819, while controversies between debtors and creditors were raging in the states, Marshall handed down two decisions bearing on the rights of contract. Of sweeping importance was *Dartmouth College* v. *Woodward*, which raised the question of whether the charter granted to the college by the legislature could subsequently be changed by the legislature. Marshall decided that the charter was a contract and that it had been unconstitutionally impaired by the legislation in question. Of great importance to colleges, this decision was of still greater importance to business enterprises operating under legislative charters; for it now appeared that these charters, defined as contracts, were secure and substantially unchangeable.

    The second decision in 1819, *Sturges* v. *Crowninshield*, dealt with a New York State bankruptcy law. Marshall found that even though Congress was empowered to pass bankruptcy laws, the states could also enact them if Congress failed to exercise its powers. But insofar as the New York law sought to relieve a debtor of the obligation to pay

[handwritten margin notes: "name to remember"; "date and name to remember"; "name and date to remember"]

477

**name and
date to
remember**

his debt, Marshall found it in violation of the contract clause
of the Constitution. Eight years later, however, in the case
of *Ogden* v. *Saunders* (1827), Marshall failed for the first and
only time to persuade the other justices to follow him in
rigidly enforcing the contract laws. Earlier bankruptcy decisions had ruled out state laws impairing debts made *before*
these laws were passed. In *Ogden* v. *Saunders*, Marshall
wanted to throw out a law impairing debts contracted *after*
its passage; but in this case the Court forsook him and upheld a state law of this kind.

**Very im-
portant
fact - get
more information**

**name and
date to
remember**

In establishing the supremacy of the federal government
and the Supreme Court over acts of states, Marshall's regime
was a spectacular success. During his 34 years as Chief
Justice, the Court acted no less than 13 times to set aside
state laws as contrary to the Constitution. In *Martin* v.
Hunter's Lessee (1816), the Court, speaking through Justice
Joseph Story, asserted its supremacy over state courts in
interpreting the Constitution. And five years later, in *Co-
hens* v. *Virginia* (1821), Marshall went out of his way to
state this principle in the broadest possible terms.

SQ3R notes

The notes shown in Figure App II–3 were taken on the preceding selection. Note that minor subheads were used for the questions in this example. After you had practiced SQ3R a while, you would ask only one
question—perhaps "What was the Era of Good Feelings?—to cover the
entire selection. *Use major headings!* Notice how little underlining is
done for the selection. Observe also how brief the SQ3R notes are. Time
and concentration were put into reading and taking notes so that memory
will be increased and later review will not be as necessary.

Suggestions for marking texts

Most students make a fatal error in marking textbooks: they mark such
large quantities of material that rereading it is tantamount to rereading
the entire book, and nothing is saved. The following suggestions, in combination with the application of SQ3R, can reduce the need for rereading
and the need for underlining paragraph after paragraph.

—Underline names, dates, places, and definitions that appear important. Mark with a red or blue pencil.

—Underline such words as *first, second,* and *last* when they point
to important statements. You may also want to write the
numbers in the margin if they are not explicit in the text.

—Place parentheses around paragraphs or lengthy selections that seem important, but be highly selective in doing so.

—Put a question mark in the margin by any section not adequately understood.

—Circle any word or phrase you do not understand; check on it later.

—What happened in election of 1816?
    — Monroe elected, large Republican sweep
—Why was there a postwar economic boom?
    — Demand from Europe for cotton, tobacco, + food
    — Purchase of manufactured goods
    — Speculation
—How did the 2nd Bank help end the boom?
    —2nd Bank made credit too easy, then too tough
    — People built up debts, couldn't pay → bust
— What was the role of the Supreme Court?
    — Broadened power of federal gov't over states

Figure Ap II–3. Notes on the "Era of Good Feelings."

—Place a star or asterisk in the margin by any selection that interests you and about which you wish further information.

—Draw a line in the margin by any statement you feel is of extreme importance.

Examinations

Most examination questions can be categorized as either objective items or essay questions. Objective test questions can be answered by one or two words or by indicating which of several alternatives is correct; essay questions require writing from as little as a couple of sentences to as much as several pages. Sometimes an examination will involve showing your skill in doing something, such as typing, performing a mechanical operation, or demonstrating proper nursing procedures upon a dummy; such examinations demand a different type of study from that described below. However, the common belief that essay exams require different types of study from objective exams is highly dubious.

A number of suggestions can be made about how students can prepare for and take examinations.

Preparing for examinations

—Try to predict what questions will be asked; the Q step of SQ3R should be helpful in this effort, and your professor has undoubtedly given hints. Perhaps you will be allowed to look at back exams your professor has given.

—Keep up-to-date in your study. This is probably the most important requirement for effective preparation, since last-minute cramming has numerous hazards.

—Get a good night's sleep before the examination.

—Schedule extra time for study before the exam, but remember that time allocated to study is worthless if not combined with concentration.

—Don't overlook cramming *in addition to* distributed learning.

—Try studying with others also taking the course, but make certain that you spend the time studying and asking each other questions, not having a bull session and debate over the merits of the instructor and the course.

—If it is to be an essay exam, practice writing answers to questions you predict.

Taking the examination

—Read *all* directions carefully.

—Try to figure out how long the exam will take; space your efforts to complete the exam and to give some answer to every item.

—Read each question all the way through, including multiple-choice questions, even though you think you know the answer after reading the first few words.

—Unless there is a penalty for guessing, put down some answer for every item, and guess on multiple-choice items.

—Don't spend too much time on any one item, but make certain to mark an omitted item so that you remember to return to it.

—If you are using an IBM answer sheet, follow directions carefully.

—Be careful to observe such words as *explain, describe, evaluate,* and *list,* or *probably, tendency,* and *always.* Answer accordingly.

—To review, if you have time, cover the answers to your questions; then try to answer the question in your mind, and compare your new answer with your previous answer.

—If the test consists of a very few, long-essay questions, spend a couple of minutes outlining each answer before writing it; also use a brief introduction and a summary or concluding statement.

—Longer answers are better than shorter answers, unless you have to "pad" or bring in irrelevant matters.

—Be as careful as possible with grammar and spelling; try to write legibly.

—Be careful to answer the question that is asked, not some related question.

—Proofread essay tests; double check objective tests to make sure you have answered every item.

—And, when you get the examination back, check over not only your errors but also your correct responses. This is an excellent way to overlearn.

Figure Ap II–4. Examples of good and poor essay answers.

1. Evaluate the French Impressionist movement in modern art:

STUDENT A:

> The French Impressionist movement included men like Van Gogh, Gauguin, Renoir, and Matisse. These men used to meet frequently in Paris cafes and discuss their progress. They didn't paint exactly what the thing they were painting looked like, but they brought in shadow effects and painted impressions, such as the name of their movement indicated. They were not very popular at that time, but have subsequently become popular, although I still think they are silly.

STUDENT B:

The French Impressionist movement signaled the breaking from traditional, Photograph-like art. Its followers made use of shadow effects and impressions rather than exact likenesses. The movement enabled painting to free itself of having to stick by so-called reality, and to make greater use of imagination. The artists became less restricted, experimented in color and form, and created many new schools of art. At the same time, freedom seemed to be licence for some artists, and they moved to painting abstractions, which - in my opinion - retarded the field of painting.

Both of these students knew the material quite well, although the latter expressed himself much better. The major difference, however, is that the first answer does not evaluate, but rather describes, the movement—until the final clause in which the writer "evaluates" by saying he doesn't like it. The second answer shows greater depth of understanding, as well as a grasp of the meaning of the question.

2. List the four presidents preceding Eisenhower and state one accomplishment of each:

STUDENT A:

Truman – War in Korea
Roosevelt – Depression, War with Europe
Hoover – helped Belgians
Coolidge – Prosperity

STUDENT B:

Harry Truman – prosecuted Korean War almost to its conclusion
F. D. Roosevelt – led the country through depression and through the Second World War
Herbert Hoover – developed programs to try to offset the depression
Calvin Coolidge – led the country during great prosperity

The first answer is satisfactory, but minimally so. Hoover's work with the Belgians took place much earlier and was not so important in its impact on the United States as his attempts to curb the depression. The second answer, although also very brief, expresses the ideas much more clearly.

3. What is SQ3R and how does it work?

STUDENT A:

SQ3R is a method for reading textbooks with greater efficiency. It works by making the student pay greater attention to what he reads. This is achieved through the five steps: (1) Survey — skim the chapter and read the summary. (2) Question — turn headings into questions. (3) Read — read the section under the heading. (4) Recite — answer the questions of the Q-step. (5) Review — review notes and perhaps skim again and read summary.

STUDENT B:

SQ3R is when you read Textbooks by using five Things — you Survey, question, read, recite, review. You Survey when you look over The chapter; you question when you make up questions; You read when you read; you recite when you answer questions; Then you review

The first answer gives a fairly good, brief response, covering both parts of the question. The second makes several errors: (1) it never states what SQ3R is; (2) it uses very poor grammar and rhetoric; (3) it answers superficially and vaguely.

4. Compare the problems of the student sitting at the back of a classroom with one sitting at the front. (This question is based on the notes taken earlier.)

STUDENT A:

At the back, the student has lots of distractions and he thinks he can dream, while he really can't because Professors Know what They are doing. Students in front dont have these problems.

STUDENT B:

Students sitting in the back of a classroom find more distractions. The heads of the students in front of them, the opportunity of looking out the window— I guess if its a fellow, good-looking girls— all these are distractions. Im back he is more likely to be with other students who are not good students, but who may be writing letters or daydreaming or goofing off. The students in front, on the other hand, may feel that other students think they're polishing the apple.

STUDENT C:

Sitting in back of a classroom brings about trouble to a lot of students. They sit back there and they find that they don't do as well as students who sit up front. Those up front, according to one experiment, get better grades. They are also better students, while the ones in the back of the class are not so good. I Think sitting in the middle is about best.

The first answer is minimal. Student A remembered two facts from the lecture and put them down with no imagination and with poor organization. He also said nothing about the problems of students up front. The lecture had made no mention of such problems, so the students answering the question were called upon to think on their own. Student B gave a very informal answer, but he covered the ground quite well. Student C used a lot of words; however, he said almost nothing, and, as he continued to write, he lost sight of the original question and began to answer a different question.

Appendix II has attempted to outline some of the more important elements of effective study, supplementing what has been written elsewhere in this book. For more thorough discussions of study methods, see the following books:

Kalish, Richard A. *Making the most of college.* Wadsworth, 1959.

Morgan, Clifford T., and James Deese. *How to study,* 2nd ed. McGraw-Hill, 1966.

Pauk, Walter. *How to study in college.* Houghton Mifflin, 1962.

Robinson, Francis P. *Effective study,* Revised. Harper, 1961.

Voeks, Virginia. *On becoming an educated person,* 2nd ed. Saunders, 1964.

Your instructor or your college counselor can suggest other books and sources of study-methods materials, some of them specifically related to the problems that concern you. The ability to study effectively is too important a matter to leave to chance or casual learning; it requires the student to be self-critical, to try new approaches, and to continue to seek methods of improving himself so as to make better use of his talents.

Glossary *

Ability: The actual power to perform an act.

Achievement: The present level of competence in performing a particular task.

Affective disorders: A group of psychotic reactions characterized by inappropriate emotional response and mood.

Agitated depression: A type of affective disorder in which depression is marked by considerable, often rapid, movement.

Alcoholic: A compulsive drinker; an individual who cannot control his drinking; an alcoholic is *not* the same thing as a heavy drinker.

Anxiety: An unpleasant emotion, similar to fear, marked by a vague feeling that something unpleasant is going to occur in the future; because of the vagueness of the cause, it is very difficult to overcome this feeling.

Anxiety reaction: A form of neurosis in which the person is in a constant state of anxiety (*see* Anxiety).

Apathy: In the sense used in Chapter 13: a withdrawal from emotional threat by retreating into a position of not caring; the unconscious feeling may be that of caring very much; sometimes used as a defense mechanism.

Approach-approach conflict: A conflict in which two positive goals are available, but the selection of one goal eliminates the possibility of selecting the other.

* In devising these definitions, the author has leaned heavily upon *A Comprehensive Dictionary of Psychological and Psychoanalytical Terms,* by Horace B. and Ava C. English, published by Longmans, Green, 1958.

Approach-avoidance conflict: A conflict in which the same goal has both positive and negative consequences, so that it attracts and repels simultaneously.

Aptitude: The potential to gain competence, assuming that training and experience are available (*see* Achievement).

Attention: The active selection of and emphasis upon one aspect of the environment at a time; the relative limiting of what is responded to.

Attitude: A continuing, learned tendency to behave in a consistent way toward an object or class of objects.

Auditory: Pertaining to hearing.

Authoritarian: A method of control or leadership, in which the individual establishes procedures and judges results without others sharing in the decision-making process.

Autonomy: Independent; self-regulating; not under the control of another.

Avoidance-avoidance conflict: A conflict in which both alternative goals are repelling; the individual believes he is faced with the necessity of selecting one or the other.

Behavior: The acts an organism performs; anything an organism does.

Belief: An emotional acceptance of an idea or statement upon what the individual considers adequate grounds; the individual has not necessarily examined the bases for his beliefs, but may have accepted them without evaluation.

Biochemical: Referring to the chemical basis for plant and animal, including human, life.

Body-image: The image or picture an individual has of his physical appearance and physical body; may include clothing, hair style, deformities, and hidden scars.

Brainwashing: The process of causing an individual to alter his attitudes, values, or behavior drastically in the direction of those guiding the process; a number of specific techniques are usually involved; brainwashing is one form of persuasion.

Case-history method: An intensive study of a single individual, utilizing a great variety of sources of information, such as school records, vocational evaluations, interviews, medical records, tests, and family history.

Catatonic schizophrenia: A form of schizophrenia marked by frequent apparent stupor; extreme excitement and activity are occasionally exhibited.

Classical conditioning: A form of learning in which two stimuli are presented close together in time on numerous occasions until the response caused by one stimulus is also elicited by the second stimulus, although the latter was originally unable to produce this response.

Clinical psychologist: The psychologist who is involved with studying or treating individuals with mental illness or personal-adjustment problems.

Compulsion: That which forces a person to do something or feel or think something against his "will"; may contribute (as a ritual form used to ward off the obsessive thought) to the form of neurosis termed obsessive-compulsive reaction.

Concept-formation: Abstracting a common quality from several stimuli, or generalizing to a common quality from several stimuli; the sky, your friend's eyes, the ink in your fountain pen, and your new sweater all share the common quality of *blue*.

Conflict: A type of stress produced by a person's being motivated by two or more needs, in such a fashion that the satisfaction of one need is believed to mean the nonsatisfaction of another need, or that the satisfaction of one need is believed to involve unpleasant consequences.

Conformity: Giving in to group pressure when the individual's judgments or behavior differ from the group's demands.

Conscious: The state of being aware of what is occurring.

Control group: A group of subjects, similar in every way possible to another group of subjects who are treated in some predetermined fashion; the control group is *not* treated in this fashion, so that any differences between the two groups after the experimental treatment can be tentatively assumed to result from the treatment conditions.

Conversion reaction: A form of neurosis in which the person displays such bodily symptoms as paralysis or sensory loss (blindness, deafness) without corresponding biochemical body changes.

Counseling psychologist: The psychologist whose primary interests are in research and treatment involving people with vocational and academic problems, those needing information and rehabilitation, and related matters; his work overlaps with that of the clinical psychologist.

Culture: The pattern of all behavior and material things that members of a society have adopted, shared, and communicated to future generations.

Defense mechanism: An attitude or other form of behavior which is used by the individual—without his awareness—to maintain the adequacy of his self-concept.

Deficiency motivation: The process of satisfying needs for things the organism lacks; hunger is a deficiency motive, while the desire (or need) to enjoy food is a growth motive.

Delusion: A false belief; a person may have the delusion that he is president of the world, that he is a great baseball player, or that his family is stealing all his money; although these delusions indicate severe personality disturbance, less serious delusions can also occur.

Demographic: Referring to the study of human population, including changes, distributions, and so forth.

Depressive reaction: A form of neurosis in which depression is the major symptom.

Derived status: To have status, or a position in the community, because of the worth or accomplishments of a parent or other relative; a type of reflected status.

Developmental psychologist: A psychologist whose primary interests are in the development of human behavior, with special emphasis upon a particular age group (e.g., children, the aged) or upon principles of development throughout the life cycle.

Discrimination: (1) In learning, the act of learning to recognize the difference between two stimuli and to respond accordingly; (2) in social psychology, the act of showing preference to one individual or group as opposed to another.

Displaced aggression: Redirected aggression, or hostile action directed away from the real cause of the aggressive or hostile feeling and onto another victim (*see* Scapegoat).

Displacement: Redirecting feelings, often anger or dislike, from the original cause usually to a less harmful person, object, or idea; the implication is that the person is prevented from directing the feelings toward the appropriate object; occurs without awareness; often a defense mechanism.

Dissociative reaction: A form of neurosis in which the primary symptom is dissociation, i.e., the separation of mental processes so that they cease to have the normal association between idea and emotion.

Distributed practice: Learning spaced out over a period of time, with intervening rest periods or periods of other activities; studying one hour each day for an examination would be an example.

Drug addict: An individual who takes drugs compulsively; he has developed a strong need for the particular drug and may display bodily changes if deprived.

Dynamic: A condition implying change, in which a change affecting one aspect of the organism instigates other changes that may affect the initial change; e.g., a gradual self-concept change, from submissive to moderately aggressive, will lead to new experiences that, in turn, may affect the self-concept.

Educational psychologist: The psychologist whose primary interests are in educational testing and measurement, curriculum planning, evaluation of teacher and pupil effectiveness, and other educational problems.

Effector organs: The cells and structures with which the organism responds: muscles and glands.

Emotion: A feeling or state of arousal of the organism which stirs it to observable action or to internal change, and which involves "sentiments."

Engineering psychologist: The psychologist whose primary interests are in studying and improving the effectiveness of man's use of machines of all sorts.

Enuresis: The act of frequent bed wetting that occurs well beyond the age at which the child can be expected to maintain control; the term can be applied to any uncontrolled act of urinating.

Esteem needs: Needs, as adapted from Maslow, for an individual to be respected by others and to respect himself.

Ethnic group: A group of individuals sharing a common language, religion, national origin, race, or cultural heritage.

Ethnic-group identification: Feeling as a member of a particular ethnic group; associating and affiliating with an ethnic group.

Experimental and physiological psychologist: The psychologist whose primary interests are in studying the biological bases for human behavior, animal behavior, learning and emotion, sensation and perception, and related matters.

Experimental method: A research method in psychology and other fields; implies a systematic approach in which one group of subjects is given one set of conditions and another group of subjects, another set; or in which the conditions are systematically varied to determine the effect of the change.

Exploratory need: The need of an individual, especially an infant or child, to examine his environment.

Extrasensory perception (ESP): Interpretation or organization of stimuli that affect the organism without processing through any of the known receptors or sense organs; this concept is not generally accepted by psychologists.

Fantasy: (1) An image that occurs as part of the thought process and that is fairly coherent; the image of a dream or daydream; (2) a type of withdrawal through daydreaming; sometimes a defense mechanism. The term may also be applied to a situation in which an individual purposely relives a previous action, rehearses a future action, or attempts some creative activity.

Fraternal twins: Twins, not necessarily similar in appearance and not necessarily of the same sex, resulting from two separately fertilized eggs.

Frustration: The unpleasant emotional state that results from a person's being blocked from his desired goal.

Fugue or fugue state: A lengthy period of amnesia or lack of recall for past events, although previous learning of skills and other aspects of life remain; the person may wander from his home and live under another identity.

Functional psychosis: Mental illness caused by stress that exceeds the individual's stress tolerance; caused by environmental stress, as opposed to direct biochemical changes.

General-adaptation syndrome (GAS): A theory to the effect that physiological changes in the human body in response to stress occur in three stages: alarm reaction, resistance, and exhaustion.

Genetic: Pertaining to, or occurring as the result of, genes; genes are elements that control many characteristics of the child and are transmitted from parents to child at the time of conception.

Group: A number of individuals having some characteristic in common.

Group decision: A decision made with the participation of the entire group and achieved with the active or tacit consent of each member of the group; a decision arrived at not by vote but by general acceptance.

Growth motivation: The process of activating behavior as the result of satisfying the need to make use of one's capacities and talents.

Growth spurt: The relatively sudden increase in growth that occurs shortly before puberty.

Guilt society: A culture in which internalized values or conscience provide the major form of social control.

Halfway house: A facility for alcoholics, addicts, delinquents, mental hospital patients, and others after their release from a hospital or other institution, to enable them to maintain some professional help while readjusting to the community; may be substituted for hospitalization.

Hallucination: A perception that occurs without relevant stimuli but which is accepted as real.

Healthy personality: A person who not only shows a relative absence of emotionally disturbed characteristics but also is able to satisfy his needs adequately, including the need for self-actualization; implies a positive, growth-motivated life.

Hebephrenic schizophrenia: A form of schizophrenia marked by silliness, giggling, and a general return to an earlier and immature condition.

Heredity: The characteristics or influences that parents transmit biologically to their children at the time of conception.

Hierarchy of needs: Associated with Maslow; a ranking of needs in terms of those that demand most immediate satisfaction, i.e., the more basic needs are ranked lowest and are placed at the base of the hierarchy; they must be reasonably well satisfied before the individual can turn his attention to the next most basic set of needs.

Homosexual: An individual who prefers sex relationships with members of his own sex rather than with the opposite sex.

Hostile-aggressive: A term used to emphasize that a particular act of aggression also involved hostility.

Hypothesis: A tentative explanation for an event, a relationship, or other form of occurrence; psychologists will frequently test hypotheses by collecting and analyzing relevant data.

Hysterical: The result of conversion reaction (*see* Conversion reaction); hysterical blindness, hysterical paralysis. Other meanings of this term are not relevant to this book.

Ideal self: The individual as he would like to be; the self the individual sees as the best "me" possible.

Identical twins: Twins, very similar in appearance and of the same sex, resulting from one fertilized egg.

Identification: Associating or affiliating with a group or another person; accepting as your own the values and purposes of another person or group; frequently used, without awareness, as a defense mechanism to improve the self-concept.

Identity: Although there are innumerable meanings for this word, only one is primarily relevant at this point: the awareness an individual has of how he relates to the rest of society, of his place in society and in the world; the awareness of himself as a unique individual.

Identity, search for: The attempt of an individual to understand his relationship to the rest of society, his place in the world, and himself as a unique individual.

Image: The "picture in the mind's eye" an individual has of a typical representative of a group of people or things; for example, many adults have an unfair image of a typical adolescent. This is only one use of this term.

Industrial psychologist: The psychologist whose primary interests are in the behavior of people at work; this field includes selection and placement of personnel; personnel testing; labor-management relations; human relations in industry; and evaluation of advertising and marketing practices.

In-group: A group whose members have a strong need for association with each other and a strong need to exclude those not of the group.

Inherited predispositions: Tendencies—to behave in particular ways or contract particular illnesses—that parents transmit genetically to their children at conception.

Insight: (1) The understanding of your own motives and other mental processes; (2) the understanding of some meaning, process, pattern, or use.

Insight learning: The process through which the meaning, significance, pattern, or use of an object or situation becomes clear.

Intellectualization: An attempt to withdraw from emotional impact by approaching a problem in purely intellectual terms; usually a defense mechanism.

Intelligence: The ability to grasp abstract concepts and symbols, to learn and to solve problems, and to cope with new situations.

IQ (intelligence quotient):   A measure of intelligence, usually based upon a test; the ratio of mental age to chronological age, multiplied by 100.

Internalization: Taking on the values, attitudes, beliefs, ideas, wishes, and goals of another person as your own; the general cultural values are transmitted from parent to child in this fashion.

Internal senses: The sense organs within the body.

Intolerance of ambiguity: A type of rigidity; an inability to deal with uncertainty; a need for clear-cut explanations.

Intra-uterine environment: The environment of the individual within the mother's womb, between conception and birth; the degree to which experiences and events involving this environment affect the later development is not well understood.

Involutional psychosis: A form of affective disorder involving depression that occurs most commonly to people in their fifties.

Job satisfaction: The degree to which an individual is pleased with his job; the amount of positive regard he has for his position.

Kinesthetic sense: The sense that enables an individual to be aware of his own movement through space.

Laissez-faire: In social psychology, a type of leadership in which the leader exerts a minimum amount of control and makes minimum demands.

Latent dream content: The "real" meaning of a dream; the meaning that underlies what the individual "sees" and recognizes (*see* Manifest dream content).

Leader: A person who modifies, directs, or controls the attitudes or actions of one or more others; especially the individual in the group who exhibits the most of such influence.

Learning: A process that occurs whenever a relatively permanent change in behavior results from experience.

Level of aspiration: The degree of competence, learning achievement, et cetera, the individual anticipates gaining.

Long-range goal: An end result, toward which a person is working and which takes a long time to achieve.

Love needs: Needs, as adapted from Maslow, to feel the love, the warmth, and the affection of physical and emotional contact with others.

Lying-in: An arrangement in the hospital whereby a new baby can be placed in the same room with the mother, who can care for the infant within a few hours of its birth; also called rooming-in.

Manic: A condition, often found in the mentally ill, of great excitability and elation.

Manic-depressive, circular type: A form of affective disorder in which the person is highly excited and elated for a period, then highly depressed for a period; there may be a period of relative normality in between.

Manifest dream content: That aspect of the dream the individual "sees" in his dream; that which is recognized (*see* Latent dream content).

Massed practice: Learning that takes place continuously without rest or other occurrences interrupting; frequently applied to study; cramming for an examination would be an example.

Maturation: Development; particularly those developmental changes that occur relatively inevitably in all normal members of the species provided with a relatively suitable environment; no special learning is required.

Menopause: The period of human development (female) during which the individual ceases to be able to become pregnant; may or may not be accompanied by physical symptoms; tends to occur during late forties or early fifties.

Mental age: The level of intellectual development, determined by comparing the person's performance on an intelligence test to the average performance of others at various chronological age levels.

Mental illness: Behavior disorder or behavior maladjustment; a breakdown in adjustment that necessitates some form of professional help or hospitalization.

Motivation: The process of setting behavior into action because of a need.

Motor skills: Those abilities related to movements, such as running, walking, hammering.

Multiple personality: A form of dissociative reaction (neurosis) in which the individual maintains two or more distinct personalities, each of which appears separately at various times; an extremely rare condition.

Natural childbirth: A process through which a pregnant woman prepares herself, both physically and emotionally, for the birth of her child with minimum dependence upon anesthetics.

Need: A lack of something in the organism which, if present, would increase the satisfaction of the organism; there are numerous ways of classifying needs, including systems by Maslow and Murray. Satisfying the need may be necessary to maintain existence, to provide stimulation, or to increase satisfactions.

Neonate: The infant between birth and about two or three weeks of age; a newly born infant.

Nervous system: The brain, the spinal cord, and the nerves.

Neurosis: A relatively mild personality disturbance, which does not incapacitate the individual nor necessitate his hospitalization; the person remains in contact with reality.

Nonverbal communication: Transmitting a message without written or oral words; e.g., through gestures or body movements.

Norm: A standard with which the performance of an individual can be compared; if, on a test of verbal ability, your score is compared to scores obtained by 1000 entering freshmen, the 1000 freshmen constitute the norm group.

Observational method: A way to study behavior; a research method; it consists of watching the relevant occurrences either in person or with some mechanical aid, such as a tape recorder; controlled observations are carefully recorded in some objective fashion.

Obsession: An idea that seems to haunt you, usually associated with dread or anxiety; may contribute to the form of neurosis termed obsessive-compulsive reaction.

Operant learning: The form of learning in which the correct response to the stimulus is gradually selected out from among all potential responses.

Organic: Referring to the body and its anatomical and biochemical make-up, rather than to the surrounding environment, the self-concept, or the personality.

Organic psychosis: Mental illness caused directly by biochemical (organic) changes in the body, particularly the brain.

Other-directed: To have internalized, or taken for yourself, only one important value, and that value is that the approval and acceptance of the group is of primary importance.

Overindulgent: Giving in to the demands and whims of another more often than is appropriate; usually used in reference to child rearing.

Overlearning: Learning in which practice goes beyond the point where the act can be performed with only the required degree of excellence; learning beyond the minimal level of adequacy, but without the implication that unnecessary learning has taken place.

Overprotection: Providing greater care than necessary, usually in reference to an infant or child; implies an unnecessary reduction in the opportunity of the individual to satisfy certain stimulation needs.

Parallel play: The play of very young children; each plays by himself in the presence of the other with only occasional interaction.

Paranoid: Marked by systematic, apparently logical, delusions; often mentally ill, but able to remain out of the hospital.

Paranoid schizophrenia: A form of schizophrenia characterized by unrealistic thinking, hallucinations, and delusions (especially of grandeur or persecution).

Percentile: One of 99 scores that divide a group of scores into 100 equal parts; thus, the student whose score is at the 53%ile (percentile) has received a higher score than 53 percent of those with whom he is being compared. (It does not mean he answered 53 percent of the questions correctly.)

Perception: The process through which the various sensations are interpreted and organized into meaningful patterns.

Personality: The dynamic organization of characteristic attributes leading to behavior and distinguishing one individual from other individuals. It refers to the total individual and includes needs, motives, methods of adjusting, temperament qualities, self-concepts, role behaviors, attitudes and values, and abilities.

Personality psychologist: A psychologist whose primary interests are in the study of personality (*see* Personality).

Phobia: A form of neurosis in which the person develops a dread, morbid, and exaggerated fear of something.

Physiological needs: Needs that result from lack of satisfaction of tissue requirements, such as hunger, thirst, oxygen, rest, and sex; physiological needs may demand satisfaction for survival or for stimulation.

Population explosion: A term applied to the rapid increase in population throughout the world, resulting primarily from the reduction in the death rate in general and infant mortality in particular.

Prejudice: An evaluation or belief, either positive or negative, developed without sufficient information and understanding and resistant to change; prejudices often form about an individual as the result of the ethnic, religious, sex, age, or vocational group to which he belongs.

Preliterate: Being without written language; usually applied by anthropologists to groups of people living under primitive conditions.

Prenatal: Pertaining to the human being during the period between conception and birth.

Primary status: To have status, or a position in the community, because of your own worth and accomplishments, rather than as a reflection of the worth and accomplishments of a parent or other relative.

Probability: The likelihood that an event would occur.

Problem solving: The process of determining a proper solution to accomplish a task; implies that some thinking was involved rather than only trial and error.

Projection: The process of attributing your own feelings, motives, shortcomings, and so forth, to others; occurs without conscious awareness; usually a defense mechanism.

Propaganda: Actions or expressions of opinion deliberately designed to influence beliefs, values, attitudes, opinions, or behavior of others; propaganda *may* have an educational value, and education *may* have propaganda value.

Psychiatrist: A medical doctor whose primary concern is with mental illness and problems of personal adjustment.

Psychoanalyst: An individual, usually a medical doctor, who studies and treats mental illness and personal-adjustment problems on the basis of Freud's principles, or upon some modification of these principles; he has completed a carefully specified course of study to become a psychoanalyst.

Psychologist: An individual who studies behavior in order to understand, describe, predict, and influence this behavior; he uses research to lead both to theories of behavior and to effective practical applications directed at immediate and long-range problems. There are many types of psychologists.

Psychosis: A relatively severe personality disturbance that often incapacitates the individual and may necessitate his hospitalization; the psychotic may lose contact with reality.

Psychosomatic: Physical symptoms produced by biochemical changes initiated by emotional stress; psychosomatic problems can do tissue damage, are often treatable through a combination of medical and psychiatric methods, and are not in the least imaginary.

Psychotherapy: The use of any psychological technique in helping an individual deal more effectively with personal or social problems; often restricted to trained psychotherapists operating in a situation in which they confront the person or persons receiving the help.

Psychotic depressive: A form of affective disorder marked by extreme depression and frequently precipitated by the immediate environment rather than by experiences in the early years of the victim's life.

Puberty: The period of human development during which the individual becomes sexually mature; usually between ages twelve and fourteen, but with wide variations.

Puberty rites: A ceremony, taking place around the time of puberty, that initiates the individual into his society as a regular member of the community.

Questionnaire: A set of questions on a given topic or several topics to investigate beliefs, attitudes, preferences, actual or potential behavior, and so forth; it is usually readily scorable.

Rationalization: An attitude or other behavior that presents a plausible reason for something that would otherwise disrupt the self-concept; the individual must be unaware of his purpose in using it; usually a defense mechanism.

Reaction formation: Establishment of a personality trait or behavior directly opposed to certain unconscious motives or feelings; usually a defense mechanism.

Receptor: A specialized part of the human or lower-animal organism sensitive to such forms of energy as light (for vision) or sound (for hearing) and changing this energy into a form that enables its impact to be transmitted to the brain.

Reference group: Those people with whom an individual compares and judges himself.

Reflex: A simple action that occurs automatically and without the control of the individual; e.g., the knee jerk in response to a tap, sneezing in response to having the nose tickled.

Regression: The return to an earlier form of behavior; sometimes a defense mechanism.

Reinforcement: The increasing of the probability that the indicated response will follow the stimulus; the strengthening of the bond between stimulus and response.

Relative deprivation, law of: The theory that a person's satisfaction or dissatisfaction will result from how much he has compared to how much he feels he should have (reflected by what he sees around him); thus, a poor Asian farmer feels less deprived than an American farmer because the latter is surrounded by wealth, but the former is surrounded by poverty.

Reliability: The consistency of a rating, a test, or other psychological measurement; if you receive the exact same grade relative to others on every quiz or examination you take in your psychology course, your scores would be considered highly reliable (or dependable or consistent).

Repression: The process leading to being unaware, or being unable to recall, as a defense against the anxiety or guilt that the awareness or recollection would produce; having such a strong need to be unaware or unable to recall, that lack of awareness or recollection results; a defense mechanism.

Response: An instance of behavior that is stirred up or stimulated by an event, a situation, or other behavior.

Retarded depressive: A type of affective disorder in which depression is marked by apathy, reduced movement, and lack of overt activity.

Reward: The satisfaction of a need in such a fashion as to increase the chance that the reward-eliciting behavior will occur the next time the need becomes motivating.

Role: The behavior expected of an individual who occupies a particular position in the social scheme; positions include age position, leadership position, vocational position, and innumerable others.

Safety needs: Needs, as adapted from Maslow, to feel safe and secure, not to fear physical violence or loss of property.

Scapegoat: The victim of displaced aggression; the person or thing that receives the displaced aggressive or hostile actions of another.

Schizophrenia: A group of psychotic reactions characterized by basic confusion regarding reality, by inappropriate emotional response, and by other forms of disturbed behavior.

School psychologist: A psychologist who functions inside a school setting, usually concerned with testing, curriculum, counseling, and related matters; tends to be concerned with day-to-day problems, rather than with more theoretical and research issues such as occupy the educational psychologist.

Segregation: To keep separate; to keep an individual separated from the group or to keep one group of individuals separated from other groups. Often used in relationship to ethnic groups.

Self: All that constitutes that individual; the "real me" (*see* Self-concept). Some authors define this term in other ways.

Self-actualization: The process of making the most of your capabilities, developing your talents, and acting naturally or being yourself.

Self-concept: The idea an individual has of himself; what a person sees himself as; the similarity between self and self-concept varies from person to person.

Self-fulfilling prophecy: A statement about what will happen in the future that helps cause the predicted circumstance to occur; a student who predicts he might fail in a course may behave in such a fashion, because of his prophecy, that he does fail.

Senile psychosis: Mental illness affecting the aged, usually assumed to have at least some organic basis.

Sensation: That which occurs when some stimulus excites a receptor; there is no meaning in the sensation, except as it is interpreted by the organism.

Separation anxiety: The concern felt by the young child because of being apart from his parents; this concern is reflected in later life when people become unhappy at temporary or permanent separations from others.

Set: A readiness to act or react; it may be a readiness to move, a readiness to perceive, or a readiness to accept a thought or idea.

Sex role: The behavior expected of an individual because of his sex.

Shame: An unpleasant emotion produced by the feeling that others disapprove of your behavior or some other characteristic; there is some implication that the individual disapproves of the behavior or other characteristic himself.

Shame society: A culture in which disapproval, ridicule, or criticism of others provide the major form of social control.

Sibling: The term used to refer to "brother" or "sister," without regard to sex; your sibling may be either a sister or a brother.

Sibling rivalry: A common occurrence among children and, often, among adults; two or more children in the same family compete for the attention and approval of the parents.

Significant figures: Those individuals who have an extremely important and continuing impact upon the development and behavior of an individual, especially of a child; the mother is most commonly a significant figure, as is the father to a slightly lesser degree. (There is also a statistical meaning to this term, but it is not mentioned in this book.)

Simple schizophrenia: A form of schizophrenia marked by limited involvement with the external world and limited adequacy in interpersonal relationships.

Social class: A grouping of individuals sharing certain social characteristics which enable them to interact with each other as approximate equals. Your social class affects your social environment, which affects values and many types of behavior.

Social-class mobility: The ability to move from one social class to another; the ability to be accepted as a member of a social-class group other than that of birth.

Social psychologist: A psychologist whose primary interests are in the study of groups, of attitudes and beliefs, of communication; in general, of the effects upon behavior of the social environment and social interactions.

SQ3R: A method for improving learning and reducing forgetting in reading, especially textbooks.

Statistical psychologist: The psychologist whose primary interests are in evolving and utilizing quantitative approaches in research.

Status: The position or standing a person is given by his group.

Stereotype: A rigid and oversimplified or biased perception or conception of an aspect of reality, especially of persons or social groups.

Stimulation needs: Those unlearned (although not uninfluenced by learning) needs that cause the individual to explore and manipulate his environment.

Stimulus: An object or event that stirs up or stimulates behavior.

Stimulus generalization: The process through which the individual learns to respond to stimuli that resemble the stimulus originally eliciting the response.

Stress: Situation or event producing strong, unpleasant emotional tension or discomfort.

Stress tolerance: The amount of stress an individual can withstand without exhibiting adjustment problems.

Suppression: An attempt to forget or ignore something, done on purpose; this is not a defense mechanism.

Survival needs: Those unlearned needs necessary to the maintenance of life of the organism, e.g., hunger, thirst, sleep.

Symptomitis: A condition occurring to students in medicine and psychology, in which they see in themselves the symptoms they are studying; this term is not likely to be found in other dictionaries.

Thinking: The process of judging, abstracting, reasoning, evaluating, recalling, imagining, anticipating, or performing a comparable intellectual task, not including perceiving.

Threshold: The point at which a stimulus is just strong enough to cause a response.

Toilet training: The process through which the child learns to control his elimination processes until he can find a socially acceptable location for eliminating.

Trait (personality):   A characteristic behavior pattern that differentiates people from each other.

Tranquilizer: A type of drug that reduces unpleasant emotional states such as anxiety and guilt and induces a feeling of calmness.

Trial: A single performance; a single attempt to respond properly to a stimulus.

Unconscious: The state of being unaware of what is occurring.

Unconscious motivation: The process of setting behavior into action because of a need or lack of something in the organism, of which the person himself has no awareness.

Validity: The capacity of a test, a rating, or other psychological measurement to measure what it is intended to measure. Your grade in psychology is valid to the extent that it measures how much you know about the material of the psychology course.

Value: A belief about what is good or bad: each individual internalizes many values, which then may serve to motivate behavior; values are often held without the individual's full awareness.

Value system: Several values related to each other and interdependent to some extent, so that a change in one value would probably produce at least a slight change in the others.

Variable: Anything that can change; in psychology, any attribute or property that changes as the result of another attribute, property, process, event; e.g., the variable *obedience* changes as the result of the event *spanking*.

Vestibular sense: The sense that enables an individual to maintain balance and to be aware of his position.

Visual: Pertaining to seeing.

Warm-up: Derived from baseball; a brief period of getting ready to do something, during which the individual gains the proper set or readiness.

Weaning: To enable a child (or young lower animal) to become accustomed to being without its mother's milk; to enable any individual to reduce his dependency upon a person or thing.

Withdrawal: An action or pattern of behavior in which an individual removes himself from a stressful situation in an attempt to reduce the feelings of tension or maintain a satisfactory self-concept.

Bibliography

Adorno, Theodore W., Else Frenkel-Brunswik, Daniel J. Levinson, and R. Nevitt Sanford. *The authoritarian personality: Studies in prejudice.* Harper, 1950. 362

Allport, Gordon W. *The nature of prejudice.* Addison-Wesley, 1954. 397

Allport, Gordon W., and B. M. Kramer. "Some roots of prejudice." Journal of Psychology, 1946. 22: 9–39. 414

——————, Philip E. Vernon, and Gardner Lindzey. *Study of values,* 3rd edition. Houghton Mifflin, 1960. 379

Alper, T. G., and Boring, E. G. "Intelligence test scores of northern and southern white and Negro recruits in 1918." *Journal of Abnormal and Social Psychology,* 1944. 39: 471–474. 367

Anastasi, Anne. *Differential psychology,* 3rd edition. Macmillan, 1958. 135, 367

Argyle, Michael. *The scientific study of social behaviour.* Methuen, 1957. 373

——————. *Religious behavior.* Free Press of Glencoe, 1959. 403

Armour, J. B. "Student attitudes in relation to classroom achievement." Unpublished master's thesis, 1954. Cited in Henry C. Smith, *Personality adjustment.* McGraw-Hill, 1961. 195

Asch, Solomon E. "Effects of group pressure upon the modification and distortion of judgment." In Harold S. Guetzkow (ed.), *Groups, leadership, and men.* Carnegie Press, 1951. 5

Astin, Alexander W., and Robert C. Nichols. "Life goals and vocational choice." *Journal of Applied Psychology,* 1964. 48: 50–58. 331

Ausubel, David P. *Theory and problems of adolescent development.* Grune and Stratton, 1954. 165, 166, 170, 200, 361, 426

Ax, Albert F. "The physiological differentiation between fear and anger in humans." *Psychosomatic Medicine,* 1953. 15: 433–442. 258

Bacon, Margaret K., Irvin L. Child, and Herbert Barry. "A cross-cultural study of correlates of crime." *Journal of Abnormal and Social Psychology,* 1963. 66: 291–300. 147

Banta, Thomas J., and Mavis Hetherington. "Relations between needs of friends and fiancés." *Journal of Abnormal and Social Psychology*, 1963. 66: 401–404. 426

Barrett, William. *Irrational man*. Doubleday, 1958. 7

Barry, Herbert, and Erich Lindemann. "Critical ages for maternal bereavement in psychoneurosis." *Psychosomatic Medicine*, 1960. 22: 166–181. 120

Bayley, Nancy. "On the growth of intelligence." *American Psychologist*, 1955. 10: 805–818. 230

——————, and Melita H. Oden. "The maintenance of intellectual ability in gifted adults." *Journal of Gerontology*, 1955. 10: 91–107. 230

Benedict, Ruth F. *The chrysanthemum and the sword*. Houghton Mifflin, 1946. 124

Bennett, Margaret E., and Molly Lewin. *Getting the most out of college*. McGraw-Hill, 1957. 183

Berelson, Bernard, and Gary A. Steiner. *Human behavior: An inventory of scientific findings*. Harcourt, Brace, and World, 1964. 215, 224, 336, 364, 386, 432

Berne, Eric. *Games people play; the psychology of human relationships*. Grove, 1964. 207

Berrien, F. Kenneth. *Values of Japanese and American students*. Technical Report 14, Group Psychology Branch, Office of Naval Research. Department of Defense, January 1964. 42

Biderman, Albert D. "The image of 'brain-washing.'" *Public Opinion Quarterly*, 1962. 26: 547–563. 12

Bieber, Irving. *Homosexuality: A psychoanalytical study*. Vintage, 1965. 315

Birren, James E. *The psychology of aging*. Prentice-Hall, 1964. 247

Block, Jack, and Hobart Thomas. "Is satisfaction with self a measure of adjustment?" *Journal of Abnormal and Social Psychology*, 1955. 51: 254–259. 40, 95

Blood, Robert O., Jr. *Anticipating your marriage*. Free Press of Glencoe, 1955. 214

——————. "Uniformities and diversities in campus dating preferences." *Marriage and Family Living*, 1956. 18: 37–45. 175

——————, and Donald M. Wolfe. *Husbands and wives*. Free Press of Glencoe, 1960. 219

Blum, Milton L. *Industrial psychology and its social foundations*, rev. edition. Harper, 1956. 237

Bogart, Leo. "American television: A brief survey of research findings." *Journal of Social Issues* (No. 2) 1962. 18: 36–42. 245

Bogdonoff, M. D., R. F. Klein, E. H. Estes, Jr., D. M. Shaw, and K. W. Back. "The modifying effect of conforming behavior upon lipid responses accompanying CNS arousal." *Clinical Research*, 1961. 9: 135. Cited in David Krech, Richard S. Crutchfield, and Egerton L. Ballachey, *Individual in society*. McGraw-Hill, 1962. 355

Bowlby, John. "Separation anxiety." *International Journal of Psychoanalysis*, 1960. 41: 89–113. 120

Boys' Clubs of America. *Needs and interests of adolescent Boys' Club members*. 1960. 166, 167, 344

Bradburn, Norman N. Achievement and father dominance in Turkey." *Journal of Abnormal and Social Psychology*, 1963. 67: 464–468. 42

Bradway, Katherine P., and Clare W. Thompson. "Intelligence at adulthood:

A twenty-five year follow-up." *Journal of Educational Psychology*, 1962. 53:1–14. 230

Brayfield, Arthur H., and Walter H. Crockett. "Employee attitudes and employee performance." *Psychological Bulletin*, 1955. 52: 396–424. 343

Bridges, Katherine M. B. "Emotional development in early infancy." *Child Development*, 1932. 3: 324–341. 259

Brown, Daniel G. "Masculinity-feminity development in children." *Journal of Consulting Psychology*, 1957. 21: 197–202. 238

Brown, William F., and Wayne H. Holtzman. "A study-attitudes questionnaire for predicting academic success." *Journal of Educational Psychology*, 1955. 46: 75–84. 195

Bruner, Jerome S., and C. C. Goodman. "Value and need as organizing factors in perception." *Journal of Abnormal and Social Psychology*, 1947. 13: 33–44. 55

Bugental, Daphne E., and George F. J. Lehner. "Accuracy of self-perception and group-perception as related to two leadership roles." *Journal of Abnormal and Social Psychology*, 1958. 56: 396–398. 371

Burgess, Ernest W., and Leonard S. Cottrell, Jr. *Predicting success or failure in marriage*. Prentice-Hall, 1939. 216

——————, and Paul Wallin. *Engagement and marriage*. Lippincott, 1953. 216

Byrne, Donn, and Barbara Blaylock. "Similarity and assumed similarity of attitudes between husbands and wives." *Journal of Abnormal and Social Psychology*, 1963. 67: 636–640. 217

Caldwell, Bettye M., and Leonard Hersher. "Mother-infant interaction during the first year of life." *Merrill-Palmer Quarterly*, 1964. 10: 119–128. 242

Calvin, A. D., and Wayne H. Holtzman. "Adjustment to the discrepancy between self-concept and the inferred self." *Journal of Consulting Psychology*, 1953. 17: 39–44. 94

Caplan, Ruth B. "Alas! for the moving generation: An essay on residential movement in the United States." *Mental Hygiene*, 1964. 48: 186–196. 232

Cattell, Raymond B., and Ivan H. Scheier. *The meaning and measurement of neuroticism and anxiety*. Ronald Press, 1961. 305

Chatterjee, M. N. *Society in the making*. Edwards Brothers, 1942. 421

Clark, Kenneth B., and Mamie P. Clark. "Racial identification and preference in Negro children." In Eleanor E. Maccoby, Theodore M. Newcomb, and Eugene L. Hartley (eds.), *Readings in Social Psychology*, 3rd edition. Holt, 1958. Pages 602–611. 364

Cohen, E. L. "The incidence and localization of acne." *British Journal of Dermatology*, 1945. 57: 10–14. 160

Cole, Luella, and Irma N. Hall. *Psychology of adolescence*, 6th edition. Holt, Rinehart and Winston, 1964. 157, 175, 176, 180

Coleman, James C. *Personality dynamics and effective behavior*. Scott, Foresman, 1960. 36, 299

——————. *Abnormal psychology and modern life*, 3rd edition. Scott, Foresman, 1964. 285, 308, 310, 314

Coleman, James S. *The adolescent society*. Free Press of Glencoe, 1961. 170

Conrad, H. S., and H. E. Jones. "A second study of familial resemblance in intelligence: Environmental and genetic implications of parent-child and sibling correlations in the total sample." *39th Yearbook National Society for the Study of Education*, 1940. Part II: 97–141. 135

Cooley, Charles H. *The nature of human nature.* Charles Scribner's Sons, 1902. 114

Coughlan, R. "Control of the brain." *Life,* 1963. 54: March 8, 90–106, and March 15, 81–94. 12

Cumming, Elaine, and William E. Henry. *Growing old.* Basic Books, 1961. 248

Deeg, Maethel E., and Donald G. Paterson. "Changes in social status of occupations." *Occupations,* 1947. 25: 205–208. 342

Dement, William. "The effect of dream deprivation." *Science,* 1960. 131: 1705–1707. 58

Diamond, Solomon. *Personality and temperament.* Harper, 1957. 91, 100

Dick-Read, Grantly. *Childbirth without fear: The principles and practice of natural childbirth,* 4th edition. Heinemann, 1960. 100

Dole, Arthur A. "College students report on their use of time." *Personnel and Guidance Journal,* 1959. 37: 633–637. 187

Dollard, John, Leonard W. Doob, Neal E. Miller, O. H. Mowrer, and Robert R. Sears. *Frustration and aggression.* Yale University Press, 1939. 283

Douvan, Elizabeth, and Joseph Adelson. "The psychodynamics of social mobility in adolescent boys." *Journal of Abnormal and Social Psychology,* 1958. 56: 31–44. 362

Durham, Philip, and Everett L. Jones, *The Negro cowboys.* Dodd, Mead, 1965. 367

Ebbs, J. H., F. F. Tisdall, and W. A. Scott, "The influence of prenatal diet on the mother and child." *The Milbank Memorial Fund Quarterly,* 1942. 20: 35–36. 99

Edwards, Allan L. *Edwards personal preference schedule.* Psychological Corporation, 1954. 38

Elkind, David, and Sally Elkind. "Varieties of religious experience in young adolescents." *Journal for the Scientific Study of Religion,* 1962. 2: 102–112. 402

English, Horace B., and Ava C. English. *A comprehensive dictionary of psychological and psychoanalytical terms: A guide to usage.* Longmans, Green, 1958. 73, 77, 132, 307, 369, 378, 431, 487

English, O. Spurgeon, and Gerald H. J. Pearson. *Emotional problems of living,* 3rd edition. Norton, 1963. 220

Erikson, Erik H. "The problem of ego identity." *Journal of the American Psychoanalytic Association,* 1956. 4: 56–121. 163

Farberow, Norman L., and Edwin S. Shneidman (eds.). *The cry for help.* McGraw-Hill, 1961. 316

Feifel, Herman. "Attitudes toward death in some normal and mentally ill populations." In Herman Feifel (ed.), *The meaning of death.* McGraw-Hill, 1959. Pages 114–130. 252

Feinberg, Mortimer R. "College student in residence." *New York Times Sunday Magazine,* Oct. 13, 1963. Page 93. 80

Fenz, Walter D., and Abe Arkoff. "Comparative need patterns of five ancestry groups in Hawaii." *Journal of Social Psychology,* 1962. 58: 67–89. 41

Festinger, Leon. "Motivations leading to social behavior." In Marshall Jones (ed.), *Nebraska symposium,* 1954. Pages 191–219. 27

————. *A theory of cognitive dissonance.* Row, Peterson, 1957. 389

Fey, William F. "Correlates of certain subjective attitudes toward self and others." *Journal of Clinical Psychology,* 1957. 13: 44–49. 115

Fisher, Sarah C. "Relationships in attitudes, opinions, and values among family members." *University of California publications in culture and society,* 1948. 2: 29–100. Cited in Henry C. Smith, *Personality adjustment.* McGraw-Hill, 1961. 403

Ford, Clellan S., and Frank A. Beach. *Patterns of sexual behavior.* Harper, 1952. 199, 315

Frankel, Edward, "Characteristics of working and non-working mothers among intellectually gifted high and low achievers." *Personnel and Guidance Journal,* 1964. 42: 776–780. 242

Freedman, Marvin B. "The sexual behavior of American college women: An empirical study and an historical survey." *Merrill-Palmer Quarterly,* 1965. 11: 38–48. 201

Frenkel-Brunswik, Else. "Intolerance of ambiguity as an emotional and perceptual personality variable." *Journal of Personality,* 1949. 18: 108–143. 57, 77

Friedan, Betty. *The feminine mystique.* Norton, 1963. 239

Fromm, Erich. *Escape from freedom.* Rinehart, 1941. 168

——————. *The art of loving.* Harper, 1956. 428

Gallup, George, and Evan Hill. "Youth: The cool generation." *Saturday Evening Post,* Dec. 23, 1961. Pages 63–80. 175, 405, 451

Gebhart, G. Gary, and Donald P. Hoyt. "Personality needs of under- and over-achieving freshmen." *Journal of Applied Psychology,* 1958. 42: 125–128. 195

Getzels, Jacob W., and Philip W. Jackson. *Creativity and intelligence: Explorations with gifted students.* Wiley, 1962. 76, 432

Gibb, Cecil A. *Leadership.* In Gardner Lindzey (ed.), *Handbook of social psychology,* Vol. II. Addison-Wesley, 1954. Pages 877–920. 370

Gibson, Eleanor J., and Richard D. Walk. "The 'visual cliff.'" *Scientific American,* 1960. 202: 64–71. 52

Gillespie, James M., and Gordon W. Allport. *Youth's outlook on the future.* Doubleday, 1955. 196

Gleazer, Edmund J., Jr. Editor's preface. In *American junior colleges,* 6th edition. American Council on Education, 1963. Pages 3–6. 180

Goldberg, Solomon C. "Three situational determinants of conformity to social norms." *Journal of Abnormal and Social Psychology,* 1954. 49:325–329. 354

Goldsen, Rose K., Morris Rosenberg, Robin M. Williams, Jr., and Edward A. Suchman. *What college students think.* Van Nostrand, 1960. 183, 192, 215, 235, 242, 329, 339, 404, 405, 408, 414

Goodenough, Florence L. *Measurement of intelligence by drawings.* World Book, 1926. 138

Gordon, Albert I. *Intermarriage: Interfaith, interracial, interethnic.* Beacon Press, 1964. 211, 212

Gorer, Geoffrey. *Himalayan village.* M. Joseph, 1938. 110

Gowan, John C. "Relationship between leadership and personality measures." *Journal of Educational Research,* 1955. 48: 623–627. 370

Grinder, Robert E., and Robert E. McMichael. "Cultural influence on conscience development: Resistance to temptation and guilt among Samoans and American Caucasians." *Journal of Abnormal and Social Psychology,* 1963. 66: 503–507. 124

Gross, Edward. *Work and society.* Crowell, 1958. 361

Gullahorn, John T., and Jeanne E. Gullahorn. "An extension of the U-curve hypothesis." *Journal of Social Issues,* July 1963. 19: 33–47.   457

Gustad, John W. "Changes in social attitudes and behavior: A review of the literature." *Educational and Psychological Measurements,* 1951. 11: 87–102.   458

——————. "Factors associated with social behavior and adjustment: A review of the literature." *Educational and Psychological Measurements,* 1952. 12: 3–19.   443

Haire, Mason. "Projective techniques in marketing research." *Journal of Marketing,* 1950. 14: 649–656.   388

Hanes, Bernard, and Edwin B. Flippo. "Anxiety and work output." *Journal of Industrial Engineering,* 1963. 14: 244–248.   236

Harlow, Harry F. "The nature of love." *American Psychologist,* 1958. 13: 673–685.   119

——————, and Margaret K. Harlow. "The effect of rearing conditions on behavior." *Bulletin of the Menninger Clinic,* 1962a. 26: 213–224.   119

——————, and ——————. "Social deprivation in monkeys." *Scientific American,* 1962b. 207: 136–146.   150

——————, ——————, and Donald R. Meyer. "Learning motivated by a manipulation drive." Journal of Experimental Psychology, 1950. 40: 228–234.   27, 29

Harrell, Ruth F. "Further effects of added thiamin on learning and other processes." *Contributions to Education,* No. 928. Teachers College, Columbia University, 1947.   137

Harris, Dale B. "Work and the adolescent transition to maturity." *Teachers College Record,* 1961. 63: 146–153.   344

Harris, Louis. "The Harris poll." In the *Los Angeles Times,* March 18, 1965. Page 12.   166, 184, 447

Harsh, Charles M., and H. G. Schrickel. *Personality: Development and assessment,* 2nd edition. Ronald Press, 1959.   97

Havemann, Ernest, and Patricia S. West. *They went to college.* Harcourt Brace, 1952.   184, 185, 441, 457

Havighurst, Robert J., Paul H. Bowman, Gordon P. Liddle, Charles V. Matthews, and James V. Pierce. *Growing up in River City.* Wiley, 1962.   184, 206, 216, 236, 331

——————, Myra Z. Robinson, and Mildred Dorr. "The development of the ideal self in childhood and adolescence." *Journal of Educational Research,* 1946. 40: 241–257.   95

Heron, Woodburn. "The pathology of boredom." *Scientific American,* 1957. 196: 52–56.   28, 51

Herzberg, Frederick, Bernard Mausner, Richard O. Peterson, and Dora F. Capwell. *Job attitudes: Review of research and opinion.* Psychological Service of Pittsburgh, 1957. Cited in Bernard Berelson and Gary A. Steiner (eds.), *Human behavior.* Harcourt, Brace, and World, 1964.   343

Hess, Robert D., and Irene Goldblatt. "The status of adolescents in American society: A problem in social identity." *Child Development,* 1957. 28: 459–468.   166

Hilgard, Ernest R. *Introduction to psychology,* 3rd edition. Harcourt, Brace, and World, 1962.   52

Himmelweit, Hilde T. "A theoretical framework for the consideration of the effects of television: A British report." *Journal of Social Issues* (No. 2) 1962. 18: 16–28.   246

Hoefer, C., and M. C. Hardy. "Later development of breast fed and artifically fed infants." *Journal of the American Medical Association,* 1929. 92: 615–619. 109

Hofstadter, Richard, William Miller, and Daniel Aaron. *The United States: The history of a republic.* Prentice-Hall, 1957. 283

Holland, James C. "Teaching psychology by a teaching machine program." Unpublished mimeographed report, 1960. 69 Cited in Bernard Berelson and Gary A. Steiner (eds.), *Human behavior.* Harcourt, Brace, and World, 1964.

Hollingshead, August B. *Elmtown's youth.* Wiley, 1949. 162, 175, 358

—————. "Factors associated with prevalence of mental illness." In Eleanor E. Maccoby, Theodore M. Newcomb, and Eugene L. Hartley (eds.), *Readings in social psychology,* 3rd edition. Holt, 1958. Pages 425–436. 305, 308

Honzik, Marjorie P. "Developmental studies of parent-child resemblance in intelligence." *Child Development,* 1957. 28: 215–228. 97

Hoppock, Robert. *Job satisfaction.* Harper, 1935. 236, 342

Hovland, Carl I., Enid H., Campbell, and T. Brock. "The effects of 'commitment' on opinion change following communication." In Carl I. Hovland, et al., *The order of presentation in persuasion.* Yale University Press, 1957. 90

Hughes, Helen MacG., and Lewis G. Watts. "Portrait of the self-integrator." *Journal of Social Issues,* (April) 1964. 20: 103–115. 368

Hurlock, Elizabeth B. *Developmental psychology,* 2nd edition. McGraw-Hill, 1959. 150, 228, 401

Hyman, Herbert H. "The value system of different classes: A social psychological contribution to the analysis of stratification." In Reinhard Bendix and Seymour M. Lipset (eds.), *Class, status, and power.* Free Press of Glencoe, 1953. Pages 426–442. 361

—————. *Political socialization: A study in the psychology of political behavior.* Free Press of Glencoe, 1959. 166, 38

Inselberg, Rachel M. "Social and psychological factors associated with high school marriages." *Journal of Home Economics,* 1961. 53: 766–772. 216, 224

Ivey, Allen E. "The academic performance of students counseled at a university counseling service." *Journal of Counseling Psychology,* 1962. 9: 347–352. 458

Izard, Carroll E. "Personality characteristics of engineers as measured by the Edwards Personal Preference Schedule." *Journal of Applied Psychology,* 1960. 44: 332–335. 41

—————. "Personality similarity and friendship: A follow-up study." *Journal of Abnormal and Social Psychology,* 1963. 66: 598–600. 426

—————, and John H. Manhold. "Correlates of peer leadership ratings. I. Medical complaints." *Medical Research Reports,* United States Naval School of Aviation, 1954. 370

Jacob, Philip E. *Changing values in college: An exploratory study of the impact of college teaching.* Harper, 1957. 185, 404

Jeans, Philip C., F. Howell Wright, and Florence G. Blake. *Essentials of pediatrics,* 5th edition. Lippincott, 1954. 109

Jeffers, Frances C., Claude R. Nichols, and Carl Eisdorfer. "Attitudes of older persons toward death: A preliminary study." *Journal of Gerontology,* 1961. 16: 53–56. 250

Jepsen, Victor L. "College activities and vocational success." *Occupations*, 1951. 29: 345–347. 443

Jones, Mary C. "A study of socialization patterns at the high school level." *Journal of Genetic Psychology*, 1958. 93: 87–111. 170

Jourard, Sidney M. *Personal adjustment: An approach through the study of healthy personality*, 2nd edition. Macmillan, 1963. 163

Kagan, Jerome, and Howard A. Moss. *Birth to maturity: A study in psychological development*. Wiley, 1962. 229

Kalish, Richard A. *Making the most of college*. Wadsworth, 1959. 80, 195, 463

——————. "An approach to death attitudes." *American Behavioral Scientist*, 1963. 6: 68–70. 414

——————. "Ethnic differences in suicide." Presentation to the Western Psychological Association, Long Beach, California, 1966.

——————, and Otomar Bartos. "Survey of student attitudes toward campus activities." *Personnel and Guidance Journal*, 1960. 39: 292–299. 443

——————, Michael Maloney, and Abe Arkoff. "Cross-cultural comparisons of college student marital-role preferences." *Journal of Social Psychology*, 1966. 68: 41–47. 219, 363

Kallmann, Franz J. *Heredity in health and mental disorder*. Norton, 1953. 97, 315

Kaplan, Max. *Leisure in America, a social inquiry*. Wiley, 1960. 245

Kelley, Harold H., and Edmund H. Volkart. "The resistance to change of group-anchored attitudes." *American Sociological Review*, 1952. 17: 453–465. 387

Kelly, E. Lowell. "Consistency of the adult personality." *American Psychologist*, 1955. 10: 659–681. 229

Keys, Ancel B., Josef Brožek, Austin Henschel, Olaf Mickelsen, and Henry L. Taylor. *The biology of human starvation*, Vol. II. University of Minnesota Press, 1950. 25

Kidd, Aline H., and Jeanne L. Rivoire (eds.). *Perceptual development in children*. International Universities Press, 1966. 101

Killian, Lewis M. "The significance of multiple-group membership in disaster." *American Journal of Sociology*, 1952. 57: 309–314. 269

Kimura, Yukiko. "War brides in Hawaii and their in-laws." *American Journal of Sociology*, 1957. 63: 70–76. 219

Kinsey, Alfred C., Wardell B. Pomeroy, and Clyde E. Martin, *Sexual behavior in the human male*. Saunders, 1948. 197, 198

——————, ——————, ——————, and Paul H. Gebhard. *Sexual behavior in the human female*. Saunders, 1953. 197, 198

Kirkpatrick, Clifford. "Religion and humanitarianism: A study of institutional implications." *Psychological Monographs*, 1949. Vol. 63. 414

Kobler, Arthur L., and Ezra Stotland. *The end of hope: A social-clinical study of suicide*. Free Press of Glencoe, 1964. 316

Kohn, Melvin L. "Social class and parental values." *American Journal of Sociology*, 1959. 64: 337–351. 359

Krech, David, Richard S. Crutchfield, and Egerton L. Ballachey. *Individual in society*. McGraw-Hill, 1962. 358, 362

Krumboltz, John D., Raymond E. Christal, and Joe H. Ward, Jr. "Predicting leadership ratings from high school activities." *Journal of Educational Psychology*, 1959. 50: 105–110.   445

Kuhlen, Raymond G. "Motivational changes during the adult years." In Raymond G. Kuhlen (ed.), *Psychological backgrounds of adult education*. Center for the Study of Liberal Education for Adults, 1963. Cited in James E. Birren, *The psychology of aging*. Prentice-Hall, 1964.   248

——————, and Martha Arnold. "Age differences in religious beliefs and problems during adolescence." *Journal of Genetic Psychology*, 1944. 65: 291–300.   402, 403

Kukuk, W. "Traits of college drinkers." Unpublished master's thesis, 1960. Cited in Henry C. Smith, *Personality adjustment*. McGraw-Hill, 1961. 455

Laird, D. A. "Experiments in the physiological cost of noise." *Journal of the National Institute of Industrial Psychology*, 1929. 4: 251–258.   8

Langhorne, M. C., and Paul F. Secord. "Variations in marital needs with age, sex, marital status, and regional location." *Journal of Social Psychology*, 1955. 41: 19–37.   218

Lee, Everett S. "Negro intelligence and selective migration: A Philadelphia test of the Klineberg hypothesis." *American Sociological Review*, 1951. 16: 227–233.   367

Lehmann, Irvin J. "Changes in critical thinking, attitudes, and values from freshman to senior years." *Journal of Educational Psychology*, 1963. 54: 305–315.   185

Lehner, George F. J., and Ella Kube. *The dynamics of personal adjustment*, 2nd edition. Prentice-Hall, 1964.   236, 246

Lenski, Gerhard E. *The religious factor*. Doubleday, 1961.   212

Leuba, Clarence J., and William F. John. *Man: A general psychology*. Holt, Rinehart, and Winston, 1961.   455

Levine, R., Isidore Chein, and Gardner Murphy. "The relation of the intensity of a need to the amount of perceptual distortion: A preliminary report." *Journal of Psychology*, 1942. 13: 283–293.   54

Lewin, Kurt. "Group decision and social change." In Eleanor E. Maccoby, Theodore M. Newcomb, and Eugene L. Hartley (eds.), *Readings in social psychology*, 3rd edition. Holt, 1958. Pages 197–211.   373

Lilly, J. C. "Mental effects of reduction of ordinary levels of physical stimuli on intact, healthy persons." Psychiatric Research Reports, 1956. No. 5: 1–28. Cited in Norman L. Munn, *Psychology: The fundamentals of human adjustment*, 4th edition. Houghton Mifflin, 1961.   27

Lindemann, Erich. "Symptomatology and management of acute grief." *American Journal of Psychiatry*, 1944. 101: 141–148.   275

Lippett, Ronald, and Ralph K. White. "An experimental study of leadership and group life." In Eleanor E. Maccoby, Theodore M. Newcomb, and Eugene L. Hartley (eds.), *Readings in social psychology*, 3rd edition. Holt, 1958. Pages 496–511.   371

Lippman, Hyman S. "Emotional factors in family breakdown." *American Journal of Orthopsychiatry*, 1954. 24: 445–453.   217

Lockman, Robert F. "An empirical description of the subfields of psychology." *American Psychologist*, 1964. 19: 645–653.   11

Lorenz, Thomas H., David T. Graham, and Stewart Wolf. "The relation of life stress and emotions to human sebum secretion and to the mechanism of acne vulgaris." *Journal of Laboratory and Clinical Medicine*, 1953. 41: 11–28.   161

Lowe, C. R. "Effect of mothers' smoking habits on birth weight of their children." British Medical Journal, 1959. 2: 673–676. 99

Luby, Elliot D., Charles E. Frohman, James L. Grisell, Joseph E. Lenzo, and Jacques S. Gottlieb. "Sleep deprivation: Effects on behavior, thinking, motor performance, and biological energy transfer systems." *Psychosomatic Medicine*, 1960. 22: 182–192. 26

Luckey, Eleanore B. "Marital satisfaction and personality correlates of spouse." *Journal of Marriage and the Family*, 1964a. 26: 217–220. 217

——————. "Marital satisfaction and its concomitant perceptions of self and spouse." *Journal of Counseling Psychology*, 1964b. 11: 136–145. 217

McClelland, David C., John W. Atkinson, Russell A. Clark, and Edgar L. Lowell. *The achievement motive.* Appleton-Century-Crofts, 1953. 41

McCord, Joan, William McCord, and Alan Howard. "Family interaction as antecedent to the direction of male aggressiveness." *Journal of Abnormal and Social Psychology*, 1963. 66: 239–242. 147

——————, ——————, and Emily Thurber. "Effects of maternal employment on lower-class boys." *Journal of Abnormal and Social Psychology*, 1963. 67: 177–182. 241, 242

McCord, William, Joan McCord, and P. Verden. "Familial and behavioral correlates of dependency in male children." *Child Development*, 1962. 33: 313–326. 127

McCormick, James H., and William Asher. "Aspects of the high school record related to the first semester college grade point average." *Personnel and Guidance Journal*, 1964. 42: 699–703. 194

McGeoch, John A., and Arthur L. Irion. *The psychology of human learning*, 2nd edition. Longmans, Green, 1952. 79

McGinnies, Elliot, and Willard Vaughan. Some biographical determiners of participation in group discussion. *Journal of Applied Psychology*, 1957. 41: 179–185. 373

McKinney, Fred. *Psychology of personal adjustment*, 3rd edition. Wiley, 1960. 445, 456

Maccoby, Eleanor E. "Developmental psychology." *Annual Review of Psychology*, 1964. 15: 203–250. 108

——————, Patricia K. Gibbs, and the staff of the Laboratory of Human Development, Harvard University. "Methods of child-rearing in two social classes." In Arthur P. Coladarci (ed.), *Educational psychology: A book of readings.* Dryden, 1955. Pages 97–121. 359

Malnig, Lawrence R. "Anxiety and academic prediction." *Journal of Counseling Psychology*, 1964. 11: 72–75. 195

Mann, Richard D. "A review of the relationships between personality and performance in small groups." *Psychological Bulletin*, 1959. 56: 241–270. 135, 371

Maslow, Abraham H. "A theory of human motivation." *Psychological Review*, 1943. 50: 370–396. 24

——————. "Deficiency motivation and growth motivation." In Marshall R. Jones (ed.), *Nebraska Symposium*, 1955. Pages 1–30. 24

——————. *Toward a psychology of being.* Van Nostrand, 1962. 420, 424

Matarazzo, Joseph D., Bernadene V. Allen, George Saslow, and Arthur N. Wiens. "Characteristics of successful policemen and firemen applicants." *Journal of Applied Psychology*, 1964. 48: 123–133. 330

Merrill, Francis E. *Courtship and marriage.* Holt-Dryden, 1959. 208, 224

Milgrim, Stanley. "Some conditions of obedience and disobedience to authority." In Ivan D. Steiner and Martin Fishbein (eds.), *Current studies in social psychology.* Holt, Rinehart, and Winston, 1965. Pages 243–262. 357

Miller, Neal E., and John Dollard. *Social learning and imitation.* Yale University Press, 1941. 67

Mishima, Yukio. "Judging the U.S. giant." *Life Magazine*, Sept. 11, 1964. 57: 81–84. 246

Moberg, David O. "Religiosity in old age." *The Gerontologist*, 1965. 5: 78–88. 403

Montagu, M. F. Ashley. "Some environmental factors which may influence prenatal development." In Jerome M. Seidman (ed.), *The child: a book of readings.* Rinehart, 1958. Pages 42–50. 99

Muensterberger, Warner. "Vom Ursprung des Todes." *Psyche*, 1963. Pages 169–184. 120

Muhyi, Ibrahim A. "Women in the Arab Middle East." *Journal of Social Issues* (No. 3) 1959. 15: 45–57. 238

Murdock, George P. *Social structure.* Macmillan, 1949. 215

——————. "World ethnographic sample." *American Anthropologist*, 1957. 59: 664–687. 199

Murray, Henry A. *Explorations in personality.* Oxford University Press, 1938. 38

Mussen, Paul H. "Some personality and social factors related to changes in children's attitudes toward Negroes." *Journal of Abnormal and Social Psychology*, 1950. 45: 423–441. 388

Newcomb, Theodore M., and G. Svehla. "Intra-family relationships in attitude." *Sociometry*, 1937. 1: 180–205. 380

Newsweek, Sept. 7, 1964. Book review of "Lament for the Molly Maguires," Arthur H. Lewis. Harcourt, Brace, and World, 1964. Page 85. 394

——————, March 22, 1965. "Campus '65." Pages 43–63. 405

Newton, Niles R., and Michael Newton. "Relationship of ability to breast feed and maternal attitudes toward breast feeding." *Pediatrics*, 1950. 5: 869–875. 109

Noel, Donald L. "Group identification among Negroes: An empirical analysis." *Journal of Social Issues*, (April) 1964. 20: 71–84. 367

Northway, M. L. "Outsiders: A study of the personality patterns of children least acceptable to their age mates." *Sociometry*, 1944. 7: 10–25. 151

Ort, Robert S. "A study of role-conflicts as related to happiness in marriage." *Journal of Abnormal and Social Psychology*, 1950. 45: 691–699. 218

Osgood, Charles E. *Method and theory in experimental psychology.* Oxford University Press, 1953. 70

Osler, William. "To the editor of the *Spectator*," Nov. 4, 1911. In L. Farmer, *Doctor's legacy.* Harpers, 1955. 247

Parker, Seymour, and Robert Kleiner. "Status position, mobility, and ethnic identification of the Negro." *Journal of Social Issues*, (April) 1964. 20: 85–102. 368

Pavlov, Ivan P. *Conditioned reflexes.* (Translated by G. V. Anrep.) Oxford University Press, 1927. 65

Peissel, Michel. "Mustang, remote realm in Nepal." *National Geographic*, Oct. 1965. 128: 579–604. 87

Pettigrew, Thomas F. *A profile of the Negro American.* Van Nostrand, 1964. 364, 368

Prince, Alfred J., and Andrew R. Baggaley. "Personality variables and the ideal mate." *Family Life Coordinator,* 1963. 3: 93–96. 215

Reichard, Suzanne, and D. Rapaport. "The role of testing concept formation in clinical psychological work." *Bulletin of the Menninger Clinic,* 1943. 7: 99–105. 72

Reiter, Henry H. "Prediction of college success from measures of anxiety, achievement motivation, and scholastic aptitude." *Psychological Reports,* 1964. 15: 23–26. 194, 195

Ribble, Margaretha A. *The rights of infants: Early psychological needs and their satisfaction.* Columbia University Press, 1943. 32

Riesman, David, with Reuel Denney and Nathan Glazer. *The lonely crowd: A study of the changing American character.* Yale University Press, 1950. 354

Robin, Stanley S., and Fae Story. "Ideological consistency of college students: The Bill of Rights and attitudes towards minority groups." *Sociology and Social Research,* 1964. 48: 187–196. 379

Robinson, Francis P. *Effective study* (revised). Harper 1961. 80, 82, 195

Roethlisberger, Fritz J., and William J. Dickson. *Management and the worker.* Harvard University Press, 1939. 237, 352

Rogers, Carl R. "This is me." From *On becoming a person.* Houghton Mifflin, 1961. 427

Rogerson, B. C. F., and C. H. Rogerson. "Feeding in infancy and subsequent psychological difficulties." *Journal of Mental Science,* 1939. 85: 1163–1182. 109

Rokeach, Milton. *The open and closed mind.* Basic Books, 1960. 282, 397

Rosen, B. C. "Socialization and achievement motivation in Brazil." *American Sociological Review,* 1962. 27: 612–624. 42

Rosenberg, Leon A. "Idealization of self and social adjustment." *Journal of Consulting Psychology,* 1962. 26: 487. 40, 95

Ross, Sherman, and Robert F. Lockman. *A career in psychology.* American Psychological Association, 1963. 10

Rosten, R. A. "Some personality characteristics of compulsive gamblers." Unpublished master's thesis, 1961. Cited in James C. Coleman, *Abnormal psychology and modern life.* Scott, Foresman, 1964. 317

Rowse, Donovan. "Nepal." *The American Annual* (Encyclopedia Americana), 1964. Pages 466–467. 206

Sanford, Fillmore H. *Psychology: A scientific study of man,* 2nd edition. Wadsworth, 1965. 50, 92

Schein, Edgar H. "The Chinese indoctrination program for prisoners of war: A study of attempted 'brainwashing.'" In Eleanor E. Maccoby, Theodore M. Newcomb, and Eugene L. Hartley (eds.), *Readings in social psychology.* Holt, 1958. Pages 311–334. 12, 265, 352

Schneider, Louis, and Sverre Lysgaard. "The deferred gratification pattern: A preliminary study." *American Sociological Review,* 1953. 18: 142–149. 360

Sears, Robert R. "Experimental studies of projection: I. attribution of traits." *Journal of Social Psychology,* 1936. 7: 151–163. 90

Sears, Robert R., Eleanor E. Maccoby, and Harry Levin. *Patterns of Child Rearing.* Harper, Row, 1957. 109, 110, 111, 112, 113, 124, 127, 139, 147, 359

Sells, Saul B. "The atmosphere effect: An experimental study of reasoning." *Archives of Psychology*, 1936, No. 200. 392

Seltzer, Carl C. "Occupation and smoking in, college graduates." *Journal of Applied Psychology*, 1964. 48: 1–6. 455

Selyé, Hans. *The stress of life*. McGraw-Hill, 1956. 278

Sewell, William H., and Paul H. Mussen. "The effects of feeding, weaning, and scheduling procedures on childhood adjustment and the formation of oral symptoms." *Child Development*, 1952. 23: 185–191. 109

Shils, Edward A. "Primary groups in the American Army." In Robert K. Merton and Paul Lazarsfeld (eds.), *Continuities in social research: Studies in the scope and method of "The American Soldier."* Free Press of Glencoe, 1950. Pages 16–40. 352

——————, and Morris Janowitz. "Cohesion and disintegration in the Wehrmacht in World War II." *Public Opinion Quarterly*, 1948. 12: 280–315. 352

Siipola, Elsa M. "A group study of some effects of preparatory sets." *Psychological Monographs*, 1935. 46: no. 210, 27–38. 19

Silberman, Charles E. *Crisis in black and white*. Random House, 1964. 137

Simon, Charles W., and William H. Emmons. "Learning during sleep?" *Psychological Bulletin*, 1955. 52: 328–342. 81

Sinnett, E. Robert, and LeRoy A. Stone. "The meaning of a college education as revealed by the semantic differential." *Journal of Counseling Psychology*, 1964. 11: 168–172. 193

Sklare, Marshall. "Intermarriage and the Jewish future." *Commentary*, April 1964. 37: 46–52. 211

Skodak, Marie, and Harold M. Skeels. "A final follow-up study of one hundred adopted children." *Journal of Genetic Psychology*, 1949. 75: 85–125. 97

Smith, Henry Clay. *Personality adjustment*. McGraw-Hill, 1961. 215, 401

Soffietti, James P. "Bilingualism and biculturalism." *Journal of Educational Psychology*, 1955. 46: 222–227. 137

Spectrum, Vol. 8, Feb. 1960. "Sex typing." Pages 40–43. 315

Spitz, Rene A. "The role of ecological factors in emotional development in infancy." *Child Development*, 1949. 20: 145–156. 27, 32, 120

Spock, Benjamin. *The common sense book of baby and child care*, revised. Pocket Books, 1957. 109, 110, 114

Stodgill, Ralph M. "Personal factors associated with leadership: A survey of the literature." *Journal of Psychology*, 1948. 25: 35–71. 370

Stone, Carol L. "Sorority status and personality adjustment." *American Sociological Review*, 1951. 16: 538–541. 443

Stright, I. L. "Some factors affecting college success." *Journal of Educational Psychology*, 1947. 38: 232–240. 443

Strodtbeck, Fred L., Rita M. James, and Charles Hawkins. "Social status in jury deliberations." In Eleanor E. Maccoby, Theodore M. Newcomb, and Eugene L. Hartley (eds.), *Readings in social psychology*. 3rd edition. Holt, 1958. Pages 379–388. 373

Sullivan, Harry Stack. *Conceptions of modern psychiatry*. Norton, 1953. 114

Sulzberger, Marion B., and Sadie H. Zaidens. "Psychogenic factors in dermatologic disorders." *Medical Clinics of North America*, 1948. 32: 669–685. 160

Sutton, R. L. "Acne vulgaris, a pustular lipoidosis." *Southern Medical Journal*, 1941. 34: 1071–1082. 161

Tanner, John M. *Education and physical growth.* University of London Press, 1961. 157

Tarnopol, Lester. "Personality differences between leaders and non-leaders." *Personnel Journal*, 1958. 37: 57–60. 371

Taylor, Ronald A. "Personality traits and discrepant achievement: A review." *Journal of Counseling Psychology*, 1964. 11: 76–82. 195, 451

Terman, Lewis M. *Psychological factors in marital happiness.* McGraw-Hill, 1938. 216

——————, and M. H. Oden. *The gifted group at mid-life. Genetic studies of genius*, vol. V. Stanford University Press, 1959. 250

Tharp, Roland G. "Psychological patterning in marriage." *Psychological Bulletin*, 1963. 60: 97–117. 218

Thigpen, Corbett H., and Hervey M. Cleckley. *The three faces of Eve.* McGraw-Hill, 1957. 306

Thompson, Helen. "Physical growth." In Leonard Carmichael (ed.), *Manual of child psychology.* Wiley, 1946. Pages 255–294. 132

Thompson, Wayne E. "Pre-retirement anticipation and adjustment in retirement." *Journal of Social Issues*, (No. 2) 1958. 14: 35–45. 250

——————, and Gordon F. Streib. "Situational determinants: Health and economic deprivation in retirement." *Journal of Social Issues*, (No. 2) 1958. 14: 18–34. 250

Thompson, William R. "Influence of prenatal maternal anxiety on emotionality in young rats." *Science*, 1957. 125: 698–699. 99

Thorne, Frederick C. "The incidence of nocturnal enuresis after age five." *American Journal of Psychiatry*, 1944. 100: 686–689. 281

Voeks, Virginia. *On becoming an educated person*, 2nd edition. Saunders, 1964.

Wallas, Graham. *The art of thought.* Harcourt, Brace, 1926. 76

Wallin, Paul. "Cultural contradictions and sex roles: A repeat study." *American Sociological Review*, 1950. 15: 288–293. 173

——————, and Rosemary Riley. "Reactions of mothers to pregnancy and adjustment of offspring in infancy." *American Journal of Orthopsychiatry*, 1950. 20: 616–622. 99

Warner, Lucien. "What younger psychologists think about ESP." *Journal of Parapsychology*, 1955. 19: 228–235. 48

Washington, Bennetta B. "Growth and cultural conflict." *Vocational Guidance Quarterly*, 1964. 12: 153–158. 117

Watson, Robert I. *Psychology of the child*, 2nd edition. Wiley, 1965. 109

Wechsler, Henry. "Halfway houses for former mental patients: A survey." *Journal of Social Issues*, (No. 2) 1960. 16: 20–26. 319

Weigand, George. "Goal aspiration and academic success." *Personnel and Guidance Journal*, 1953. 31: 458–461. 195

Wenger, Marion A., F. N. Jones, and M. H. Jones. *Physiological psychology.* Holt, 1956. 279

White, Robert W. *The abnormal personality*, 3rd edition. Ronald, 1964. 312

Whiting, John W. M., and Irvin L. Child. *Child training and personality: A cross-cultural study.* Yale University Press, 1953. 110, 113

Will, Caroline F. "A survey of problems confronting Frear Hall residents." Bureau of Testing and Guidance Research Studies on University of Hawaii Student Behavior, 1957, #1. 449, 458

Winch, Robert F., Thomas Ktsanes, and Virginia Ktsanes. "The theory of complementary needs in mate selection: an analytic and descriptive study." *American Sociological Review*, 1954. 19: 241–249.   217

Witty, Paul A., and M. A. Jenkins. "Intra-race testing and Negro intelligence." *Journal of Psychology*, 1936. 1: 179–192.   367

Wolfe, J. B. "Effectiveness of token-rewards for chimpanzees." *Comparative Psychology Monographs*, 1936. 12: No. 60.   69

Wolff, Kurt. "Personality type and reaction toward aging and death—a clinical study." Presentation, Gerontological Society meetings, Los Angeles, 1965.   250

Wrenn, C. Gilbert. "Editor's Introduction" In Norman T. Bell, Richard W. Burkhardt, and Victor B. Lawhead (eds.), *Introduction to college life.* Houghton Mifflin, 1962.   183

———, and Elizabeth B. Crandall. "Behavior ratings and scholarship among college freshmen." *Journal of Educational Research*, 1941. 34: 259–264.   195

Yarrow, Marian, P. Scott, L. deLeeuw, and C. Heinig. "Child-rearing in families of working and nonworking mothers." *Sociometry*, 1962. 25: 122–140.   243

Zander, Alvin, and Robert Quinn. "The social environment and mental health: A review of past research at the Institute for Social Research." *Journal of Social Issues* (No. 3), 1962. 18: 48–66.   343

Zollitsch, Herbert G. "Fringes—benefits or burdens?" *Personnel*, July/August 1964. 41: 54–59.   342

Index

Abilities
  and career planning, 331–333
Achievement, 349
  in college, 449–450
Acne, 160–161
Activity needs, 28–29
Adjustment, in old age, 248–252
  related to job success, 235–238
  and religion, 409–410
  to stress, 294–295
Adolescence, 155–178
  acne, 160–161
  age discrimination, 164–166
  body-image, 158–161
  dating, 170–177
  derived status, 162
  emancipation, 166–168
  going steady, 176–177
  physical growth, 157–158
  popularity, 169–170
  primary status, 166–168
  puberty, 157
  religious beliefs, 400–403
  self-concept, 162–164
  social relationships, 168–177
  "typical" adolescent, 161–162
Adult life cycle, 228–231
  career opportunities, 235
  changes in family structure, 232–233
  opportunities and responsibilities, 231–246
  sex role, 238–243

Affective disorders, 312
  agitated depressive, 312
  involutional psychotic, 312
  manic-depressive psychosis, circular type, 312
  manic state, 312
  retarded depressive, 312
Aggressive behavior, 127–129
  "anti-parent" weapons, 148
  and displacement, 260–261
  as factor in stress, 272–273
  and play, 151
  as result of stress, 283
  and social class, 359–360
  traced from childhood to adulthood, 229
Air hunger, 25
  influence upon fetus, 99
Alcohol, 314–315
  influence upon fetus, 99
  -ism, 314–315
  use in college, 454–456
American Psychological Association, 11
Amnesia, 306–307
Anger
  expression, 262
Anxiety, 263–264, 269–270
Anxiety reaction, 305
Aptitudes, 349
Athletics
  in college, 445–446
  and popularity, 170

Attention, 53–54
Attitudes (*See* specific attitudes)
Authority figures
  factor in stress, 273
Bedwetting, 281
Bereavement, 275
Body-image, 158–161
  acne, 160–161
  obesity, 160
  physical handicaps, 158–160
Brainwashing, 12, 265, 352
Breast feeding, 109–110
Campus activities, 443–449
Career planning, 327–349
  abilities and, 331–333
  adult opportunities, 235
  demographic characteristics and, 335–337
  education and, 333
  influence upon values, 386
  job description, 340–341
  job market, 338
  job requirements, 339–340
  of Negro, 335–336, 365–366
  personal characteristics and, 329–331
  selected by women, 242
  sources of information for, 346–348
Cheating, 192–193
Childhood (*See* Parent-child relationships; Child-rearing methods)
Child-rearing methods, 108–114
  breast feeding, 109–110
  development of attitudes and values, 121–125
  discipline, 145–148
  feeding (early), 108–110
  religion, 400–403
  sex training, 112–114
  and social class, 359
  toilet training, 110–112
  weaning, 110
Classical conditioning, 65–66
  in bedwetting, 281
Clinical psychologist, 9, 12
College, 179–204
  academic achievement in, 449, 450
  and active students, 191–192
  activities, 443–449
  arts, 446–447
  aspirations and social class, 360–362
  athletics, 445–446

College (continued)
  catalogue, 441–442
  cheating, 192–193
  courses, 440–441
  definition of, 180, 182
  emotional problems in, 450–451
  enrollment, 180
  factor in stress, 274
  finances in, 451–453
  freedom from supervision, 185–188
  goals, 195–197
  grades, 193–194, 442
  instructors, 441
  learning tasks in, 182–183
  library, 460
  major, 439–440
  orientation to, 439–461
  politics, 447–448
  psychological help in, 321–322, 458–460
  reasons for going, 183–184
  religious beliefs, 404–405
  religious problems, 405–409
  search for identity, 188–189
  as seen by students, 183–185
  sex behavior in, 197–203
Communication
  difficulties in, 87, 89
  effectiveness in, 87, 89
  language, 74–75
  in marriage, 221–222
  nonverbal, 75–76
  use of symbols in, 91
Community, 243–244
  influence upon values, 383–386
  participation, 243
  world, 243–244
Compulsive gambling, 316–317
Concept formation, 71–72
Conflict, 265, 267–269
Conformity, 354–357
Conscience (*See* Internalization)
Conversion reaction, 305–306
  hysterical paralysis, 306
Courtship and engagement, 206–214
  purposes of, 206–208
  problems in, 208–212
Counseling in college, 457–460
  centers, 459
  faculty adviser, 458
  medical, 460
Creativity, 72–73
  and healthy personality, 430–433

Creativity (continued)
in play, 151
in thinking, 76
Cross-cultural comparisons
adolescent growth, 157–158
dating, 174–175
definition of adolescence, 156
dress, 91
emotional expression, 87, 262
ethnic-group prejudice, 395
female sex role, 238–239
food preferences, 30–31
grading, 193–194
language, 74–75
manners, 56–57
marital success, 219
marriage, 87, 206, 215
needs, 41–42
non-verbal communication, 75–76
normal and abnormal behavior, 299
parent-child relationship, 144
sex behavior, 199–200
shame society vs. guilt society, 123–125
toilet training, 110–111
Dating, 170–177
cross-cultural comparisons, 174–175
going steady, 176–177
interfaith, 210–212
and marriage, 171–172
parental attitudes, 175
Daydreams, 60, 72
Death
factor in stress, 275
in old age, 248, 250
as separation from significant figures, 120
Defense mechanisms, 284–293
displacement, 288
fantasy, 288
identification, 291
intellectualization, 289
projection, 287
psychological "crutches," 292–293
rationalization, 286–287
reaction formation, 287–288
regression, 288–289
repression, 285
Deficiency motivation, 36–37
Delusions, 304–305, 310–311, 312–313
Dependent behavior, 127–129

Depressive reaction, 308
Derived status, 166
Discipline
in childhood, 145–148
maturation level, 146–147
punishment, 147–148
Displacement
of aggressions upon scapegoat, 260–261
as defense mechanism, 288
Dissociative reactions, 306–307
amnesia, 306–307
fugue state, 307
multiple personality, 306–307
Distractions in learning, 80–81
people, 80
personal problems, 81
noise, 80
study area, 81
Divorce, 224
Dreams, 58–60
latent content, 58
manifest content, 58
sexual, 197
Drug addiction, 314–315
Education
and career planning, 333
goals in, and social class, 360–362
influence upon values, 382–383
Edwards Personal Preference Schedule, 38
Elderly, 246–252
attitudes toward, 246–247
death, 248, 250
IQ change, 247
religious associations, 403–404
retirement, 229
Elimination pressures, 26
Emotions, 257–276
definition, 258
development of, 259
expression of, 87, 259–262
and learning, 259
and maturation, 259
and motivation, 258–259
physiological changes, 258
Engagement (*See* Courtship and engagement)
Enuresis (*See* Bedwetting)
Esteem needs, 33
Ethnic groups
discrimination towards, 363–368, 392–397
Examinations, 79, 479–483
Experimental method, 18–19
Exploration needs, 28–29

Extra-sensory perception (ESP), 48
Fantasy, 60
  as defense mechanism, 288
Fatigue, 26
  as response to stress, 280–281
  in college, 453
Fear
  expression of, 260, 263
Feeding (in infancy and child-hood), 108–110
Finances
  adult responsibilities, 234–235
  and career planning, 341–342
  factor in stress, 274
  as problem during college, 451–453
  as problem during courtship, 210
  working women, 239–243
Foreign students, 457
Freud, 13
  development of sex role, 125–127
Friends (*See* Social relationships)
  characteristics of, 150–151
  in childhood, 150–151
  and healthy personality, 425
  and play, 150–152
  as problem in courtship, 209
  and social class, 358
  values of, 381–382
Frustration, 265–267
Fugue state, 307
General-adaptation syndrome, 278
Genetic, 96–98
Going steady, 176–177
Grades, 193–194
Group discussion, 371–373
Group pressure, 353–358
Groups (*See also* Values, Religion), 351–374
  conformity, 354–357
  discussions, 371–373
  ethnic, 363–368
  group pressure, 353–358
  leaders, 369–371
  opposing standards, 272, 353–358
  religious, 413
  social class, 357–363
Growth motivation, 36–37
Guilt, 123–125, 265, 269–270
  guilt society, 123–125
  and religion, 411–413
Hallucinations, 60, 304–305, 310–311
Healthy personality, 419–434
  characteristics of, 420–425

Healthy personality (continued)
  and creativity, 430–433
  development of, 425–427
  and friends, 425
  and love, 427–428
  and self-actualization, 419–425
Heredity, 96–98, 298–299
Hierarchy of needs, 24–38
Homosexuality, 198, 315
Hunger, 24–25, 29–31
  and diet during pregnancy, 99
Hypothesis, 5
Ideal self, 95
Identification, 291
  role of Negroes, 364–367
Identity
  in adolescence, 162–164
  in college, 188–189
Infancy (*See* Parent-child relationships)
Inherited factors in personality (*See* Heredity)
Insight
  and stress, 293–294
Intellectualization, 289
Intelligence (and IQ), 132–139, 230
  changes as adult, 230
  definition of, 132–134
  family influences, 135–139
  influences upon, 135–139
  inherited qualities in, 97
  measurement, 134–135, 137
  in old age, 247
  and race, 367–368
Interaction between heredity and environment in personality, 98
Interests
  and career planning, 328–331
  evaluation of, 348–349
Interfaith dating and marriage, 210–212
Internalization
  of attitudes, 121–125
  of guilt, 123–125, 270
  proper sex behavior, 199–200
  of sex role, 125–127, 219–220
  of shame, 123–125
Internal senses, 48
Intolerance of ambiguity, 281–282
Job description, 340–341
  advancement opportunities, 341
  benefits, 342–343
  income, 342–343
  working conditions, 341
Job information, 346–348

Job market, 338
Job requirements, 339–340
Job satisfaction, 328, 342–344
Job search, 337–338
Job success
  factor in stress, 274
  factors in, 235–238
  significance of, 235, 328
  supervision, 236–238
Junior college
  enrollment, 180
  and careers, 333
Kinesthetic sense, 48
Language
  and intelligence, 136–137
  in learning, 69
  nonverbal, 75–76
  and symbols, 74–75
Latent dream content, 58
Leaders, 369–371
  methods, 371
  qualities of, 370–371
  types of, 369–371
Learning (*See* Study methods),
    63–72, 78–83
  about religion, 407–408
  classical conditioning, 65–66
  concept formation, 71–72
  definition, 64
  and effective study, 78–83
  and emotions, 259
  insight learning, 69–71
  operant learning, 67–69
  and perception, 52
  problem solving, 69–71, 74
  reinforcement, 66
  symbols in, 69
  through dating, 171
  through play, 151
  trial-and-error, 70–71
Lecture notes, 78–79, 466–470
Leisure, 244–246
  television, 245–246
Level of aspiration, 39–42
  and stress, 293–294
Library, 460
Love, Love needs, 32–33, 143–144
  in courtship and marriage, 213–
    214
  development of, 117–121
  factor in stress, 271
  and healthy personality, 427–42
  unhealthy expressions of, 428–
    430
  withdrawal of, 124–125

Lying-in, 101
Manifest dream content, 58
Manipulation needs, 28–29
Marriage, 205–225
  average age at, 206
  behavior in, 220–221
  and college attendance, 185
  and dating, 171–172
  factors leading to, 215–216
  interfaith, 210–212
  need satisfaction in, 217–218
  roles in, 218–220
  student, 223–224
  successful, 216–224
  unmarried, 225
  unsuccessful, 216–217
Maturation, 101, 103
  and discipline, 146–147
  and emotions, 259
  and perception, 52–53
Meaningful material, learning of,
    79–80
Menopause, 231
Mental hospitals, 318–319
Mental illness, 297–322
  symptoms of, 300–302
  1965 fact sheet on, 302–303
Military service
  as a career, 346
Mind-reading, 12, 48
Motivation (*See* Needs, Emo-
    tions), 21–44
Motor development
  in children, 101–102
  in neonates, 101
Narcotics
  influence upon fetus, 99
Natural childbirth, 100
Needs
  activity, 28–29
  air hunger, 25
  and career planning, 329–331
  complementarity of, 217–218
  elimination pressures, 26
  esteem, self-esteem, 33, 143–144
  and ethnic prejudice, 397
  exploration, 28–29
  fatigue, 26
  and friendship, 168–169
  hunger, 24–25, 29–31
  love, 32–33, 143–144
  manipulation, 28–29
  novelty, 28–29
  pain avoidance, 26
  and perception, 54–56

Needs (continued)
  physiological, 24–31
  safety, security, 31–32, 143–144
  satisfaction in marriage, 217–218
  satisfaction through groups, 352
  self-actualization, 22–24, 33–38,
    142–144
  sex, 27–28
  stimulation, 26–29, 32, 51, 142–
    143
  survival, 24–26
  thirst, 25
Negro
  family, 365–366
  intelligence of, 367–368
  job discrimination, 335–336
  middle class, 368–369
  role, 364–368
Neonate, 99–101
  behavior differences in, 100
  physical development, 101
Neurosis, 303–304, 305–308
  anxiety reaction, 305
  conversion reaction, 305–306
  depressive reaction, 308
  dissociative reactions, 306–307
  obsessive-compulsive behavior,
    307–308
  phobic reactions, 307
Norm group, 17
Notebook, 470–473
Novelty needs, 28–29
Obedience, 357
Obsessive-compulsive behavior,
  307–308
Operant learning, 67–69
Optical illusions, 52
Organic (*See* Stress, Psychosis)
Other-directed, 354–355
Overlearning, 78
Overprotection, 142–143
Pain avoidance, 26
Paranoid reactions, 312–313
Parent-child relationships
  in adolescence, 166–168
  aggressive behavior, 127–129
  "anti-parent" weapons, 148
  child-rearing methods, 108–114
  and dating, 175
  dependent behavior, 127–129
  development of sex role, 125–127
  discipline, 145–148
  during college, 185–186
  expression of feelings, 142
  factor in stress, 270–271
  freedom in, 140–142

Parent-child relationships (contin-
    ued)
  guilt, 123–125
  healthy relationships, 139–140
  and intelligence, 135–139
  internalization, 121–125
  love, 32–33, 117–121
  overprotection, 142–143
  as problem in courtship, 208–209
  purpose of children, 233
  responsibility in, 140–142
  and self-actualization, 142–144
  separation, 119–121
  shame, 123–125
  significant figures, 114–117
  stimulation needs, 28–29
  working mother, 241–243
Pavlov, 65–66
Perception, 47–61
  and experiences, 56–57
  and learning, 52
  and maturation, 52–53
  and needs, 54–55
  perceiver characteristics in, 54–
    57
  and prejudice, 57
  and rigidity, 57
  stimulus characteristics in, 53–54
  without external stimuli, 58–60
Personality (*See also* Self-concept,
    Parent-child relationships,
    Child-rearing methods), 85–
    153
  at birth, 100
  and career planning, 329–331
  changeability versus consistency,
    87
  changes in old age, 247–249
  changes with age, 230
  complexity versus predictability,
    89–90
  control of, 10, 12
  definition, 92–93
  differences between twins, 97–98
  and effectiveness of communica-
    tion, 87, 89
  and ethnic prejudice, 397
  human, as different from lower
    animal, 90–92
  heredity-environment interac-
    tion, 98
  inherited factors in, 96–98
  inherited predispositions, 96–98
  and intelligence, 137–139
  and marital success, 216–217
  prenatal influences, 98–99

Personality (continued)
  rigidity versus adaptability, 86–87
  roles, 95–96
  and self-concept, 93–94
  significant figures, 114–117
  theories of, 6–7
Personality disorders, 313–317
  alcoholism, 314–315
  compulsive gambling, 316–317
  drug addiction, 314–315
  homosexuality, 315
  sexual deviation, 315
  suicide, 315–316
Physical development and change
  in adolescents, 157–158
  in adulthood, 230–231
  and body-image, 158–161
  menopause, 231
  in neonates, 101
  in old age, 247
Physical illness and handicaps
  in adolescence, 158–161
  in college, 453–454, 460
  factor in stress, 274–275
  influence upon fetus, 99
Physiological needs (*See* Needs), 24–31
  social aspects of, 29–31
Play, 151–152
  importance of, 151–152
  development of, 152
Politics
  campus, 447–448
  off-campus, 448
Popularity, 169–170
  qualities leading to, 169–170
Population explosion, 99–100
Practice, distributed vs. massed, 79
Prejudice (*See also* Groups, Values, Negro)
  and age discrimination, 164–166, 246–247
  and ethnic discrimination, 392–397
  meaning of, 391–392
  racial, and perception, 76–77
  racial, and rigid thinking, 76–77
  and segregation, 392–397
Prenatal influences, 98–99
  psychological factors, 99
Primary status, 166–168
Probabilities, 6
Problem solving, 69–71, 74
  insight, 69–71
  trial-and-error, 70

Projection, 287
Propaganda, 389–391
  terms, 390
Psychiatrist, 12, 13
Psychoanalyst, 13
Psychological "crutches," 292–293
Psychologist (*See* Psychology)
  clinical, 9, 12
  developmental, 9–10
  industrial, 10
  jobs, 10
  physiological, 9
  social, 9
  specialities, 9–10
  training, 9–10
Psychology (*See* Psychologists)
  applied, 6–7
  art of, 6–7
  case history, 15–17
  control group, 18–19
  defined, 4–7
  experimental, 18–19
  methods in, 13–19
  observation, 14–15
  questionnaire, 17–18
  relationships with other disciplines, 7–8
  science of, 4–7
  surveys, 17–18
  test, 15–17
Psychosis, 303–305, 308–314
  affective reactions, 312
  functional, 308–310
  organic, 308–310
  paranoid reactions, 312–313
  schizophrenic reactions, 310–312
  senile, 308
Psychosomatic, 279–280
Psychotherapy, 9, 319–321
Puberty, 157–158
Punishment
  in childhood, 146–148
Questionnaire method, 17–18
Rationalization, 286–287
Reaction formation, 287–288
Receptor organs, 48
Reference group, 41
Regression, 288–289
Reliability, 16–17
Religion (*See also* Groups, Values), 399–415
  and adjustment, 409–410
  beliefs of others, 407–408
  church affiliation, 413
  college student problems, 405–409

Religion (continued)
    development of beliefs, 400–404
    as factor in career planning, 335–336
    and faith, 409–410
    freedom of, 408–409
    and guilt, 411–413
    nonbeliever, 413–414
    as problem during courtship, 210–212
    purpose of life, 408
    rituals, 410–411
    and science, 405–407
Repetitions in learning, 78–79
Repression, 43–44
    of emotions, 262
    as defense mechanism, 285
Retirement, 229
Rigidity, 57
    intolerance of ambiguity, 281–282
    result of stress, 281–282
    in thinking, 76–77, 185
    versus adaptability in personality, 86–87
Role, 95–96
    elderly, 246–247
    ethnic group, 363–368
    marital, 218–220
    Negro, 364–368
    sex, 125–127, 238–243
Safety needs, 31–32
Scapegoat, 260–261
Schizophrenic reactions, 310–312
    catatonic, 311
    hebephrenic, 311
    paranoid, 312–313
    simple, 310
Scientific method, 5–6
Self
    and identity in adolescence, 162–164
Self-actualization, 22–24, 33–38
    and career planning, 342–344
    and children, 142–144
    and healthy personality, 419–425
    and working women, 239–241
Self-concept (*See* Personality), 93–94
    and adjustment, 94
    and age discrimination in adolescence, 164–166
    and body-image, 158–161
    conscious versus unconscious, 94
    and dating, 170
    defense mechanisms, 284–293

Self-concept (continued)
    development of, 114–116
    ideal self, 95
    and love, 117–121
    and marriage, 216–217
    self-perpetuating aspects of, 116–118
    and significant figures, 114–116
Self-esteem, 33, 284–286, 342–344
Self-fulfilling prophecy, 77
Sensation, 48, 50–51
Sensory development
    handicaps, 50–51
    in neonates, 101
Sensory threshold, 50
Separation anxiety, 119–121
Set, 57, 74
    as aid in learning and recall, 82–83
Sex behavior (*See* Sex training)
    in college, 197–203
    in courtship, 213
    factor in stress, 272–273
    freedom and responsibility, 198–200
    and guilt, 201–203
    homosexuality, 198
    masturbation, 197
    "new" morality, 200–201
Sex needs, 27–28
Sex role, 125–127
    adult, 238–243
    as factor in stress, 272–273
    female discrimination, 239–241
Sex training (in infancy and childhood), 112–114
Sexual deviation, 315
Shame, 123–125
    shame society, 123–125
Sibling rivalry, 149–150
Significant figures, 114–117
    when absent, 119–121
    death of, 120
    and development of self-concept, 114–116
    and development of sex role, 125–127
    and internalized attitudes, 121–125
    and love, 117–121
Smoking
    influence upon fetus, 99
    in college, 454–456
Social class, 357–363
    and child-rearing methods, 359

Social class (continued)
  and educational goals, 360–362
  and IQ, 136–137
  mobility, 362–364
  Negro middle class, 368–369
  and vocational goals, 360–362
Social class mobility, 362–364
Social needs, classification of, 38
  differences in strength, 39, 41–42
Social relationships (*See* Friends)
  in adolescence, 168–177
  in college, 189–190
  dating, 170–177
  popularity, 169–170
SQ3R, 82–83, 473–479
Stereotype, 77
Stimulation needs, 26–29, 32, 51,
  142–143
  and self-actualization, 342–344
Stress (*See also* Emotion, Neurosis, Psychosis), 265–295
  aggression, 283
  and anxiety, 265
  bodily changes, 278
  defense mechanisms, 284–293
  disorganized behavior, 283–284
  effects upon acne, 161
  factors in, 270–276
  growth responses, 293–295
  inevitability, 275
  reactions to, 277–295
  rigidity, 281–282
  types of, 265–270
  withdrawal, 282–283
Study methods, 78–83
  and college success, 195
  distractions in, 80–81
  and examinations, 79, 479–483
  lecture notes, 78–79, 466–470
  meaningful material, 79–80
  notebooks, 470–473
  overlearning, 78
  practice, distributed vs. massed,
    79
  repetition in, 78–79
  SQ3R, 82–83, 473–479
  time schedule, 463–466
  warm-up, 78
Suicide, 315–316
Supervision, 236–238
Suppression, 285–286
Survey method, 17–18

Survival needs (*See* Needs), 24–26
Symptomitis, 301
Teaching machines, 68–69, 83
Television, 245–246
Temperature regulation, 26
Tests, 15–17
  as method in psychology, 15–17
  intelligence (and IQ), 134–135
Thinking, 73–78
  and college attendance, 185
  creative, 76
  definition, 72
  and language, 74–75
  rigidity in, 76–77
  without conscious control, 73–74
Thirst, 25
Time schedule, 187–188, 463–466
Toilet training, 110–112
Trait, 95
Tranquilizers, 321
Twins, identical vs. fraternal, 97–
  98
Unconscious motivation, 42–43
  internalization of attitudes, 121–
    125
Validity, 16–17
Values (*See also* Groups, Religion), 377–397
  in adolescence, 166
  and career planning, 329–331
  change of, 387–391
  financial, 234–235
  formation of, 379–381
  internalization of, 121–125, 379–
    381
  and prejudice, 392–397
  propaganda, 389–391
  related to marital success, 218–
    220
  Study of Values, 379
Variables, 5
Vestibular sense, 48
Warm-up, 78
Weaning, 110
Withdrawal, 282–283
Work (*See also* Career)
  in adolescence, 164–168
  experience, 344–346
  job success, 235–238
  as student, 256–257
Working women, 239–243
  and self-actualization, 239–241